"Phil Ryken writes with practical pastoral wisdom and sound theological judgments. These are the traits of Ecclesiastes and consequently this commentary. This volume is a much needed addition to the dearth of commentaries on this wonderful slice of biblical literature. Insightful. Readable. Recommended."

Anthony Carter, Lead Pastor, East Point Church
East Point, Georgia

"Philip Ryken's commentary on Ecclesiastes is a good, faithful exposition of the text, adorned with delightfully helpful pastoral applications all along the way. Thanks, Phil, for feeding our souls again."

Sandy Willson, Second Presbyterian Church, Memphis

"Phil Ryken's *Ecclesiastes* exposes the futility of chasing after everything under the sun. While reading it I thought of God decidedly and mercifully bending his head beneath the lintel of our impoverished existence. In kindness he steps across the threshold of our vain pursuits and shows us a better way. Here we have one of America's foremost preachers taking a text written by 'the Preacher,' faithfully nourishing the lives of pastors who are called to do the same."

David Helm, Pastor, Holy Trinity Church, Chicago

PREACHING THE WORD
Edited by R. Kent Hughes

Genesis | R. Kent Hughes

Exodus | Philip Graham Ryken

Leviticus | Kenneth A. Mathews

Numbers | Iain M. Duguid

Deuteronomy | Ajith Fernando

Joshua | David Jackman

Judges and Ruth | Barry G. Webb

1 Samuel | John Woodhouse

2 Samuel | John Woodhouse

1 Kings | John Woodhouse

Job | Christopher Ash

Psalms, vol. 1 | James Johnston

Proverbs | Raymond C. Ortlund Jr.

Ecclesiastes | Philip Graham Ryken

Song of Solomon | Douglas Sean O'Donnell

Isaiah | Raymond C. Ortlund Jr.

Jeremiah and Lamentations | R. Kent Hughes

Daniel | Rodney D. Stortz

Matthew | Douglas Sean O'Donnell

Mark | R. Kent Hughes

Luke | R. Kent Hughes

John | R. Kent Hughes

Acts | R. Kent Hughes

Romans | R. Kent Hughes

1 Corinthians | Stephen T. Um

2 Corinthians | R. Kent Hughes

Galatians | Todd Wilson

Ephesians | R. Kent Hughes

Philippians, Colossians, and Philemon | R. Kent Hughes

1–2 Thessalonians | James H. Grant Jr.

1–2 Timothy and Titus | R. Kent Hughes and Bryan Chapell

Hebrews | R. Kent Hughes

James | R. Kent Hughes

1–2 Peter and Jude | David R. Helm

1–3 John | David L. Allen

Revelation | James M. Hamilton Jr.

The Sermon on the Mount | R. Kent Hughes

(((PREACHING *the* WORD)))

ECCLESIASTES

WHY EVERYTHING MATTERS

PHILIP GRAHAM RYKEN

R. Kent Hughes
Series Editor

:: CROSSWAY

WHEATON, ILLINOIS

Ecclesiastes

Copyright © 2010 by Philip Graham Ryken

Published by Crossway
        1300 Crescent Street
        Wheaton, Illinois 60187

Cover design: Jon McGrath, Simplicated Studio

Cover image: Adam Greene, illustration

First printing 2010

Printed with new cover 2014

Printed in the United States of America

Hardcover ISBN: 978-1-4335-4888-8
ePub ISBN: 978-1-4335-4891-8
Mobipocket ISBN: 978-1-4335-4890-1
PDF ISBN: 978-1-4335-4889-5

Library of Congress Cataloging-in-Publication Data

Ryken, Philip Graham, 1966–
    Ecclesiastes : why everything matters / Philip Graham Ryken;
R. Kent Hughes, general editor.
      p. cm. (Preaching the Word)
    Includes bibliographical references and index.
    ISBN-13: 978-1-4335-1375-6 (hc)
    ISBN-10: 1-4335-1375-7 (hc)
    ISBN-13: 978-1-4335-1376-3 (pbk)
    ISBN-13: 978-1-4335-2441-7 (ebk)
    1. Bible. O.T. Ecclesiastes—Commentaries. I. Hughes, R. Kent.
II. Title. III. Series.
BS1475.53.R95   2010
223'.8077—dc22   2009038318

Crossway is a publishing ministry of Good News Publishers.

VP		31	30	29	28	27	26	25	24	23	22	21
15	14	13	12	11	10	9	8	7	6	5	4	3

To
Karoline Jorena Ryken,
in the hope that Jesus will give her victory over life's vanity

and

to everyone who desires to know the true meaning of life

The words of the wise are like goads,
and like nails firmly fixed are the collected sayings;
they are given by one Shepherd.

ECCLESIASTES 12:11

Contents

A Word to Those Who Preach the Word

There are times when I am preaching that I have especially sensed the pleasure of God. I usually become aware of it through the unnatural silence. The ever-present coughing ceases, and the pews stop creaking, bringing an almost physical quiet to the sanctuary—through which my words sail like arrows. I experience a heightened eloquence, so that the cadence and volume of my voice intensify the truth I am preaching.

There is nothing quite like it—the Holy Spirit filling one's sails, the sense of his pleasure, and the awareness that something is happening among one's hearers. This experience is, of course, not unique, for thousands of preachers have similar experiences, even greater ones.

What has happened when this takes place? How do we account for this sense of his smile? The answer for me has come from the ancient rhetorical categories of *logos*, *ethos*, and *pathos*.

The first reason for his smile is the *logos*—in terms of preaching, God's Word. This means that as we stand before God's people to proclaim his Word, we have done our homework. We have exegeted the passage, mined the significance of its words in their context, and applied sound hermeneutical principles in interpreting the text so that we understand what its words meant to its hearers. And it means that we have labored long until we can express in a sentence what the theme of the text is—so that our outline springs from the text. Then our preparation will be such that as we preach, we will not be preaching our own thoughts about God's Word, but God's actual Word, his *logos*. This is fundamental to pleasing him in preaching.

The second element in knowing God's smile in preaching is *ethos*—what you are as a person. There is a danger endemic to preaching, which is having your hands and heart cauterized by holy things. Phillips Brooks illustrated it by the analogy of a train conductor who comes to believe that he has been to the places he announces because of his long and loud heralding of them. And that is why Brooks insisted that preaching must be "the bringing of truth through personality." Though we can never perfectly embody the truth we preach, we must be subject to it, long for it, and make it as much a part of our ethos as possible. As the Puritan William Ames said, "Next to the Scriptures, nothing makes a sermon more to pierce, than when it comes out of the inward affection of the heart without any affectation." When a preacher's *ethos* backs up his *logos*, there will be the pleasure of God.

Last, there is *pathos*—personal passion and conviction. David Hume, the Scottish philosopher and skeptic, was once challenged as he was seen going to hear George Whitefield preach: "I thought you do not believe in the gospel." Hume replied, "I don't, but he does." Just so! When a preacher believes what he preaches, there will be passion. And this belief and requisite passion will know the smile of God.

The pleasure of God is a matter of *logos* (the Word), *ethos* (what you are), and *pathos* (your passion). As you preach the Word may you experience his smile—the Holy Spirit in your sails!

R. Kent Hughes
Wheaton, Illinois

Preface and Acknowledgments

Eutropius had fallen into disgrace. As the highest-ranking official in the Byzantine Empire (late fourth century), he served as the closest adviser to the emperor Arcadius, then ruling in Constantinople. But Eutropius abused his imperial power and aroused the anger of the empress Eudoxia, who orchestrated a campaign against him that resulted in a sentence of death.

Desperate to save his life, Eutropius slipped away from the palace and ran to the Hagia Sophia, where he clung to the altar and claimed sanctuary. Soon an angry mob of soldiers surrounded the great church, denouncing Eutropius and demanding his summary execution. Eventually the crowds dispersed, but the next day was Sunday, so they returned the following morning to see whether the pastor would give in to their demands.

The preacher was John Chrysostom, the famous orator who served as the Bishop of Constantinople. As he mounted his pulpit, Chrysostom could see a church thronged with worshipers and thrill-seekers. They, in turn, could see Eutropius groveling at the altar. The great man had become a pitiable spectacle, with his teeth chattering and abject terror in his eyes.

The dramatic sermon Chrysostom gave that day may have been the finest he ever preached.[1] For his text Chrysostom took Ecclesiastes 1:2 ("Vanity of vanities! All is vanity"), and for his primary illustration he used the decline and fall of Eutropius.

Here was a man, Chrysostom noted, who had lost everything—position, wealth, freedom, safety. Only days before, he had been the second most powerful man in the world. But it was all vanity, as events had proven, for now Eutropius had become "more wretched than a chained convict, more pitiable than a menial slave, more indigent than a beggar wasting away with hunger." "Though I should try my very best," Chrysostom said, "I could never convey to you in words the agony he must be suffering, from hour to hour expecting to be butchered."

Chrysostom did not stop there, however. His purpose was not to condemn Eutropius but to save him, and also to give his listeners the gospel. To that end, he challenged his listeners to recognize the vanity of their own existence. Whether rich or poor, one day they would all have to leave their possessions behind. They too would face a day of judgment—the judgment of a holy God. Their only hope then would be the hope that they should offer to Eutropius now—mercy at the table of Christ.

The sermon must have hit its mark, for as Chrysostom came to a close, he could see tears of pity streaming down people's faces. Eutropius was spared—a life saved by the preaching of Ecclesiastes.

By the grace of God, Ecclesiastes can have the same impact in our lives. By cautioning us not to put our hope in earthly pleasures and worldly treasures, Ecclesiastes teaches us to put our hope in God instead. The book also reminds us, especially in its closing verses, that a day of judgment is coming. Like everything else in the Bible, therefore, Ecclesiastes points us to the gospel of salvation. Our only safety is in the mercy of Jesus Christ.

This expositional commentary originated with a sermon series at Philadelphia's Tenth Presbyterian Church. I praise God for the people who came to Christ through those sermons and for the many others (including me) who gained a deeper grasp of the gospel and came to a clearer understanding of the Christian life.

I also praise God for the many people who helped bring this commentary into print. I am grateful to Kent Hughes and to Crossway Books for the privilege of contributing again to this fine series of commentaries. A generous sabbatical provided by the session and congregation of Tenth Presbyterian Church afforded the time needed to finish the book. Lois Denier, Randall Grossman, Elaine Maxwell, Jonathan Rockey, Leland Ryken, and Mary Ryken made necessary corrections to the original manuscript and had valuable suggestions for its improvement. Robert Polen entered the final editorial changes.

Some people think that Ecclesiastes is about the meaninglessness of human existence. This perspective is not quite correct, however. Ecclesiastes is really about the meaninglessness of life *without God*. But because the writer never gives up his belief in God, his ultimate purpose is to show us how meaningful life can be when we see things from God's perspective. His message is not that nothing matters, but that everything does. The more we study Ecclesiastes, the better we understand why.

Philip Graham Ryken
Philadelphia, Pennsylvania

1

Vanity of Vanities

ECCLESIASTES 1:1–2

*The words of the Preacher, the son of David,
king in Jerusalem. Vanity of vanities, says the
Preacher, vanity of vanities! All is vanity.*

1:1–2

SOCIOLOGIST Jonathan Kozol met Mrs. Washington in the South Bronx. She and her young son, David, were living at a homeless hotel close to East Tremont Avenue, in a first-floor room with three steel locks on the door.

Mrs. Washington was dying, and each time Kozol came for a visit, she was visibly weaker. But, oh, the stories she could tell about life on the underside of urban America—stories about poverty and injustice, drugs, violence, and rape. Mrs. Washington told Kozol about children in her building born with AIDS and about the twelve-year-old at the bus stop who was hit by stray gunfire and paralyzed. She told him about the physical abuse she had suffered from Mr. Washington and about all the difficulties poor people had getting medical care in the city.

The woman and her son also talked about spiritual things. "I wonder how powerful God is," David admitted in one interview. "He must be wise and powerful to make the animals and trees and give man organs and a brain to build complex machineries, but he is not powerful enough to stop the evil on the earth, to change the hearts of people." On a subsequent visit Kozol looked down and saw that Mrs. Washington's Bible was open on the quilt next to her. So he asked what part of the Bible she liked to read. "Ecclesiastes," she said. "If you want to know what's happening these days, it's all right there."[1]

Why Study Ecclesiastes?

Not everyone would agree with Mrs. Washington. Ecclesiastes seems to take such a gloomy view of life that some people doubt the spiritual value of reading it or even question whether it belongs in the Bible at all. When one of the ancient rabbis read Ecclesiastes he said, "O Solomon, where is your wisdom? Not only do your words contradict the words of your father, David; they even contradict themselves."[2] Closer to our own times, scholars have described the book as "the low-water mark of God-fearing Jews in pre-Christian times."[3] Some have even doubted whether its author had a personal relationship with God at all, since his "gloomy sub-Christian attitude" seems so "far removed from the piety of the Old Testament."[4] So what is Ecclesiastes doing in the Bible, and why should we take the trouble to study it?

Mrs. Washington was right: if we want to know what is happening these days or have trouble understanding why a powerful Creator allows evil on the earth or struggle to resolve life's other inconsistencies, it is all right here in this book.

We should study Ecclesiastes *because it is honest about the troubles of life*—so honest that the great American novelist Herman Melville once called it "the truest of all books."[5] More than anything else in the Bible, Ecclesiastes captures the futility and frustration of a fallen world. It is honest about the drudgery of work, the injustice of government, the dissatisfaction of foolish pleasure, and the mind-numbing tedium of everyday life—"the treadmill of our existence."[6] Think of Ecclesiastes as the only book of the Bible written on a Monday morning. Reading it helps us to be honest with God about the problems of life—even those of us who trust in the goodness of God. In fact, one scholar describes Ecclesiastes as "a kind of back door" that allows believers to have the sad and skeptical thoughts that we usually do not allow to enter the front door of our faith.[7]

We should also study Ecclesiastes *to learn what will happen to us if we choose what the world tries to offer instead of what God has to give*. The writer of this book had more money, enjoyed more pleasure, and possessed more human wisdom than anyone else in the world, yet everything still ended in frustration. The same will happen to us if we live for ourselves rather than for God. "Why make your own mistakes," the writer is saying to us, "when you can learn from an expert like me instead?"[8]

Then too we should study Ecclesiastes *because it asks the biggest and hardest questions that people still have today*. As we shall see, there is some debate as to when this book was actually written. But whether it was written during the glory days of Solomon's golden empire or later, when Israel was in exile, it addresses the questions that people always have: What is the meaning of life? Why am I so unhappy? Does God really care? Why is there so much suffering and injustice in the world? Is life really worth living? These are the kinds of intellectual and practical questions that the writer wants to ask. "Wisdom is his base camp," writes Derek Kidner, "but he is an explorer. His concern is with the boundaries of life, and especially with the questions that most of us would hesitate to push too far."[9] Nor is he satisfied with the kind of easy answers that children sometimes get in Sunday school. In fact, part of his spiritual struggle is with the very answers that he has always been given. He was like the student who always says, "Yes, but . . . "

Here is another reason to study Ecclesiastes: *it will help us worship the one true God.* For all of its sad disappointments and skeptical doubts, this book teaches many great truths about God. It presents him as the Mighty Creator and Sovereign Lord, the transcendent and all-powerful ruler of the universe. Reading Ecclesiastes, therefore, will help us grow in the knowledge of God.

At the same time, this book *teaches us how to live for God and not just for ourselves.* It gives us some of the basic principles we need to build a God-centered worldview, like the goodness of creation and our own absolute dependence on the Creator. Then, on the basis of these principles, Ecclesiastes gives many specific instructions about everyday issues like money, sex, and power. It also has many things to say about death, which may be the most practical issue of all.

In short, there are many good reasons to study Ecclesiastes. This is especially true for anyone who is still deciding what to believe and what not to believe. It is a book for skeptics and agnostics, for people on a quest to know the meaning of life, for people who are open to God but are not sure whether they can trust the Bible. If Ecclesiastes serves as a back door for believers who sometimes have their doubts, it also serves as the gateway for some people to enter a personal relationship with Jesus Christ that leads to eternal life, which is why for some people it turns out to be one of the most important books they ever read.

Who Is Qoheleth?

Once we start to read Ecclesiastes for ourselves, the first question we need to consider is authorship. Who wrote this book? The opening verse seems to give us the answer, but it also raises a number of questions. It says, "The words of the Preacher" (Ecclesiastes 1:1). This seems straightforward enough, except that "Preacher" is not the only way to translate the Hebrew name *Qoheleth.* Some translators refer to the author as the Teacher, the Philosopher, or the Spokesman. Others prefer to leave his name untranslated and simply call him Qoheleth. So which translation should we choose?

Certainly it is safe to call the author "Qoheleth," as I will often do in this commentary. Qoheleth is perfectly good Hebrew even if no one knows exactly how to put it in English. "Teacher" is also defensible, especially given what is said at the end of the book, that he "*taught* the people knowledge" (Ecclesiastes 12:9). Qoheleth was a public teacher. Yet "Preacher" may be the best translation of all. Let me explain.

The Hebrew root of the word *qoheleth* literally means "to gather, collect, or assemble." Some scholars take this as a reference to the way the author collected various proverbs and other wise sayings together into one book. However, that is not the way this form of the word is used anywhere else in the Bible or other Hebrew literature. Instead, the verb *qoheleth* refers to the gathering or assembly of a community of people, especially for the worship of God. So Qoheleth is not so much a teacher in a classroom but more like a pastor in a church. He is preaching wisdom to a gathering of the people of God.

This context is clearly reflected in the title this book is usually given in English. "Ecclesiastes" is a form of the Greek word *ekklesia*, which is the common New Testament word for "church." An *ekklesia* is not a church building but a congregation—a gathering or assembly of people for the worship of God. The word "ecclesiastes" is the Greek translation of the Hebrew word *qoheleth*. Literally, it means "one who speaks in the *ekklesia*"—that is, in the assembly or congregation.[10] So Qoheleth is a title or nickname for someone who speaks in church. In a word, he is the "Preacher."

In this case, we can be even more specific because the Preacher is further identified as "the son of David, king in Jerusalem" (Ecclesiastes 1:1). Naturally we think first of King Solomon, for although many kings came from the royal line of David, Solomon is the only immediate son of King David who ruled after him in Jerusalem.

Furthermore, many of the things that Qoheleth tells us about his life sound exactly like King Solomon. Who else could say, "I have acquired great wisdom, surpassing all who were over Jerusalem before me" (Ecclesiastes 1:16; cf. 2:9)? No one but Solomon, because God promised him "a wise and discerning mind" like no one before or after, with riches beyond compare (see 1 Kings 3:12–13). Then, as the Preacher goes on to describe the houses he built, the gardens he planted, and the women he kept as concubines, we are reminded of the power and luxury of King Solomon. The description of the Preacher at the end of the book, where he is described as "weighing and studying and arranging many proverbs with great care" (Ecclesiastes 12:9; cf. 1 Kings 4:32), also sounds exactly like Solomon, who fits the context of Ecclesiastes far better than any of Israel's other kings.

From the earliest days of the church, many teachers have identified Solomon as the Preacher. After wandering away from God and falling into tragic sin, Solomon repented of his sinful ways and returned to the right and proper fear of God. Ecclesiastes is his memoir—an autobiographical account of what he learned from his futile attempt to live without God. In effect, the book is his final testament, written perhaps to steer his own son Rehoboam in the right spiritual direction.

In more recent times, some Bible scholars have moved away from identifying Solomon as the author of Ecclesiastes. They point out that he is never mentioned by name (the way he is named at the beginning of Proverbs, for example). If the author wanted to claim full Solomonic authority for his book, why didn't he come right out and say that it was written by Solomon?[11] Instead the opening verse leaves a sense of distance between Solomon and Ecclesiastes; the famous king is obviously associated with the book, but never explicitly identified as its author. Furthermore, the events that tie in well with the life of Solomon mainly appear in the first two chapters, after which he seems to get left behind. In fact, later the Preacher says some things that some people find it hard to imagine Solomon ever saying, such as when he starts to criticize wealthy kings and their officials for oppressing the poor (e.g., Ecclesiastes 5:8).

Then there is the ending of the book to consider. Most of Ecclesiastes is written in the first person. "This is what I saw," the Preacher says; "this is what I said in my heart." Yet at the very end he is referred to in the third person: "Besides being wise, the Preacher also taught the people knowledge" and so forth (Ecclesiastes 12:9ff.). Thus many scholars conclude that at some point Ecclesiastes must have had an editor, and some believe that it was written after the days of Solomon, possibly during Israel's exile in Babylon or even later.

So why does Ecclesiastes give the impression that it was written by King Solomon? Because, it is said, in ancient times it was fairly common for people to write fictional autobiographies.[12] In order to communicate his message, a writer would take on the persona of someone famous. This was not done in order to deceive anyone. In fact, most of these fictional autobiographies were based on the life of someone from history. To illustrate this, the conservative Lutheran scholar H. C. Leupold quotes the opening line of *Sir Galahad*, by the Victorian poet Alfred Lord Tennyson. The poem begins, "My good blade carves the casques of men." Leupold rightly points out that no one would ever accuse Tennyson of impersonating an Arthurian knight.[13] Rather, by putting words into Galahad's mouth, the poet was using a well-known literary convention.

Many scholars (including some evangelicals) think that Ecclesiastes is the same kind of book—a fictional royal autobiography. The author has taken a well-known figure from history and used that person's life to make a spiritual point. With Qoheleth, writes Derek Kidner, "we put on the mantle of a Solomon."[14] Who better than King Solomon to illustrate the futility of life without God? The man had everything that anyone could ever want. But the world is not enough. If it could not satisfy the richest, wisest king in the world, it will never satisfy anyone.

Judging by what the book says, Ecclesiastes may well have been written by Solomon himself; this is the most natural way to read the Biblical text. But even if another author used Solomon to help make his point, the words of Ecclesiastes are the very words of God, inspired by the Holy Spirit. The end of the book tells us that whatever wisdom we find in this book has been "given by one Shepherd" (Ecclesiastes 12:11), meaning God himself. Furthermore, Solomon's life is clearly presented as the Biblical context for what we read in Ecclesiastes. The book's real-life background—and we need to see it from this perspective—is the story we read about Solomon in 1 Kings and other places.

When we read that story carefully, we discover—somewhat surprisingly—that "Preacher" is a very appropriate title for Solomon. He was the king, of course, so we do not usually think of him as a preacher. Yet when Solomon dedicated the temple in 1 Kings 8, the Bible says that he "assembled" Israel (v. 1), and then it repeatedly says that the Israelites formed an "assembly" (e.g., v. 14). Thus the vocabulary in 1 Kings 8 is closely related to the terminology of Ecclesiastes 1, where we read the words of Qoheleth— the person who speaks to the assembly. Ecclesiastes is Solomon's sermon to people gathered for the worship of God.

What Does the Preacher Say?

What, then, does the Preacher say? His opening words hardly sound very encouraging: "Vanity of vanities, says the Preacher, vanity of vanities! All is vanity" (Ecclesiastes 1:2). With these encapsulating superlatives, Qoheleth takes the whole sum of human existence and declares that it is utterly meaningless. Then he takes the next twelve chapters to prove his point in painful detail, after which he returns to the very same statement: "Vanity of vanities, says the Preacher; all is vanity" (Ecclesiastes 12:8).

Like the name Qoheleth, the word "vanity" is notoriously difficult to define. But since it shows up dozens of times in the book of Ecclesiastes, it is important for us to try to understand this "multipurpose metaphor."[15] Taken literally, the Hebrew word *hevel* refers to a breath or vapor, like a puff of smoke rising from a fire or the cloud of steam that comes from hot breath on a frosty morning. Life is like that. It is elusive, ephemeral, and enigmatic. Life is so insubstantial that when we try to get our hands on it, it slips right through our fingers.

Life is also transitory. It disappears as suddenly as it comes. Now you see it, now you don't! We are here today and gone tomorrow. Thus the Bible often compares our mortal existence to a vapor. According to the psalmist, we are "mere breath" (Psalm 39:5); our days will "vanish like a breath" (Psalm 78:33; cf. Job 7:7). The Apostle James said something similar when he described life as "a mist that appears for a little time and then vanishes"

(James 4:14). So too when the Preacher says "vanity of vanities," he is partly making a comment on the transience of life. Breathe in; now breathe out. Life will pass by just that quickly.

Some versions translate this word literally and use a word like "vapor" or "smoke" for the Hebrew word *hevel*. For example, here is Eugene Peterson's paraphrase of Ecclesiastes 1:2: "Smoke, nothing but smoke. There's nothing to anything—it's all smoke" (MESSAGE). When we look at the way this word is used throughout the book, however, it takes on broader significance. The word *hevel* comes to express the absurdity and futility of life in a fallen world. Thus in the New International Version, the Preacher says, "Meaningless! Meaningless! Utterly meaningless! Everything is meaningless." But perhaps the old King James Version and newer translations like the English Standard Version say it the best way that we can say it in English: "vanity of vanities." To use the word "vanity" like this is to say that our brief lives are marked by empty futility, which is what Qoheleth says all the way through his book.

Notice the vast scope of the claim that he makes: "*all* is vanity" (Ecclesiastes 1:2). There is not one single aspect of human existence that is not frustrated by futility. It is all empty, pointless, useless, and absurd. To prove this point, the Preacher will take everything that people ordinarily use to give meaning or to find satisfaction in life and then show how empty it really is. In doing this, he will speak from experience, because he had tried it all—money, pleasure, knowledge, and power.

Some people try to find meaning in what they can know and learn about life, but when the Preacher tried to pursue knowledge he discovered that "in much wisdom is much vexation, and he who increases knowledge increases sorrow" (Ecclesiastes 1:18). Some people think they will be satisfied with all of the pleasures that money can buy. The Preacher was rich enough to conduct a thorough experiment with this as well, but in the end he learned that "all was vanity and a striving after wind, and there was nothing to be gained under the sun" (Ecclesiastes 2:11). He immersed himself in his work, trying to do something significant with his life or to make a name for himself, but this also proved to be a vexation to his soul; he had nothing to show for all of his heavy labor.

Sooner or later we all have the same experience. We try to find the meaning of life but come up empty. We indulge in certain pleasures, only to end up more dissatisfied than ever. Or we are unhappy because we feel that we will never do anything important or be anybody special. Then there is the biggest vanity of all, the emptiest of all futilities—death, in all of its dreadful finality. Death is the vanity of all vanities.

What makes everything even worse for the Preacher is that somehow God is at the bottom of it. Qoheleth never gives up his faith in the power and sovereignty of God. But rather than making him feel better, the truth of

God's existence often seems to make things worse. Whatever frustrations he has with the world are also frustrations with the God who made it. So what hope does he have that life will ever make sense? Anyone who has ever felt that life was not worth living—that nothing ever turns out the way one wants or hopes and that not even God can make a difference—knows exactly what the Preacher was talking about.

The End of the Matter

Given everything that Ecclesiastes says about the vanity of life, one might think that the book is depressing. Admittedly, some people think that the Preacher is too much of a pessimist (although the average pessimist would probably say that Solomon is actually a realist!). Certainly the experiences of life have taught him to take a darker view. He still believes in God, so he is not an atheist, or even an agnostic. But there do seem to be times when he is tempted to be a cynic, if not a fatalist. The Old Testament scholar Gerhard von Rad went so far as to describe the author as a bitter skeptic "suspended over the abyss of despair. . . . Nothing remained for Ecclesiastes but to submit in deep resignation to this tragic existence."[16] Can we really trust a man like this to give us wisdom for life?

Some Bible scholars complain that Qoheleth never seems to make any spiritual or intellectual progress, that his book does not seem to have a clear structure, and that he ends up right back where he began. In the words of one scholar, there is "no progression of thought from one section to another," and the author "offers no universal or satisfactory answer" to any of the problems he raises.[17] To quote from another source, the author of Ecclesiastes "seems rather disorganized," moving "from one topic to another without any evident organizing principle embracing all the parts."[18] Other scholars say that although the words of the Preacher are not entirely trustworthy, they get corrected by the book's conclusion, which was written by a true and orthodox believer in the God of Israel.[19]

Over against these contemporary perspectives on Ecclesiastes, I believe that the book does have a coherent message and that there is wisdom for us all the way through. It may well be the case that the last six verses were written by someone other than Qoheleth. This conclusion does not contradict what comes before, however, but brings the message to its proper conclusion—the one that Qoheleth has had in view from the beginning. What purpose would the final editor have in publishing a book with which he disagreed almost entirely?[20] While it is true that the Preacher takes a sober view of life, never flinching from any of its complexities and confusions, it is equally true that he has solid hope in the goodness of God as well as lasting joy in the beauty of his many gifts. This is exactly why he has shown us the futility of everything earthly: it is so we will put our hope in the everlasting God.

The Preacher hints at his evangelistic purpose by using an important phrase almost thirty times over the course of his argument: "under the sun." As he describes the absurdity and futility of work and wisdom and pleasure and everything else, he repeatedly says that this is what things are like "under the sun" (e.g., Ecclesiastes 1:3). In other words, this is what life is like when we view it from a merely human perspective, when we limit our gaze to this solar system, without ever lifting our eyes to see the beauty and glory of God in Heaven. If that is all we see, then life will leave us empty and unhappy. But when we look to God with reverence and awe, we are able to see the meaning of life, and the beauty of its pleasures, and the eternal significance of everything we do, including the little things of everyday life. Only then can we discover why everything matters.

We catch glimpses of this eternal perspective throughout the book of Ecclesiastes, but it becomes even clearer at the very end. Vanity does not have the last word. Instead, the author says, "The end of the matter; all has been heard. Fear God and keep his commandments, for this is the whole duty of man" (Ecclesiastes 12:13). Similarly, the book of Proverbs says, "The fear of the LORD is the beginning of knowledge" (1:7). Here in Ecclesiastes, Solomon says that the fear of God is not just the beginning but also the end—the goal of our existence. But in order to know and enjoy God properly, we first have to see the emptiness of life without him, becoming thoroughly disillusioned with everything the world has to offer. To this end, Ecclesiastes gives us a true assessment of what life is like apart from the grace of God. This makes it a hopeful book, not a depressing one; ultimately its worldview is positive, not negative. Like a good pastor, Qoheleth shows us the absolute vanity of life without God, so that we finally stop expecting earthly things to give us lasting satisfaction and learn to live for God rather than for ourselves.

The great English preacher John Wesley once preached his way through this great book of the Bible. In his personal journal he described what it was like to begin that sermon series. "Began expounding the Book of Ecclesiastes," he wrote. "Never before had I so clear a sight either of its meaning or beauties. Neither did I imagine, that the several parts of it were in so exquisite a manner connected together, all tending to prove the grand truth, that there is no happiness out of God."[21] What Wesley discovered was a life-changing truth, which we can pray that Ecclesiastes will also teach us: we will never find any true meaning or lasting happiness unless and until we find it in God.

If we learn this lesson well, it will draw us closer to Jesus, the Son of God. The Bible says that because of our sin, creation itself "was subjected to futility" (Romans 8:20). When the Bible says "futility," it uses the standard Greek translation for the word we encounter in Ecclesiastes—the Hebrew word for vapor or vanity (*hevel*). This is why life is always so frustrating and sometimes seems so meaningless: it is all because of sin. But Jesus suffered the curse of sin in all its futility when he died on the cross (see Galatians 3:13). Now, by the power of his resurrection from the grave, the emptiness of life under the sun will be undone: "the creation itself will be set free from its bondage to corruption and obtain the freedom of the glory of the children of God" (Romans 8:21). Thus Ecclesiastes helps us see our need for the gospel of Jesus, which is the most important reason of all to study it.

2

Same Old, Same Old

ECCLESIASTES 1:3–11

All things are full of weariness;
a man cannot utter it;
the eye is not satisfied with seeing,
nor the ear filled with hearing.
What has been is what will be,
and what has been done is what will be done,
and there is nothing new under the sun.

1:8–9

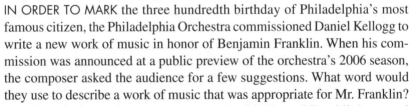

IN ORDER TO MARK the three hundredth birthday of Philadelphia's most famous citizen, the Philadelphia Orchestra commissioned Daniel Kellogg to write a new work of music in honor of Benjamin Franklin. When his commission was announced at a public preview of the orchestra's 2006 season, the composer asked the audience for a few suggestions. What word would they use to describe a work of music that was appropriate for Mr. Franklin?

"Revolutionary," someone answered, thinking of Franklin's central role in freeing the United States from English tyranny. "Electric!" shouted another member of the audience, thinking of the famous experiment with the kite, the key, and the bolt of lightning. But the man who drew the biggest laugh told Mr. Kellogg to make sure that his composition was "profitable." After all, what would be more in keeping with the entrepreneurial spirit of Benjamin Franklin than making a little money?

Many of Franklin's famous maxims promote good honest capitalism. He commented on the worth of money ("Nothing but money is sweeter than honey"). He praised the virtue of hard work ("Early to bed and early to rise makes a man healthy, wealthy, and wise"). He encouraged people to be frugal ("Beware of small expenses; a small leak will sink a great ship"). Then there is his most famous proverb: "A penny saved is a penny earned." As a successful businessman, these were all principles he put into practice. If anyone knew how to make a profit, it was Benjamin Franklin.

Profit Motive

The man who wrote Ecclesiastes had the same motivation. His Hebrew name was Qoheleth; in English we know him as the Preacher. From the statement made in the opening verse and from other details in the book we know that he was either Solomon himself or else someone who wanted to present that famous king's tragic downfall as a cautionary tale. But however we identify him, the man wanted life to pay him some dividends. Like Benjamin Franklin, he had many wise things to say about daily life, and he was looking constantly for anything he could turn to his advantage.

We see this from the Preacher's opening question. In verse 2 he states the theme of his book and his motto for life: "Vanity of vanities! All is vanity." Then in verse 3 he begins to make his case for the emptiness of our existence by asking, "What does man gain by all the toil at which he toils under the sun?" (Ecclesiastes 1:3). The same question will come up again in chapter 3: "What gain has the worker from his toil?" (v. 9). The idea of gaining some profit will come up repeatedly as well; it appears nearly a dozen times in the book of Ecclesiastes (e.g., Ecclesiastes 5:9).

The word "gain" (Hebrew *yitron*) is a commercial term ordinarily used in the context of business. It refers to a surplus, to something left over after all the expenses have been paid. This is the goal toward which anyone in business is working. The goal is to turn a profit as the reward for one's labor. Gain is the return on investment for hard work.

As a bottom-line thinker, the Preacher was looking to get a good return. He was willing to work hard, but first he wanted to know the cash value. So he asks the question that people have about every job: Is it worth it? Am I really accomplishing anything? What will I have to show for all my toil? People usually assume that if they work a little harder, they will get something extra—more than they would have had otherwise. But the Preacher had started to doubt whether this was really true in life. Thus he asks us to consider what we will have to show for ourselves when life on earth is finished.

The answer the Preacher gives here is, absolutely nothing. He asks in order to draw us into the discussion, but his question is purely rhetorical. Qoheleth already knows the answer; he is only asking to make a point. As far as he could tell, no matter how hard people work, they never really gain anything. The word he uses for "toil" is simply the ordinary Hebrew word for "work" ('*amal*), but sometimes it has a negative connotation, as seems to be the case here. People work hard, laboring for some kind of profit, but what do they really get for all their effort? Precious little, if anything at all.

The problem of fruitless effort—and the difficulty some people have perceiving it—may be helpfully illustrated from a short poem by Stephen Crane:

> I saw a man pursuing the horizon;
> Round and round they sped.
> I was disturbed at this;
> I accosted the man.
> "It is futile," I said,
> "You can never—"
> "You lie," he cried,
> And ran on.[1]

Going around in Circles

To prove his point—that we have nothing to show for all our effort—the Preacher lists a series of things that never seem to go anywhere or gain anything. The first half of his introductory poem gives examples from creation—the natural world (vv. 4–7). The second half gives examples from human experience (vv. 8–11). But whether we look at the world around us or consider our own life experience, the point is the same: there is nothing to gain. People like to talk about progress—economic development, technological advances, evolutionary improvements—but it is all a myth. There is never any progress: just the same old, same old.

Start with nature—earth, wind, fire, and water. Qoheleth says, "A generation goes, and a generation comes, but the earth remains forever" (Ecclesiastes 1:4). When people think about the next generation, they usually think in terms of progress. Our children are our future; they will be able to accomplish things that go beyond anything we could ever dream. Whether it is generation X, generation Y, or generation Z, there is always another generation to give us hope for the future.

But, as usual, Ecclesiastes takes a gloomier view. Generations come and go, the writer says. One generation may be rising, but at the same time another generation is dying off. Soon the younger generation will become the older generation, and then there will be a generation after that. It is always the same. The generation gap never seems to change either. To the rising generation, anyone over thirty seems old-fashioned and out of touch. On the other hand, older folks are often shocked by the lack of respect they get from the younger generation. But it has always been this way. Socrates spoke about it in ancient times: "The children now love luxury. They have bad manners, contempt for authority, they show disrespect to their elders."[2] Similarly, Peter the Hermit is sometimes quoted as saying, "The young people of today think of nothing but themselves. They have no reverence for parents or old age. They are impatient of all restraint. They talk as if they alone knew everything."

Meanwhile, the world itself remains the same. There is never any progress. The rise of each generation gives the impression that something actually is happening, but nothing really is. A seemingly endless procession of people comes and goes, "but the earth remains forever" (Ecclesiastes 1:4). The world is a very repetitive place. Nothing ever changes. So what profit is there? What do we gain? Jerome said, "What is more vain than this vanity: that the earth, which was made for humans, stays—but humans themselves, the lords of the earth, suddenly dissolve into the dust?"[3]

Here is another illustration of the same principle: "The sun rises, and the sun goes down, and hastens to the place where it rises" (Ecclesiastes 1:5). This is the verse that Ernest Hemingway made famous as the title of his greatest novel—*The Sun Also Rises* (1926). Hemingway originally began his novel by quoting verse 4, about generations coming and going, but the publisher suggested that verse 5 would work well for a title. Hemingway agreed, presumably because he took the same basic perspective as Ecclesiastes on the meaninglessness of life under the sun.

Even the daily journey of the sun seems pointless. Around and around it goes, without ever actually ending up anywhere. Day after day the fire in the sky rises and sets and rises again. Its movement is repetitive but not progressive, just like life. Pink Floyd said something similar in a song on the album *The Dark Side of the Moon*:

> So you run and you run to catch up with the sun but it's sinking
> Racing around to come up behind you again
> The sun is the same in a relative way but you're older,
> Shorter of breath and one day closer to death.[4]

According to Ecclesiastes, even the sun itself gets short of breath. The word "hastens" is really the Hebrew word for "pant" (*sha'ap*), which may suggest that the sun is racing from east to west and back again; but more likely it means that the sun is weary of its slow and endless journey across the sky. Usually we turn to nature to find encouragement for the soul, but when the Preacher looks at the sun, he simply sees the monotony of life in a static universe.

The wind shows us the same thing, for it fails to accomplish anything more than the sun: "The wind blows to the south and goes around to the north; around and around goes the wind, and on its circuits the wind returns" (Ecclesiastes 1:6). Usually we think of the wind blowing from west to east, like the jet stream, but in Palestine the wind sometimes comes from a northerly or southerly direction. Presumably that phenomenon is mentioned here to complete the points on a compass: the sun crawls from east to west, while the wind restlessly blows from the north and the south. It may seem free to blow wherever it pleases, and in fact Jesus used this truth as the basis for one of his most famous analogies—being born again by the power of the Holy Spirit (see John 3:8). Yet the wind also follows its customary currents. It blows past, and then it comes back again. Around and around it goes, following its circular course but never reaching a destination. For all its constant movement, there is never any progress.

The flow of water seems just as profitless. "All streams run to the sea," the Preacher says, "but the sea is not full; to the place where the streams flow, there they flow again" (Ecclesiastes 1:7). When he talks about water flowing and flowing again, he is not describing the water cycle, in which water evaporates into the clouds and eventually returns to water the earth in the form of rain. Rather, Quoheleth is talking about the way that all rivers and streams flow forever to the sea. There is an especially vivid example of this in Israel, where Qoheleth lived. The Dead Sea is landlocked; it has no outlet to another body of water. Yet for all the centuries that the Jordan River has been flowing down into the Dead Sea, the sea is not yet full, and thus the water continues to flow.

Life is the same way. Everything seems to be in a rut. Where is the progress? What is the profit? You spend your whole life working for one company after another, but what do you gain for all your toil? These days it is hard to get a retirement dinner anymore, let alone a gold-plated watch. Or what do you have to show for all the work you do around the house? There are always more meals to prepare, more floors to scrub, and more clothes to wash.

Daily life is like the famous song from the musical *Show Boat*, in which Old Man River just keeps rolling along. The song is sung by Joe, a dock worker on the Mississippi River, who is worn out by all his hard work. What he sings sounds a lot like Ecclesiastes:

Ah gits weary,
An' sick o' tryin',
Ah'm tired o' livin',
And skeered o' dyin',
But Ol' Man River,
He jus' keeps rollin' along![5]

What's New?

If the sun and the wind and the mighty rivers have nothing to show for their constant labor, then what hope do we have of ever accomplishing anything in life? It makes the Preacher tired just thinking about it. So he takes what he has observed in nature and summarizes it like this: "All things are full of weariness; a man cannot utter it" (Ecclesiastes 1:8). Life is such a wearisome, toilsome trouble that it is hard even to put into words. The Contemporary English Version says it like this: "All of life is far more boring than words could ever say."

With this statement, the Preacher reiterates the central theme of his poem. He is trying to show how tiresome life is. Yet he is not finished making his argument. It is not just the natural world that proves how little there is for us to gain in life, but also our own personal experience.

Start with sensory perception. Here is a notable example of the weariness of all things: "the eye is not satisfied with seeing, nor the ear filled with hearing" (Ecclesiastes 1:8). People are always looking and listening. This is especially true now in the information age. Every day we see an endless procession of visual images: Comcast, YouTube, BlackBerry, Netflix. We can also listen to an endless stream of sounds: iPod, iPhone, iTunes, TVs, CDs, and mp3s.

Yet even after all our looking and listening, our eyes and our ears are not satisfied. We still want to see and hear more. Soon we are back to take in more of the endless procession of sounds and images. We can never get enough. There is always one more show to watch, one more game to play, one more song to which to listen. So we keep text-messaging, webcasting, Facebooking, Twittering, and Flickring. But what have we gained? What have we accomplished? Is there any profit? These are important questions to ask ourselves about everything we see and hear: Is this helping me make some kind of progress, or is it the same old, same old? Like the sea that is never full, "the eye is not satisfied with seeing, nor the ear filled with hearing" (Ecclesiastes 1:8).

Or consider the endless weariness of human history, which always seems to be repeating itself: "What has been is what will be, and what has been done is what will be done, and there is nothing new under the sun" (Ecclesiastes 1:9). Nations rise and fall, but human nature remains the same. There are times of war and times of peace, but even in peacetime we know that war will come again. In fact, some conflicts never seem to end, like the endless struggle between Jews and Arabs for control of Palestine. When Russian tanks rolled into Georgia during the 2008 Summer Olympics, it was (to quote Yogi Berra's famous redundancy) "déjà vu all over again," just like the Soviet invasion of Hungary in 1956. There is nothing new under the sun—only reruns.

This is such a sweeping claim that someone may be tempted to think of a counterexample. Surely there must be at least one thing that is new under the sun. For a moment the Preacher seems almost willing to consider this possibility. He asks, "Is there a thing of which it is said, 'See, this is new'?"

But just as quickly, he denies it. Whatever seems new "has been already in the ages before us" (Ecclesiastes 1:10).

To give just one example, consider the discovery of the New World. As every schoolchild knows, "In 1492 Columbus sailed the ocean blue." But was Christopher Columbus really the first European to set foot on North America? What about the Basque fishermen who were already crossing the Atlantic to fish for cod off the coast of Newfoundland? Or the merchants from Bristol in England who wrote to Columbus after his triumphant return in order to complain that he knew perfectly well *they* had been to America before him?[6] What about the fifteenth-century voyages of Zheng He and the imperial fleet of China? Or for that matter, what about Leif Ericson and the other Norse explorers who reached the New World four hundred years before that?

Perhaps it would be possible to think of some discovery or invention that represents a real advance in knowledge or technology. But even the latest developments fall into the same categories of human experience, like transportation or communication. Wireless telecommunication may be a legitimate advance of the twenty-first century, but there is also something familiar about it: people felt the same sense of progress when the first telegraph wire was connected or the first telephone call was placed.

Furthermore, the people who come up with these new inventions have the same fallen nature as ever. They have the same basic problems, the same moral deficiencies, and the same underlying insecurities that people have always had. This explains why history does not seem to be going anywhere, why it seems to be circular rather than linear, like the tread wheel in a hamster cage. What we see now is what people have seen before and will see again. Former linebacker Matt Millen said it well when people at his alma mater (Penn State University) were complaining about misconduct by members of the football team: "If people out there are thinking that this is new, let me just give you a little bit of Scripture. Ecclesiastes. Nothing is done that hasn't been done before."[7]

The more things change, the more they stay the same. And if it ever seems like there really is something new under the sun, it is only because we have forgotten what happened before. The Preacher's poem about life's weary repetition ends with a line about memory loss: "There is no remembrance of former things, nor will there be any remembrance of later things yet to be among those who come after" (Ecclesiastes 1:11).

How quickly people forget! What Ecclesiastes describes here is a kind of historical amnesia. People generally do not know their history very well, so what seems new to us may in fact be something ancient that we have long forgotten. For example, we often think of the United States as the first great civilization of North America. But there were people here long before us— people loving and fighting and living and dying. More than a thousand years ago the Anasazi peoples built a large city in New Mexico's Chaco Canyon, with five-story buildings containing hundreds of rooms. The Cahokia community near St. Louis grew as large as 40,000 people—the largest city in North America until Philadelphia surpassed it in the nineteenth century.[8] But who remembers any of these things now?

One day we too will be forgotten. Centuries from now, the common experiences of our own time will be among the "former things" that are mentioned in Ecclesiastes 1. What we have accumulated will be lost; what we have accomplished will be forgotten. Our descendants will not remember us any better than we remember our ancestors. Eventually, when things that have yet to happen are forgotten, those people will no longer be remembered either.

The same memory failure happens at the individual level. There are many things we find hard to remember—the experiences of early childhood, the math skills that we learned last year in school, the place where we last saw whatever it is for which we are looking. It is hard to remember. Soon most of us will face the memory loss that comes with old age, when our own experiences become inaccessible to us. Will we still be who we are when we have all but forgotten who we were? Or will every last memory of us be forgotten? This is part of the weariness of life, that there is no remembrance of former things.

All Things New

"Vanity of vanities!" "All things are full of weariness." Are you starting to agree with the Preacher's philosophy of life? Do you think there is anything to gain for all your hard work, or has his litany of failure convinced you that life is nothing but toil and trouble?

Here it is crucially important to understand the Preacher's purpose. There is a reason why he wants us to feel the full weight of the weariness and futility of life under the sun. "The function of Ecclesiastes," writes Derek Kidner, "is to bring us to the point where we begin to fear that such a comment (all is vanity) is the only honest one. So it is, if everything is dying. We face the appalling inference that nothing has meaning, nothing matters under the sun."[9]

This is not the whole story, however. Remember that this is only the way things are *if* we look at them "under the sun." This phrase, which occurs here in verse 3 and again in verse 9, as well as dozens of other places in Ecclesiastes, is one of the keys to understanding the book. It partly expresses the extent of our problem. Where do we experience life's futility and frustration? Everywhere in the world—wherever the sun shines.

Yet this phrase also leaves open the possibility of a different perspective. When he says "under the sun," the Preacher "rules out all higher values and spiritual realities and employs only the resources and gifts that this world offers. The use of this phrase is equivalent to drawing a horizontal line between earthly and heavenly realities."[10] To see things "under the sun," then, is to look at them from ground level. It is to take an earthly point of view, leaving God out of it for the moment.

But of course this is not the only way to look at things, or even the right way to look at them. There is a God in Heaven who rules *over* the sun. Therefore, we are not limited to the terrestrial; by the revelation of the Word of God, we can also see things from the celestial. The reason the Preacher shows us the weariness of our existence, making us more and more disillusioned with life under the sun, is so we will not expect to find meaning and satisfaction in earthly things, but only in God himself. Here is how the nineteenth-century English commentator Charles Bridges explained the Preacher's strategy: "We are permitted to taste the bitter wormwood of earthly streams, in order that, standing by the heavenly fountain, we may point our fellow sinners to the world of vanity we have left and to the surpassing glory and delights of the world we have newly found."[11]

This does not mean that if we believe in God all our troubles will be over or that we will never again feel the weariness and vanity of life under the sun. For one thing, believers often forget to remember God, and when we do, we are right back "under the sun" again. But Ecclesiastes does open up the possibility of an "above the sun" perspective that can bring joy and refreshment to life as we learn everything matters.

One way to see this is to take all of the things that make life so wearisome—all of the dreary repetitions in nature and human experience—and see what a difference it makes to bring God back into the picture. What happens when we take the vanity of all these vanities into the Holy of Holies and see them from God's point of view?

The Preacher looks at the natural world and fails to see any progress. But there is another perspective. The psalmist says, "The heavens declare the glory of God, and the sky above proclaims his handiwork" (Psalm 19:1). To prove his point, he looks at the same old sun and says it "comes out like a bridegroom leaving his chamber, and, like a strong man, runs its course with joy" (Psalm 19:5). Whether the sun seems to make any progress or not, it bears witness to the joy and strength of its Creator. Therefore, "From the rising of the sun unto the going down of the same the LORD's name is to be praised" (Psalm 113:3, KJV).

The repetition that we see in nature is a testimony to the goodness and orderliness of God. The regularity of the created world shows the constancy of its Creator. The winds blow at his bidding, the waters flow at his command, and this is for the blessing of every creature. The Scripture says, "He lays the beams of his chambers on the waters; he makes the clouds his chariot; he rides on the wings of the wind" (Psalm 104:3; cf. 147:18).

Again, Scripture says, "He draws up the drops of water; they distill his mist in rain, which the skies pour down and drop on mankind abundantly" (Job 36:27–28). So rather than seeing the day-in, day-out routines of nature the way Qoheleth saw them, we can see them the way Jeremiah saw them when he said, "The steadfast love of the LORD never ceases; his mercies never come to an end; they are new every morning; great is your faithfulness" (Lamentations 3:22–23).

Looking above the sun also gives us a different perspective on our experience. Is there anything new? Maybe not under the sun, but the God who rules over the sun is always doing something new. There is a "new covenant" in the blood of Jesus Christ (Luke 22:20)—the blood that he shed on the cross for the forgiveness of all our sins. There is the new life that came up from the empty tomb when Jesus rose from the dead with the power of eternal salvation. There is the "new heart" that God gives to everyone who believes in Jesus (Ezekiel 36:26). There is the "new self" that the Holy Spirit starts to grow in the knowledge and the holiness of God (Ephesians 4:24). This new self is so new that the Bible calls it "a new creation" (2 Corinthians 5:17), which is a way of saying that when we trust in God, his work in us will re-create our whole world. The Christian life is not the same old, same old. The living God who sits on the throne of the universe says, "Behold, I am making all things new" (Revelation 21:5). This is the promise to hold on to whenever we are tired of life and all its troubles. The God we worship is the God who says, "Behold, I am doing a new thing" (Isaiah 43:19).

One day this God will make new heavens and a new earth. Not everyone believes this, of course. In fact, the Bible says that some people deny the coming judgment and the final salvation because they think "all things are continuing as they were from the beginning of creation" (2 Peter 3:4). What they say sounds a lot like Ecclesiastes: "there is nothing new under the sun." But the Bible goes on to promise that when this weary old world is destroyed, God will make "new heavens and a new earth" (2 Peter 3:13). This promise gives hope to the people of God and enables us to persevere even when we are weary. Life's frustrations will not last forever; we live in the hope of a new day. In one of the earliest commentaries ever written on Ecclesiastes, Didymus the Blind wrote, "A person who is enlightened by the 'sun of righteousness' is not 'under' it but 'in' it. Thus it is said in the Gospel: 'The righteous will shine like the sun in the kingdom of their Father,' not 'under' the sun."[12]

When the great day comes, our restless ears and roving eyes will be fully and finally satisfied to see Jesus Christ and to hear the sound of his glorious worship. "What no eye has seen, nor ear heard, nor the heart of man imagined," this is "what God has prepared for those who love him" (1 Corinthians 2:9). We will no longer look this way and that for something to satisfy us, but our senses will be saturated with the glory of God. This is something to remember whenever we are frustrated or angry or sad or disappointed with everything in life that is getting broken, falling apart, or going wrong. Remember that this life is not our final existence. We were made for a better world. The very fact that we are weary of life is pointing us to the only God who can satisfy our souls.

All of this brings us back to the question that the Preacher asked at the very beginning: "What does man gain by all the toil at which he toils under the sun?" (Ecclesiastes 1:3). The answer here is, nothing. T. M. Moore writes:

> Although Solomon intends his readers to understand that life under the sun is a gift from God and should be received and enjoyed as such, he is at pains to show us that life *looked at from that perspective alone* never quite seems to make sense. The phrase "under the sun" repeatedly punctuates the futility and meaninglessness of life lived only for self and the moment, without gratitude to or regard for God and his ways.[13]

Yet the question of profit or gain is still a good question. We know this because Jesus put things almost exactly the same way. "What will you gain?" he asked. Except that Jesus turned the whole question on its head. He did not ask what in the world we would gain for all our work. Instead he asked what we would really gain if we had the whole world: "What will it profit a man if he gains the whole world and forfeits his soul?" (Matthew 16:26; cf. Mark 8:36). The implication is that not even the entire world is enough to compensate for the loss of one eternal soul.

If we are looking to make a profit, we should not live for what this world seems to offer, but only for the everlasting gain that comes with trusting Jesus for the free gift of eternal life.

3

Humanity's Search
for Meaning

ECCLESIASTES 1:12–18

*I have seen everything that is done
under the sun, and behold, all is
vanity and a striving after wind.*

1:14

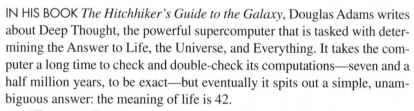

IN HIS BOOK *The Hitchhiker's Guide to the Galaxy,* Douglas Adams writes about Deep Thought, the powerful supercomputer that is tasked with determining the Answer to Life, the Universe, and Everything. It takes the computer a long time to check and double-check its computations—seven and a half million years, to be exact—but eventually it spits out a simple, unambiguous answer: the meaning of life is 42.

"Forty-two!" someone yells at the computer. "Is that all you've got to show for seven and a half million years' work?"

"I checked it very thoroughly," Deep Thought replies, "and that quite definitely is the answer. I think the problem, to be quite honest with you, is that you've never actually known what the question is."[1]

Everyone wants to know the meaning of life, but to get the right answer we have to ask the right question. This is our quest in Ecclesiastes—to come to a true and accurate understanding of life, the universe, and everything. As we join Qoheleth (the Preacher) on his spiritual journey, which fortunately takes somewhat less than seven and a half million years (!), we discover the meaning of life for ourselves.

The Seeker's Quest

The book opened with an introduction of the author (Ecclesiastes 1:1), a statement of theme (Ecclesiastes 1:2), and a poetic summary (Ecclesiastes 1:3–11), in which a series of examples drawn from nature and human experience prove that the world is "endlessly busy and hopelessly inconclusive."[2] Now the quest begins in earnest. It is possible that the first eleven verses came from the book's final editor—someone who referred to the Preacher in the third person and wanted to summarize the book's message. But in verse 12 Qoheleth speaks for himself, telling us who he is: "I the Preacher have been king over Israel in Jerusalem."

A statement like this is typical in Ancient Near Eastern literature: "an old man, sometimes a king or one who for literary purposes claims to be a king, draws on the experiences of a lifetime to give advice to his son or successor."[3] The writer is speaking autobiographically. He is describing his personal experiences for the moral benefit of his readers.

Obviously, in this case the old man is meant to be Solomon. This was evident already in verse 1, where Qoheleth described himself as "the son of David, king in Jerusalem." Here in verse 12 he further identifies himself as "king *over Israel* in Jerusalem." This description only fits the life of Solomon, because although Rehoboam and other descendants of David ruled in Jerusalem, none of them ruled over Israel. After Solomon the kingdom was divided between north and south, and whoever was king in Jerusalem only ruled over the southern kingdom of Judah, not over the northern kingdom of Israel. So this king must be Solomon.

As we have seen, some scholars take a slightly different perspective. Since the Preacher does not come right out and call himself Solomon, they believe that Ecclesiastes was written by someone else—a second "Solomon" who used the life of Israel's famous king to illustrate his own philosophy of life. To put this literary strategy in a contemporary context, it would be something like a drama on television in which the President of the United States is one of the main characters. Even if the drama is not a documentary, the President on such a program often has personal characteristics or political views that are reminiscent of John F. Kennedy or George W. Bush or someone else who sat in the Oval Office. Similarly, the argument goes, Ecclesiastes is modeled on the life of Solomon.

It is equally likely, if not more so, that the book was written by Solomon himself. But either way, the life of that famous king provides the Biblical context for Ecclesiastes. Here he introduces himself as Qoheleth, which means "the Collector" or "the Convener." He uses this title because one of the duties of his royal office is to gather his subjects and instruct them in spiritual wisdom, as Solomon did in 1 Kings 8 when he assembled Israel to dedicate the holy Temple in Jerusalem. Thus, the king is also the Preacher.

The fact that he speaks in the perfect tense ("I . . . have been king") tells us further that he is writing near the end of his reign, after he has been king for some time. Writing from the vantage point of age and experience, he is telling us the story of what he has learned about life.

The Solomon of Ecclesiastes was a seeker; he was on a personal quest for wisdom and knowledge. He says, "I applied my heart to seek and to search out by wisdom all that is done under heaven" (Ecclesiastes 1:13). The Preacher-King was asking the ultimate questions. He wanted to know the meaning of life.

This quest fits everything we know about King Solomon from other places in the Bible. When Solomon became king, God gave him the opportunity of a lifetime: he could ask for anything he wished. Solomon chose wisely. Rather than asking for money or fame, he asked for wisdom to govern the people of God. God was so pleased with Solomon's request that he said, "Behold, I give you a wise and discerning mind, so that none like you has been before you and none like you shall arise after you" (1 Kings 3:12). This precious gift of wisdom did not mean that the king instantly understood everything. He still had to apply himself to the pursuit of knowledge, which is exactly what Solomon did: he devoted his life to learning.

Solomon's quest was sincere. When he says, "I applied my heart," he means that the pursuit of knowledge came from the very core of his being. The Preacher-King focused his mind and disciplined his heart to know the truth.

His quest was also comprehensive. The words "to seek" and "to search" indicate the seriousness of his efforts. Although some scholars have tried to distinguish the meaning of these two words, here they are used fairly synonymously. Together they show Solomon's diligence. He wanted to understand life—not just one part of life but life taken as a whole. His quest was as extensive as it was intensive. The Preacher was an ancient-day Renaissance man. He wanted to know as much as he could about as many things as he could. He wanted to take it all in, leaving nothing out, so that his conclusions would be as definitive as possible. He wanted to investigate every area of human endeavor—"all that is done under heaven" (Ecclesiastes 1:13). In short, he wanted to know everything about everything under the sun.

This was a commendable quest. Rather than seeking pleasure or looking for popularity or finding significance in his personal accomplishments, the Preacher first used wisdom to find meaning for life. As a wisdom writer, he viewed wisdom as the highest virtue. Rather than living for lower pleasures, he pursued the life of the mind.

The kind of wisdom the Preacher had in mind was not divine wisdom but human wisdom—the very best that human beings have ever thought or said. Although wisdom generally has very positive connotations in the Bible, it does not always refer to spiritual wisdom that comes from God.

The Hebrew word for wisdom (*hochma*) is a broad term. Here it refers to what human beings can learn about the world without any special revelation from God.

Seeking such wisdom is a worthy pursuit, as far as it goes. All truth is God's truth, wherever it may be found. If we learn anything that is true to the world as it truly is, that truth ultimately comes as a gift from God. Even false religions contain some words that are true. Even people who do not know God nevertheless have practical wisdom for daily life. By God's "common grace," as theologians call it, even books in the "Religion and Self-Help" section of a secular bookstore give people some of the knowledge they seek. The question is, how far will such wisdom take us? Will it help us to know and to worship Jesus Christ as the Son of God? Will it lead us in the way of life everlasting? Will it help us understand why everything matters?

A Bad Business

One good way to answer these questions is to see the result of the Preacher's quest. What did he discover? And what would we learn if we devoted our lives to a similar quest for knowledge?

The reality is that the Preacher came up totally empty. Rather than adding up to 42, the Preacher found that the meaning of life was nothing at all. So in verses 13–15 he describes the unhappiness, the emptiness, and the futility of his own efforts to understand the universe—the end of his first quest.

The mood of these verses is unmistakably gloomy. Qoheleth says, "It is an unhappy business that God has given to the children of man to be busy with" (Ecclesiastes 1:13). Sooner or later most people end up feeling the same way. Many things make us feel unhappy. The bad relationship that our parents have, unkind comments that people make about us, things we do not have but wish we did, the recognition we think we deserve but never get, even the ordinary frustrations of daily life—all of these circumstances make us feel unhappy.

But Ecclesiastes is saying something even more depressing. His word for unhappiness (Hebrew *ra'*) is more negative. Properly speaking, it refers to something bad or evil.[4] Thus it describes a moral category rather than an emotional state. The problem is not simply that life makes us unhappy, but that it is evil in itself. It is not just an *unfortunate* business,[5] but a *bad* business.

There are at least two different ways to understand this statement. When the Preacher talks about "business," he may be referring to everything that people do—human activity in general. If so, what he says about that business is certainly true. Ever since the sin of our first parents, work has been a bad experience. Leonard Woolf, the British publisher and political theorist who helped begin the Bloomsbury Group (also the husband of Virginia Woolf), had this to say about his life and work:

> I see clearly that I have achieved practically nothing. The world today and the history of the human anthill during the past five to seven years would be exactly the same as it is if I had played Ping-Pong instead of sitting on committees and writing books and memoranda. I have therefore to make a rather ignominious confession that I must have, in a long life, ground through between 150,000 and 200,000 hours of perfectly useless work.[6]

These are the words of someone who wrote more than twenty books on literature, politics, and economics. Yet in the end it all seemed useless to him, a complete waste of time. As we think about all our own hard work—whether it is at home, at school, on the job, or in ministry—it is tempting to feel the same way: life is a bad business.

There is another way to take this verse, however. The "unhappy business" the Preacher mentions may in fact be his very quest to understand the meaning of life.[7] It is the pursuit of knowledge itself that turns out to be such a bad business. The longer he looked for answers and the harder he tried to understand life, the more burdened he became. Sometimes the more we try to know, the more frustrated we get with life and all its unanswerable questions.

The Preacher believed that the quest for knowledge was his God-given task. As a person made in God's image, he could not help but ask the ultimate questions, trying to understand the meaning of life. This is part of the spiritual business that God has given to humanity. As Francis Schaeffer once wrote, "All men . . . have a deep longing for significance, a longing for meaning . . . no man, regardless of his theoretical system, is content to look at himself as a finally meaningless machine which can and will be discarded totally and for ever."[8] Even people who deny God's existence search for the meaning of their own existence. The famous astrophysicist Stephen Hawking was grasping at this truth when he said, "We are just an advanced breed of monkeys on a minor planet of a very average star. But we can understand the universe."[9] Or at least we can *try* to understand the universe. Yet the very business of that quest leads to unhappiness.

Striving after the Wind

It also leads to emptiness, as the Preacher also discovered. After going everywhere to make a thorough investigation of everything that people do, he came to this conclusion: "I have seen everything that is done under the sun, and behold, all is vanity and a striving after wind" (Ecclesiastes 1:14).

Once again the Preacher is using some of his favorite phrases. He says that he is looking "under the sun." In other words, he is seeing what people do from an earthly perspective. He also repeats the word "vanity," which literally means "smoke" or "vapor" and refers more broadly to the meaninglessness of life. Then he introduces a new phrase, another metaphor that encapsulates his philosophy of life. Life under the sun is "a striving after wind." The word "behold" makes this statement emphatic. We might translate the verse like this: "I observed all that is done under the sun. And really, it is all meaningless and a chasing of the wind."[10]

There is some uncertainty about the best way to translate the word "striving" (Hebrew *re'ut*). It can mean "chasing." It can also mean things like "feeding" or "shepherding." But whatever translation we choose, none of these activities has any hope of mastering the wind. Whether we are chasing it or feeding it or striving after it, there is nothing we can do to catch the wind. Today when individuals talk about how difficult it is to get people to do something, they say it is like herding cats. But if you think herding cats is difficult, try shepherding the wind!

So it is with life and all our human efforts to understand it. In one of Solomon's many famous proverbs we hear wisdom say, "Whoever finds me finds life and obtains favor from the LORD" (Proverbs 8:35). But here in Ecclesiastes that quest seems futile. From what the Preacher has seen, based purely on his personal experience, without the benefit of divine revelation, figuring out the meaning of life is as unattainable as striving after the wind.

Many good minds have reached the same conclusion. Before he died, the modernist poet Ezra Pound said, "All my life I believed I knew something. But then one strange day came when I realized that I knew nothing; yes, I knew nothing. And so words became void of meaning."[11] Similarly, the infamous atheist and evolutionist Richard Dawkins has concluded that human existence is "neither good nor evil, neither kind nor cruel, but simply callous: indifferent to all suffering, lacking all purpose."[12]

The Preacher concludes his own empty, unhappy quest for the meaning of life with a proverb. We know this couplet is a proverb because of its parallel grammatical structure and also because it expresses truth in an enigmatic way that takes careful thought to understand. This is what it says: "What is crooked cannot be made straight, and what is lacking cannot be counted" (Ecclesiastes 1:15).

Even if we cannot understand the meaning of life, we still have to face up to its hard realities. Some things in life are crooked—not in the sense that they involve criminal or immoral activity, but in the sense that they are so bent out of shape that they resist all our efforts to straighten them out again. There are many things in life that we wish we could straighten out but cannot, any more than we can mend a crumpled fender. We suffer arguments at home, conflicts in the church, wrongs done in the workplace, mistakes made by the government, our own moral failings, financial troubles, physical disabilities—the list goes on and on. There is always something in life we wish we could bend back into shape. Yet the Preacher has learned that "what is crooked cannot be made straight" (especially if it turns out to be something God wants to leave crooked; see Ecclesiastes 7:13). Some of our circumstances cannot be corrected. No matter how hard we try, we cannot bend them in a different direction.

Nor are we able to make life add up, which is the point of the second line in this proverb: "What is lacking cannot be counted." This may simply mean that we cannot count what we do not have. Today's English Version says it like this: "You can't straighten out what is crooked; you can't count things that aren't there." The problem may go even deeper, however. The Preacher may be saying that we do not even know what we are missing or that what is missing from life is beyond measure. But no matter how we look at this verse, the point is that life fails to add up. In the words of the Turkish novelist Orhan Pamuk, "unfinished, the world is somehow lacking."[13]

Taking both parts of the proverb together, life is what it is, and there is nothing we can do to fix it. There are so many things that we are powerless to change: people we cannot manage, problems we cannot solve, longings we cannot satisfy. We certainly cannot bend life to our own will simply by the exercise of human wisdom. To put it another way, life is like an account that refuses to balance. We can tell that something is missing, but we cannot figure out what it is, and even when we make an adjustment to get everything to balance, deep down we know that we are fudging the figures. So it was for the Preacher. His quest failed. Human wisdom could not give him the answer to the meaning of life.

The Quest Continued

This does not mean that he was ready to give up, however. In verses 16 to 18 the Preacher describes his continued quest for meaning. After his first attempt ended in failure, he had a heart-to-heart talk with his own soul, a running internal dialogue about what he had discovered thus far. He said to himself, "I have acquired great wisdom, surpassing all who were over Jerusalem before me, and my heart has had great experience of wisdom and knowledge'" (Ecclesiastes 1:16).

This was all true, and again it reminds us of Solomon. Who had ever acquired more wisdom or had greater knowledge than Israel's wisest king? This was no idle boast, but a statement of Biblical fact. Solomon was the wisest man who ever lived, and he had taken the quest as far as he could, which made him the ultimate test case. If Solomon was unable to figure out the meaning of life, then no one can.

Admittedly, some scholars have wondered why Solomon would talk about all the men who ruled Jerusalem before him if King David was his only predecessor. So they say that perhaps Ecclesiastes is presenting this Preacher-King as some sort of super-Solomon. Yet Jerusalem had been the home of the Jebusites for centuries before David conquered the city. Thus many men had ruled in Jerusalem before Solomon (most famously, Melchizedek; see Genesis 14:18), who, with regard to his intellectual capacity, surpassed them all.

But Solomon had not yet considered the claims of morality, so his quest was not complete. He had tried to learn everything he could about life, like someone who attends the best universities and reads all the latest books claiming to reveal the mysteries of human existence. But he had not yet fully investigated the difference between right and wrong or tried to find meaning and purpose in life by becoming a better person. So he said, "I applied my heart to know wisdom and to know madness and folly" (Ecclesiastes 1:17).

Formerly the Preacher had been seeking and searching for wisdom, but now he would take a comparative approach, contrasting wisdom with folly. When he says "madness and folly," he is not talking about insanity but immorality. In other words, Qoheleth was using "madness and folly" the way they are usually used in the Old Testament—to refer to the mad foolishness of living in disobedience to God. Solomon was not trying to see if losing his right mind would help him understand the meaning of life. Rather, he was trying to understand the difference between right and wrong.

Many people take the same approach to life today. Even if they are not sure where God fits in, or whether there is a god at all, they still believe that there is a difference between right and wrong. They still want to lead good, moral lives. The Preacher who wrote Ecclesiastes wanted to be a good person, too, so he sought to understand both wisdom and folly. When we consider the life of Solomon, it is hard not to think that he studied folly a little *too* well. Part of the back story to Ecclesiastes is 1 Kings 11, in which King Solomon fell tragically into foolish sin. He married many wives and worshiped many idols. In the process, the man who knew so much wisdom learned more about folly than anyone ever should.

What was the result of this new quest? Did knowing the difference between right and wrong help him find meaning and purpose in life? Not at all. The claims of conventional morality failed to satisfy his soul. It was all a waste. So he said, "I perceived that this also is but a striving after wind" (Ecclesiastes 1:17).

Once again the Preacher quoted a proverb that summarized the conclusion of his quest. Human wisdom failed because it could not straighten things out or make life add up (Ecclesiastes 1:15). But knowing the difference between right and wrong failed for an additional reason: "For in much wisdom is much vexation, and he who increases knowledge increases sorrow" (Ecclesiastes 1:18).

Like most proverbs, this statement is open-ended. It applies to so many situations in life that it is hard to know precisely what it means here. The Preacher talks about "vexation," which is an irritation, a frustration of the soul verging on anger. He says that rather than helping us understand life, more knowledge actually increases this kind of vexation. As H. C. Leupold puts it, gaining wisdom "leads a man to find out many disturbing things that may militate strongly against his peace of mind."[14]

Maybe this is because we learn so many things that we would rather not know at all—things about the frailty of other human beings, for example, or about how many problems there are in the world. Children often wish they knew more about some of the things their parents talk about. Eventually we get older and supposedly wiser, but by then we wish we could go back to the innocence of childhood. The same thing happens in ministry: knowing more about people's spiritual weakness and the problems of the church brings us sorrow and vexation. This is why people say that ignorance is bliss. The more we know about things, the more trouble it brings.

A Hopeful Conclusion

Once again the Preacher has succeeded in making us feel even worse about life than we did before. At first his honesty may seem refreshing, but the more we study his book, the more convinced we become that all is vanity—a depressing conclusion.

If it all sounds hopeless, this means that the writer is achieving his purpose. Remember that he is showing us the world from an earthly perspective—"the best thinking that man can do on his own."[15] The Preacher believes in God, of course, and even mentions him by name (Ecclesiastes 1:13), but he made his spiritual quest without God's help. Solomon once said that "the fear of the LORD is the beginning of knowledge" (Proverbs 1:7). But what role did godly fear play here in Ecclesiastes? The Preacher did not pray. He did not consult Scripture. Instead he was off and running on his quest for knowledge without ever stopping to consider the majesty of God. He was probing "into the depth of matters by his unaided and unenlightened reason apart from any disclosures of truth that God has granted to man."[16]

If we take a secular perspective, trying to understand the world on our own terms rather than on God's terms, we will never escape Ecclesiastes 1. Study all the philosophy, research all the religion, take all the personal improvement courses, and it will still end in frustration and vexation. Human reason will only take us so far, which is why God tells us not to boast in our own wisdom, but only in our knowledge of him: "Let not the wise man boast in his wisdom . . . but let him who boasts boast in this, that he understands and knows me" (Jeremiah 9:23–24). In the New Testament, God goes even farther and says, "I will destroy the wisdom of the wise" (1 Corinthians 1:19; cf. Isaiah 29:14). Ecclesiastes is one of the sources that demonstrate God destroying the pretensions of human wisdom by showing how empty all our learning is without him.

But God does not leave us in despair. At the end of all our questing, he comes to find us in the Person of his own Son, Jesus Christ, whom the Bible describes as "the wisdom of God" (1 Corinthians 1:24). Jesus entered into all the vexation of life in this fallen world in order to show us the wise way to live. His way is the way of faith, in which we trust God to be true to his word. It is the way of hope, in which we look forward to what God has for us in the future. It is the way of love, in which we find meaning in life by living for others rather than for ourselves.

If we follow Jesus and his wisdom, we will not keep trying to bend what is crooked back to our own purpose but will humbly submit to the way God wants things to be, just like Jesus did when he went to the cross and died for our sins (see 1 Peter 2:21–24). If we follow his wisdom, life will add up. It will never add up to something as simple as 42, of course, and it may not always seem to add up on this side of eternity. Therefore, we need to be content to leave the final calculations to God. Jesus will see to it that all of God's books balance in the end, including our own personal account, which he will reconcile by his own blood. Thus our present vexation will not last forever, including all the struggles we have to understand the meaning of life. Soon all our sorrows will be over. To our everlasting joy, we will be with Jesus forever, and we will find in him the answer to all our questions.

4

Meaningless Hedonism

ECCLESIASTES 2:1–11

I said in my heart, "Come now, I will
test you with pleasure; enjoy yourself."
But behold, this also was vanity.

2:1

MOST AMERICANS TODAY are richer than most people in the history of the world. Yet in spite of our material prosperity—or maybe because of it—we still suffer from poverty of soul. The taste of pleasure has grown our appetite for this world beyond satisfaction. Meanwhile, we are still searching desperately for meaning in life.

Peggy Lee talked about this problem in the song "Is That All There Is?" In the second stanza she describes the childhood experience of going to the circus:

> When I was 12 years old, my father took me to a circus, the greatest show on earth. There were clowns and elephants and dancing bears, and a beautiful lady in pink tights flew high above our heads. And so I sat there watching the marvelous spectacle. I had the feeling that something was missing. I didn't know what, but when it was over, I said to myself, "Is that all there is to a circus?"

Then Peggy Lee croons her famous refrain: "Is that all there is? Is that all there is? If that's all there is, my friends, then let's keep dancing. Let's break out the booze and have a ball, if that's all there is."[1]

The Pleasure Test

The Solomon of Ecclesiastes had the same question as Peggy Lee: Is this all there is to life, or is there something more? First he tried to think his way to an answer, using his mind to figure out the mysteries of human existence. But his quest for knowledge ended in vexation and sorrow.

At this point it must have been tempting to give up, or else sink into depression. Yet the Preacher decided to take another approach. He started talking to himself—not about something life-changing like the beauty of God or the good news of his grace—but about doing something new to get more out of life. So he said to his soul, "Come now, I will test you with pleasure; enjoy yourself" (Ecclesiastes 2:1).

Every term in this short statement is important. The word "test" indicates that what follows is an experiment, a deliberate attempt to learn something from personal experience. The word "pleasure" shows what he wants to experience—the pleasures of life. He is like "The Wanderer" in the song based on Ecclesiastes that U2 wrote, featuring Johnny Cash on lead vocals: "I went out there / In search of experience / To taste and to touch and to feel as much / As a man can before he repents."[2]

The other important word, which gets repeated in every single verse in this passage, is the word "I." Admittedly, the writer is speaking autobiographically, so there are times when he needs to refer to himself. But does he need to do it quite so often? There is so much "me, myself, and I" in these verses that we get a strong sense of self-indulgence in the pursuit of self-centered pleasure.

So Qoheleth becomes an experimental hedonist. In other words, he chooses to make his own personal happiness his chief end in life. This is the way that many people live today, and it is a temptation for all of us—to live for ourselves rather than for God.

Let the Good Times Roll

Immediately the Preacher tells us that this quest failed as spectacularly as the first one. Pleasure did not satisfy his soul any more than wisdom did. "Behold," he says, demanding our attention, "this also was vanity" (Ecclesiastes 2:1). In other words, it was vapor and smoke. Pleasure seemed to hold out the promise of purpose in life, but it didn't last. In the end it turned out to be empty, elusive, and ephemeral. By the time his pleasures floated away, the Preacher was left with absolutely nothing. His hedonism proved to be meaningless.

In announcing the result of his quest right at the beginning, Qoheleth was not prejudging things. On the contrary, this was a comprehensive experiment, as he proceeds to explain. In verses 2–8 he lists all of the pleasures he tried, followed in verses 9–11 by a personal reflection on what he learned from his experience.

First he experimented with comedy, an entertainment that many people use to make it through life. When they feel insecure, they make a joke about something. When they get down on themselves, they make fun of other people. When they are bored, they look for something to give them a giggle, like one of the sitcoms on television or a funny video clip on YouTube—anything to get a laugh.

The Preacher tried this sort of thing too; yet it failed to bring him any lasting fulfillment. Listen to his conclusion: "I said of laughter, 'It is mad,' and of pleasure, 'What use is it?'" (Ecclesiastes 2:2). Here "mad" does not refer to being out of one's mind, the way we might use the word today, but to something sinful. According to Derek Kidner, it indicates "moral perversity rather than mental oddity."[3] A lot of laughter is like that: it is morally perverse. Not all of it, of course, because there is a kind of joyful laughter that brings glory to God (see, e.g., Proverbs 31:25). But a lot of joking is frivolous and superficial, or else cynical, sarcastic, and even cruel (see Proverbs 10:23; 26:19; 29:9). To honor God, we need to ask whether our laughter is rejoicing in the goodness of God or is coming at someone else's expense.

Qoheleth discovered that when it comes to understanding the meaning of our existence, laughter turns out to be a useless pleasure. Here is how T. M. Moore paraphrases verse 2: "I concluded that laughter and merriment for their own sakes were madness. What did they accomplish to help me find lasting meaning and purpose in life?"[4] Life is no laughing matter. Some people laugh all their way to the grave, but there is nothing funny about the deathbed of someone who dies without Christ.

The next pleasure the man tried was alcohol, and this too is a popular way to find enjoyment in life, or else to escape from its troubles. The Preacher-King found a lubricant for his laughter: "I searched with my heart how to cheer my body with wine—my heart still guiding me with wisdom—and how to lay hold on folly, till I might see what was good for the children of man to do under heaven during the few days of their life" (Ecclesiastes 2:3).

This verse turns out to be surprisingly difficult to interpret. To "cheer [one's] body with wine" strikes a decidedly negative note. The Preacher seems to be abusing alcohol the way so many people abuse drugs and alcohol today. Rather than receiving wine as a gift and drinking it with thanksgiving to God, he took it for himself as a selfish pleasure. If that is what he did, then what he said next is totally untrue—namely, that "his heart [was] still guiding [him] with wisdom." As we know from one of Solomon's other proverbs, "Wine is a mocker, strong drink a brawler, and whoever is led astray by it is not wise" (Proverbs 20:1).

Some scholars interpret this verse a different way. When Qoheleth says that his heart was still guiding him with wisdom, he means that his wine-tasting was a controlled experiment. He was not giving himself over to drunken debauchery but was drinking in moderation and then soberly and thoughtfully assessing his experience. The man was not an alcoholic but a connoisseur making careful use of wine "so that appetite is sharpened, enjoyment enhanced, and the finest bouquets sampled and enjoyed."[5]

Either way—whether his wine-drinking was characterized by sophistication or inebriation—the man was looking for pleasure while he still had the time. The end of verse 3 introduces a theme that will become increasingly prominent throughout the rest of the book, namely, the brevity of life. One of the main reasons people pursue pleasure is because life is so short. As the advertiser said in one of the popular beer commercials I remember from my childhood, "You only go around once in life, so you have to grab for all the gusto you can get!"

The Solomon of Ecclesiastes grabbed for all of that gusto, but he still came up empty. To quote again from T. M. Moore's translation, "I resolved to cheer my body with wine, still seeking after wisdom, mind you, and to lay hold on revelry in order to see whether this might yield the good I was seeking. Perhaps, since life is so short, folly and revelry might be the meaning of it all? But no."[6]

The Finer Things in Life

In addition to wine and laughter, there are many other pleasures in life, and the Preacher-King was rich enough to try almost all of them. He lived the lifestyle of the rich and famous, building a beautiful home and planting many magnificent gardens: "I made great works. I built houses and planted vineyards for myself. I made myself gardens and parks, and planted in them all kinds of fruit trees. I made myself pools from which to water the forest of growing trees" (Ecclesiastes 2:4–6).

Exercising almost God-like creativity and control, the Preacher made better homes and gardens. The man was an architect, a builder, and a developer. He designed and built mansions of pleasure. Once again this reminds us of King Solomon, who spent more than a decade building his royal palace, and at great expense (1 Kings 7:1–12). He was equally skilled in viniculture, the production of wine. He planted many vineyards (see Song 8:11), which presumably were necessary to supply all the grapes to produce the wine for his royal banqueting hall. He was equally involved in horticulture and silviculture, planting flowers and fruit trees. The lush vegetation he planted was irrigated by reservoirs large enough to water a small forest.

These projects were so large that only a great man could even attempt them. The scope of Solomon's grand achievement is indicated by the fact that everything occurs in the plural—houses and vineyards, gardens and parks, trees and pools. It sounds like a second Garden of Eden, especially with all the fruit trees (see Genesis 1:29; 2:9). In the words of Derek Kidner, "He creates a little world within a world: multiform, harmonious, exquisite: a secular Garden of Eden, full of civilized and agreeably uncivilized delights, with no forbidden fruits."[7] The palace of the Preacher-King was paradise regained.

Best of all, it was all for him. The Bible describes Qoheleth's building and landscaping projects as "great works" (Ecclesiastes 2:4), but they were not public works. They were part of the man's private residence. He was living large in the garden of his own pleasure. But that is not all. Beyond his building projects, the Preacher was pleasurably and enjoyably wealthy, as we can see from his many possessions: "I bought male and female slaves, and had slaves who were born in my house. I had also great possessions of herds and flocks, more than any who had been before me in Jerusalem" (Ecclesiastes 2:7). Given the scope of his building projects and the size of his property, the Preacher-King needed a huge workforce to run his daily operation. So he purchased many slaves, and the slaves he owned bore many children, who also belonged to their master's house. To feed them all, he had to keep flocks of cattle and herds of sheep and goats all over his royal ranch.

We observe all of this in the life of King Solomon, who had countless servants waiting on him hand and foot (see 1 Kings 10:4–8). He also had so many animals that every day the chefs in his royal kitchen would prepare "ten fat oxen, and twenty pasture-fed cattle, a hundred sheep, besides deer, gazelles, roebucks, and fattened fowl" (1 Kings 4:23).

Needless to say, the Preacher-King also had a lot of money. Some of his treasure came from taxes on his own people and some from the tribute of foreign powers, but all of it came from someone else: "I also gathered for myself silver and gold and the treasure of kings and provinces" (Ecclesiastes 2:8; cf. 1 Kings 9:26–28; 10:14ff.). Then he used some of this money to make beautiful music, both literally and figuratively: "I got singers, both men and women, and many concubines, the delight of the children of man" (Ecclesiastes 2:8). Music was a rare pleasure in those days, but the man who wrote Ecclesiastes could afford to bring it into his own home, engaging entire choirs to sing for his pleasure.

Sex is a more common pleasure, but few people have ever experienced it on quite the scale as King Solomon. Here he speaks of many concubines, but 1 Kings 11:3 gives us the raw statistics—seven hundred wives and princesses, with three hundred concubines—more sexual partners than anyone could imagine. The erotic luxury of this vast harem was the royal icing on his cake of pleasure.

Foolish Pleasure

Wine, women, and song—the Solomon of Ecclesiastes had it all. Today his face would be on the cover of *Fortune* magazine, in the annual issue on the wealthiest men in the world. His home would be featured in a photo spread with *Architectural Digest*—the interior and the exterior, from the wine cellar to the lavish gardens. Pop stars would sing at his birthday party; supermodels would dangle from his arms.

Don't you find it hard not to envy the man? Wouldn't *you* like to live like a king? All other things being equal, wouldn't you rather have a bigger, nicer house with better, more beautiful views? Don't you wish that you had someone to do all your work for you, or at least all the work that you don't enjoy doing? Think of all the money that Solomon had, with all of the choirs and concubines. Honestly, if you could get away with it, wouldn't you be tempted to grab some of his gusto for yourself?

Here is how the Preacher-King summarized his experiment with pleasure: "So I became great and surpassed all who were before me in Jerusalem. Also my wisdom remained with me. And whatever my eyes desired I did not keep from them. I kept my heart from no pleasure, for my heart found pleasure in all my toil, and this was my reward for all my toil" (Ecclesiastes 2:9–10).

The Bible warns against "the lust of the flesh, and the lust of the eyes, and the pride of life" (1 John 2:16, KJV). The psalmist was heeding this warning when he prayed, "Turn my eyes from looking at worthless things; and give me life in your ways" (Psalm 119:37). But Solomon disregarded God's warning completely. Whenever he spied something he wanted, he took it. Whenever he was tempted to indulge in a fleshly pleasure, he did so. There was nothing he denied himself—nothing "visibly entertaining or inwardly satisfying."[8] He did this because he thought he had it coming to him. "I deserve it," he would tell himself, "as the reward for all my hard work."

Since he was living the lifestyle of the rich and foolish, it sounds strange to hear him say that his wisdom remained with him. Obviously he could not possibly be talking about the kind of wisdom that begins with the fear of God. Maybe he was referring to his raw intelligence—he was still as smart as ever. More likely, he meant that he was still serious about conducting his experiment, about testing his heart to see whether pleasure would show him the meaning of life. In the words of Derek Kidner, "Part of him stands back from it all to see what frivolity does to a man."[9]

So what was the result? What happens to people who pursue any and every pleasure as their main passion in life?

The answer Ecclesiastes gives is one that we ought to know already, based on what happens to us when we pursue our own pleasures. Like Solomon, we have ample opportunity to indulge many sinful and selfish desires. In fact, maybe Solomon would envy us. Generally speaking, we live in better homes than he did, with better furniture and climate control. We dine at a larger buffet; when we go to the grocery store, we can buy almost anything we want, from anywhere in the world. We listen to a much wider variety of music. And as far as sex is concerned, the Internet offers an endless supply of virtual partners, providing a vast harem for the imagination.

By every indication, then, we are living in the godless times that Paul described for Timothy, when people would be "lovers of pleasure rather than lovers of God" (2 Timothy 3:4). Everything is offered to us. Nothing is unavailable.

So are we satisfied, or do we still want more? Gregg Easterbrook gives us the answer in his book *The Progress Paradox*, which is subtitled *How Life Gets Better While People Feel Worse*. Easterbrook proves that we have more of almost everything today . . . except happiness. In fact, the more we have, the unhappier we are, because we know we will never be able to get all the new things that we want.[10]

At the end of his quest, the Preacher-King reached the same conclusion. Even after experiencing all the pleasure that he could afford, he still had not gained anything out of life. On "the morning after," while he was still suffering the effects of his pleasure trip, he said, "Then I considered all that my hands had done and the toil I had expended in doing it, and behold, all was vanity and a striving after wind, and there was nothing to be gained under the sun" (Ecclesiastes 2:11).

The verb "consider" (Hebrew *pana*) literally means "to face," to look someone or something right in the eye (cf. Job 6:28). So Solomon is facing up to his situation, seeing his life as it really is, and he wants us to know that it isn't pretty. The word "behold" is emphatic. Life is vanity; there is nothing to it. Life is striving after wind; you can never catch it. Squeeze out all the pleasure you can, and there is still nothing to be gained from living under the sun.

Pleasure, pursued for its own sake, does not and cannot satisfy the soul. Learn this lesson from Ecclesiastes, or else learn it from sad experience, like the woman whom Rabbi Harold Kushner writes about in *When All You've Ever Wanted Isn't Enough*. She married a successful corporate executive and bought her dream house in the suburbs. But now she "cannot understand why she goes around every morning saying to herself, 'Is this all there is to life?'"[11]

Longing for God

Is this all there is? And if it is all there is, what should we do about it? What do you do when you have everything you thought you ever wanted and it still isn't enough?

Football star Tom Brady was asked this question on *60 Minutes*. Brady had just quarterbacked the New England Patriots to their third Super Bowl. He said, "Why do I have three Super Bowl rings and still think there's something greater out there for me? I mean, maybe a lot of people would say, 'Hey man, this is what is.' I reached my goal, my dream, my life. Me, I think, ' . . . It's got to be more than this.' I mean this isn't, this can't be what it's all cracked up to be." When the interviewer asked, "What's the answer?" Brady could only say, "I wish I knew. I wish I knew."[12]

At this point Peggy Lee comes in to sing her song about breaking out the booze and having a ball, but that isn't the answer either. Isn't there anything else that we can try?

The answer is that our dissatisfaction with life should point us back to God—not away from him but toward him. If all the pleasures under the sun cannot satisfy our souls, then we need to look beyond this world to God in Heaven. C. S. Lewis writes:

> Most people, if they had really learned to look into their own hearts, would know that what they do want, and want acutely, is something that cannot be had in this world. There are all sorts of things in this world that offer to give it to you, but they never quite keep their promise. The longings which arise in us when we first fall in love, or first think of some foreign country, or first take up some subject that excites us, are longings which no marriage, no travel, no learning, can really satisfy. . . . There was something we grasped at, in that first moment of longing, which just fades away in the reality.[13]

Our unsatisfied longings give us a spiritual clue that we were made for the pleasure of God. The pleasures of this world—especially all of the pleasures we experience today—leave us with what social critic Andrew Delbanco has described as an "unslaked craving for transcendence."[14] This is exactly the way that God has designed us. If we were able to find lasting satisfaction in earthly pleasure, then we would never recognize our need for God. But satisfaction does not come in the pleasures themselves; it comes separately. Satisfaction only comes in God himself, so that our dissatisfaction may teach us to turn to him.

This is one of the main reasons why Ecclesiastes is in the Bible. It is here to convince us not to love the world or live for its pleasures. This message is not intended to discourage us or to make us any more depressed than we already are, but to drive us back to God. This is not all there is. There is also a God in Heaven, who has sent his Son to be our Savior. That Son resisted the pleasures of this life to fulfill the purposes of God for our salvation. As Mark Driscoll has said, "Everything Solomon pursued, Jesus was tempted by, but resisted."[15] This is the man that Johnny Cash was looking for in "The Wanderer" and that every dissatisfied sinner needs: "Lookin' for one good man / A spirit who would not bend or break / Who could sit at his father's right hand."

Now the crucified and risen Christ offers himself to us as the source of all satisfaction. By faith we respond to him the way Christina Rossetti responded in a poem that is really a confession of faith: "Lord, I have all things if I have but Thee."[16]

Meaningful Hedonism

When we turn back to God, asking him to save us in the name of Jesus Christ, something very surprising happens: the very pleasures that once failed to satisfy us now help us find even greater joy in the goodness of God. This is not true of foolish and sinful pleasures, of course, which we are still warned against (e.g., Romans 13:13–14). Like Moses, we are called to suffer for the cause of Christ rather than to "enjoy the fleeting pleasures of sin" (Hebrews 11:25). But there is such a thing as holy and legitimate pleasure. For the people of God there is *meaningful* hedonism—pleasure that comes in the enjoyment of God.

This will never happen when we pursue pleasure for its own sake or take pleasure for ourselves or make it our main passion in life. But it will happen when we receive every pleasure as a gift from God. He is the God of pleasure; thus, whatever legitimate pleasure we experience is a gift of his goodness. So it was that Solomon's father rejoiced in the pleasures of his God. King David said, "You will fill me with joy in your presence, with eternal pleasures at your right hand" (Psalm 16:11, NIV). This is mainly a promise about Heaven, where the pleasures of God endure forever. But we can begin to taste that pleasure right now.

We taste God's pleasure when we receive laughter as a gift from him—not mocking other people or joking in a vulgar way, but laughing at ourselves and our limitations, knowing that one day we will enter our Master's joy (see Matthew 25:21).

We taste true pleasure when we receive wine as a gift from God. Later Ecclesiastes will teach us how to drink wine "with a merry heart" (Ecclesiastes 9:7), for as the psalmist also says, the gift of wine "gladden[s] the heart of man" (Psalm 104:15).

We taste God's pleasure when we design good homes and other buildings, provided that we build them for the good of other people and the glory of God (e.g., Nehemiah 12:27–30), not just for our own grandeur.

We taste God's pleasure when we go for a walk in the park or plant a beautiful garden. I have had the joy of visiting famous botanical gardens on four continents. I have been to Penshurst, Hampton Court, Blenheim Palace, Rydal Mount, Kensington Gardens, and many other English Gardens.

I have seen the begonias at Vancouver's Butchart Gardens, the proteas at Kirstenbosch in Cape Town, and the orchids in the national gardens of Singapore. In every park and garden, as my eyes have feasted on the colors of creation, I have seen the beauty of God.

There is pleasure in all of the other things that Solomon mentions as well. There is pleasure in rewarding work that is done for the glory of God (Colossians 3:23). There is pleasure in feasting at a banquet table and then returning our thanks to God (1 Timothy 4:3–4). There is pleasure in silver and gold that is given for the kingdom of God, with the guarantee of an eternal return on our investment (see Matthew 6:19–21). There is pleasure in music that delights the ear and moves our emotions to the worship of God.

There is pleasure in sexual relations when they are shared as the Designer intended. Back in the 1960s when people were arguing for unrestrained sexual freedom, *Time* magazine (of all publications) offered this rebuttal: "When sex is pursued only for pleasure, or only for gain, or even only to fill a void in society or in the soul, it becomes elusive, impersonal, and ultimately disappointing."[17] By contrast, when sex is given to someone else, rather than taken for ourselves, and when it is shared exclusively between one man and one woman who are bound by a love covenant for life, then sexual intercourse finds its highest pleasure. No one has explained this principle better than Martin Luther, who said, "If the Lord has given one a wife, one should now hold on to her and enjoy her. If you want to exceed these limits and add to this gift which you have in the present, you will get grief and sorrow instead of pleasure."[18]

God is not a spoilsport. He is not trying to take pleasure away from us but to give it to us. Once we learn how to find our satisfaction in God himself, then all of his other gifts become the best and truest pleasures. Happily, we do not have to be as rich as Solomon to experience meaningful hedonism. We simply have to see what is in the world around us and know that it comes to us as a gift from God.

A marvelous example of knowing the pleasure of God comes from the testimony of a poor Christian woman. Her name is so long forgotten that now it is known only to God, but sometime in the eighteenth century she wrote these contented words:

> I do not know when I have had happier times in my soul than when I have been sitting at work, with nothing before me but a candle and a white cloth, and hearing no sound but that of my own breath, with God in my soul and heaven in my eye. I rejoice in being exactly what I am—a creature capable of loving God, and who, as long as God lives, must be happy. I get up and look a while out the window. I gaze at the moon and stars, the work of an

Almighty Hand. I think of the grandeur of the universe and then sit down and think myself one of the happiest beings in it.[19]

Have you experienced this kind of satisfaction? Like that godly woman, you were made with the capacity to be one of the happiest beings in the universe. But you will never find it by living for your own pleasure. You will only find it when you learn to glorify God and enjoy him forever.

5

Wisdom and Mad Folly

ECCLESIASTES 2:12–17

Then I said in my heart,
"What happens to the fool will happen to me also.
Why then have I been so very wise?"
And I said in my heart that this also is vanity.

2:15

EVERYTHING ABOUT THE WASP, except why." Thus says the narrator in "A Child's Christmas in Wales," by the poet Dylan Thomas, as he laments the "Useful Presents" that he received for Christmas when he was a small boy. In addition to all of the scarves and hats and mittens and galoshes he needed to survive the cold winter, he was often given the kind of educational books that taught him, he said, "everything about the wasp, except why."[1]

Apparently the boy had an inquiring mind. He loved to ask, "Why?" Most children are equally inquisitive—not just about insects but about everything. Why do you do what you do? Why don't you do it another way? Why is the universe this way rather than that way? Why? Why? Why?

Eventually most people stop asking so many questions. We get enough answers that we can live with, or else we learn to be content without knowing all the answers. But some people never lose their intellectual curiosity. They never stop asking, "Why?"—especially when it comes to the big questions about God, the universe, and the meaning of human existence. They want to know the "why" about everything, including (but not limited to) the wasp.

Qoheleth's Quest

The man who wrote Ecclesiastes had this insatiable curiosity about life. He called himself Qoheleth (Ecclesiastes 1:1, 12), which means "the Assembler," because his calling in life was to gather God's people for spiritual instruction. Today we would call him "the Preacher," or maybe, since he also identifies himself as the king of Jerusalem, we would call him the Preacher-King. Although he never comes right out and mentions his name, from the way he describes his wealth and his wisdom, Qoheleth seems to identify himself with King Solomon.

Whether he was Solomon himself or Solomon's ghostwriter, Qoheleth loved to ask, "Why?" In order to make sense of his world, he went on a long and difficult quest to find meaning in life. When he failed to find the answers he was looking for, he did not give up but kept looking even harder.

At first the Preacher thought that the pursuit of wisdom would give him all the answers (Ecclesiastes 1:12–15), but there were so many things in life that he couldn't straighten out or that didn't add up that his quest soon ended in failure. Information failed to bring transformation. So Qoheleth turned to morality. Perhaps knowing the difference between right and wrong would give him a sense of purpose (Ecclesiastes 1:16–18). Yet this only added to his sorrow and vexation.

Next the Preacher-King pursued pleasure (Ecclesiastes 2:1–11). If wisdom ended in sorrow, maybe self-indulgence would lead to happiness. So he built magnificent buildings and created beautiful gardens. He savored the luxuries of wine, women, and song. Never abstaining from pleasure or restraining his appetites, Solomon grabbed for all the gusto he could get. Yet even the greatest pleasures in life failed to satisfy his soul. If he said it once, he said it a thousand times: it was all vanity and a striving after wind. There was nothing to be gained under the sun.

Still, Qoheleth continued his quest. He couldn't help it. The man wanted to know "Why?" and he refused to give up until he knew he had the answer. So with persistent perseverance, he kept looking for the meaning of life. Anyone who wants to know the truth about things should follow his example. Do not shy away from the difficult questions. Do not settle for easy explanations that will not hold up to careful scrutiny. Keep searching until you find your way to God.

With the goal of understanding, the Preacher tells us that he "turned to consider wisdom and madness and folly" (Ecclesiastes 2:12). If these words sound familiar, it is because Qoheleth said almost exactly the same thing in Ecclesiastes 1:13, when he applied his heart "to seek and to search out by wisdom," and again in Ecclesiastes 1:17, when he applied his heart "to know wisdom and to know madness and folly." The seeker has returned to look again at something he has considered before.

This is what people often do when they are looking for something that is missing. First they look in the most logical place to find it. When that fails, they start to look elsewhere. But if they still can't find what they are looking for, they say to themselves, "Maybe I missed something. I should probably go back where I started and look more carefully."

I witnessed this common phenomenon the night before my wedding. Some of my friends (so-called) kidnapped me, blindfolded me, tied me up, and threw me in the trunk of a car. To their dismay and my delight, I managed to wriggle out of the ropes, so that when they opened the trunk, I leaped out of the car and ran away. While they scoured the neighborhood, I carefully worked my way back to a hiding place where I could keep an eye on the car. About fifteen minutes later, two of them came back to the car and opened the trunk to make *sure* that I wasn't there. Apparently they had trouble believing that I was really gone because they did the same thing fifteen minutes after that!

This is the way we operate. When something is missing, we go back to the place where it ought to be, even if we have looked there before. So Qoheleth returned "to consider wisdom and madness and folly."

"Madness" and "folly" go together. The Preacher is not describing three different categories but only two. On the one hand there is "wisdom," which is used here in its most general sense to refer to human thinking at its very best. Wisdom in this sense is not the deep spiritual understanding that begins and ends with the fear of the Lord, but simply good, moral, practical advice for daily life that comes from people like Benjamin Franklin, Emily Post, Oprah Winfrey, and Dr. Phil.

On the other hand, there is "madness and folly," or maybe it would be better to say "mad folly" because these terms belong together. Here Ecclesiastes uses a figure of speech called *hendiadys*, in which two words are joined by the word "and" to express a single idea. For example, when Shakespeare's Macbeth says that life is "a tale told by an idiot, full of sound and fury,"[2] he is not making a careful distinction between sound and fury but is putting them together to describe the furious sound that comes from someone who cannot speak but only roars and groans.

What the Preacher is telling us, therefore, is that after pursuing pleasure, he reconsidered the claims of wisdom and mad folly. He wanted to compare the two, studying the difference between the right way and the wrong way to live, and then see if that would help him understand the purpose of life.

His reason for reconsidering is to make sure that life has been considered from every conceivable angle. The Preacher wanted to write the last word about the meaning of life. Thus he desired to make his quest as comprehensive as possible, a desire that comes through in what he says next: "For what can the man do who comes after the king? Only what has already been done" (Ecclesiastes 2:12).

Admittedly, this is a difficult verse. As it stands in most English translations, it seems to be another way of saying that there is "nothing new under
the sun"—a common theme in Ecclesiastes (e.g., 1:9). On this reading, the
verse means that even when a new king follows the old king, he will not do
anything that is really new. Others are not so sure of this meaning, however,
or even that the verse has a meaning at all. One well-known commentator
claims that the verse "makes no sense as it stands."[3]

But I believe that the verse does make sense and that it helps us understand the purpose of Ecclesiastes. Michael Eaton offers the following literal
translation: "And I turned to consider wisdom and madness and folly, for
what kind of person is it who will come after the king, in the matter of
what has already been done?"[4] When he speaks of "the matter of what has
already been done," Qoheleth seems to be referring to his present struggle
to understand the meaning of life. When he speaks of the person "who will
come after the king," he is looking ahead to the future and is wondering who
else will have the same questions that he has about human existence. With
those people in mind, he wants to write a definitive statement about wisdom
and mad folly. As the wisest and wealthiest king, he is in a unique position
to do this. Who could ever add anything to the experience of someone like
Solomon? He is the ultimate test case. If he cannot find the meaning of life,
who can? What hope is there for anyone to answer these questions? But if
the Preacher-King is able to understand the purpose of our existence, then
what he says about the meaning of life will stand.

A Brief Glimmer of Hope

As he compares wisdom to mad folly, Qoheleth offers us a brief glimmer of
hope. After announcing the goal of his quest, he proceeds to tell us what he
discovered: "Then I saw that there is more gain in wisdom than in folly, as
there is more gain in light than in darkness" (Ecclesiastes 2:13).

Until now, everything has been vanity and striving after wind. But
here, as the Preacher-King praises the relative value of wisdom, we see
some progression in his thought. Perhaps it is true that wisdom is unable to
straighten out what is crooked or to count what is missing. It may well be
the case that having more wisdom increases vexation and sorrow. But all
other things being equal, having wisdom is still better than the alternative.
Earlier Qoheleth said there is nothing to be gained in life, but here he admits
that wisdom is at least somewhat advantageous. Though limited, its value is
legitimate, for it is better to be a wise person than a mad fool!

Qoheleth expresses the contrast between wisdom and folly in terms of
light and darkness. It is better to be in the light than to be in the dark, as
everyone knows. We notice this when the lights are out. Even if we think
we know where everything is, we often end up tripping over things that

turn out to be in our way. In the same way, foolish people go stumbling through life.

Then the Preacher extends his comparison by saying, "The wise person has his eyes in his head, but the fool walks in darkness" (Ecclesiastes 2:14). The value of wisdom is not simply that it gives light, but that it enables us to see. It gives vision, not just illumination. To say that the wise person has "eyes in his head" means that he can actually see what he is doing and where he is going. He has a useful perception of life. By contrast, the fool does not have eyes at all but walks in darkness. This darkness is not just around him but inside him because he has no eyes with which to see.

I witness the difference between light and darkness whenever I spend time with my brother-in-law, whose blindness often puts him at a relative disadvantage. He is able to live and work and play to the glory of God. But his blindness makes it impossible for him to see the beauty of nature (even though he can hear it, taste it, and touch it). Light *is* better than darkness.

The Bible often makes this contrast. Sometimes it uses light and darkness to show the absolute difference between knowing God and living without him or between living in holiness and stumbling through life in the darkness of sin (e.g., John 3:19; Ephesians 5:8; 1 Peter 2:9). Here the Bible simply says that the difference between wisdom and folly is like light and darkness. According to the paraphrase by T. M. Moore, "I saw that wisdom was more valuable by far than folly. It makes more sense to pursue the course of wisdom than to waste one's life in revelry and merriment. This was as clear as night and day to me."[5]

The Great Equalizer

To this point the Preacher has given us the conventional wisdom about wisdom—that it is better to be wise than to be a mad fool. We find the same perspective in many of Solomon's proverbs. "A wise son makes a glad father," he says, "but a foolish son is a sorrow to his mother" (Proverbs 10:1). Again he says, "The wise of heart will receive commandments, but a babbling fool will come to ruin" (Proverbs 10:8).

So far so good; but then the Solomon of Ecclesiastes has a troubling thought. This is typical of him. Never content simply to accept the conventional wisdom, he always wants to press an issue.

Here the Preacher explores wisdom and folly to the absolute value, pushing them all the way to the edge of life: "And yet I perceived that the same event happens to all of them" (Ecclesiastes 2:14). To translate this verse as it appears in the New International Version, "the same *fate* overtakes them both."

This verse may simply mean that the wise and the foolish experience the same ups and downs in life. In that case the word "fate" is not being used fatalistically but refers generally to anything and everything that happens in life. Whether we live by wisdom or by mad folly, we will get caught up in many of the same events, including the same calamities and catastrophes. As Jesus says, the rain falls on the just and the unjust alike (Matthew 5:45). It does not matter how smart we are, many things in life are beyond our control. Thus many of the same incidents will happen to us that happen to everybody, both for good and for ill.

Yet when he talks about "the same event," or "the . . . fate" that overtakes us all, the Preacher seems to have something more specific in mind. He is talking about the one thing that happens to everyone—death. This becomes perfectly clear in verse 16, where he says that "the wise dies just like the fool!" But already in verse 14 he is talking about the fate that awaits us all. As we go through life, it is better to be wise than foolish. But what will happen to us in the end? We will all die anyway. So what really is the use of being wise? Once we are dead, our wisdom will not do us any good. Whatever advantage we gain from wisdom is strictly temporary. Whether we are wise or foolish, either way we will soon be dead, and who will remember us then? Death is the great equalizer.

Many years ago, when I heard Dr. Haddon Robinson preach from Ecclesiastes, he recounted what it was like for him to stand at the graveside of a man who had a working knowledge of thirty-four languages. Most people know only one or two languages, at the most, but here was a man who understood nearly three dozen. Yet in the end it didn't matter how smart he was—he was still as dead as could be. "Even the wise die," the psalmist says; "the fool and the stupid alike must perish" (Psalm 49:10).

Death is no respecter of persons. This tragic absurdity frustrates all of our efforts to find meaning in life. We go through life desperately trying to deny the reality of our mortality; yet we are haunted by death just the same. Gregg Easterbrook writes about this in *The Progress Paradox*. First Easterbrook demonstrates that even though the lives of average Americans are constantly improving in material terms, we never get any happier. Then he tries to figure out why people are feeling worse at the very time that life supposedly is getting better.

Easterbrook has a variety of answers to this question, many of them based on sociological research. But at a certain point he wonders whether perhaps the problem might have something to do with death. Maybe "people grow steadily better off," he says, "yet seemingly no happier, because there is a baseline anxiety in all our hearts, and that anxiety is the fear of death."[6] For a brief moment Easterbrook opens a window to the human soul. If only he had the answer for our anxiety!

It is one thing to believe that all men are mortal, accepting the reality of death in intellectual terms, but it is something entirely different to recognize that we ourselves must die. This is something every soldier confronts in wartime. Many soldiers go into their first battle with the naive expectation that although other men will die, somehow they will manage to survive. But when they see their first comrade fall in battle, they think, "That could have been me" and are compelled to confront their own mortality.

When the Preacher confronted his mortality, he talked to himself in the privacy of his innermost soul. "Then I said in my heart, 'What happens to the fool will happen to me also. Why then have I been so very wise?' And I said in my heart that this also is vanity" (Ecclesiastes 2:15). Sooner or later everyone comes to the same shocking realization: *One day I am going to die; my heart will beat one last time, my lungs will exhale one final breath, and that will be the end of my days on this earth.*

This painful reality makes the wise man wonder how wise it really is to pursue wisdom. In view of his impending demise, figuring out the meaning of life now seems like a lot of wasted effort. Jean-Paul Sartre would have agreed, for the famous existentialist has been quoted as saying, "Life has no meaning the moment you lose the illusion of being eternal."

There is a further problem with death, and again it is a problem that afflicts the wise every bit as much as the foolish: death has the power to erase the very memory of our existence. Sometimes people try to overcome this problem by earthly achievement, but death still wins out in the end. The filmmaker Woody Allen acknowledged this when he said, "I don't want to achieve immortality through my work. I want to achieve it by not dying."[7] Yet the reality is that we all must die. And who will remember us when we are gone?

In the introduction to his book, Qoheleth said, "There is no remembrance of former things" (Ecclesiastes 1:11). Here he says, "For of the wise as of the fool there is no enduring remembrance, seeing that in the days to come all will have been long forgotten. How the wise dies just like the fool!" (Ecclesiastes 2:16). Earlier, in one of his many famous proverbs, Solomon said that "the memory of the righteous is a blessing" (Proverbs 10:7; cf. Psalm 112:6), but now he is not so sure. Will anyone remember us after all?

Apparently not. Alexander the Great learned this lesson in a dramatic way from his friend Diogenes, a famous philosopher. Alexander found Diogenes standing alone in a field, looking intently at a large pile of bones. When Alexander asked what he was doing, Diogenes gave this reply: "I am searching for the bones of your father Philip, but I cannot seem to distinguish them from the bones of the slaves."[8]

Whether we are rich or poor, death will bring an end to every advantage we have in life. So Qoheleth's quest has failed again. A fresh investigation has come up with the same old findings. Human wisdom cannot overcome death, and therefore it cannot solve the problem of meaning in life. Death brings everything to a halt. "If *one fate comes to all*," writes Derek Kidner, "and that fate is extinction, it robs every man of his dignity and every project of its point."[9]

Hating Life Itself

By this point in Ecclesiastes, the Preacher's refrain is all too familiar. The equalizing power of death leads him to conclude—yet once more—that life is only vanity, like the steam that rises from a boiling kettle and then disappears. But this time his attitude seems much more negative. The repeated failure of his ongoing quest is in danger of embittering his heart: "So I hated life, because what is done under the sun was grievous to me, for all is vanity and a striving after wind" (Ecclesiastes 2:17; cf. Job 7:16).

It is one thing to be disappointed with life and all its frustrations, but hating life is another thing entirely. The Solomon of Ecclesiastes seems to be spiraling down into absolute despair. It is not just *his* life that he hates but life in general—the whole enterprise of human existence. So he has reached what one scholar calls "a nadir of anger and despair."[10]

What his experience shows, maybe more clearly than anything else in the Bible, is the reality of life without God. Remember that we are still looking at things from a merely human perspective, based on the worldly wisdom of people living "under the sun." From that perspective, life is so pointless that eventually it leads to despair.

Many thinkers have reached the same conclusion. Like Qoheleth, the philosopher Voltaire, when writing to a close friend, said, "I hate life, and yet I am afraid to die."[11] The young C. S. Lewis, in the days when he was still an atheist, said, "Come let us curse our Master ere we die, / For all our hopes in endless ruin lie. / The good is dead. Let us curse God most High."[12] Or consider these words from Francois Mauriac, who won the Nobel Prize for Literature in 1952: "You can't imagine the torment of having had nothing out of life, and of having to look forward to nothing but death, of feeling that there is no other world beyond this one, that the puzzle will never be explained."[13]

Such is life under the sun. The Preacher hated life because of the certainty of death and the absurdity of losing all his wisdom as a result. Maybe you hate life for some other reason—for its physical pain perhaps or its unjust suffering or its broken relationships or its financial hardships or its many other disappointments. But whatever the reason, as long as we look at things from an under-the-sun perspective, there are many things to hate about life.

Wisdom beyond the Grave

The only way out of that hatred is to find wisdom that comes from above the sun and life that comes from beyond the grave. Providentially, and graciously, the Bible shows us where to find that life-giving wisdom when it invites us to "seek the things that are above, where Christ is, seated at the right hand of God. Set your minds on things that are above, not on things that are on earth. For you have died, and your life is hidden with Christ in God. When Christ who is your life appears, then you also will appear with him in glory" (Colossians 3:1–4; cf. Ephesians 2:6).

These words open up a perspective that can help us love life instead of hating it. Rather than only looking at things "under the sun," the apostle tells us to lift our gaze higher, to the throne of the universe, where Jesus Christ is seated at the right hand of God. Rather than limiting ourselves to human wisdom, as useful as it is in many ways, we are encouraged to set our minds on heavenly things.

What do we see when we look at life from this lofty vantage point? We see Jesus Christ, who is the perfection of all wisdom, the one "in whom are hidden all the treasures of wisdom and knowledge" (Colossians 2:3). Jesus Christ is the very wisdom of God. Furthermore, he is the life of God. Jesus Christ is "the true God and eternal life" (1 John 5:20; cf. John 17:3). We see his life in Colossians 3:1, where the Scripture declares that Jesus has been raised to the right hand of God. After Jesus was crucified for our sins, after he was dead and buried, he was raised back from the dead by the power of the Holy Spirit. Then he was exalted to the right hand of God, which is the place of all authority and power over the universe. Jesus Christ is alive from the dead.

Because Jesus is alive, the grave is not the end for anyone who is wise enough to trust in him. The Preacher hated life because he saw that it would bring an end to all his wisdom. But he was only looking at things from an earthly perspective—"under the sun." For those who set their minds on things that are above, not on things that are on earth, there is life and wisdom beyond the grave.

This means that who we are will not be forgotten but will be remembered for all eternity. Jesus is our very life, and the Bible promises that when the risen Jesus comes to earth again, we will be with him, alive in glory. The Bible assures us further that our lives are "hidden with Christ in God" (Colossians 3:3). This verse implies not so much that our lives are concealed but that they are protected. All our memories are safe with God in Christ. The word the apostle uses for "hidden" comes from the Greek root (*krupto*) that forms the basis for English words like *encryption*, which is one helpful way to think about the spiritual implications of this verse: our lives are encrypted with Christ in God. God so preserves us in his Son that nothing essential to who we are will be lost forever. God will remember us even when we can scarcely remember him and when we fear that no one else will remember us at all.

Are you afraid of death? Do you hate life? Do you ever worry that you will be forgotten? Are you discouraged by the vanity of your existence? Do you feel like you have been striving after the wind? Look above the sun to the Son of God. He will raise you up from the dead and will protect your life forever.

6

Working Things Out

ECCLESIASTES 2:18–26

What has a man from all the toil and striving
of heart with which he toils beneath the sun?
For all his days are full of sorrow, and his
work is a vexation. Even in the night his
heart does not rest. This also is vanity.

2:22–23

IF ANYTHING is striving after wind, it would have to be the labor and travail of our everyday work.

> Up every mornin' just to keep a job
> I gotta fight my way through the hustling mob
> Sounds of the city poundin' in my brain
> While another day goes down the drain.

These lyrics from the Vogues' 1965 hit single "Five O'Clock World" capture the futility and frustration of working on the job. You work away day after day, but what do you have to show for all your effort? Another day working is another day wasted.

The Solomon who wrote Ecclesiastes felt the same way. He never had to commute in heavy traffic, push for a sale to make his commission, or cover for all the coworkers who got laid off, but the Preacher-King did suffer the curse of work, and thus he found that this too was vanity and striving after wind.

You Can't Take It with You

Remember Qoheleth's quest. In headlong pursuit of the meaning of life, he explored the claims of wisdom and folly. Then he indulged in all the pleasures of the flesh (and I do mean all). After that, he reconsidered the advantages of wisdom, as over against folly. But no matter what he tried, his quest failed. Eventually he ended up hating life entirely, everything under the sun (Ecclesiastes 2:17). One of the things that he hated the most was his work—not just life in general, but work in particular: "I hated all my toil in which I toil under the sun" (Ecclesiastes 2:18).

Many people still expect work to give them a sense of purpose in life. This explains why one of the first things people ask when they meet someone new is, "What kind of work do you do?" or "What do you do for a living?" We are defined by our jobs. But according to Ecclesiastes, work is the wrong place to look for meaning in life.

There are many problems with work. Leland Ryken has listed some of them in an essay on business ethics:

- an anemic work ethic coexisting with an undervaluing of work;
- on the part of others, an overvaluing of work that takes the form of workaholism;
- a sense of alienation from corporate goals, often accompanied by resentment against the corporation as an employer;
- working for a corporation whose ethical standards have long been suspect;
- anxiety stemming from job insecurity in a corporate milieu that feels no long-term loyalty to employees; and
- viewing workers and work in purely economic terms as a means of production.[1]

And so on. These problems affect all of us. Every time we get sick and tired of doing the same thing over and over, every time we are inconvenienced by someone else's laziness or incompetence, every time our families suffer from the demands of our employer, every time we are pressured to practice business unethically, we are struggling with the vanity of work.

As far as Ecclesiastes is concerned, there are two main problems with our earthly business. The first is that in the end someone else will profit from all our hard work. As a bottom-line thinker, the Preacher wanted to know what kind of return he would get on his investment. He had been thinking about death (see Ecclesiastes 2:16), and as he looked ahead, he realized that one day he would have to leave everything behind: "I must leave it to the man who will come after me" (Ecclesiastes 2:18).

You can spend your whole life gathering a collection of some kind or building a business or making a home or establishing a school or amassing a large fortune, but you can't take it with you. Maybe you will lose it before you die, through some misfortune (the collapse of a financial market, for example). But whether it happens sooner or later, one day you will have to leave it *all* behind. Your collection will go to a dealer. The contents of your home will be sold at auction. Someone else will manage your portfolio. Then everything that you have worked a lifetime to gain and to maintain will be gone.

Maybe our possessions will end up in good hands. Then again, maybe they won't. This was part of the Preacher's frustration: "Who knows whether he will be wise or a fool? Yet he will be master of all for which I toiled and used my wisdom under the sun. This also is vanity" (Ecclesiastes 2:19). We could almost accept the loss of our possessions if they went to someone we loved and respected, but we can never be sure what will happen, especially after we die. The question "Who knows?" invites a negative response. The person who comes after us may be wise, but with so many fools in the world, chances are that everything will fall into the wrong hands.

Besides, even if the person who gets our property is wise, he still won't deserve it. What we gain from our work ought to belong to us, as the reward for all our labor. Instead it will go to someone else. This is part of the Preacher's frustration: "So I turned about and gave my heart up to despair over all the toil of my labors under the sun, because sometimes a person who has toiled with wisdom and knowledge and skill must leave everything to be enjoyed by someone who did not toil for it. This also is vanity and a great evil" (Ecclesiastes 2:20–21).

One man does the work, but another man gets the wealth. It just doesn't seem fair! Rather than working for your own profit, you actually end up working for someone else—the slacker who gets your stuff when you die. Qoheleth felt this loss very keenly. When he talks about someone working "with wisdom and knowledge and skill," he is speaking in general terms, but he is also describing himself. Remember the buildings he built and the gardens he planted. Remember the large workforce he supervised, the huge fortune he accumulated, and all of the property he owned (see Ecclesiastes 2:4–9). Here was a man with a lot of know-how—an excellent administrator, as the Bible describes King Solomon (see 1 Kings 10). He was the world's most successful businessman.

But when Solomon died, he left all of his earnings as a bequest for his oldest son, King Rehoboam. Solomon may not have known whether or not his successor would be wise, but *we* certainly do: Rehoboam was such a fool that he lost ten-twelfths of his father's kingdom (see 1 Kings 12).

Here is one of the great frustrations of our existence. We are born with a longing for permanence, a deep desire to do something that will endure or to make something that will last. Yet the under-the-sun reality is that we will spend our whole lives working to gain something we cannot keep. It was enough to drive the Preacher to despair.

The great Russian novelist Leo Tolstoy had the same experience. He wrote:

> My question—that which at the age of fifty brought me to the verge of suicide—was the simplest of questions, lying in the soul of every man . . . a question without an answer to which one cannot live. It was: "What will come of what I am doing today or tomorrow? What will come of my whole life? Why should I live, why wish for anything, or do anything?" It can also be expressed thus: Is there any meaning in my life that the inevitable death awaiting me does not destroy?[2]

The Curse of Work

Leaving it all behind is bad enough, but there is another serious problem with work. It was not just the loss of work's reward that the Preacher hated, but the work itself! The first problem is that our work will be someone else's reward. The second problem is that the work itself is toil and trouble. "What has a man from all the toil and striving of heart with which he toils beneath the sun? For all his days are full of sorrow, and his work is a vexation. Even in the night his heart does not rest. This also is vanity" (Ecclesiastes 2:22–23).

To emphasize the weariness of work, the Preacher describes it as "toil and striving." When he talks about toiling "beneath the sun," we imagine someone working long, hot hours out in the fields, sweating under the burning heat. But work also makes its mental demands, which is why he calls it "striving of heart." Every occupation has its own unique demands, but no matter what kind of work we do, it always takes its toll on us. Hard work can be exhausting for the soul as well as for the body. There is "too much strain," writes James Limburg, "without much gain."[3]

Work is also "sorrow" and "vexation." Think of all the worry that work brings. Sometimes we are anxious about having enough work to support ourselves and our families. At other times we have so much work that we worry about getting it all done. It would help if we could get a full night's sleep; instead we are awake in the night obsessing about today's on-the-job conflict or worrying about tomorrow's project. "Even in the night" the weary laborer's "heart does not rest" (Ecclesiastes 2:23; cf. 8:16).

Day and night, there is no rest for the weary, and the worker is always weary. Notice how long his problems will last: "all his days" (Ecclesiastes 2:23). From beginning to end, life is a weary labor, with little or nothing to show for it. Therefore, work is as vain as every other aspect of our existence.

If we try to find significance in our work, it will only end in disappointment. If you make your work your life, it will leave you empty.

Warren Schmidt learned this lesson in the 2002 film *About Schmidt*. After retirement, as Schmidt looks back on his life as an actuary for an Omaha insurance company, he realizes that he has little or nothing to show for all his hard work. Here is what he writes to the poor, needy child he has started to sponsor in Africa:

> I know we're all pretty small in the big scheme of things, and I suppose the most you can hope for is to make some kind of difference. But what kind of difference have I made? What in the world is better because of me? . . . Once I am dead and everyone who knew me dies too, it will be as though I never even existed. What difference has my life made to anyone? None that I can think of. None at all. Hope things are fine with you. Yours truly, Warren Schmidt.[4]

What kind of difference have you made? Do you have anything to show for all your work? Qoheleth would have given the same answer as Warren Schmidt. When he considered what a man gains from his labor under the sun, the Preacher came to this conclusion: "all his days are full of sorrow, and his work is a vexation" (Ecclesiastes 2:23).

Take This Job and Love It

Nothing can prepare us for what happens next in Ecclesiastes because suddenly the book takes a surprising turn. Without warning, the Preacher says the first truly positive thing in the entire book: "There is nothing better for a person than that he should eat and drink and find enjoyment in his toil. This also, I saw, is from the hand of God, for apart from him who can eat or who can have enjoyment?" (Ecclesiastes 2:24–25).

These verses are an oasis of optimism in a wilderness of despair. As such, they mark a turning point in Ecclesiastes—not just on the subject of work, but for the argument of the book as a whole. "Having experienced the bankruptcy of our pretended autonomy," writes Michael Eaton, "the Preacher now points to the God who occupies the heavenly realm, and to the life of faith in him."[5] Martin Luther called the end of Ecclesiastes 2 "a remarkable passage, one that explains everything preceding and following it." It is "the principal conclusion," he said, "in fact the point of the whole book."[6]

Not everyone would agree with Luther. Some scholars think that the perspective on life in these verses is still fairly negative and that there is nothing constructive in Ecclesiastes until we get to the end of chapter 12.[7] The words "there is nothing better," they say, express only a grudging appreciation of the good things in life. The author "couches his language in a way that communicates his reluctance and lack of enthusiasm,"[8] as if to say, "It isn't much, but this is what life has to offer." If that is true, then we had better seize the day—*carpe diem!* So the Preacher is like the rich fool in the parable that Jesus told, the man who said to his soul, "eat, drink, be merry" (Luke 12:19) or like the victims doomed to be torn apart by wild beasts in the Roman amphitheaters: "Let us eat and drink, for tomorrow we die" (1 Corinthians 15:32).

Yet I believe that Ecclesiastes 2:24–26 is much more positive. The Preacher is not giving in to despair but is beginning to see the difference it makes to live with God instead of without him. Unless we see this progression in his thought, we will miss the practical benefit of his book. His message is not simply that all is vanity under the sun, but also that joy comes from the hand of God, giving meaning to everything in life:

> Qohelet clings tenaciously to both claims: all life is *hebel* [vanity], and yet joy is both possible and good. It is important not to make one of these claims the only message of the book and dismiss the other as either a distraction or a grudging qualification. Qohelet insists on both, and often in the same passage.[9]

One is reminded of an old cartoon in which a publisher is pleading with Charles Dickens to change the most famous opening line in the history of the novel: "Mr. Dickens, either it was the best of times or it was the worst of times. It can't be both."[10] But of course it *can* be both, and often is. We live in a world that is cursed by sin (see Genesis 3:17–19), but it is also a world that God created essentially good (see Genesis 1—2) and that he has visited in the flesh and is working to redeem through the life, death, and resurrection of his Son. Thus we experience joy as well as sorrow, especially if we know God in a personal and saving way.

Notice what brings the joy. In verse 24 the Preacher embraces some of the very activities that he has already rejected as failing to bring meaning to life. Earlier he concluded that work was a total drag and that even the pleasures of food and drink could not satisfy his soul. But now he eats and drinks and finds enjoyment in his toil.

What makes the difference between joy and sorrow? God makes the difference! Up to this point in Ecclesiastes, God has hardly been mentioned, and when he was mentioned (1:13), he seemed to be part of the problem. But here God's presence makes all the difference. According to verse 25, no one can ever find any true joy in anything apart from him. So if anyone is having trouble finding enjoyment in life, it must be because God is not at the center of things. By contrast, the eating and drinking that the Preacher enjoys in verse 24 come directly "from the hand of God." He has stopped trying to take pleasure for himself and has started receiving it as a gracious gift. He has started putting into practice the principle that Paul later taught to young Timothy—a basic principle we can apply to many situations in life: "Everything created by God is good, and nothing is to be rejected if it is received with thanksgiving, for it is made holy by the word of God and prayer" (1 Timothy 4:4–5).

Paul's affirmation is not an argument for total license when it comes to the choices we make about what to eat and drink, but it is a call to thankful liberty. Earthly pleasures are gifts from God. They have their limits, of course, so they will never give us eternal satisfaction. But the legitimate enjoyment they bring encourages us in the worship of God. Few things are better in life than to receive his earthly blessings as gifts and then return thanks to him. "Isn't it strange," asks Ray Stedman, "that the more you run after life, panting after every pleasure, the less you find, but the more you take life as a gift from God's hand, responding in thankful gratitude for the delight of the moment, the more that seems to come to you."[11] It is strange, but true: when we learn to receive the good things in life as gifts rather than taking them as entitlements, we experience genuine joy and true thanksgiving. "So, whether you eat or drink," the Scripture says, "or whatever you do, do all to the glory of God" (1 Corinthians 10:31).

Work too is a gift that we receive from the hand of God. This has been true since the very beginning. Sometimes we imagine that Adam and Eve had nothing to do in the Garden of Eden, but in fact God gave them good hard work to do (Genesis 1:28; 2:15). Work is one of the ordinances of creation—part of God's original goodness to humanity. In John Milton's epic poem *Paradise Lost*, Adam celebrates the goodness of God in the gift of work: "Man hath his daily work of body or mind / Appointed, which declares his dignity, / And the regard of Heaven on all his ways."[12]

Unfortunately, because of Adam's sin our work has been cursed, which turns our labor into toil and trouble. But there is still a basic goodness about work that comes from our Creator. We were made in the image of a working God, and thus we have the capacity to find his pleasure in work itself, even apart from anything that we gain by working. According to Dorothy L. Sayers, "Work is the natural exercise and function of man—the creature who is made in the image of his Creator."[13] When we work, therefore, we feel his pleasure.

The way to experience this pleasure is to work for God and not simply for ourselves. It is so easy to get caught up in our career ambition, our work schedule, and our paycheck without ever stopping to consider whether our work is pleasing to God—both what we do and the way we do it. Difficult work is more satisfying and even more enjoyable when it is done for the greater glory of God.

For the believer in Christ, our true Boss and ultimate Master is the

Savior who gave his life for our sins. Whatever our job happens to be—whether we work as a teacher or a student, a homemaker or a cabinetmaker, a buyer or a seller, an office worker or a factory worker, in food service or financial services, we are working for Christ and for his kingdom. To put this another way, we are working under the Son, and not simply under the sun. So the Scripture gives us this command: "Whatever you do, work heartily, as for the Lord and not for men, knowing that from the Lord you will receive the inheritance as your reward. You are serving the Lord Christ" (Colossians 3:23–24; cf. Ephesians 6:5–8).

The Fruit of Our Labor

The inheritance of a reward takes us back to an issue we considered earlier: What does the worker gain for all his toil? The Preacher had started to wonder whether he would gain anything at all under the sun, partly because he would have to leave it all behind and partly because his work seemed to be nothing but toil and trouble. But when he brought God back into the picture, he found this reward: "For to the one who pleases him God has given wisdom and knowledge and joy, but to the sinner he has given the business of gathering and collecting, only to give to one who pleases God. This also is vanity and a striving after wind" (Ecclesiastes 2:26).

Here the Preacher makes a clear distinction between two kinds of people: those who are under the favor of a gracious God and those who are lost in their sins. This may seem like a form of works-righteousness: good things happen to good people, while bad things happen to bad people. There are also some scholars who see this verse as arbitrary and capricious: God rewards some people and punishes others, and there is nothing we can do about it—it is all part of the vanity of life. But what we see here instead is a careful distinction between people who live under the mercy of God and people who persist in their sins.

Notice how the people who please God are described—as the grateful recipients of *spiritual* blessings. God has given them "wisdom," which for the first time in this book is described as a divine gift rather than a human enterprise. With wisdom comes "knowledge" and also true spiritual "joy." The reason these people are pleasing to God is because they have been blessed by God. The contrast here, says Derek Kidner, "is between the satisfying spiritual gifts of God (wisdom, knowledge, joy), which only those who please Him can desire or receive, and the frustrating business of amassing what cannot be kept, a business which is the chosen lot of those who reject Him."[14] If we live for God's pleasure, we will be richly rewarded with all of the spiritual blessings that God loves to give.

But for the impenitent sinner there is no reward, only loss. This is the first time the Preacher has spoken directly about sin, which will become an important theme throughout the rest of his book. One of the biggest vanities under the sun is human depravity. It is "the sinner," especially, who finds work to be a total frustration and thus suffers the vanity of verse 26. His business is to gather and to collect; in other words, his life is dominated by the acquisition and accumulation of consumer goods. But sooner or later he will have to leave them all behind. Then he will turn them over to someone who is pleasing to God—this, indeed, is vanity.

Sometimes the transfer of property takes place in the present life. There are some good examples of this in the Bible, like the Canaanites who lost their cities to the children of Israel, or wicked Haman who had to dress his mortal enemy in the royal robes he thought to have claimed for himself (see Esther 6).

A more recent example comes from the history of the Dutch community near Pella, Iowa. During World War I, when my grandfather was a boy, local Dutch farmers were the victims of organized persecution. This was largely because their language sounded so close to German, but there may have been other reasons as well—their prosperity, their work ethic, their strong commitment to Christ. Whatever the reason, their farms were vandalized, their property was burned, and their lives were threatened. Soon the FBI sent men to investigate. They cracked the case wide open when one of the ringleaders boasted about his plans to a secret agent at a local saloon. The criminals were arrested. In following years they suffered further loss when many of them were forced to foreclose on their own property. Their farms were snatched up at bargain prices by local Dutch farmers, of all people, and thus the Scripture was fulfilled: the sinners gathered and collected, only to give what they had to people whose work was pleasing to God.

This doesn't always happen, of course—at least not right now. In fact, one of the vanities of a fallen world is that while the righteous suffer afflic- tion, many sinners seem to prosper. But it will not always be like this. At the end of history, the wealth of all nations will be brought into the kingdom of Heaven (see Revelation 21:24). The meek really will inherit the earth, as Jesus promised (Matthew 5:5). According to the justice of God's sovereign providence, his people will receive what sinners have gathered. As Jesus said, "To everyone who has, more will be given, but from the one who has not, even what he has will be taken away" (Luke 19:26).

In the meantime, we have the reward of our work—not just the fruit of our labor, but the labor itself. God has given us good work to do. We do this work knowing that Jesus has already done the hard work of our salvation. One of the reasons why Christians often talk about "the work of Christ" is because this is the way Jesus talked. "My Father is working until now," Jesus said, "and I am working" (John 5:17). "My food is to do the will of him who sent me and to accomplish his work" (John 4:34). Jesus Christ was a work- ing man. Think especially of all the heavy lifting he did on the cross, where he carried the full weight of our sin all the way to death—what theologians call "the finished work of Christ."

Jesus is still working today, not by adding anything to his sacrifice for sin but through the ministry of his church (see John 9:4; Acts 1:1; Ephesians 4:12). We share in that good work by giving people the gospel, by singing God's praise, by loving our neighbors, by praying for God's kingdom to come, by giving generously to Christian ministry. We also share in that good work by doing our own ordinary daily tasks in a way that gives glory to God. This, too, is kingdom work. As Martin Luther once said, "The entire world [should] be full of service to God, not only the churches but also the home, the kitchen, the cellar, the workshop, and the field."[15]

Are you finding God's strength in the work that he has given you to do? Thomas Hughes captures the joy of kingdom work in his novel *Tom Brown's Schooldays*. One of Tom Brown's classmates at Rugby School is George Arthur, a frail boy who contracts a life-threatening fever. Arthur has never been strong enough to run and climb and play and fight like other boys. During his illness he fears that he will never be able to work like other men. Yet one night he has a dream that fills his heart with joy—a vision of the kingdom of God. Here is how Arthur described it:

> And on the other bank of the great river I saw men and women and chil-
> dren; the tears were wiped from their faces; they put on glory and strength;
> and all weariness and pain fell away. And they worked at some great work.
> They *all* worked. Each worked in a different way, but all at the same work.
> And I saw myself, Tom; and even *I* was working and singing.[16]

Whatever you do in life, are you busy with the great work of Jesus? Each of us works in a different way, but it is all part of the same work, to the glory of God. So "be steadfast, immovable, always abounding in the work of the Lord, knowing that in the Lord your labor is not in vain" (1 Corinthians 15:58).

7

To Everything a Season

ECCLESIASTES 3:1–8

For everything there is a season,
and a time for every matter under heaven.

3:1

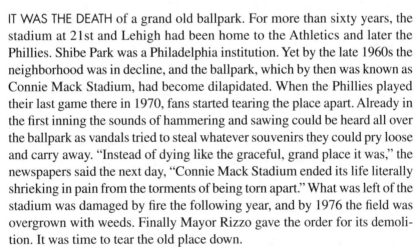

IT WAS THE DEATH of a grand old ballpark. For more than sixty years, the stadium at 21st and Lehigh had been home to the Athletics and later the Phillies. Shibe Park was a Philadelphia institution. Yet by the late 1960s the neighborhood was in decline, and the ballpark, which by then was known as Connie Mack Stadium, had become dilapidated. When the Phillies played their last game there in 1970, fans started tearing the place apart. Already in the first inning the sounds of hammering and sawing could be heard all over the ballpark as vandals tried to steal whatever souvenirs they could pry loose and carry away. "Instead of dying like the graceful, grand place it was," the newspapers said the next day, "Connie Mack Stadium ended its life literally shrieking in pain from the torments of being torn apart." What was left of the stadium was damaged by fire the following year, and by 1976 the field was overgrown with weeds. Finally Mayor Rizzo gave the order for its demolition. It was time to tear the old place down.

Yet soon it was time to build again. In 1981 Deliverance Evangelistic Church bought the parcel of land with a vision to serve the city with a gospel-centered community. The church made space for ministry and Christian education, built homes for the elderly, and eventually constructed a huge sanctuary for the worship of God.

These events are beautifully described by historian Bruce Kuklick in his book on Shibe Park and urban Philadelphia. Kuklick borrowed his title from Ecclesiastes 3: *To Every Thing a Season.*[1] In the economy of God, there is a time and a season for everything, including both a time to tear down and a time to build up. While there is a season to play baseball, there is also a season for advancing the ministry of the church—everything in its God-given time.

A Time for This, A Time for That

After everything else he has said about the vanity and futility of human existence, we might well have expected the Preacher to say something different and more discouraging about time. He might have said that the time is short, for example, and that therefore we never have enough time to do all the things we want to do.

Or the Preacher might have talked about the tyranny of time—the way it seems to control our lives down to the millisecond. Plautus wrote about this. Bemoaning the stress caused by the latest device for keeping time, the Roman playwright said, "The gods confound the man who first found out how to distinguish hours! Confound him who has cut and hacked my days so wretchedly into small pieces. Confound him who in this place set up a sundial."[2]

The Preacher who wrote Ecclesiastes might also have said that time is fleeting, that we are running out of time, and that once it is gone, it can never be recovered. With this thought in mind, the American educator Horace Mann once wrote the following want ad: "Lost, yesterday, somewhere between Sunrise and Sunset, two golden hours, each set with sixty diamond minutes. No reward is offered, for they are gone forever."[3]

These are all things that the Preacher might have said but decided not to. Instead he wrote a poem about the orderliness of every time that God has ordained—the world's most famous poem on the subject of time. The poem is so famous, in fact, that even people who don't know the Bible have often heard it. The folk singer Pete Seeger set it to music in the 1950s, with a tune that the Byrds popularized a decade later in their hit single "Turn, Turn, Turn." But long before it was put to music, the Preacher's song had struck a responsive chord in the human heart.

The Preacher begins with a summary statement: "For everything there is a season, and a time for every matter under heaven" (Ecclesiastes 3:1). Then, by way of explanation, he penned the following lyric:

> a time to be born, and a time to die;
> a time to plant, and a time to pluck up what is planted;
> a time to kill, and a time to heal;
> a time to break down, and a time to build up;
> a time to weep, and a time to laugh;

a time to mourn, and a time to dance;
a time to cast away stones, and a time to gather stones together;
a time to embrace, and a time to refrain from embracing;
a time to seek; and a time to lose;
a time to keep, and a time to cast away;
a time to tear, and a time to sew;
a time to keep silence, and a time to speak;
a time to love, and a time to hate;
a time for war, and a time for peace. (Ecclesiastes 3:2–8)

Everyone recognizes the beauty of these lines—their rhythm, their repetition, and their orderly completeness. Yet some scholars believe that the perspective of this poem is almost totally pessimistic. The Preacher is so trapped in the tyranny of time that he is fatalistic about his existence. There is a time for this, and a time for that, but no matter what time it is, there is nothing that anyone can do about it. Thus the critics complain that the God of Ecclesiastes 3 is an "absolute and arbitrary master."[4] Although one scholar admits that this passage "is one of great beauty and poetry," he also says, "Koheleth feels imprisoned by this sequence of times, and he rebels because this is what he must go through without knowing why."[5]

Part of the difficulty for these scholars seems to be their discomfort with the doctrine of the sovereignty of God. Rather than finding encouragement in his governance of time and his predestination of human events, they see him as a random deity. Thus the *Abingdon Bible Commentary* provides the following heading for Ecclesiastes 3: "Hopelessness of Struggle against an Arbitrary God." But is this really the perspective that Ecclesiastes gives us about the God of time?

Keep in mind that chapter 2 ended with a declaration of the enjoyment we find whenever God is present and we receive life's blessings as a gift from him. Notice as well the strong affirmation that Ecclesiastes 3:11 gives of God's timeliness in ordering human events: "He has made everything beautiful in its time." Far from being a fatalist, the Preacher has come to a proper appreciation of the sovereignty of God over time and eternity. Life is not uniformly bad but includes both positive and negative experiences. From this beautifully balanced poem we learn many important truths about God, about his Son, and about our own stewardship of time, which may be our most precious possession.

The God of Time

A Biblical understanding of time and its place in the Christian worldview begins with the sovereignty of God. Although he is not mentioned by name in the first eight verses of Ecclesiastes 3, God is mentioned in the verses that follow. Furthermore, the opening verse talks about what happens "under heaven." Many scholars see this phrase as virtually identical to the more common expression "under the sun." However, the words "under heaven" seem to have much more positive connotations. Later the Preacher will say explicitly that "God is in heaven" (Ecclesiastes 5:2). So everything that happens in this time-bound universe is under the authority of the God who rules in Heaven.

God is sovereign over time and whatever happens in time. This is evident from the sweeping breadth of verse 1: "For everything there is a season, and a time for every matter under heaven." Nothing happens outside the will of God. In the words of the *Westminster Shorter Catechism*, his "holy, wise, and powerful" providence governs "all his creatures, and all their actions" (A. 11).

The scope of God's sovereignty is further emphasized in the poem that follows, with its parallel series of related opposites. Each pair forms a *merism*, a figure of speech in which two polarities make up a whole. For example, when the Bible says that God created "the heavens and the earth" (Genesis 1:1), it means that God created the entire universe. Similarly, each of the pairs in Ecclesiastes 3 makes up a larger whole. Together birth and death comprise the whole of human existence, weeping and laughing summarize the full range of human emotion, and so on. There is something comprehensive about each pair.

There is also something comprehensive about the list as a whole. There are fourteen pairs in all, which is twice the Biblical number (seven) of perfection and completion. Not surprisingly, the pairs themselves seem to take in the whole sweep of human experience, from birth to death, from war to peace (which is where the poem ends), and everything in between. In the words of H. C. Leupold, the pairs in Qoheleth's poem "cover the widest possible range and thus practically every aspect of human life."[6]

God is the King of Time. He regulates our minutes and our seconds. He rules all our moments and all our days. Nothing happens in life without his superintendence. Everything happens when it happens because God is sovereign over time as well as eternity.

Furthermore, there is a definite orderliness to the way God does things. He is a precise God. Absolute in his authority over space and time, he puts everything in its own time and place. God's sovereignty has a chronology. This has been true from the very beginning of time, when God divided the days of creation. We see it with every change of season—the turning of summer into autumn and the coming of springtime after winter. The rhythms of creation testify to the orderliness of their Creator (see Genesis 8:22).

In Ecclesiastes 3 we see the same sovereign order applied to human activities and relationships. As the Preacher says, "for everything there is a season"—not just the four seasons, but for everything that happens under Heaven. A "season" in this sense is "a fixed time, a predetermined purpose."[7] The standard Greek translation of the Old Testament (known as the Septuagint) uses the term *kairos* (time viewed as opportunity) for this passage rather than the term *chronos* (time considered as duration). In the divine economy there is a suitable occasion or appropriate opportunity for everything that happens.

This perspective is far from fatalistic. The Preacher is *not* saying that God is arbitrary and thus there is nothing we can do about what happens. His point rather is that there is a "fitness" to what happens. According to one old commentator, Ecclesiastes 3 demonstrates

> the wise, and regular, and orderly administration of One, who sees the end from the beginning, and to whom there is no unanticipated contingency; and whose omniscient eye, in the midst of what appears to us inextricable confusion, has a thorough and intuitive perception of the endlessly diversified relations and tendencies of all events, and all their circumstances, discerning throughout the whole the perfection of harmony.[8]

To put it very simply, God does everything at just the right time.

Both/And

Usually people think of the actions in Ecclesiastes 3 as things that people do, which of course they are. We could demonstrate this from the life of King Solomon, who was a builder of great buildings, a planter of magnificent gardens, and a gatherer of many proverbs. But this poem is not limited to the human level. The activities listed are also things that *God* does, and that he is said to do in the Old Testament. For example, in Jeremiah 1:12 God says to his prophet: "You have seen well, for I am watching over my word to perform it." The verbs in Ecclesiastes 3:1–8 are divine actions before they become human activities.

It is important to see the completeness of what God does. The sovereign God who gives order to time is not one-dimensional. Each activity in this poem has its opposite, and together *both* of them tell us what God does in the world.

Consider birth and death—the two most momentous experiences in life, and the two appointments that every person must keep. Both the cradle and the deathbed follow God's timetable. He is the one who brings life into the world. So David praised him by saying, "You formed my inward parts; you knitted me together in my mother's womb" (Psalm 139:13; cf. Job 33:4). God is also the one who appoints the time of death. Man's "days are determined," Job said to his Creator, "and the number of his months is with you, and you have appointed his limits that he cannot pass" (Job

14:5–6). The Lord of life also has sovereign power over death. "You cannot live any longer than the Lord has prescribed," said Martin Luther, "nor die any sooner."⁹ The initiation, duration, and termination of our existence are all under his authority.

The same is true of planting and harvesting. In the Old Testament, these verbs are often used to describe God's relationship with his people. God planted his people as a fruitful vineyard (e.g., Isaiah 5:1; Jeremiah 2:21). But when they turned against him in wild rebellion, God dug up the vine, sending his people into captivity. He said through the prophet Isaiah, "And now I will tell you what I will do to my vineyard. I will remove its hedge, and it shall be devoured; I will break down its wall, and it shall be trampled down" (Isaiah 5:5).

Notice that God is involved both in planting *and* uprooting. Similarly, there is a time for building up as well as breaking down, and God does them both. God broke down the Tower of Babel that was built because of human pride (Genesis 11:8–9). He also built up a house for Israel and a kingdom for David. The complete work of God includes both creation and devastation.

Many people prefer a one-dimensional deity. They like to think of God giving life, but not appointing the time of death. They would rather see God planting and building than uprooting and tearing down. But instead of taking him by halves, we must consider his complete character. There is a time for him to kill as well as a time for him to heal—in other words, a time for capital punishment (see Genesis 9:6; Romans 13:3–5) as well as for skilled medical care and the healing of a nation's soul (2 Chronicles 7:14). This is part of God's perfection in his sovereign dealings with the human race. As God said in the days of Moses, "there is no god beside me; I kill and I make alive; I wound and I heal" (Deuteronomy 32:39).

God is not either/or; he is both/and, depending on what time it is. According to God's schedule, there is both "a time to love, and a time to hate." Again, many people like to think of God as love without considering the reality of his wrath. But the hatred of God is one of his perfections. It is right and good for God to oppose every wicked deed and to bring evil to judgment. We see this in the Second Commandment, where the holy God tells us that he will hate idolatry to the third and the fourth generation, while at the same time showing love to a thousand generations of people who love him and keep his commandments (see Exodus 20:4–6). We also see it in Proverbs, where Solomon tells us seven things that the Lord hates: "haughty eyes, a lying tongue, and hands that shed innocent blood, a heart that devises wicked plans, feet that make haste to run to evil, a false witness who breathes out lies, and one who sows discord among brothers" (6:17–19).

With God there is both "a time for peace, and a time for war." Yes, God has promised peace on earth. But until the second coming of the "Prince of Peace" (Isaiah 9:6), we are living in wartime. This is true spiritually, for we use the weapons of the Word of God and prayer to fight against Satan. But there are also times when there is warfare in the world as righteous nations fight to protect their people and battle for justice.

We need the complete picture. To know God and to understand our own place in his world, we need to accept that both halves of each pair tell us the truth about his character. Many people have an unbalanced view of God. They never take into account the full Biblical teaching about his character, and thus they end up with only half the equation. God makes "time for every matter under heaven" because at the right time, everything in this poem is fully in keeping with his character—birth and death, mourning and laughter, love and hate, exclusion and embrace, war and peace.

Perfect Timing

This is as far as most people go in connecting Ecclesiastes 3:1–8 to the character of God, but we can go one step farther by connecting this great poem to the person and work of Jesus Christ. The lyric that teaches us about the character of almighty God also teaches us about the Son who shares in all divine perfections.

If God is sovereign over the seasons, then Jesus Christ is the Lord of time. As the Creator God, Jesus ordered the rhythms of creation. Now, by his resurrection from the dead, Jesus rules the universe with sovereign authority over time and eternity. Matthew Bridges aptly said in his marvelous hymn "Crown Him with Many Crowns" that Jesus Christ is "the Lord of years" and "the Potentate of time."

When we witness the work of Jesus in the Gospels, we see a Savior who always knew what time it was. There was a time for him to be born: "when the fullness of time had come, God sent forth his Son, born of woman" (Galatians 4:4). There was also a day appointed for Jesus to die. He died on that day, and not a day before or a day later. The religious leaders were plotting against him, trying to put him to death as soon as they could. But they were not able to crucify him until the day that God had appointed. Before that time, "his hour had not yet come" (e.g., John 7:30). But when the hour did come, Jesus died on the cross. So the Scripture says, "at the right time Christ died for the ungodly" (Romans 5:6). Jesus rose again at the right time too—on the third day, as the Scriptures had promised (Hosea 6:2; cf. Luke 24:45–46; 1 Corinthians 15:4). From his birth to his death and then on to his resurrection, Jesus did everything timely in his saving work.

During his earthly ministry, Jesus knew the right time for every activity. When he said, "I am the vine; you are the branches" (John 15:5), he was using his disciples to replant the vineyard of the people of God. As Lord of the harvest, he also knew when it was time to uproot. Jesus said, "Every plant that my heavenly Father has not planted will be rooted up"

(Matthew 15:13). Jesus knew when it was time to heal. As he performed the miracles of the kingdom, he made the lame to walk, the deaf to hear, and the blind to see. Jesus knew when it was time to break down—think of the way he drove the moneychangers out of the temple, for example (Luke 19:45)—and also when it was time to build up, such as the time he built his church on the rock of Peter's confession that he was and is the Christ (Matthew 16:15–18; cf. 7:24).

Jesus knew the right time for every emotion. There were times to mourn. So this "man of sorrows" (Isaiah 53:3) grieved at the tomb of Lazarus (John 11:35, 38) and shed a good shepherd's tears for the lost sheep of Jerusalem (Luke 19:41–44; cf. Matthew 9:36). But there were also times for him to laugh and to dance. So he rejoiced in the Holy Spirit when his disciples came back from their first mission trip, having started to do the work of the kingdom (Luke 10:21).

When it came to personal relationships, Jesus knew when it was time to seek lost sheep and when it was time to lose the goats that refused to hear his voice. He embraced the tax collectors, the prostitutes, and other lost sinners who knew how much they needed a Savior. But Jesus refrained from embracing the scribes, the Pharisees, and other proud people who insisted that they were already righteous enough for God.

Jesus also knew when it was time to speak and when it was time to keep silent. He did a lot of talking during the three short years of his public ministry—telling stories, explaining the Law, preaching the gospel. Jesus fulfilled his purpose "to bear witness to the truth" (John 18:37). But when it came time for the trial of his life, he did not speak in his own defense (Matthew 27:14) but suffered in silent innocence. It was time for him to maintain silence, for "like a sheep he was led to the slaughter and like a lamb before its shearer is silent, so he opens not his mouth" (Acts 8:32; cf. 1 Peter 2:21–23).

To the day he died, Jesus knew the right time for everything. He still does. He knows the time to love, showing mercy to lost and needy sinners who ask him to be their Savior. He knows the time to hate, standing against evil and injustice. He knows the time for war, as his church does battle against Satan and all the enemies of God. Soon it will be the time for peace, when the Son of God will "make wars cease to the end of the earth" (Psalm 46:9) and bring us the everlasting *shalom* of the kingdom of God. From beginning to end, Jesus has perfect timing. God's sovereignty over the seasons is gloriously displayed in his life and saving work.

Redeeming the Time

The example of Jesus calls us to make the best use of our time. This is one of the best ways to avoid the vanity of life without God—by knowing what to do with our time. The way we spend our time is the way we spend our lives. If we call ourselves the followers of Christ, then we need to know what time it is, not measuring time merely in terms of hours and days, but viewing it as an opportunity to serve God. So consider three practical ways to apply this poem to the life of Christian discipleship.

First, wait for God's timing. If it is true that God is sovereign over time and that Jesus always makes perfect use of time, then we should trust God to know the right time for everything. This is one of the reasons why David was able to "bless the LORD at all times" (Psalm 34:1); he knew that whatever time it was, God was still in control. Some of the times on the Preacher's list are beyond our control—like the times of birth and death, for example, or the times of war and peace. This is true of many events in life: they are beyond our control. Most of us would prefer to manage our own agenda, which makes us quick to criticize God's timing. But instead of getting impatient or pushing ahead of God's timetable, we ought to hurry up and wait for God.

Whenever we find ourselves facing uncertainty, we should wait for God. It is not for us "to know the times or seasons that the Father has fixed by his own authority" (Acts 1:7). In the meantime, we are called to wait for God's timing. We should wait like Isaiah, who promised that those "who wait for the LORD shall renew their strength" (Isaiah 40:31; cf. 30:18) or like David, who said, "I trust in you, O LORD. . . . My times are in your hand" (Psalm 31:14–15). These words should be the prayer of every believer, as they were for William Lloyd when he turned David's psalm into a hymn:

> My times are in thy hand;
> My God, I wish them there;
> My life, my friends, my soul I leave
> Entirely to Thy care.[10]

Second, live your whole life knowing that there is a time for you to die. As the Scripture says, "it is appointed for man to die once, and after that comes judgment" (Hebrews 9:27). Will you be ready when the time comes? Many people aren't. When the Vicomte de Turenne was mortally wounded at the Battle of Salzbach in 1675, he wistfully said, "I did not mean to be killed today."[11] By contrast, one sixty-five-year-old widow from Amsterdam was totally prepared. After the death of her husband in 2005, she carefully planned her own funeral, including the music. One day the next year, when she went to pay her respects where her husband was buried, she lay down and died right next to the family grave, perhaps of a heart attack. The woman's name was already inscribed on the headstone, and her will was found inside her handbag.[12]

It would be hard for anyone to be better prepared to die than she was, although in truth anyone who trusts in Christ ought to be ready to die at any time, because Heaven is God's promise to every believer. Are you ready for eternity? There is no time to lose. Whatever time it is right now, this is a good time to give your life to Christ—a time to be born again, for when it comes to receiving the free gift of eternal life, there is no time like the present: "Behold, now is the favorable time; behold, now is the day of salvation" (2 Corinthians 6:2).

Third, make good use of whatever time you have. Time is the most precious commodity we have. It is the priceless currency that God has given for doing the work of his kingdom—what Stephen Olford has called "a fragment of eternity given by God to man as a solemn stewardship."[13] Time also happens to be one of the most difficult things we have to manage. We all have the same amount of time on a daily basis; the question is how we will spend it . . . or whether we will waste it. Thus the Bible tells us to use our time wisely, "redeeming the time, because the days are evil" (Ephesians 5:16, KJV).

The best way to use our time is for the glory of God and the kingdom of Christ. But redeeming the time requires the wisdom of the Holy Spirit. There are times in life and ministry to start something, planting and building and giving birth. There are also times when something is supposed to come to an end—a project, a ministry, or an institution. Knowing when it is time to uproot and break down always takes wisdom because these are some of the hardest decisions in life.

God calls us to be timely in our emotional responses, both in private (weeping and laughing) and in public (mourning and dancing). Having the heart of Jesus means knowing when it is time to "weep with those who weep" and when it is time to "rejoice with those who rejoice" (Romans 12:15; cf. John 16:20). We need wisdom for the timing of our relationships, knowing when it is time to embrace someone and when it is time to exclude them from our plans, from our priorities, and sometimes even from the church. There are times when it is important to speak up, speaking a word in season (see Proverbs 15:23; 25:11) or giving a reason for the hope that is in us (1 Peter 3:15). But there are also times to shut up—times when silence would be golden or when it would be better to hold our tongue (see Psalm 141:3; Proverbs 27:14; James 1:26).

Redeeming the time also requires wisdom in the use of our possessions. There are times to gather and times to scatter.[14] There are times to keep looking for what is lost, but also times to stop looking and give something up for lost instead. There are times to keep something that we may need later, but also times to cast it away for someone else to use.

If there is "a time for every matter under heaven" (Ecclesiastes 3:1), then redeeming the time will require wise decision-making. Learn to ask what time it is. Is this a time to break down or build up? Should I embrace or exclude? Is this something that God wants me to love or to hate? Am I speaking because I want to say something or because I really have something to say? Ask God for help, and he will give you the wisdom to know what time it is (see James 1:5).

One day soon Jesus will come again—"a second time" (Hebrews 9:28), indeed at just the right time, at the hour his Father has appointed (Matthew 24:36)—and then time will be no more. In the meantime, we pray that the Lord will bless us the way he blessed the sons of Issachar in the time of David. Those men "had understanding of the times, to know what Israel ought to do" (1 Chronicles 12:32; cf. Esther 1:13). To that end, we pray the timeless words of the prophet Moses: "teach us to number our days that we may get a heart of wisdom" (Psalm 90:12).

8

All in Good Time

ECCLESIASTES 3:9–15

I have seen the business that God has given to the children of man to be busy with. . . . I perceived that there is nothing better for them than to be joyful and to do good as long as they live.

3:10, 12

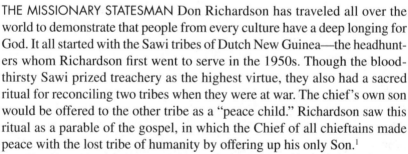

THE MISSIONARY STATESMAN Don Richardson has traveled all over the world to demonstrate that people from every culture have a deep longing for God. It all started with the Sawi tribes of Dutch New Guinea—the headhunters whom Richardson first went to serve in the 1950s. Though the bloodthirsty Sawi prized treachery as the highest virtue, they also had a sacred ritual for reconciling two tribes when they were at war. The chief's own son would be offered to the other tribe as a "peace child." Richardson saw this ritual as a parable of the gospel, in which the Chief of all chieftains made peace with the lost tribe of humanity by offering up his only Son.[1]

Based on his experiences with the Sawi, Richardson began to wonder if any other people groups had similar traditions—sacred rituals that served as redemptive analogies for the gospel. He discovered that many people groups—both ancient and modern—have partial knowledge of religious truth. Whether these beliefs come from what God has revealed in creation or from remnants of a faith passed down since Biblical times, they bear witness to God and to the gift of his atoning grace.

Richardson tells the story of the Inca king who rejected the sun god Inti in favor of an older and greater deity—the life-giving and merciful Viracocha, who dwells in uncreated light. He gives examples of tribes like the Karen people of Burma, who had legends of a lost book that one day the

Supreme God *Y'wa* would send to set them free from oppression. He even describes tribal rituals that make atonement for sin. For example, one day every year the Dyaks of Borneo put their sins on a little boat and sail it down the river—a "scapeboat," so to speak.[2]

According to Richardson, all of these stories prove the truth of something written in Ecclesiastes: God "has put eternity into man's heart" (Ecclesiastes 3:11). We are born with the longing for another world—a life with God that is beyond the reach of mortal time.

The Beauty of God's Sovereignty

The Preacher-King who wrote Ecclesiastes acknowledged this longing in the verses immediately following his famous poem about time (Ecclesiastes 3:1–8). From birth to death, there is a time and a season for everything under Heaven.

Then, having said that God is sovereign over time, the Preacher returned to the subject of work and asked a question he had asked before (and would be sure to ask again): "What gain has the worker from his toil?" (Ecclesiastes 3:9). In his ongoing quest to find meaning in life, the Preacher always wanted to know what kind of return he would get for the investment of his time and effort. Knowing how hard people work, he said, "I have seen the business that God has given to the children of man to be busy with" (Ecclesiastes 3:10). But he still wanted to know whether it was all worth it.

Some scholars believe that his answer was an emphatic "No!" The Preacher still believed what he said in chapter 2—namely, that work under the sun is vexation. Thus his question in Ecclesiastes 3:9 is rhetorical. What gain does the worker get? The implication is that he gets nothing at all. The trouble with this interpretation is that verse 11 makes such a strong affirmation of the goodness of God, who "has made everything beautiful in its time." Some people resent God's control over time and eternity; they would rather set their own agenda. But the Solomon of Ecclesiastes could see the beauty of God's sovereignty. Not only is there a time for everything, but God always does things at just the right time. Therefore, the Preacher praised God for his beautiful timing.

In the Old Testament, "beautiful" is first of all a visual term; ordinarily it refers to something that we can see. For example, the word is used to describe Job's daughters as the best-looking women in the country (Job 42:15). In time, however, the word took on a wider range of meaning, just like the word *beautiful* in English. Something beautiful is something good; it is right, pleasing, and appropriate.

It is in this sense that God can be said to have beautiful timing. At whatever time he does things, God is always right on time. He knows when it is time for breaking down and building up, for keeping and casting away, for war and for peace. When the Preacher says that God "has made every-thing beautiful in its time" (Ecclesiastes 3:11), he is not just talking about the way that God made the world in the first place, but about the way that he has ruled it ever since. The seasons of nature and the patterns of human activity are under his sovereign superintendence and providential care. From beginning to end, God does everything decently and in order. Derek Kidner thus speaks of "the kaleidoscopic movement of innumerable processes, each with its own character and its period of blossoming and ripening, *beautiful in its time* and contributing to the over-all masterpiece which is the work of one Creator."[3]

Do you believe in the timeliness of God, not just for the world in general but for your own case in particular? Do you trust his timing for the seasons of your own life? People often criticize God for being too late, or else too early. Yet in retrospect we discover that his agenda was better all along. Because a door was closed when we wanted it open, we ended up going a different direction, which turned out to be the right direction all along. We were not ready for the relationship we wanted when we wanted it, but only later. Something happened to change our schedule, and we ended up hav-ing an unexpected conversation that changed our whole direction in life, or maybe someone else's direction.

Sometimes being in the right place at God's time instead of at the wrong place on your own schedule can even save your life. By way of example, a group of students from Wheaton College was frustrated one morning when their sightseeing in London was delayed by slow service at breakfast. They thought they were running late, but when they walked up to their subway sta-tion, they discovered that they had just missed an underground explosion. To give another example, a friend from college was supposed to be at the top of the World Trade Center on 9/11, but a double-booking forced his company to relocate their meetings.

It is all in the timing. Rather than insisting on having everything run according to our own schedule, we need to learn to trust God's timetable. Know this: the Savior who was born "when the fullness of time had come" (Galatians 4:4) and died for our sins at just "the right time" (Romans 5:6) has a beautiful sense of timing.

Between Time and Eternity

Knowing that God is in control does not necessarily mean we always under-stand or appreciate his timing. Often we do not, and this can be a real frus-tration for us. So having affirmed the beauty of God's sovereign authority over time, the Preacher pointed out one of the basic dilemmas of our earthly existence: God "has put eternity into man's heart, yet so that he cannot find out what God has done from the beginning to the end" (Ecclesiastes 3:11).

Here the Preacher finds himself caught between time and eternity. On the one hand, God has put eternity into our hearts.[4] We were made to live forever (see Genesis 3:22), and thus we have a desperate longing for never-ending life with God. Many of the Bible's most precious promises offer us everlasting blessing. The eternal God (Psalm 90:2) has made an "everlasting covenant" (Genesis 9:16) to give us a kingdom that will last "forever" (2 Samuel 7:13). He has kept these promises by giving eternal life to anyone who believes in his Son, who offered his life for our sins before rising from the grave with power over death.

The trouble is that we are still living in a time-bound universe. There is a huge gap between our present mortality and our future destiny. The eternity in our hearts gives us a deep desire to know what God has done from beginning to end. Each of us is born with "a deep-seated desire, a compulsive drive . . . to know the character, composition, and meaning of the world . . . and to discern its purpose and destiny."[5] But as finite creatures living in a fallen world, there are so many things we do not understand. No matter how hard we look—and the Preacher-King who wrote Ecclesiastes had looked as hard as anyone—we "cannot find out what God has done from the beginning to the end" (Ecclesiastes 3:11).

Whereas God has a complete view, all we have is a point of view. Our limited perspective is unable to span the mind of God. This has been part of the Preacher's frustration from the beginning. He is looking for meaning in life but finds it hard or even impossible to understand. "The human being has 'eternity' in his heart—his Creator has made him a thinking being, and he wants to pass beyond his fragmentary knowledge and discern the fuller meaning of the whole pattern—but the Creator will not let the creature be his equal."[6]

All of this explains why some commentators see Ecclesiastes 3:11 as very negative. Having eternity in our hearts, they say, only leads to more frustration. As far as God is concerned, there is a time for everything. But we do not always know what time it is, and thus it is hard for us to know when to embrace and when to refrain from embracing, for example, or when to speak and when to stay silent. Thus we cannot make sense of our world. We desperately want to understand what is going on, but only God knows.

Some people respond to this frustration by leaving God out of it entirely and coming up with their own interpretation of the universe. According to filmmaker Woody Allen, "The universe is indifferent . . . so we create a fake world for ourselves, and we exist within that fake world . . . a world that, in fact, means nothing at all, when you step back. It's meaningless. But it's important that we create some sense of meaning, because no perceptible meaning exists for anybody."[7]

There is another way to respond, however. Knowing that we are caught between time and eternity can help us find our way to God. Up to this point in his quest, Qoheleth has failed to find anything on earth that can fully satisfy the human mind or heart. But this still leaves open the possibility of finding satisfaction in God and in his Heaven. So rather than giving up on our desire for understanding, we should conclude instead that our longing for eternity proves that we were made for another world.

No one has ever explained the implications of our longing for eternity better than C. S. Lewis, who said, "If I find in myself a desire which no experience in this world can satisfy, the most probable explanation is that I was made for another world. If none of my earthly pleasures satisfy it, that does not prove that the universe is a fraud. Probably earthly pleasures were never meant to satisfy it, but only to arouse it, to suggest the real thing."[8] "The sweetest thing in all my life," Lewis wrote in one of his novels, "has been the longing . . . to find the place where all the beauty came from."[9] Elsewhere he describes this longing as "the scent of a flower we have not found, the echo of a tune we have not heard, news from a country we have never yet visited."[10]

Have you caught the scent of God's aroma or heard an echo from the song of his redemption? God has put the beauty of eternity into our hearts so that we will find our way to him. Our deepest longings will never be satisfied until we come to a personal knowledge of God and of his Son Jesus Christ, who is "the beginning and the end" (Revelation 21:6). When we find our way to him, we are finally able to say, as Charles Bridges once said, "I have found more in Christ, than I ever expected to want."[11]

Doing God's Business

One day we will know what God has done from beginning to end—or at least as much of what he has done as he wants us to know. In the meantime, the Preacher tells us two things that we should all be doing. Verse 12 and verse 14 both begin with the words "I perceived." In his struggle to understand how to live as a man caught between time and eternity, the Preacher had gained two very important insights: one about doing God's business and one about trusting God's sovereignty.

First, we should take whatever time we have been given and use it joyfully in the service of God. In verses 12–13 the Preacher tells us to get busy: "I perceived that there is nothing better for them than to be joyful and to do good as long as they live; also that everyone should eat and drink and take pleasure in all his toil—this is God's gift to man." Back in verse 10 the Preacher had talked about "the business that God has given to the children of man." Here he tells us how to go about that business—joyfully and energetically, with gratitude to God for the pleasure of serving him.

Some commentators have viewed these verses much more negatively. The Preacher's attitude, they say, is one of "resignation, not enthusiasm."[12]

On this reading, the words "nothing better" are faint praise. In fact, Today's English Version translates the verse like this: we should "do the best we can." In other words, the Preacher is trying to make the best of a bad situation. He wishes there were something better in life, but there isn't. And if this is all that life has to offer, the best thing that he can do under the circumstances is to enjoy the moment, grasping for the lower pleasures of eating and drinking and working. This is the best that a man can get. Thus the Preacher is saying something similar to the existentialist philosopher Jean-Paul Sartre, who wrote:

> It was true, I had always realized it—I hadn't any "right" to exist at all. I had appeared by chance, I existed like a stone, a plant, a microbe. I could feel nothing to myself but an inconsequential buzzing. I was thinking . . . that here we are eating and drinking, to preserve our precious existence, and that there's nothing, nothing, absolutely no reason for existing.[13]

There are a number of problems with a negative interpretation of Ecclesiastes 3. One is that nearly all the terms in these verses are positive. The Preacher speaks of pleasure and enjoyment. He talks about eating and drinking—the good things of life. He encourages us "to do good." Best of all, he reminds us that all of these things are "God's gift to man." So when he says that there is "nothing better" than doing God's business, he is not settling for something second best but is telling us that there is meaning and joy in the regular things of everyday life.

One good way to understand and apply this verse is to put it in the first person and use it as a job description: "There is nothing better than to be joyful and to do good as long as I live, and to eat and drink and take pleasure in all my work—this is God's gift to me." Imagine how much good a person could do over the course of a lifetime simply by putting these verses into daily practice. Then imagine how much kingdom work a church could do if it approached everything with this kind of joy, this kind of hard work, and this kind of gratitude to God.

The Preacher tells us to be joyful. We may not always be happy about the way things are going in life, but we can always find joy in the grace of our God and the work he has given us to do. No matter how bad our circumstances may be—whether through the natural hardships of life or the harm done to us by others or the painful consequences of our own rebellious sin—in every situation there is always a way for us to glorify God, and this should give us joy.

The Preacher also tells us to "do good"—a phrase that should be taken in its moral and ethical sense. To "do good" is to do good works. This does not mean that we could ever earn our way to Heaven, of course, but it does mean that we should do the good work that God has given us to do, for as long as he gives us to do it. Out of gratitude for what God has done for us in Jesus, forgiving all our sins, we should get busy doing the work of his kingdom. Indeed, this is the very reason for our existence: we are God's "workmanship, created in Christ Jesus for good works, which God prepared beforehand, that we should walk in them" (Ephesians 2:10).

In his grace, God has given every one of us something good to do for him. We do not work because we have nothing better to do, but because God has called us to work for him. Every believer should do good work at home, loving the people with whom he or she lives. Every believer should do good work on the job, serving God in the ordinary duties of an earthly calling. Every believer should do good work in the church, using his or her spiritual gifts in at least one regular ministry. Every believer should do good work in society, showing the love of Jesus through practical deeds of mercy.

We should do all these things as long as we live, working right to the end of our lives. When the Preacher says "as long as they live," he is remembering what he said back in verse 2, namely, that there is a time for us to die. Until that time comes, however, we must spend our time wisely, using it for Jesus. The Presbyterian pastor and theologian Thomas Boston once said to his congregation in rural Scotland:

> Each generation has its work assigned it by the sovereign Lord; and each person in the generation has his also. And now is our time. We could not be useful in the generation that went before us; for then we were not: nor can we [be useful] personally in that which shall come after us; for then we shall be off the stage. Now is our time; let us not neglect usefulness in our generation.[14]

As we do good work in our generation, the Preacher gives us permission to celebrate the good things of life—eating and drinking and enjoying the pleasures that God has made for us to enjoy. Of course, it is always a temptation for us to live for earthly pleasure, serving our appetites instead of serving Jesus (see Romans 16:18). The good things in life so easily become our gods, which is absolute vanity, as the Preacher has already told us (see Ecclesiastes 2:1ff.). But the way to resist this temptation is not by avoiding everything. Rather, we avoid idolatry by gratefully receiving the good things of life as blessings from God. Do not be a user and a taker; be a receiver and a thanker. This is all part of offering back to God what he has given to us in joyful service, while we have the time.

Trusting God's Sovereignty

The other thing that the Preacher tells us to do—his second insight—is to let God be God, reverently accepting his sovereignty over time and eternity.

He said, "I perceived that whatever God does endures forever; nothing can be added to it, nor anything taken from it. God has done it, so that people fear before him. That which is, already has been; and God seeks what has been driven away" (Ecclesiastes 3:14–15).

When he says, "whatever God does," the Preacher may be thinking back to the beginning of the chapter, when he said that there is "a season . . . for everything . . . and a time for every matter under heaven" (Ecclesiastes 3:1). "Whatever God does" includes everything sailing that God does, at whatever time he does it. He is sovereign over the times and the seasons. Whatever he does will endure: no one can add to it or subtract from it—now until forever.

Once again, however, some scholars see these verses as depressing and fatalistic. God does whatever he does, and there is nothing we can do about it. In the words of Michael Fox, "God's works steamroller over man's puny efforts, and nothing substantially new can interrupt the awesome course of events that God has ordained."[15] If we cannot add anything to what God has done or take anything away from it, then there is absolutely nothing that we can do about our situation in life.

Is this a good thing or a bad thing? In other words, is the absolute rule of God a source of hope or discouragement? Ecclesiastes gives us the answer when it tells us why God does what he does: "so that people fear before him" (Ecclesiastes 3:14).

Even at this point some scholars try to claim that God is trying "to frighten people into submission, not to arouse a sense of respectful awe of his power and might."[16] The trouble with this interpretation is that the fear of God is one of the most positive concepts in the entire Bible. To fear God is to revere him and to tremble at his mighty power. Both the Psalms and the Proverbs say that such fear of the Lord is the very beginning of wisdom and that anyone who fails to see this is a fool (Psalm 111:10; Proverbs 1:7). In fact, when we get to the end of Ecclesiastes, we will discover that this is the point of the whole book. After saying everything else that he has to say, the Preacher will leave us with this simple instruction: "Fear God" (Ecclesiastes 12:13).

To fear God is not to give up on finding meaning in life, but to rest our lives on the only solid foundation for time and eternity. To fear God is to trust in his foreknowledge, believing that he knows all things, including our present joys and trials. Martin Luther said, "This is what it means to fear God: to have God in view, to know that He looks at all our works, and to acknowledge Him as the Author of all things."[17]

To fear God is also to believe that he is still in control, even when we cannot see (or do not understand) what he is doing. The early church father Didymus the Blind used a marvelous illustration to explain this. Didymus compares us to passengers on a large sailing vessel who have never met the captain, yet still know that he is steering the ship: "God himself manages the cosmos and looks after it. . . . When you see a ship which is piloted and holds its course, you perceive the idea of a helmsman even if he is not visible. . . . Likewise the Creator is known by his works and the order of his providence."[18]

Do you believe in the doctrine of divine sovereignty? Can you accept that God is really God? Have you learned to fear your Maker? Far from discouraging us into giving up, knowing that God is in control of everything from here to eternity encourages us to keep pressing on. Michael Eaton explains how trusting God's sovereignty helps us live the Christian life. The fear of God that Qoheleth is talking about, he says,

> is not only the beginning of wisdom; it is also the beginning of joy, of contentment and of an energetic and purposeful life. The Preacher wishes to deliver us from a rosy-colored, self-confident, godless life, with its inevitable cynicism and bitterness, and from trusting in wisdom, pleasure, wealth, and human justice or integrity. He wishes to drive us to see that God is there, that He is good and generous, and that only such an outlook makes life coherent and fulfilling.[19]

Even verse 15 is encouraging. The first part of the verse sounds similar to something we heard in chapter 1, that there is nothing new under the sun. According to the prologue of Ecclesiastes, "What has been is what will be, and what has been done is what will be done" (Ecclesiastes 1:9). Here we read, "That which is, already has been; that which is to be, already has been" (Ecclesiastes 3:15). In other words, whatever happens now has happened before; it is the same old, same old over and over again. The difference is that chapter 3 explicitly puts everything under the sovereignty of God. Thus the book is helping us make progress in understanding the universe. The things that are outside our control should not cause us to despair but to hope in God, who is sovereign over everything that happens.

The last part of verse 15 is more difficult: "God seeks what has been driven away." This seems to be a poetic way of talking about things that have happened in the past.[20] We tend to think that bygone days are gone forever, but this verse tells us that God is looking to recover the past. Maybe this means that he will bring former deeds to judgment. This is the interpretation given by the New International Version, which reads, "God will call the past to account." Judgment is a prominent theme in Ecclesiastes, which ends with a promise that "God will bring every deed into judgment" (Ecclesiastes 12:14), whether past or present. Yet the language of seeking is so positive that it suggests that God is looking to redeem the past, and not simply to render judgment. By his grace he will recover and restore what seems, from our vantage point, to be lost forever.

Eternal redemption is our hope whenever we feel caught between time and eternity. What we do in this life matters. The work of God endures forever, including whatever good work we are busy doing in the name of Jesus. Therefore our lives and our labor are not in vain. The same God who put eternity into our hearts will make everything beautiful, including things past that now seem lost or broken. All in his good time.

9

From Dust to Glory

ECCLESIASTES 3:16—4:3

For what happens to the children of man and what happens to the beasts is the same; as one dies, so dies the other. They all have the same breath, and man has no advantage over the beasts, for all is vanity. All go to one place. All are from the dust, and to dust all return.

3:19–20

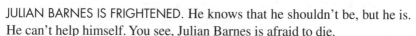

JULIAN BARNES IS FRIGHTENED. He knows that he shouldn't be, but he is. He can't help himself. You see, Julian Barnes is afraid to die.

The famous English writer—the author of *Flaubert's Parrot* and other prize-winning novels—formerly called himself an atheist. Then he claimed to be an agnostic, because in his opinion there is no good reason to think there is a God. This would further imply that there is no such thing as life after death, and therefore *Nothing to be Frightened Of*, which is the title of one of his latest books.

Yet the sober truth is that Julian Barnes is desperately afraid to die. *The New York Times Book Review* correctly diagnoses his condition as *thanatophobia*—the fear of death. Barnes thinks about death every day and admits that sometimes in the night he is "roared awake" and "pitched from sleep into darkness, panic and a vicious awareness that this is a rented world." Awake and utterly alone, he finds himself beating his pillow with a fist and wailing, "Oh no Oh No OH NO."

Julian's dreams are even darker. Sometimes he is buried alive. Other times he is "chased, surrounded, outnumbered." He finds himself "held hostage, wrongly condemned to the firing squad, informed that there is even less time" than he thought. "The usual stuff," he calls it.[1] And perhaps this *is* the usual stuff, because death is the sum of all our fears—of being alone, of being abandoned, of being condemned. When you wake up in the middle of the night, what are you afraid of?

Man's Inhumanity to Man

Ecclesiastes faces up to our fears by asking the hardest questions that anyone can ask about the meaning of the universe, the existence of God, and the life to come. The difficult question of death comes up again at the end of chapter 3, where the Preacher poses a problem and comes up with an answer, only to discover that there is a problem with the answer too. He has been thinking about all the injustice in the world and about his longing for God to address it at the Final Judgment. But thinking about that great and terrible day causes him to wonder again what will happen when we die.

The starting point is verse 16, where the author introduces a new subject: "Moreover, I saw under the sun that in the place of justice, even there was wickedness, and in the place of righteousness, even there was wickedness" (Ecclesiastes 3:16). As we have seen before, the phrase "under the sun" describes "the futility and meaninglessness of life lived only for self and the moment, without gratitude to or regard for God and his ways."[2] What we see "under the sun" in this instance is rampant injustice—man's inhumanity to man.

Here Qoheleth sounds like one of the Biblical prophets. Men like Amos and Jeremiah were always crying for justice, and rightly so because justice is one of the deep longings of the human heart. It starts during childhood: "Hey, that's not fair!" Unfortunately, unfairness does not stop at the playground but goes all the way through life. We are members of an unjust race.

The problem here is that even "the place of justice" is unjust. The very place where we most expect and most need to receive justice turns out to be a place of unfairness. Even the court system is corrupt. This is not merely a frustration, like some of the other problems we read about in Ecclesiastes, but a manifestation of genuine evil. Innocent people are convicted for crimes they never committed. They were simply in the wrong place at the wrong time, or maybe the wrong color in the wrong neighborhood. Just as frequently, other people get away with murder. They have the money to hire better lawyers, or else they hide behind the structure of a large corporation to take advantage of people who are less fortunate.

Even worse, there is nothing that can be done about this. The Preacher's frustration is not simply that injustice is done, but that it goes unpunished. According to Martin Luther, he is "not complaining because there is wickedness in the place of justice but because the wickedness in the place of justice cannot be corrected."[3] When the halls of justice become corridors of corruption, where can righteousness be found?

The Preacher revisits this theme at the beginning of chapter 4, where he says, "Again I saw all the oppressions that are done under the sun. And behold, the tears of the oppressed, and they had no one to comfort them! On the side of their oppressors there was power, and there was no one to comfort them" (Ecclesiastes 4:1). By this reasoning, there are two kinds of people in the world: the oppressed and their oppressors. The oppressors are the ones who have all the advantages. The power is all on their side, leaving their victims with nothing but tears.

As we read the Bible, we quickly discover that this is a conflict in which God chooses sides. He is not on the side of injustice but stands against it with all his power. We see this again and again in the Biblical prophets. Amos preached against people who "oppress the poor" and "crush the needy" (Amos 4:1; cf. Proverbs 14:31). Ezekiel warned about extortion and stealing from foreigners (Ezekiel 22:12). Zechariah listed the people who were most likely to be oppressed: widows, orphans, travelers, and the poor (Zechariah 7:9–10; cf. Exodus 22:21–22). It is not just words and actions that bring oppression but also legislation. Thus Isaiah pronounced God's woe against "those who decree iniquitous decrees, and the writers who keep writing oppression" (Isaiah 10:1).

The words of these prophets speak to the sins that we see in our own country—the poorest of the poor getting poorer, legal immigrants finding it hard to get a decent job, school systems failing our children, fathers abusing their wives and children. Then there is all the oppression we see around the world—genocide, terrorism, slavery, sex trafficking, street children. Oh, the injustice of it all!

When the Preacher saw what was really happening in the world, he longed for someone to comfort the oppressed and dry their tears. In a culture of exploitation, he wanted to rectify wrongs and console the victims of injustice. Twice he lamented that no one was able to offer any comfort.

The Preacher had an intense emotional response to both groups of people—the same holy response that we see in the life of Jesus Christ. On the one hand, he responded to the plight of the oppressed with lamentation, like the tears that Jesus shed for the harassed and helpless people of Israel (Matthew 9:36). On the other hand, he responded to their oppressors with indignation, like the angry words that Jesus had for the moneychangers at the temple (e.g., Luke 19:45–46). But what the Preacher mostly felt was frustration that he could not bring an end to oppression.

We feel the same frustration today when we learn about the plight of the persecuted church. Consider the true story of "Lana," a nineteen-year-old Egyptian girl who was raised in a devout Muslim home. Lana had always been taught to despise Christianity, but one day a friend from school invited her to listen to a radio program on which she heard the gospel. Lana began to wonder whether Jesus Christ was truly God or whether he was merely a messenger from God as she had always been told. As she read the Bible, she came to a clear conviction that Jesus is the Christ.

Sadly, when Lana accepted Jesus as her Savior and her Lord, she was attacked by her own family. Her father beat her. Her mother would not allow her to sit with the family at meals. Eventually they declared that Lana was as good as dead to them. But even after they threw her out of the house, they continued to persecute her. She was kidnapped and beaten until she was broken and unconscious.[4]

This is the kind of oppression that we see under the sun—persecution that we are sometimes powerless to prevent. So how should we respond? Where does this kind of suffering fit in with our theology?

A Time for Justice

The writer of Ecclesiastes had a good answer to the problem of injustice. He said in his heart, "God will judge the righteous and the wicked, for there is a time for every matter and for every work" (Ecclesiastes 3:17).

Here we see the Preacher applying an old sermon to his own heart. By way of comparison, consider something encouraging that happened to me after preaching from Ecclesiastes 3:2, which tells us that there is both "a time to be born, and a time to die." A few days later I received a note from one of the fathers in our church. He told me how he had sat down with his seven-year-old son to tell him that his grandmother was very sick and probably not going to recover. "It's just like Pastor Ryken said," his son responded. "God has a time for everything." The boy took the truth about time and used it to make sense of life and death.

The Preacher does something similar in verse 17: he takes a spiritual principle that he taught earlier in chapter 3 and applies it to the issue of injustice. If there is a season for everything and "a time for every matter under heaven" (Ecclesiastes 3:1), then there must be a time for justice. Therefore, rather than simply getting angry and sad about all the oppression we see in the world, we can trust God to make things right in the end.

This does not mean that there is never a time for us to pursue justice. Depending on our place in society—the spiritual or civil authority that God has given to us—it is our responsibility to fight against oppression. As fathers and mothers, as pastors and elders, as citizens and public officials, we are called to do what is right in the home, in the church, and in society.

Yet, unfortunately, even our very best efforts will not bring an end to all oppression. There will still be violence against women and children. Police officers will still get killed in the line of duty. There will still be structures of corruption in business and government. Foreign powers will still abuse their own people in defiance of world order. But in all the situations that we do not have the power or authority or wisdom to resolve, God will see to it that justice is done.

Our confidence does not lie in a justice system but in the Chief Justice himself, Jesus Christ. God has promised a day when his Son will judge the righteous and the wicked (Acts 17:30–31). The time for his work of divine retribution is the Day of Judgment, when he will render his final verdict on all mankind. "Shall not the Judge of all the earth do what is just?" (Genesis 18:25). Indeed, the wicked will be punished forever (Matthew 25:41–46), and the righteous will be comforted by the Spirit of God, who will wipe away every tear from their eyes (Revelation 21:4). As the Preacher will go on to say at the very end of his book, "God will bring every deed into judgment, with every secret thing, whether good or evil" (Ecclesiastes 12:14).

We live in the sure hope and certain expectation of that great day. Whenever we see injustice—especially acts of oppression that we are powerless to prevent—we can still pray for justice, leaving things in God's hands. This requires faith in God's promises and also the patience to wait for his timing. Like the martyrs who have gone ahead of us to glory, we cry out, "O Sovereign Lord, holy and true, how long before you will judge?" (Revelation 6:9–10). Jesus has promised that when his people cry out day and night, God "will give justice to them speedily" (Luke 18:8). If justice seems a long time coming, as it often does, we should believe the words of the prophets, who said, "If it seems slow, wait for it; it will surely come; it will not delay" (Habakkuk 2:3).

Dust to Dust

Some people may still wonder why justice is delayed. Why doesn't God judge people right away? Why does he wait until the Final Judgment? The Preacher had a good answer to this question as well: "I said in my heart with regard to the children of man that God is testing them that they may see that they themselves are but beasts" (Ecclesiastes 3:18).

Our present existence is a proving ground. It is a test, not simply in the sense of something we pass or fail, but also in the sense of something that demonstrates our true character.[5] One of the purposes of life is to examine and ultimately to reveal our place in the universe and our true relationship to God. This test is not for God's benefit, as if there were anything about us that he does not know already, but for our benefit, so that we learn to recognize our mortality. Will we see ourselves for who we really are?

At first Qoheleth's comparison to animals may seem un-Biblical, like something an evolutionist would say. Doesn't the Bible say that we are only a little lower than the angels, with all of the animals under our dominion (see

Psalm 8)? Didn't God make us in his own image (see Genesis 1:27), and doesn't this distinguish us from every other creature in the world?

All of this is true, but what Ecclesiastes says is also true: men are beasts. In saying this, the Preacher is not commenting on our biology but our destiny. He is making a specific comparison, as he goes on to explain: "For what happens to the children of man and what happens to the beasts is the same; as one dies, so dies the other. They all have the same breath, and man has no advantage over the beasts, for all is vanity. All go to one place. All are from the dust, and to dust all return" (Ecclesiastes 3:19–20).

This is one of the Bible's strongest statements of the inevitability of death. The Preacher's point is that people die, just like the animals. For all the differences between us, we do share this one thing in common: whether man or beast, we will all meet the same fate, at least with regard to our physical bodies.

Death is the great equalizer. We are reminded of this every time we see a dead animal. Living in the city, I often see corpses when I walk to church—pigeons and other birds, squirrels . . . even rats occasionally. When we see something like this, do we remember that we too are mortal, or do we look away?

Animals are living creatures, just like us. Like us, they have been given life and breath by their Creator. But that life will not last forever. The day will come when they breathe their last, just like us. With our parting breath, we will all go to the same place, falling to the earth and returning to dust (see Job 10:9; Psalm 22:15). By using this language, the Preacher is reminding us of God's curse against Adam's sin: dust we are, and to the dust we shall return (Genesis 3:19; cf. Psalm 90:3; 104:29). "Ashes, ashes, we all fall down." To this extent, we are no better than animals. In the words of the Psalmist, "Man in his pomp will not remain; he is like the beasts that perish" (Psalm 49:12).

What is your response to the certainty of your own mortality? The approach taken by one order of Trappist monks is worthy of emulation. Together they dig a grave. Every day they go out to the grave site, peer over the edge, and ponder their own mortality. When one of their number dies, they lower him into the grave and cover him with dirt. Then they dig a new grave and start the ritual all over again, never knowing for certain who will be the next to die.[6]

Not everyone responds to death in such a sober or practical way. Some people try to laugh it off, like Woody Allen who famously said, "I'm not afraid to die; I just don't want to be there when it happens!" Other people *are* afraid, like Julian Barnes. Without any comfort for their fears, they have terrors in the night and despair of ever finding meaning in life. The Preacher seems to be at that point here; "all is vanity," he says (Ecclesiastes 3:19).

If everyone dies, then life has no meaning. The English writer Somerset Maugham reached the same conclusion:

> If one puts aside the existence of God and the survival after life as too doubtful . . . one has to make up one's mind as to the use of life. If death ends all, if I have neither to hope for good nor to fear evil, I must ask myself what I am here for, and how in these circumstances I must conduct myself. Now the answer is plain, but so unpalatable that most will not face it. There is no meaning for life and [thus] life has no meaning.[7]

Is There Life after Death?

Meaningless, meaningless, it's all meaningless. For a moment it seemed as if the Final Judgment would solve the problem of injustice. But whatever relief the Preacher felt was only temporary. The answer to his problem turned out to be another problem! As he reflected further on the delay of divine justice and started thinking about the implications of his own mortality, he ended up right back where he started: vanity of vanities!

Qoheleth knew there was one thing that could make a difference in the face of death, however. Even if it is true that our bodies will return to the dust, maybe our souls will live forever. If they do, then this would clearly distinguish man from beast. It would also give the Preacher some reassurance that oppressors will come to justice. It all depends on whether or not there is life after death. If there isn't, then there is no way out of despair; but if there is, then everything may still come out right in the end.

For the moment, the Preacher is not entirely sure about the life to come. In fact, he seems downright uncertain: "Who knows whether the spirit of man goes upward and the spirit of the beast goes down into the earth?" (Ecclesiastes 3:21). Obviously the Preacher had heard the conventional wisdom that when animals die, they just die, but when people die, their spirits rise to Heaven. Although some scholars still doubt whether people in Old Testament times believed in life after death, it is clear from this and many other verses that they generally did. Yet Qoheleth was starting to have his doubts. So he asked the agnostic questions: Who knows? Can we really be sure? How can we know for certain that after we die we will go to Heaven and live with God?

These are the most fundamental questions that we can ask about our destiny. We know that one day the time will come for us to die. The question is, will we live again? Knowing what will happen when we die would help us understand how to live. Yet the Preacher was struggling to find certainty. Although some scholars have viewed verse 21 as an affirmation,[8] it seems to be a genuine question: Who knows?

As he wrestled with this uncertainty, the Preacher's first impulse was to throw himself back into his work: "So I saw that there is nothing better than that a man should rejoice in his work, for that is his lot. Who can bring him to see what will be after him?" (Ecclesiastes 3:22). If we are facing an uncertain future, perhaps the best thing that we can do right now is to be productive. This may seem like small comfort, but the Preacher is not completely cynical. Even if what he says about finding joy in our work rings a little hollow, it fits what he says elsewhere about the ordinary pleasures of daily life.

Unless we have the assurance of eternal life, however, finding joy in our everyday work will never give us lasting satisfaction. We see this in the opening verses of chapter 4, where the Preacher quickly spirals back down into despair. Once again he witnesses ungodly oppression by evil men (Ecclesiastes 4:1). This makes him envy the dead and the unborn: "And I thought the dead who are already dead more fortunate than the living who are still alive. But better than both is he who has not yet been and has not seen the evil deeds that are done under the sun" (Ecclesiastes 4:2–3).

This bitter comparison echoes the words of faithful prophets like Elijah and Jeremiah, who sometimes despaired of life itself (see 1 Kings 19:3–5; Jeremiah 20:14–18). Have you ever wished that you had never been born, or else wanted your life to end so that all your troubles would be over? If the question is "to be or not to be," then maybe it is better not to be. "It's all a big nothing," says one of the characters on the television drama *The Sopranos*. "In the end, you die in your own arms."

Given all of the depressing things that happen in this depraved world, maybe we are better off never having lived at all. If we had the certainty of our own salvation and knew that justice would be done, then our lives would be full of hope and joy. But when we have our doubts, like the Preacher often did, it is tempting to think that we would be better off dead.

Dust to Glory

By this point in Ecclesiastes, it is clear that the Preacher-King does not have all the answers. For all the progress he had made in understanding the meaning of life, there were still many things he could not understand. But at least he was asking the right questions! Maybe better than anyone else in history, Qoheleth accurately identified the problems of human existence. If we continue to ask his questions today, and look for the answers that God has for us in the gospel of his Son, the Holy Spirit will lead us to the truth of everlasting life. One of the early church fathers said, "Ecclesiastes, instructing us through enigmas, guides us to the other life."[9]

One way to find this other life is by giving the full Biblical answers to the questions that the Preacher raises in this passage. He asks, "Who knows whether the spirit of man goes upward and the spirit of the beast goes down into the earth?" (Ecclesiastes 3:21). Further, he asks, "Who can bring him to see what will be after him?" (Ecclesiastes 3:22).

These are great questions. If we wanted, we could answer them from the Old Testament. The very same Psalm that talks about people dying "like the beasts that perish" goes on to make this promise: "But God will ransom my soul from the power of Sheol, for he will receive me" (49:15). In fact, when he talked about men and beasts going down to the dust of death, Qoheleth may have assumed that his readers would remember this psalm, including its promise of life after death. He certainly came to believe in life afterward for himself, because when he talks about death at the end of his book he says, "the dust returns to the earth as it was, and the spirit returns to God who gave it" (Ecclesiastes 12:7).

The best answer of all, however, is the one that God has given through the person and work of his Son, Jesus Christ. Anyone who wants to know what will happen after death should ask Jesus. He is able to "bring [us] to see what will be after [us]" because he has been through death and reached the other side. Jesus was put to death on a cross, but he did not stay dead. On the third day he was raised again. His body and his spirit ascended to the glory at the right hand of God. Now everyone who believes in him will "rise again to a better life" (Hebrews 11:35). Jesus has gone to Heaven to prepare a place for us, so that we may be where he is (see John 14:3). This is why we can be certain of going to Heaven. It is because Jesus "abolished death and brought life and immortality to light through the gospel" (2 Timothy 1:10).

The Civil War correspondent Samuel Wilkerson claimed this great promise as he surveyed the carnage after the Battle of Gettysburg. In the providence of God, the journalist discovered the body of his own son, who had fought for the Union and had fallen in battle. In his grief, Wilkerson did not despair but claimed the promise of the resurrection, that those who die in Christ will rise again. Here is what he wrote for the *New York Times*, standing next to the body of his beloved son:

> Oh, you dead, who at Gettysburg have baptized with your blood the Second birth of Freedom in America, how you are to be envied! I rise from a grave whose set clay I have passionately kissed, and I look up and see Christ spanning this battlefield with his feet and reaching fraternally and lovingly up to heaven. His right hand opens the gates of Paradise—with his left he beckons to those mutilated, bloody, swollen forms to ascend.[10]

Have you claimed this promise, by the death and resurrection of Jesus Christ, that when you go down to the dust of death, you will rise again to glory? If so, then you have the comfort of the resurrection in all your sorrows. By the grace of God you can rejoice in whatever work God has given you to do as you wait for the Day of Judgment. You have the faith and hope to persevere in the face of injustice and oppression.

Earlier I told the story of "Lana," a young Egyptian convert who was persecuted for her faith in Jesus Christ. When Lana was disowned by her family, what kept her from despair was her faith in the resurrection power of God, in life after death with Jesus. "I'm in real danger," she testified, "but I trust God because He is alive. My comfort is that it is only a short time I'm spending here on earth, but there will be a long time that I'll spend with Him. . . . We know there will come a time when there will be no more sorrow or suffering. This is our hope in the Lord Jesus."[11] Yes, this is our hope in the Lord Jesus—that after all our troubles and sorrows, the risen Lord will raise us up to glory.

10

Two Are Better Than One

ECCLESIASTES 4:4–16

Two are better than one, because they have a good
reward for their toil. For if they fall, one will lift
up his fellow. But woe to him who is alone when
he falls and has not another to lift him up!

4:9–10

PEOPLE LOVE TO MAKE COMPARISONS: "This one is better than that one."
"The original movie was better than the sequel." "Those are more expensive,
but they're worth it because they're better made." These are the kinds of
comparisons that people make every day.

When he was younger, one of my boys liked to compare football teams.
"Dad," he would say, "what do you think is the best team in college football?" "What about the pros?" "Who's better—the Bears or the Eagles?"
Finally, in exasperation, I would say, "Look, that's enough for right now. I'm
not going to answer any more questions about which teams are the best."
After a long and thoughtful pause, my son tried another approach: "Dad,
who do you think has the *worst* team in pro football?"

The writers of the Old Testament often used a similar strategy. In order
to show the way of wisdom or the path of obedience, they would compare
one thing to another. For example, when Samuel wanted to say that loving
God is more important than simply going through the religious motions,
he said, "To obey is better than sacrifice" (1 Samuel 15:22). Or when
Solomon wanted to praise the harmony of a loving home, he said, "Better
is a dinner of herbs where love is than a fattened ox and hatred with it"
(Proverbs 15:17).

The Preacher-King who wrote Ecclesiastes used the same strategy.

Given all the trouble there is in the world, sometimes he was tempted to think that it might be better not to live at all, and he said as much at the beginning of chapter 4. Then he made several more comparisons that were based on what he saw happening around him and that give practical wisdom for daily life in this transient world. By the grace of God, it is better for us to live with contentment (Ecclesiastes 4:4–6), to lead with a teachable spirit (Ecclesiastes 4:13–16), and to work in partnership with other people (Ecclesiastes 4:7–12).

Living with Contentment

The first comparison was about contentment, and it began with an observation about the working world: "Then I saw that all toil and all skill in work come from a man's envy of his neighbor. This also is vanity and a striving after wind" (Ecclesiastes 4:4).

Qoheleth has told us already that work is a gift from God (e.g., Ecclesiastes 2:24). But like all of God's blessings, work can be distorted by sin. Here the Preacher points out that much of our work is motivated by envy, by the sinful desire to get ahead in life by getting ahead of other people. Economists sometimes identify the competitive urge of self-interest as the engine that drives a capitalist economy. But Ecclesiastes sees a deeper motivation at work, a motivation that comes from a selfish heart.

Envy is not the only reason that people work, of course, and if we took this verse by itself it would sound like an exaggeration. There certainly are some exceptions that prove the rule. But the Preacher still has a point—one of the reasons we work so hard is to get what our neighbor has. This is why some people shortchange the government on their taxes, or cheat their customers, or get into debt with their credit cards. It is because we envy what other people have and will do anything to get it.

There are many things we are tempted to envy—for example, someone's looks or abilities or situation in life. Someone else has the job or the grades or the girlfriend that we always wanted. But of all the things that we are tempted to envy, usually our neighbor's possessions are near the top of the list. Just look at the Tenth Commandment: most of the things it tells us not to covet are things that money can buy. We work hard to get more money to buy more things, or else we pull out the plastic to engage in what one economist has called "retail therapy."[1] If we get everything we covet, someone else will envy us, and the cycle will continue. The world is full of Joneses trying to keep up with the other Joneses.

In 2008 I flew into Philadelphia on the travel day between the second and third games of the World Series. The man sitting next to me had it made. Every year his company flies him to the Fall Classic—great seats for two games and three nights at a nice hotel, complete with restaurant vouchers and limousine service. He also happened to mention that he has six season tickets on the thirty yard line at Texas Stadium. Sitting next to him, editing a sermon manuscript but also anticipating the next two games between the Phillies and the Rays, I felt a sudden surge of envy. But then I heard Qoheleth whisper in my ear, reminding me that wanting what God has given to someone else instead of what he has for me is vanity, a striving after wind.

There was something else the Preacher had observed. The opposite of the man who worked too much, it was a man who refused to work at all: "The fool folds his hands and eats his own flesh" (Ecclesiastes 4:5).

Rather than joining the rat race, some people drop out altogether. They know they can't keep up with the Joneses, so they don't even try. All they do is fold their lazy hands. But this turns out to be deeply self-destructive. As the Preacher describes it, the fool eats what he has until he has nothing left at all:

> He is the picture of complacency and unwitting self-destruction, for this comment on him points out a deeper damage than the wasting of his capital. His idleness eats away not only what he has but what he is: eroding his self-control, his grasp of reality, his capacity for care and, in the end, his self-respect.[2]

These verses describe two equal and opposite errors. "As toil can be all-consuming, so idleness is self-cannibalizing."[3] Which of these errors is more of a temptation for you? Maybe you are tempted to envy what other people have and then wear yourself out trying to get it. Or maybe you think you are above all of that, yet you have such a negative attitude about work that sometimes you avoid it altogether. Either way Qoheleth has some good advice: "Better is a handful of quietness than two hands full of toil and a striving after wind" (Ecclesiastes 4:6).

This beautiful comparison is built on a double contrast. "Quietness" is contrasted with "toil and . . . striving." A good synonym is "contentment." The quiet person is peaceful and composed. Rather than always striving for more, he or she is satisfied already. The contrast is reinforced by the difference between having a single handful and having "two hands full." The person with two hands full is a two-fisted consumer, always grabbing as much as he can and always grasping for more. But sometimes less *is* more, and the quiet person has found the right balance. His hands are not folded, like the fool. He is working hard enough to have a decent handful of what he needs in life. But that is enough for him. He does not keep demanding more and more but accepts what God has given.

Have you learned to be content? The quiet person is like Jesus, who always shows us the best way to live. Jesus did not fold his hands in idleness. Neither did he envy people who had more possessions than he did, which included almost everyone. He simply worked hard in the calling that his Father had given him—the calling to seek and to save lost sinners. As he worked, Jesus trusted his Father to provide for his daily needs; he was content with the basic things in life.

Now Jesus invites us to live the same way—the better way that we see in Ecclesiastes. Work hard, but be content with what you have. Find your satisfaction in the goodness of God, like the little girl who misquoted Psalm 23 but spoke better than she knew. Rather than saying, "The Lord is my shepherd; I shall not want," she said, "The Lord is my shepherd; that's all I want."[4] Most of us want so many other things in life that it is hard for us to say that, but whether Jesus is all we want or not, the truth is that he is all we need.

Leading with a Teachable Spirit

The Preacher makes another helpful comparison at the end of chapter 4, which we should consider briefly before coming back to the heart of the passage. The point of this closing comparison is that it is better to lead with a teachable spirit than to be too proud to let anyone teach us anything at all.

This time the Preacher makes his comparison first, then tells a real-life story to illustrate it. The comparison goes like this: "Better was a poor and wise youth than an old and foolish king who no longer knew how to take advice" (Ecclesiastes 4:13). Then he tells the rest of the story: "For he went from prison to the throne, though in his own kingdom he had been born poor. I saw all the living who move about under the sun, along with that youth who was to stand in the king's place. There was no end of all the people, all of whom he led. Yet those who come later will not rejoice in him. Surely this also is vanity and a striving after wind" (Ecclesiastes 4:14–16).

This "rags to riches" story is about a man who rose from obscurity to royalty. If Solomon wrote it, as many people think, then obviously he could not have been referring to himself, since that great king was raised in a royal palace. It sounds more like the story of David, who served as a shepherd before claiming his crown. Yet the mention of prison sounds like something from the life of Joseph. So perhaps the story comes from somewhere else entirely.

The story's transitions are somewhat hard to follow, but apparently what happened was this: a young man unexpectedly rose to power, taking the place of the king who ruled before him. Though he had been born in poverty, he rose to the highest office in the land. Some scholars think that verse 14 refers to the old king in his younger days, but more likely it refers to the younger and better man who took his place. This new king ruled over a vast empire; there seemed to be no end to the people who followed him. Yet even the new king could not rule forever. Taken literally, verse 15 refers to a second youth, whom some scholars take to be the new king's eventual successor. Whether this is the right way to read the verse or not, verse 16 makes it clear that one day this king and every king will be forgotten.

Part of the lesson here is that fame is fleeting. No matter how popular a ruler is, the day will come when someone else takes his place and all his glory fades away. In the end, everyone turns out to be expendable. The old king may be past his prime, but the young upstart will not live forever either. According to Derek Kidner, the new king "has reached a pinnacle of human glory, only to be stranded there. It is yet another of our human anticlimaxes and ultimately empty achievements."[5] We are thus reminded not to put too much stock in earthly position—either our own or anyone else's.

But there is another lesson here that we should be sure not to miss. Of all the contrasts between the two kings—youth versus age, poverty versus wealth, wisdom versus folly—the most important is their attitude toward advice. The old king "no longer knew how to take advice" (Ecclesiastes 4:13). In earlier days he had listened to his advisors, but now he kept his own counsel, and for this reason he had ceased to be of any real use to his people. This tragedy has been repeated many times in the history of nations (and also, sadly, in the ministry of the church) as old men cling to positions of power, refusing to let go.

This story stands as a warning to older Christians. We usually think that gray hair brings wisdom, and often it does. But whether they are young or old, the wisest Christians are the ones who listen to counsel and, if necessary, accept correction. At the same time, this verse is an encouragement to younger Christians. Even someone young and poor can do valuable work for the kingdom of God. The way to do such work is not by telling other people what to do or seeking a more prominent position. The way to do it is by having the wisdom to say, "I still have a lot to learn about life and ministry, and when the time is right, God will give me the right place to serve."

The best way to gain this wisdom is by turning to Jesus Christ, the only King whose fame will last forever. The life of the Reformer John Calvin illustrates this principle well. When he described his conversion to faith in Christ, Calvin said that God subdued his mind and brought it to "a teachable frame."[6] The word "teachable" occurs with some regularity in his famous *Institutes of the Christian Religion*.[7] A Christian is simply a teachable follower of Christ.

The end of Ecclesiastes 4 is really the story of Jesus and his humble, teachable spirit. The Bible says that when he was a young boy, living in the home of Joseph and Mary, "Jesus increased in wisdom" (Luke 2:52). He must have been willing to listen to his parents. He certainly listened to his Heavenly Father because he followed his Father's counsel all the way to the cross where he died for our sins. Then, when the time was right, the Father raised Jesus up from the grave to be our King. Thus the man born in poverty and obscurity was exalted to the throne of everlasting glory.

Now there is no end to all the people that Jesus leads—people all through history, from all over the world. If we are wise, we will follow his example and live by his grace. We will ask God to give us a teachable heart, without which we will never be ready to lead or to be useful in any other way for the kingdom of God.

Working in Partnership

To do good kingdom work we need something else besides contentment and a teachable spirit. To see what it is, we need to go back to the middle of the chapter, where we see yet another comparison, one that has to do with partnership.

Once again the Preacher-King makes careful observation of the way people live: "Again, I saw vanity under the sun: one person who has no other, either son or brother, yet there is no end to all his toil, and his eyes are never satisfied with riches, so that he never asks, 'For whom am I toiling and depriving myself of pleasure?' This also is vanity and an unhappy business" (Ecclesiastes 4:7–8).

Here the Preacher tells us the sad tale of a solitary individual. The man is not mentioned by name, but he lives and works alone. If he has a wife, she is not mentioned, so perhaps this is the biography of a bachelor. But even if he does have a wife, he does not have an heir—a son or a brother to inherit his wealth. So he is only working for himself, not for the blessing or benefit of anyone else.

As the Preacher looked at the man's life, he saw that it was vanity from beginning to end. There seemed to be no end to the man's work. Day after day after day he kept working away, from dawn until dark. How long was his workweek? Sixty hours? Seventy hours? Yet the miser was never satisfied; he always wanted more. Derek Kidner calls him "the compulsive money-maker."[8] But for what purpose? No matter what he gained, the man had no one with whom to share it. He was working too hard to make any friends or to start a family.

Apparently the man did not even take the time to stop and ask himself what he was doing with his life. Or if he did ask the question, he could not answer it. Here he was, making costly sacrifices to advance his career and build up his bank account, yet never even considering whether it was all worth it. The Preacher could see that it *wasn't* worth it; the man's sacrifices were worthless. His possessions could never satisfy his soul, and without anyone to share it with, his life would end in unhappiness.

What the Preacher saw is a warning for all of us against isolation, self-ishness, greed, and a sinful addiction to work. Yet most Americans continue to believe that we can make it on our own—rugged individualism, we call it. Consider the words of Carolyn Burnham, in the film *American Beauty*, who tries to teach her daughter Jane how to cope with the disappointments of life: "You're old enough now to learn the most important lesson in life. You cannot count on anyone except yourself. . . . It's sad but true, and the sooner you learn it the better."[9]

Living and working for ourselves is one of the fastest ways to turn the American dream into a nightmare. Ecclesiastes has taught us that work can be a pleasure, but not if we pursue it for our own selfish purposes. To find pleasure in our work, we need to ask ourselves the question in verse 8 and come up with the right answer: "For whom am I toiling?" Not for myself, the Christian says, but for the glory of God and the good of other people, including the people I love in the family of God.

Otherwise we will end up like the businessman whom Ellen Goodman described in a provocative column for the *Minneapolis Tribune*. Goodman told the tragic story of a man who worked as hard as the man in Ecclesiastes 4. When he died at the age of fifty-one, his obituary said the cause of death was coronary thrombosis, but most people knew better. At the office six days a week, often until 8 or 9 at night, his friends and family said that he had simply worked himself to death. Yet on the day of his funeral, when the company was already making inquiries about his replacement, the president looked around the office for candidates and said, "Well, who's been working the hardest?" But the killer line was delivered by the dead man's wife. When a friend said, "I know how much you will miss him," she said, "Oh, I already have."[10]

There is a better way to live and work, and the Bible tells us how when it says, "Two are better than one" (Ecclesiastes 4:9). According to this simple comparison, it is better to share our life and work than to try to make it on our own. The Preacher is not simply talking about marriage here, although of course every God-centered marriage is living proof of this principle. But the Preacher is talking about all of our other relationships too. We were never designed to go it alone, but always to live in community with other people. The "buddy system" is not just for school field trips and swimming in the ocean; it is God's plan for our life and service to him. It has been this way since the beginning, when God created Adam and said, "It is not good that the man should be alone" (Genesis 2:18). Togetherness is better than loneliness. Connection is better than competition.

The Preacher gives us a number of reasons why partnership is better than personal isolation. Two are better than one because they are more productive in their work—"they have a good reward for their toil" (Ecclesiastes 4:9). The man in verse 8 had no one for whom or with whom to work. But when two people work together well, they accomplish more than twice as much as either one could accomplish alone. I have seen this again and again in the church as other pastors or elders have challenged my ideas and improved my ideas for ministry. I have seen it in writing and publishing, especially in working on books with my father. I have seen it in the kitchen, where Lisa and I do the dishes together. Whether we are in the church, in the workplace, or at home, our work is more rewarding when we share it with someone else.

Two are also better than one because they can help one another in times of trouble. "If they fall," the Preacher says, "one will lift up his fellow. But woe to him who is alone when he falls and has not another to lift him up!" (Ecclesiastes 4:10). This warning is reminiscent of the famous television commercial in which an old woman has an accident at home and says, "I've fallen and I can't get up!" Sometimes this happens in life, not only literally but also metaphorically. We get knocked down by life's trials and troubles. Sometimes somebody pushes us, and sometimes we just trip over our own two feet, but either way we end up on the ground. We try something and end up failing. Relationships get broken. Financial difficulties make us feel desperate. Against our own better judgment we fall into grievous sin.

If we were all alone, we might go down and stay down. But we are not alone. A brother or sister in Christ is there to lift us up with words of encouragement, to remind us of the love and mercy of God, and to help us rise again.

Then two are better than one because they can keep each other warm. "Again," the Preacher says, "if two lie together, they keep warm, but how can one keep warm alone?" (Ecclesiastes 4:11). At first we may think that he is talking about the marriage bed, but the implications of what he says are much wider. What the Preacher has in mind is someone traveling through the wilderness. The desert gets cold at night, and if a pilgrim is walking alone, he will freeze, maybe even to death. But not if he has a companion! Two of them can sleep back to back and stay warm all night. And sometimes, of course, the traveling companion is also a lover, who gives the most warmth of all:

> The snow is snowing, the wind is blowing
> But I can weather the storm!
> What do I care how much it may storm?
> I've got my love to keep me warm.[11]

This is not just good travel advice but wisdom for the soul. There is spiritual warmth in going through life with other believers. It is easy to grow cold in the Christian life, to become numb to the work of God, and eventually to freeze almost to spiritual death. But when we are growing cold, the heat of another Christian can warm us up. The prayer of an elder or deacon, the verse that a friend shares from Scripture, an exhortation to turn our hearts back to God—these are some of the sparks that God uses to keep the fire burning.

Cold is not the only danger that travelers face along the open road. This was especially true in the days of King Solomon, when there was always the danger of getting attacked by robbers. This is yet another reason why two are better than one: they can protect one another. For although "a man might prevail against one who is alone, two will withstand him" (Ecclesiastes 4:12).

There is safety in numbers. Two people are more than twice as hard to defeat as one. Therefore, sometimes all it takes to protect us is one person who "has our back," a comrade at arms. A simple illustration comes from the 2005 film *Batman Begins*. Police Commissioner Gordon wonders how he can ever bring a dangerous criminal to justice. The Commissioner is just one man, after all. How can he stand against all the forces of darkness in the city? But then Batman comes forward and says, "Now we are two!"

Even if we do not travel the open road or live in Gotham City, we still face spiritual danger every day. The world is full of temptation—the desire of the eyes, the lust of the flesh, and the pride of life (1 John 2:16). Satan is always prowling around like a lion to devour us (1 Peter 5:8). When it comes to facing these spiritual dangers, two are better than one. If we live close with other believers, there is always someone to stand with us in the fight and to cover us with the protection of prayer.

The Best Friend of All

Two really are better than one—better for work and for warmth, better in times of woe and of warfare. But for us to have this advantage we need to live in close fellowship with the people of God. Who are your partners in ministry? Are you in relationships that are strong enough to help you grow in Christ? If you are married, are you spending time with your spouse in prayer? If you live with other Christians, are you speaking to one another about spiritual things? Do you belong to a small-group Bible study? Is anyone holding you accountable in your most vulnerable areas of temptation? Does anyone in the world know you well enough to guard your back through prayer?

The children of God were never designed to live alone, but always with the help and support of their brothers and sisters in Christ. Every ministry of the church—from working in the nursery to planting a new church—depends on working partnerships. Sooner or later we all need someone to reheat us with the gospel, or pick us back up when we have fallen, or help us fight a spiritual danger. Do not wait until you get into trouble to start looking for a friend; by then it might be too late! Rather than assuming that you can manage your ministry or your sanctification on your own, open your arms to spiritual partnership. As you have the opportunity, be the friend that someone else needs.

And remember, too, that when it comes to spiritual friendship, the best partner of all is Jesus Christ, the "friend of . . . sinners" (Matthew 11:19; Luke 7:34). One of the climactic moments in this passage in Ecclesiastes is when the Preacher does gospel arithmetic to turn two into three. His argument all along has been that two are better than one. But at the end of verse 12 he turns a dynamic duo into a powerful trinity, saying that "a threefold cord is not quickly broken."

By adding a third strand to this cord, the Preacher is making the simple point that for everything from work to warfare, three people are even better than two. This is the law of larger numbers. If the Preacher were talking only about marriage, then a third strand would be an intruder (unless perhaps he was referring to the blessing of children). But apart from marriage, in most of the dangerous and difficult situations that we face in life, three people are stronger than two.

This is especially true if the third person is God himself. I am not saying that Qoheleth had God in mind here, necessarily, or that this is one of the many places where the Old Testament gives us an explicit prophecy about Jesus Christ. But I am saying that of all the friendships that give us strength for life, Jesus is the best friend of all.

Jesus said that we are not simply his servants but truly his friends. We find the greatest reward when we work in partnership with him, relying on his grace to help us with every difficult task and asking for his blessing to take what we do, in all its weakness, and use it for his glory. When our hearts are cold, Jesus wraps us in the arms of his love to warm us up again. When we fall down, he picks us up, reminding us that our sins really are forgiven and that by the power of the Holy Spirit he can help us stand. When we are in desperate danger, fighting against the very powers of Hell, Jesus defends us and rescues us—not just by his death, but also by the power of his eternal life.

Jesus is the friend we need most of all. Have you become his friend by putting your trust in him? Two really are better than one when one of the two is the Best One of all.

11

In Spirit and in Truth

ECCLESIASTES 5:1–7

*Be not rash with your mouth, nor let your
heart be hasty to utter a word before God,
for God is in heaven and you are on earth.
Therefore let your words be few.*

5:2

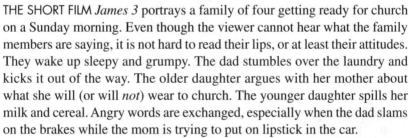

THE SHORT FILM *James 3* portrays a family of four getting ready for church on a Sunday morning. Even though the viewer cannot hear what the family members are saying, it is not hard to read their lips, or at least their attitudes. They wake up sleepy and grumpy. The dad stumbles over the laundry and kicks it out of the way. The older daughter argues with her mother about what she will (or will *not*) wear to church. The younger daughter spills her milk and cereal. Angry words are exchanged, especially when the dad slams on the brakes while the mom is trying to put on lipstick in the car.

As they get ready for church, no one in the family smiles or exchanges even one friendly word . . . until they walk into church and it is time to put on a happy face. The mom and the dad smile at the first people they meet. Joyfully they take their places in the sanctuary. When they stand to sing, their eyes are closed in reverent adoration. As the film ends, the sound begins, and we can hear what they are singing: "Praise God from whom all blessings flow."

Which is reality? Which is fantasy? And which is the real you? Is it the person who treats people badly at home or the person who acts nice to people in the house of God? When you go to worship, is it really worship, or are you just pretending?

Listen Up!

Ecclesiastes 5 opens with an exhortation to have truth and reverence in the worship of God. Qoheleth, the Preacher-King, began his book by talking about the meaninglessness of our existence. "Vanity of vanities," he said. "All is vanity." At first he just seemed to be complaining about all the problems in the world. But the longer he wrote, the more advice he had about the way we ought to live—wise and practical advice about everyday concerns like work, death, time, and possessions.

In chapter 5 he addresses us directly, telling us what to do. Now he really does sound like a preacher! This is the section of his message where he gives practical application to teach people the right way to live. The Preacher's admonitions and imperatives are as much for us as they were for people who lived in his day. According to Derek Kidner, they are for "the well-meaning person who likes a good sing and turns up cheerfully enough to church; but who listens with half an ear, and never quite gets round to what he has volunteered to do for God."[1]

In other words, the Preacher is speaking to just about everyone who ever goes to church. His words are not for people who never go to church at all. On the contrary, for all his frustration with life, he not only believed in God but was fully committed to worship. So his exhortations are for people who *do* go to church but sometimes find it hard to pay attention, whose thoughts wander when they pray, and who are full of good intentions about serving God but have trouble following through. They are for people who know they need to get involved in outreach but usually come up with some excuse for not joining a ministry right now. They have started a serious program for personal Bible study several dozen times but have never finished. They try to pay attention in church but usually spend half their time thinking about the upcoming week.

To people like that—to people like us—Ecclesiastes says, "Guard your steps when you go to the house of God. To draw near to listen is better than to offer the sacrifice of fools, for they do not know that they are doing evil" (Ecclesiastes 5:1; cf. 1 Samuel 15:22). This is Qoheleth's first exhortation, which pertains to the way we approach the worship of God. He is telling us to pay attention to God's Word.

The context is that of a worshiper walking into the house of God, the holy sanctuary. In the days of Solomon, "the house of God" would have been the temple in Jerusalem, but what he says applies to any sacred place that is set aside for the worship of God. As we go to worship, the Preacher is telling us to watch our step! There is a right way and a wrong way to enter the courts of thanksgiving and the gates of praise.

The right way to approach God in worship is to come with our ears wide-open. The Preacher assumes that when people go to the house of God, there will be something for them to hear. That "something" is the Word of the living God. The house of God is a place for the reading and the preaching of the Word of God. So the first questions we need to ask ourselves as we prepare for worship are: Am I ready to listen to the voice of God? Is my heart open to spiritual instruction? Are my ears attentive to the message I will hear from the Bible?

The worship of God at Philadelphia's Tenth Presbyterian Church begins even before the musical prelude with a verse or two from Scripture—something related to the main theme of the worship service to follow. Even before the formal call to worship, God speaks to us so that we can begin to hear our Savior's voice. If we are wise, we will listen, for the Scripture says, "faith comes from hearing, and hearing through the word of Christ" (Romans 10:17; cf. Acts 10:33).

The trouble, of course, is that it is hard for us to listen. So many other voices clamor for our attention. Even when we enter a quiet place for worship, the noise of the surrounding culture is still ringing in our ears. It is easy to let our thoughts wander, but hard for us to hear the voice of God. Like headless chickens, sometimes we go through the motions of worship without ever getting our minds engaged.

It is better to listen, the Preacher says, making another one of his wise comparisons. It is not just a little better for us to listen to the Word of God but totally better. The Preacher uses harsh language to condemn people who fail to pay attention. Instead of offering God a sacrifice of praise, they offer him "the sacrifice of fools." If they hear God's message at all, they do not receive it by faith, and therefore they are not saved (see Hebrews 4:2). Whatever sacrifices they offer are insincere. Such hypocrisy is not just foolish, it is also evil. Remember, the Preacher is talking about people in the church. Yet they have so little understanding of who God is or what it means to worship him "in spirit and truth" (John 4:24) that they do not even realize that what they are doing is wicked. The worship of the hypocrite is sin.

Understand that whenever we go to worship, we enter the presence of a holy God who has gathered his holy people to hear his Holy Word. If we take this for granted, not listening to what God says, then the Bible says that we are guilty of great evil, for we have despised the gospel of the cross and the empty tomb. This explains why some people have been struck dead on the doorstep of God's house—like Nadab and Abihu, who offered unholy fire (Leviticus 10:1ff.), or Ananias and Sapphira, who lied to God about how much they had put in the offering plate (Acts 5:1–11). Each of these dreadful acts of judgment took place at the beginning of a new era of worship (when tabernacle worship was inaugurated and in the days of the early church), showing for all time how zealous God is for proper worship.

When we consider the holiness of God and compare it with our own unholy worship, it is a wonder that any of us is still alive. Thank God for

Jesus! It is not only his sufferings that save us but also his obedience, including the perfect worship he offered to his Father. Jesus died for all our sins, including all the sins we have committed in the very act of worshiping God. But Jesus also did something more. According to Hebrews, he took the words of Psalm 22:22 and made them his own: "In the midst of the congregation I will sing your praise" (Hebrews 2:12). These words refer to the worship that Jesus offered at the temple and the synagogue. Envision the Son of God singing the psalms the Spirit inspired and using them to praise the Father. By faith in Christ, that perfect worship now belongs to us, as if we ourselves had offered it to God. This is part of what it means for us to know Christ: our imperfect worship is accepted by the Father because of the perfect worship offered by the Son.

When we know that even our worship is forgiven, then we can approach God with joyful confidence. Rather than saying, "If I worship the right way, then God will accept me," we say, "I am already accepted through the crucifixion and resurrection of Jesus Christ, and now it is my privilege to worship God the way he wants to be worshiped." We come to worship the way that the Solomon of Ecclesiastes tells us to come—paying attention to God, watching our step when we enter his sanctuary, and listening to the truth of his Word. We hear that word with the confidence of Solomon, who said, "Every word of God proves true" (Proverbs 30:5). We hear it with the expectancy of Mary, who sat at her Master's feet in Bethany, hanging on every word (Luke 10:38–39). We hear it with the faith of Peter, who said to Jesus, "You have the words of life" (John 6:68).

Watch What You Say!

The Preacher is concerned not only with how we listen, but also with how we speak. His first exhortation was to listen up. His second exhortation—which pertains primarily to prayer—is to watch what we say: "Be not rash with your mouth, nor let your heart be hasty to utter a word before God, for God is in heaven and you are on earth. Therefore let your words be few" (Ecclesiastes 5:2).

People do tend to be rash with their words. They tell lies, make rude comments, and lash out in anger. They utter murderous threats and use ugly racial slurs. They make promises they will never keep. They even swear against God. Every time a mouth is open, a heart is on display, and we are as likely to hear a word from Hell as a word from Heaven.

Of all our rash words, Qoheleth was most concerned about the ones we speak in the house of God. Verse 2 refers to a word spoken "before God." There is a sense in which every word we speak is spoken before God. If God is everywhere, then every word we utter goes from our mouth to God's ear. He is always listening, which ought to make us careful about what we say, wherever we are. But the phrase "before God" refers specifically to public worship, especially in this context, where the Preacher has been talking about guarding our steps on our way to the house of God. He wants us to be careful what we say in worship, when we pray and when we preach.

Do we really mean what we say when we stand and worship in the house of God? It is easy to read a psalm or sing a hymn or confess a creed without ever thinking about what it means. Sometimes even a prayer can be prayerless! Simply repeating pious words does not mean that our words come from a pious heart.

The God we worship—or pretend to worship—is the sovereign and mighty God who rules the entire universe. The Preacher reminds us of this in verse 2, when he says, "God is in heaven and you are on earth." This is one of the Bible's best verses for putting us back in our place. John Calvin said that knowing God and knowing ourselves is the sum of all wisdom.[2] Ecclesiastes 5:2 gives us that wisdom. God is in Heaven; he is the eternal Deity who made the entire universe. We are on earth; we are mortal beings, limited in time and space. There is a vast distance between the finite and the infinite. The distance between God in Heaven and us on earth is important to the theological geography of Ecclesiastes in providing the context for everything Qoheleth says about life "under the sun" and also in opening up the possibility of an above-the-sun perspective on life's vanity. More generally, the difference between God in Heaven and us on earth is fundamental to any proper view of the world—what theologians call the Creator/creature distinction.[3]

The Creator/creature distinction has practical implications for what we say when we worship. We need to know our place, remembering both who God is and who we are. Isaiah said in one of his famous prophecies, "My thoughts are not your thoughts, neither are your ways my ways, declares the LORD. For as the heavens are higher than the earth, so are my ways higher than your ways and my thoughts than your thoughts" (Isaiah 55:8–9). If this is true, then we should think before we speak. Gregory of Nyssa wrote, "Knowing how widely the divine nature differs from our own, let us quietly remain within our proper limits."[4]

Ecclesiastes helps us set those limits when it says, "Let your words be few," and then explains why: "For a dream comes with much business, and a fool's voice with many words" (Ecclesiastes 5:2–3). The Preacher's comparison is familiar to anyone who sleeps, and perchance also dreams. When we have been working hard to get caught up in our earthly business, we are likely to have many strange dreams at night. There is a natural connection. Similarly, there is a close connection between folly and verbosity. It is hard to be wise all the time, and the more talking we do, the greater the chance that we will say something foolish, especially when we worship. As a general rule, fools are loquacious (cf. Ecclesiastes 10:14). They rarely keep their thoughts to themselves but tend to do a lot of talking. Tremper Longman paraphrases verse 3 like this: "Work leads to many dreams; foolishness leads to many words."[5]

The Preacher tells us to be more circumspect. Instead of going on and on about things, we should be economical with our speech. The actual number of words that we use is not the issue, however. The real issue is whether the words that we do speak are sincere. According to Charles Bridges, "The fewness of the words is not the main concern; but whether they be the words of the heart."[6] We can apply this principle to all the words that we speak, asking questions like: Am I speaking from the heart? Do my words of encouragement reflect my real opinion, or am I only trying to flatter someone? When I use words to give someone the gospel, do I believe the good news that I am trying to share?

Sincerity is especially important when we worship. When we sing a hymn of praise, it should be with thoughts of God in our minds and love for God in our hearts. The Boardwalk Chapel in Wildwood, New Jersey has a sign to help its worship leaders remember this. The sign reads, "Sing it like you mean it," but the word "like" is crossed out and replaced with the word "because": "Sing it *because* you mean it." Our prayers should be just as sincere. Jesus taught us not to keep babbling on and on like pagans but simply to go to our Father with our requests (see Matthew 6:7ff.).

Jesus is our perfect example for all of this. The Bible says, "if anyone does not stumble in what he says, he is a perfect man" (James 3:2). Jesus Christ is that perfect man. Every word he ever spoke is true. Jesus never made a rash comment. Even when he was persecuted, he did not respond in unrighteous anger. To the end of his life, when he was dying on the cross, every word that Jesus ever spoke was carefully chosen.

Jesus has grace to help us speak words that are pleasing to God. The Savior of perfect speech can touch our lips with his grace. By the power of the Holy Spirit, he will teach us how to use the words we speak for the glory of God.

Words, Words, Words!

A good summary of everything we have been saying so far comes from the Apostle James, who said, "let every person be quick to hear, slow to speak" (James 1:19). But the Preacher also had a third exhortation, and it too was on a subject near and dear to James's heart. James talked about not just hearing the Word but also doing it (see James 1:22). Qoheleth said it like this: "When you vow a vow to God, do not delay paying it, for he has no pleasure in fools. Pay what you vow. It is better that you should not vow than that you should vow and not pay" (Ecclesiastes 5:4–5; cf. Deuteronomy 23:21–23).

After telling us to listen up and to watch what we say, the Preacher now tells us what to do. He says, "*Do* what you say." Or to be more precise, he says, "Pay what you vow." Here Ecclesiastes is talking about one very specific kind of speech—the promises that we make before God.

In Biblical times people often made vows to God, usually in the context of public worship (see Leviticus 22:18–20). We find this language in some of the psalms, like Psalm 50:14 ("Offer to God a sacrifice of thanksgiving, and perform your vows to the Most High") or Psalm 65:1 ("Praise is due to you, O God, in Zion, and to you shall vows be performed"). We also see examples in stories from the Old Testament, such as the story of Hannah, who vowed to dedicate her firstborn son to the ministry of a priest (1 Samuel 1:11), or Jephthah, who rashly made a vow that cost him his daughter (Judges 11:29–40).

Here in Ecclesiastes we are not talking about a sinful vow but about a holy promise to offer God a gift or sacrifice, like the vow Asaph described in Psalm 76:11: "Make your vows to the LORD your God and perform them; let all around him bring gifts to him who is to be feared." The point the Preacher makes is very simple: if we make a vow, we need to be sure that we do what we say and pay God what we owe.

It is much easier to make a promise than to keep it. People do this with God all the time, especially when they are bargaining with him in prayer. They say things like, "God, if only you will forgive me just this once, I swear I will never commit that sin again," or "I promise that as soon as I get more money, I will start giving 10 percent back to you." If you have ever offered a prayer like that—as many people have—then you also know how easy it is to forget what you promised! Before we know it, we are committing that same old sin again or being just as selfish with our money as ever, in which case it would be better if we had never made God a promise at all.

Jesus told a parable about someone like that—a son who said he would do what his father said and go out to work in the fields, but never went (Matthew 21:28–31). The Preacher who wrote Ecclesiastes would have called the boy a fool because he never did what he said. It is not just our words that we owe to God but also our works. If we tell him we will do something—if we make a commitment to ministry, for example, or if we pledge to give our money for kingdom work—then we need to do what we promised and pay what we owe. In fact, Ecclesiastes says that we need to do it without delay. Following through promptly on our commitments is an important part of practical godliness.

Another way to say this is, don't play games with God! If you promise him something, be a man or a woman of your word. In some cases this means that it would be better for us not to promise God anything at all. But the Bible assumes that there are times when it is appropriate for us to take spiritual vows, like the vows of covenant matrimony, for example, or the promises people make when they become members of a church. When we are considering a vow, here is some good advice for us to follow, from the worthy old preacher Charles Bridges:

> A solemn engagement advisedly made with God is a transaction needing much prayer and consideration. It should rest on the clear warrant of God's word. It should concern a matter really important, suitable, and attainable. It should be so limited, as to open a way for disentanglement under unforeseen contingencies, or altered circumstances.[7]

These are wise principles to follow, because if we make a vow that we fail to keep, we are guilty of sin and may fall under the judgment of God. Ecclesiastes issues a strong warning: "Let not your mouth lead you into sin, and do not say before the messenger that it was a mistake. Why should God be angry at your voice and destroy the work of your hands?" (5:6). There are many ways that our mouths can lead us into sin (just read James 3!). But presumably what the Preacher has in mind here is the great sin of failing to keep the promises that we make to God.

People usually try to make excuses for their sin, and the Preacher talks about that here. "The messenger" he mentions might be an angel, but more probably it refers to someone from the temple who came around to collect the offerings and sacrifices that people had vowed to pay. Some scholars believe that "during Qohelet's time there were people whose duty it was to check up on those who had not fulfilled their public vows."[8] Today we would probably call them "the tithe police," but in those days spiritual leaders held people accountable for their stewardship. The trouble was that some people tried to get out of their commitments by coming up with all kinds of lame excuses. ("Vow? What vow? There must be some kind of mistake!")

When we fail to do what we say—especially what we promise to God— the Bible says that we are guilty of sin, that God will be angry with us, and that he will destroy what we have done. This is why people sometimes say that "the road to Hell is paved with good intentions." However good our intentions may be, they will not get us to Heaven. In fact, they may only add to our condemnation. If we keep promising God that we will do this, that, and the other thing, but never do it, then we are more guilty than ever.

Once again we can only cast ourselves on the mercy of God, pray that he will forgive us for everything we have failed to do, and ask him to accept us through Jesus Christ. Jesus is the only one who ever kept all his promises to God, including his own vow to offer a holy sacrifice—the sacrifice of his body for our sins. By the mercy of Jesus, we are forgiven for all our failures. And now, by the grace of Jesus, we have help in keeping our commitments to God. When we pray for the grace to follow through, we are praying to a Savior who knows what it means to keep a commitment, who did everything he promised to the very death.

From Vanity to Reverence

The Preacher closes this passage by describing the heart attitude that we ought to bring to everything we say and do in worship: "For when dreams increase and words grow many, there is vanity; but God is the one you must fear" (Ecclesiastes 5:7).

If "the fear of the LORD is the beginning of knowledge" (as Solomon once said; Proverbs 1:7), then this is one of the wisest verses in Ecclesiastes. It brings together the two grand themes of this great book. Ecclesiastes began with the vanity of vanities—the futility of life in a fallen world. Here we see such vanity in the idle daydreams and foolish words of a churchgoer who only pretends to worship, without ever really offering his mind and his heart to God.

We also see the Preacher's answer to life's vanity. At the end of Ecclesiastes, when he finally reaches the conclusion of his spiritual quest, he will say that the goal of life is the fear of God (Ecclesiastes 12:13). The book thus moves from vanity to reverence. That transition is introduced here, where Qoheleth is preaching to us about worship. God is the one whom we must revere.

Charles Bridges defined the fear of God as "the grand fundamental of godliness."[9] To fear God is to recognize his might and majesty. It is to acknowledge that he is in Heaven and we are on earth, that he is God and we are not. It is to say, "Who among the heavenly beings is like the LORD, a God greatly to be feared in the council of the holy ones, and awesome above all who are around him?" (Psalm 89:6–7).

When we fear God in this way, we will come to worship with expectancy and awe. We will be ready to listen to what he says (he is God, after all). We will be careful what we say, limiting our speech to words that are pleasing to him. We will give God what he deserves, including whatever time or talent or treasure we have promised to give.

Ecclesiastes 5 was written to help us take God more seriously when we worship. T. M. Moore has written a loose poetic paraphrase of these verses that can help us remember its spiritual lessons.

> How brazen and dishonest people are
> with their religion. They will go as far
> with it as suits their needs; so they attend
> the services and sing the hymns, and when
> they have to, give a little money to
> the Lord. But do they live as one should do
> who's made a vow to God? Don't kid yourself.
> Among their friends their faith is on the shelf. . . .
>   Remember, God knows everything.
> He knows our hearts when we before him bring

our worship, and you can't fool him. So take
a good look at yourself before you make
your next appearance before the Lord. And go
to listen, not to speak, for he will know
just what you need. Why, any fool can spout
a lovely prayer or sing a hymn about
his faith. His words are mindless, like a dream,
although to people looking on they seem
impressive. Not to God. . . .
    For words are cheap,
just like the dreams you have while you're asleep.
God wants your heart, my son, not just a show.
Get right with him before you to him go.[10]

The way to get right with God before we go to worship is very simple.
The right way to worship is to be honest with him about our hypocrisy and
all our other sins and then ask him to forgive us, for Jesus' sake.

12

Satisfaction
Sold Separately

ECCLESIASTES 5:8–20

*He who loves money will not be satisfied
with money, nor he who loves wealth
with his income; this also is vanity.*

5:10

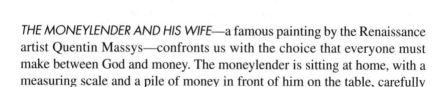

THE MONEYLENDER AND HIS WIFE—a famous painting by the Renaissance artist Quentin Massys—confronts us with the choice that everyone must make between God and money. The moneylender is sitting at home, with a measuring scale and a pile of money in front of him on the table, carefully assessing the value of a single coin.

Yet our eye is also drawn to the woman sitting next to him, the money-lender's wife. She is leafing through a Bible or a book of spiritual exercises, which presumably was bought by her wealthy husband. She is having her devotions, except she is distracted by all the money being counted. As she turns the page, her gaze is captivated by the coin in her husband's hand.

Massys painted this image to make a serious point. His adopted city of Antwerp had become a world center for business and trade. But Massys saw how easily money can pull our souls away from the worship of God.

All of us feel this tension. We know that God demands our highest allegiance. We believe that nothing is more precious than the message of his gospel—the forgiveness of our sins and the free gift of eternal life through faith in Jesus Christ. Yet we are easily distracted. Sometimes we would rather thumb through a mail-order catalog than listen to what God has said in his Word.

The Vanity of Injustice

The Solomon of Ecclesiastes wants to help us win this spiritual struggle by showing us the vanity of money. He starts by talking about the injustice that people suffer from the sinful structures of society. In a moment he will make this personal, but he starts by talking about the system: "If you see in a province the oppression of the poor and the violation of justice and righteousness, do not be amazed at the matter, for the high official is watched by a higher, and there are yet higher ones over them" (Ecclesiastes 5:8).

The Preacher sees something that we all see—oppression and injustice at every level of society. We see it in communism, where the state seizes control of the means of production. But we also see it in capitalism whenever profit is pursued without regard for the well-being of other persons. Somehow poor people always seem to get the worst end of the bargain. Ecclesiastes tells us not to be surprised by the vanity of all this injustice. This is not to excuse unrighteousness; it is simply being realistic about life in a fallen world.

What is hard to understand is exactly why Qoheleth thinks we should not be surprised by all this injustice. He refers to an official hierarchy, in which one person oversees another. But it is not entirely clear why this causes injustice. Maybe the issue here is government bureaucracy—what Tremper Longman calls the "red tape" interpretation.[1] Somehow a multilevel bureaucracy always seems to open more doors to injustice. In the words of one scholar, this verse is about "the frustrations of oppressive bureaucracy with its endless delays and excuses, while the poor cannot afford to wait, and justice is lost between the tiers of the hierarchy."[2]

Or perhaps the point is that each level of government takes something from the level below. We should not be surprised when people in authority abuse their power. Eventually injustice reaches all the way down to the poor, who would probably oppress someone if they could, but they can't because they are at the bottom. On this interpretation, the problem is not bureaucracy but tyranny.

The right way to interpret the verse partly depends on the meaning of the word for "watched" (*shomer*). Occasionally this word has a negative connotation. So it might refer to the way that different branches of government tend to be suspicious of one another. To "watch" in this sense is to keep people under surveillance, looking for a way to take advantage of them. But "watch" can also be taken more positively, in which case it would imply that people in government are watching out for one another, protecting each other. This kind of cronyism creates a political machine that leaves poor and ordinary people on the outside looking in.

It is hard to be certain exactly which kind of injustice Ecclesiastes has in mind, but even the uncertainty helps prove the Preacher's point. There are so many kinds of injustice in society that we should never be surprised by sin. Unless there is "some Solomon to exhort and console him," said Martin Luther, "government crushes the man, extinguishes him, and utterly destroys him."[3]

Verse 9 seems to offer at least a partial solution to this perennial problem. The Preacher says, "But this is gain for a land in every way: a king committed to cultivated fields" (Ecclesiastes 5:9). This is another hard verse to translate. The way the English Standard Version has it, the best defense against government corruption is a godly king. Society needs a ruler with wisdom like Solomon, someone who values economic freedom, who encourages his people to prosper by cultivating their own fields. Many scholars read this verse more negatively, however, and translate as follows: "The profit of the land is taken by all; even the king benefits from the field."[4] On this reading, the king is not part of the solution but another part of the problem. Certainly this is the way most rulers operated in the ancient world, and ever since: they claimed the profits of the land for themselves.

Our experience with injustice in this fallen world leads us to expect corruption at every level of government, right up to the very top. Although some leaders are motivated by a pure desire to serve society, many others are like the notorious Philadelphia politician who used public funds to sustain his own lavish lifestyle and then boasted to his friends about spending "Other People's Money."

The best governments assume from the outset that people are sinners and that therefore they need checks and balances to restrain unrighteousness. But even the best governments are far from perfect. As long as we live on this earth, we will see people buying their way to power, using public position for personal gain, and manipulating the system for their own advantage.

Rather than looking for the government to solve our problems, we need to acknowledge that even the best rulers fall well short of perfection. Therefore, we live in the hope of a better administration—one that we may not find in Ecclesiastes but do find in the gospel:

> For to us a child is born,
> to us a son is given;
> and the government shall be upon his shoulder,
> and his name shall be called
> Wonderful Counselor, Mighty God,
> Everlasting Father, Prince of Peace.
> Of the increase of his government and of peace
> there will be no end,
> on the throne of David and over his kingdom,
> to establish it and to uphold it

with justice and with righteousness
    from this time forth and forevermore.
The zeal of the LORD of hosts will do this. (Isaiah 9:6–7)

The Vanity of Prosperity

To this point the Preacher has been talking about wealth and poverty on the national scale, but beginning in verse 10 he brings things down to the personal level. Public officials are not the only people who want to get more money; this is a temptation for all of us. So the Preacher warns us about the vanity of prosperity: "He who loves money will not be satisfied with money, nor he who loves wealth with his income; this also is vanity" (Ecclesiastes 5:10).

Here we have a well-known truth, stated as a proverb, to which the Preacher adds his typical editorial comment about vanity. No matter how much money they have, people who live for money are never satisfied. They always want more. John D. Rockefeller was one of the richest men in the world, but when someone asked him how much money was enough, he famously said, "Just a little bit more."

The contemporary author Jessie O'Neill has diagnosed this spiritual problem. She calls it "affluenza," which is "an unhealthy relationship with money" or the pursuit of wealth.[5] Most Americans have at least a mild case of this deadly disease. Even if we are thankful for what we have, we often think about the things that we do not have and how to get them. This explains the sudden pang of discontent we feel when we realize that we cannot afford something we want to buy or the guilt we feel because we bought it anyway, and now we are in debt as a result.

The appetite for what money can buy is never satisfied. The only way to curb it is to be content with what God provides. Charles Bridges said that when our desires are running ahead of our needs, it is better for us "to sit down content where we are, than where we hope to be in the delusion of our insatiable desire."[6] Rather than always craving more, we are invited to be happy with less because we are satisfied with God.

This is a lifelong struggle. The fact that we have resisted the temptation of money before does not make us immune to it from now on. One day we may say, "I don't care too much for money." But soon we are singing a different tune, like the Beatles did: "Money don't get everything, it's true / What it don't get, I can't use. / Now give me money (that's what I want)."[7]

Ecclesiastes warns our divided hearts that living for the things that only money can buy is vanity. To help us avoid coming down with a bad case of "affluenza," the book gives us a long list of reasons why.

The first problem with money is that *other people will try to take it from us.* "When goods increase," the Preacher says, "they increase who eat them, and what advantage has their owner but to see them with his eyes?" (Ecclesiastes 5:11). The phrase "they increase who eat them" refers in some way to people who consume our wealth. It might be the oppressive government described in verses 8– 9, which takes away our money through higher taxes. It might be our children or other dependents—the hungry mouths around our table. Or it might be the people who come begging for us to give them something—the spongers, the freeloaders, and the hangers-on. But no matter who they are, the more we have, the more other people try to get it.

No one knew this better than King Solomon. He was the richest man in the world, but given the many thousands of people whom he had to feed (see 1 Kings 4:22–28), he almost needed to be! Here he warns us that the more we have, the more people will want it. If they succeed in getting it, we will never be able to enjoy it ourselves. We may see it, but it will be gone before we ever get the chance to use it. This is vanity.

A second problem with having more money is that *it will keep us up at night.* The Preacher-King makes this point by drawing a contrast: "Sweet is the sleep of a laborer, whether he eats little or much, but the full stomach of the rich will not let him sleep" (Ecclesiastes 5:12).

As a general rule, people who work hard all day, especially if they work with their hands, are ready for a good night's sleep. Whether they have had a decent supper or else are so poor that they go to bed hungry, they will be tired enough to go right to sleep. The idle rich do not enjoy this luxury but are up all night. This is not because they are worrying about all their possessions, like the rich fool in the parable that Jesus told (Luke 12:13–21), but because a gluttonous diet of fatty foods gives them a tummy-ache. Their insomnia is caused by indigestion.

Having a lot of money can be very unhealthy—not just spiritually but also physically. People who work hard should count their blessings, even if they cannot always count on getting a fat paycheck. Refreshing sleep is the blessing of manual labor. But the lifestyle of the rich and lazy tends not to be very restful. Derek Kidner points out one of the ways that we see this in the West, where almost everyone is wealthy. Kidner looks at all our "modern exercise-machines and health clubs" and says it is "one of our human absurdities to pour out money and effort just to undo the damage of money and ease."[8] One is reminded of Oliver Goldsmith's warning: "Ill fares the land, to hast'ning ills a prey, / Where wealth accumulates, and men decay."[9]

Temporary Prosperity

Thus far Qoheleth has been talking about the vanity of having a lot of money. In verses 13–14 he talks about the vanity of losing it: "There is a grievous evil that I have seen under the sun: riches were kept by their owner to his hurt, and those riches were lost in a bad venture. And he is the father of a son, but he has nothing in his hand."

This is a third reason why living for money is meaningless: *it may be here today, but it will be gone tomorrow.* The Preacher calls this "a grievous evil," which literally means that it makes him sick even to think about it. To explain why, he gives us a case study, the point of which, said Martin Luther, is to show that "God permits the very riches in which people trust to bring about the ruin of those who own them."[10]

The story Qoheleth tells concerns a wealthy man who tried to hoard his wealth, yet lost it all in some risky investment. Today people lose their money in places like the stock market. In those days their ships foundered at sea or their camel trains were attacked in the wilderness. But whatever the reason, this man took a gamble and ended up destitute as a result.

Even worse, the man was a father, and now he had nothing to leave his son. The story thus assumes what the Bible teaches in other places: parents should leave a legacy for their children (e.g., Proverbs 13:22). In financial planning for the future, we should think not only of ourselves, but also about what we can give to our families, including our spiritual family in the church. Fathers and mothers have a duty to save and sacrifice for their sons and daughters. Yet this does not mean that getting and keeping more money should be our primary focus. Just the opposite: the whole point of this story is that counting on money is vanity and striving after the wind.

Then the Preacher-King gives us a fourth reason to resist the fevers of "affluenza." The reason this time is that *we can't take it with us.* Here is how the story of the man who lost his money continues: "As he came from his mother's womb he shall go again, naked as he came, and shall take nothing for his toil that he may carry away in his hand. This also is a grievous evil: just as he came, so shall he go, and what gain is there to him who toils for the wind?" (Ecclesiastes 5:15–16).

The language of these verses is familiar to anyone who knows the story of Job. When that poor man lost everything that he had, he said, "Naked I came from my mother's womb, and naked shall I return. The LORD gave, and the LORD has taken away; blessed be the name of the LORD" (Job 1:21). The Apostle Paul took the same truth and applied it to all of us: "We brought nothing into the world, and we cannot take anything out of the world" (1 Timothy 6:7).

One day all our labors will be lost. This is the tragic reality that every one of us must face—the reality of our mortality. At the end of one of his most profitable years on the European Tour, someone asked the English golfer Simon Dyson if there was anything that he was afraid of. "Death," Dyson replied. "I'm in a position now where I can pretty much do as I want. . . . Dying wouldn't be good right now."[11]

Whether or not we make as much money as a professional golfer, like it or not, the day will come when we have to leave it all behind. So what gain is there in living for money? Some people wait until their deathbed to think about that—if then!—but if we are wise like the Solomon of Ecclesiastes, we will think about it now. Martin Luther said, "As I shall forsake my riches when I die, so I forsake them while I am living."[12]

One way to forsake our wealth is simply to look around at what we have and say to ourselves, "Now here is something that God has given me to enjoy for the time being, or maybe to give away for the work of his kingdom, but I need to remember that I will never be able to take it with me when I die." This is a good thing for girls to say about their dolls and for boys to say about their video games. It is a good thing for teenagers to say about their clothes and their music. It is a good thing for men and women to say about their homes and automobiles, if they have them. We are headed for eternity! Therefore, we should travel light.

Everything that Solomon says about money is beautifully paraphrased by Randy Alcorn in his book *The Treasure Principle*, under the heading "Chasing the Wind." Alcorn quotes each of Solomon's insights in Ecclesiastes 5:10–15, and then adds his own paraphrase:

- "Whoever loves money never has money enough" (v. 10). *The more you have, the more you want.*
- "Whoever loves wealth is never satisfied with his income" (v. 10). *The more you have, the less you're satisfied.*
- "As goods increase, so do those who consume them" (v. 11). *The more you have, the more people (including the government) will come after it.*
- "And what benefit are they to the owner except to feast his eyes on them?" (v. 11). *The more you have, the more you realize it does you no good.*
- "The sleep of a laborer is sweet, whether he eats little or much, but the abundance of a rich man permits him no sleep" (v. 12). *The more you have, the more you have to worry about.*
- "I have seen a grievous evil under the sun: wealth hoarded to the harm of its owner" (v. 13). *The more you have, the more you can hurt yourself by holding on to it.*
- "Or wealth lost through some misfortune" (v. 14). *The more you have, the more you have to lose.*
- "Naked a man comes from his mother's womb, and as he comes, so he departs. He takes nothing from his labor that he can carry in his hand" (v. 15). *The more you have, the more you'll leave behind.*[13]

Solomon summarizes the many reasons not to live for money in verse 17: "Moreover, all his days he eats in darkness in much vexation and sickness and anger." This verse gives us a pathetic picture of where greed will lead. "If anything is worse than the addiction money brings," writes Derek Kidner, "it is the emptiness it leaves."[14] The miser will end up alone in his misery. Because he lives in spiritual darkness, his soul will be vexed with many anxieties. The ungodly pursuit of wealth will take its physical toll, leaving him in poor health. He will also be very angry—a bitter old man—for who has ever heard of a happy miser? People who live for money try to hold on to as much of it as they can, but when they have to let it go—as everyone does eventually—it makes them angry with everyone and everything.

This gives us a helpful question to ask about our own anger, some of which may well be caused by excessive love for the things of this world. When we get angry, what is the reason? When husbands and wives have arguments about how much to spend, for example, and what to spend it on, are they disagreeing about the principles of Biblical stewardship, or are they really just fighting for what they want to have? The unsatisfied desire for worldly possessions is one powerful producer of anger.

The Power to Enjoy

When we hear the story of the angry old man in Ecclesiastes 5, we cannot help but think that there must be a better way to live, and there is. The Bible tells us not to put our "hope in wealth, which is so uncertain," but to put our "hope in God, who richly provides us with everything for our enjoyment" (1 Timothy 6:17, NIV). Ecclesiastes says it like this:

> Behold, what I have seen to be good and fitting is to eat and drink and find enjoyment in all the toil with which one toils under the sun the few days of his life that God has given him, for this is his lot. Everyone also to whom God has given wealth and possessions and power to enjoy them, and to accept his lot and rejoice in his toil—this is the gift of God. (5:18–19)

Some scholars find these verses so completely contrary to what the Preacher has already said that they think he must be speaking sarcastically, or at least stoically. "In the light of the absence of a meaningful life," they tell us, "Qohelet advocates a life pursuing the small pleasures afforded by food, drink, and work."[15] The Preacher does not really believe that life is very enjoyable, but he is trying to help us enjoy it while we can. So he tells us to eat, drink, and be industrious, for tomorrow we die.

That is not all the Preacher says, however. He is giving us a balanced, God-centered view. Just as he has been honest about the vanity of our existence, so also he wants to tell the truth about finding joy in the everyday things of life, like working and feasting. He has talked about these blessings before, in the so-called "enjoyment passages" of Ecclesiastes (e.g., 2:24–26). He knows that joy is real because he has experienced it himself. He also knows that joy is "good and fitting"—something appropriate for the people of God. Yes, our time on earth is short, but whatever time we do have is a sacred gift. When the Preacher calls life "the gift of God," he is giving it the highest praise. This is not stoicism or sarcasm but godly gratitude.

The Preacher can say this because he believes in the God of joy. Earlier in this passage, when he was talking about the vanity of money, the Preacher hardly mentioned God at all. But in verses 18–20 he mentions him repeatedly. Whatever enjoyment he finds is God-centered. Without God, life is meaningless and miserable, especially if we are living for money. But when we know the God of joy, even money can be a blessing.

To understand this, we need to pay attention to the phrasing of verse 19. Earlier the Preacher listed some of the many reasons why accumulating money is vanity. Yet here he tells us explicitly that if we are wealthy, we should enjoy it. It almost sounds like a contradiction, but notice where the power of enjoyment comes from: it comes from God. Both having things and enjoying things are gifts from God.

This profound insight helps us have a balanced view of our earthly possessions. The world that God created is full of many rich gifts, but the power to enjoy them does not lie in the gifts themselves. This is why it is always useless to worship the gifts instead of the Giver. The ability to enjoy wealth or family or friendship or food or work or sex or any other good gift comes only from God. Satisfaction is sold separately. So the God-centered verses at the end of Ecclesiastes 5 call us back to a joy that we can only find in God. The person who finds the greatest enjoyment in life is the one who knows God and has a relationship with him through Jesus Christ.

The English poet George Herbert wrote about the power of enjoyment in his poem "The Pulley."[16] Herbert began by saying that when God first made man, he took his glass and poured out as much blessing as he could—riches, beauty, wisdom, honor, and pleasure. But when the glass was almost empty, he decided to stop pouring. "When almost all was out," Herbert wrote, "God made a stay, / Perceiving that alone of all his treasure / Rest in the bottom lay." In other words, the one gift that God decided not to grant was rest, or perhaps we could say, satisfaction: "For if I should (said he) / Bestow this jewel also on my creature, / He would adore my gifts instead of me." In wisdom and love, God thus decreed that we should be "rich and weary," so that our very weariness would turn our hearts back to him.

Have you turned away from the weariness of wealth to find your joy in God? This is part of the Preacher's answer to the problem of life's vanity. He is teaching us to depend on God for our enjoyment rather than depending on one of his many gifts. The person who learns this lesson well "will not much remember the days of his life because God keeps him occupied with joy in his heart" (Ecclesiastes 5:20). Although some scholars have misread this verse as a desperate attempt to forget the troubles of life, here the Preacher uses positive words to make a positive point about the joy that God alone can bring to the human heart. When we learn to enjoy God, we experience so much joy that life's short vanity is all but forgotten.[17]

Quentin Massys appears to have learned this spiritual lesson. We know this from a striking detail in *The Moneylender and His Wife*. Remember that in this masterpiece both husband and wife turn away from God to focus on their money. On the table between them, Massys cleverly painted a small round mirror, which reflects a little scene that is taking place just outside the frame of the painting. If we look at the image in the mirror closely, we see the dark lines of a window frame intersecting to make the form of a cross. We also see a small figure reaching out for the frame, as if to hold on to the cross. His face is familiar to art historians: it is Massys himself.

The artist—like the Preacher-King who wrote Ecclesiastes—is reminding us not to look for money to give us any satisfaction in life. Instead we are invited to reach out for the cross where Jesus gave his life for all our greedy sins, to hold on to Jesus and to find our full satisfaction in him.

13

Here Today,
Gone Tomorrow

ECCLESIASTES 6:1–12

*There is an evil that I have seen under the sun,
and it lies heavy on mankind: a man to whom God
gives wealth, possessions, and honor, so that he
lacks nothing of all that he desires, yet God does
not give him power to enjoy them, but a stranger
enjoys them. This is vanity; it is a grievous evil.*

6:1–2

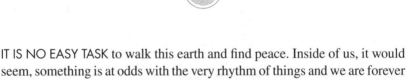

IT IS NO EASY TASK to walk this earth and find peace. Inside of us, it would seem, something is at odds with the very rhythm of things and we are forever restless, dissatisfied, frustrated, and aching. We are so overcharged with desire that it is hard to come to simple rest. Desire is always stronger than satisfaction."[1] Thus writes Ronald Rolheiser in his book *The Holy Longing: The Search for a Christian Spirituality*. As we walk this restless earth, full of desire, we are never fully satisfied.

Jonathan Clements reached a similar conclusion in the pages of the *Wall Street Journal*. "We may have life and liberty," he wrote. "But the pursuit of happiness isn't going so well. . . . We constantly hanker after fancier cars and fatter paychecks—and, initially, such things boost our happiness. But the glow of satisfaction quickly fades and soon we're yearning for something else."[2]

It happens every year after we open our Christmas presents. We get what we thought we wanted, and we enjoy it for a little while. But soon there is something else that we wish we had instead, or in addition. Our longings never go away for long; they always return.

Satisfaction *Not* Guaranteed

The disappointment of unsatisfied desire is as old as Ecclesiastes. Qoheleth said, "He who loves money will not be satisfied with money" (Ecclesiastes 5:10). After considering the vanity of prosperity, the Preacher-King concluded that the only way to find any true satisfaction in life is to trust in the God of joy (see Ecclesiastes 5:18–20). But he did not stay satisfied for long. Soon he was lamenting more of the many problems he saw with life under the sun.

Ecclesiastes 6 is one of the Bible's darkest chapters. As we hear what the Preacher has to say, we are reading what the Russian poet Alexander Pushkin called "reason's icy intimations, and records of a heart in pain."[3] The writer lists a series of disappointments that left him deeply dissatisfied, followed by several questions that are hard for anyone except God to answer. Many people think about life the same way: a long list of disappointments has left them with serious questions about God.

The Preacher's first disappointment related to people's possessions. Satisfaction, he saw, is not guaranteed: "There is an evil that I have seen under the sun, and it lies heavy on mankind: a man to whom God gives wealth, possessions, and honor, so that he lacks nothing of all that he desires, yet God does not give him power to enjoy them, but a stranger enjoys them. This is vanity; it is a grievous evil" (Ecclesiastes 6:1–2).

The man in these verses seemed to have it all. Not only was he worth a fortune, but he was also famous, which many people value even more highly than money. Yet for some unspecified reason he was unable to enjoy what he had. Martin Luther called these verses "a description of a rich man who lacks nothing for a good and happy life and yet does not have one."[4]

Unlike the man described at the end of Ecclesiastes 5, the man in chapter 6 had the acquisition without the satisfaction. In the end he lost everything, and thus he never had the chance to enjoy what he worked a lifetime to gain. Perhaps he lost his property in wartime or through theft or threw it away in some risky investment (see Ecclesiastes 5:13–14). Maybe he was too sick to make good use of his money or died before he reached retirement (see Ecclesiastes 2:18), as many people do. But for some providential reason, someone who seemed to have everything that he could want never had the chance to enjoy it. It was here today but gone tomorrow, and when it left, it went to someone else entirely—somebody the man didn't even know.

The Preacher called this "a grievous evil." He also described it as something that "lies heavy on mankind" (Ecclesiastes 6:1). While this expression may refer to the severity of the situation, more likely it refers to its frequency. It happens all the time: one person loses everything he has worked so hard to gain, and then someone else comes along to enjoy it. As David wrote in one of his psalms, "man heaps up wealth and does not know who will gather!" (Psalm 39:6).

If anything good can come from this unfortunate situation, it is the recognition that our possessions can never bring us lasting joy. The gifts that God gives us and the power to enjoy those gifts come separately. This is why having more money can never guarantee that we will find any enjoyment. Without God, we will still be discontent. It is only when we keep him at the center of our existence that we experience real joy in the gifts that God may give. The fear of the Lord is not just the beginning of knowledge; it is also the source of satisfaction.

Better Off Dead

If satisfaction is not guaranteed, then maybe we would be better off dead. This is the dark possibility that the Preacher considers next:

> If a man fathers a hundred children and lives many years, so that the days of his years are many, but his soul is not satisfied with life's good things, and he also has no burial, I say that a stillborn child is better off than he. For it comes in vanity and goes in darkness, and in darkness its name is covered. Moreover, it has not seen the sun or known anything, yet it finds rest rather than he. Even though he should live a thousand years twice over, yet enjoy no good—do not all go to the one place? (Ecclesiastes 6:3–6)

This is another one of the Preacher's "better than" statements, in which he compares one thing to another. In this case, he compares a man whose life is full of blessing to a child who never sees the light of day. Given the vanity of life in this fallen world, Qoheleth bitterly concludes that the stillborn child gets the better end of the bargain.

The man described in these verses had the best life that anyone in Old Testament times could imagine. Ecclesiastes does not tell us how wealthy he was, but in a culture that rightly considered children to be a blessing from the Lord, he had fathered a hundred sons and daughters. He also lived for many years—two thousand, to be exact, which made him more than twice as old as Methuselah (see Genesis 5:27). Yet the man still wasn't satisfied, presumably because he did not have God in his life. Notice that it was his soul, specifically, that was dissatisfied. Something was missing in his life spiritually. There was a hole in his heart.

Sadly, when the man died, he did not even receive the honor of a decent burial. The Bible does not tell us why his body was left unburied. Maybe he died in battle, or perhaps he was despised by his family. But whatever the reason, the fact that he went unburied would have led many people to conclude that he was under the curse of God. It all goes to show that a person can "have the things men dream of—which in Old Testament terms meant children by the score, and years of life by the thousand—and still depart unnoticed, unlamented and unfulfilled."[5]

As he thinks about this hypothetical situation, the Preacher entertains the thought of non-existence. A person can have everything that life has to offer and still be miserable. But if we are so unhappy with life, then maybe we would be better off never having lived at all.

So the Preacher considers the strange blessedness of a stillborn child. The child "comes in vanity" because its delivery is fruitless (Ecclesiastes 6:4). It "goes in darkness" because it dies before ever seeing the light of day (cf. Job 3:16). Even its name is covered in darkness—not because the child is never named by his or her parents, but because death shrouds his or her identity and personality. No one ever gets to know the child's character or abilities. Nor does the child ever get to know this world: "it has not seen the sun or known anything" (Ecclesiastes 6:5).

Maybe it is better that way. "Better to miscarry at birth," says one commentator, "than to miscarry throughout life."[6] The stillborn child never has to endure pain, or see suffering, or struggle with the guilt of conscious sin. Best of all, the child is the first to die and therefore the first to find its eternal rest.

This thought has given at least some consolation to many parents who have suffered the all but unbearably painful loss of an infant. As the Preacher considers that thought here, he is almost tempted to envy: "If this life is all, and offers to some people frustration rather than fulfillment, leaving them nothing to pass on to those who depend on them; if, further, all alike are waiting their turn to be deleted, then some indeed can envy the stillborn, whose turn comes first."[7]

Even someone who lived for two millennia would come to exactly the same end as a stillborn child. Death is the great leveler. No matter how long we live, we all die eventually. The famous neoorthodox theologian Karl Barth took that stark reality very personally. He said, "Some day a company of men will process out to a churchyard and lower a coffin and everyone will go home; but one will not come back, and that will be me."[8] But if in the end we all die anyway, then what is the advantage in going on living, especially when life does not happen to be especially enjoyable?

Remember that when the Preacher says all of this, he is leaving God out of it for the moment. He is thinking mainly in terms of life under the sun, but not in terms of life after death and all the promises God has made about the coming of his kingdom. This life is not all there is. Jesus proved that when he died and rose again, bringing the light of the resurrection out of the darkness of the grave. When believers are buried—and when they bury their little children—it is always in the sure and certain hope of the resurrection of the dead.

But the Preacher-King is not yet ready to give us that gospel. Instead he is writing to show us our need for God. He does this by telling us that no matter how long we live or how much money we have, it is all meaningless unless we can enjoy it, which we will never be able to do without the power of God.

Insatiable in Appetite

The Preacher's dissatisfaction returns again in the verses that follow. In verses 1–2 he talked about a man who had everything he wanted in life, except the chance to enjoy it. In verses 3–6 he used a comparison to argue that if we cannot enjoy life, we might be better off dead. Now he wonders if we will ever be satisfied: "All the toil of man is for his mouth, yet his appetite is not satisfied. For what advantage has the wise man over the fool? And what does the poor man have who knows how to conduct himself before the living? Better is the sight of the eyes than the wandering of the appetite: this also is vanity and a striving after wind" (Ecclesiastes 6:7–9).

If people have trouble enjoying life—if satisfaction is not guaranteed, no matter how long we live—then maybe we could avoid disappointment by wanting less out of life. The trouble is that we always have an appetite for more. In verse 7 the Preacher tells us what happens when we feed that appetite: we get hungry all over again; the same cravings return day after day. We eat food to give us strength to work to earn our daily bread, which we eat to give us strength to work again tomorrow, and so it goes, day after day.

Nor does it matter how wise we are or how much money we have—we all have unfulfilled longings. It is better to be wise than foolish, of course, but even wise people have desires that life does not fully satisfy. Nor can noble poverty deliver us from desire. The poor man described in verse 8 is wise enough to know the right way to live. So maybe he can avoid all of the disappointments that rich people have when they expect money to give them meaning and purpose in life. Yet when it comes to satisfying desire, the poor man will be as disappointed as anyone. Neither wisdom nor poverty proves to be an advantage.

Usually we think we can find satisfaction in everything that life has to offer—food and drink, music and beauty, family and friends. Yet desire is a tramp. Never content to stay at home, it always wants to go out wandering. This is the Preacher's vivid image in verse 9, where he talks about "the wandering of the appetite." Our desires are always traveling, but never arriving. This is the wanderlust of the human soul.

A striking example of perpetual dissatisfaction comes from the excavations at the city of Pompeii. When Vesuvius erupted and Pompeii was buried, many people perished, with their body shapes, postures, and in some instances their facial expressions preserved in volcanic ash. One woman's feet were pointed in the direction of the city gate, headed for safety. Yet her face was turned back to look at something just beyond the reach of her outstretched hands. She was grasping for a prize—a bag of beautiful pearls. Whether suddenly she remembered that she had left the pearls behind or else saw that someone else had dropped them as she was running for her life, the woman was frozen in a pose of unattainable desire.[9]

This is a temptation for all of us: to turn from life to death by reaching for something we think will satisfy us—a string of pearls perhaps or some other kind of jewelry. Some people reach for food and drink or some other substance they can put into their bodies. Others are allured by sexual pleasure. Still others turn to their toys and games or to some other hobby. Or maybe they just spend more time watching television or playing on the computer. But whatever it is, our wandering appetites are always reaching for something we hope will satisfy us.

The truth is that only God can fully satisfy—through his word, through his worship, and through the help that comes from the Holy Spirit when we turn to him in prayer. This is important to remember whenever we feel unhappy about anything in life. We need to ask ourselves what we truly need and remind ourselves what God wants to give us. Before we buy something or eat something or turn something on, it is better for us to talk things over with our Father in Heaven, saying something like, "Lord, you know how empty I feel right now. Help me not to run away from my problems but to turn them over to you. Teach me that you are enough for me. And by your grace, give me the peace and the joy that you have for me in Jesus."

Same Old, Same Old

Unfortunately, the writer of Ecclesiastes was not yet ready to pray through his disappointments with life. Rather than turning to the Lord, he kept adding to his list of complaints. He has said that satisfaction is not guaranteed. He has wondered if he would be better off dead. He has admitted the wanderlust of his insatiable appetite. Now he says that life is just the same old, same old until you die, and who knows what happens after that?

Here is how Qoheleth said it:

> Whatever has come to be has already been named, and it is known what man is, and that he is not able to dispute with one stronger than he. The more words, the more vanity, and what is the advantage to man? For who knows what is good for man while he lives the few days of his vain life, which he passes like a shadow? For who can tell man what will be after him under the sun? (Ecclesiastes 6:10–12)

These verses fall virtually at the midpoint of Ecclesiastes, but the Preacher is still saying some of the same things he said at the beginning of his book. If he has said it once, he has said it a dozen times: there is nothing new under the sun. The names have already been assigned; everything is labeled and categorized. Furthermore, the human condition is what it always has been ever since the fall of Adam and Eve: vanity and a striving after wind. This lament reminded Martin Luther of an old German proverb: "As things have been, so they still are; and as things are, so they will be."[10]

If we are unhappy with the way things are, there is no sense arguing with God about it. This seems to be what the Preacher means when he talks about disputing with someone stronger than we are. The "one stronger" is Almighty God. Sometimes people do try to argue with God—like Job, for example—but usually they come to regret it. After God answered him out of the whirlwind, Job had to confess, "I have uttered what I did not understand . . . therefore I despise myself, and repent in dust and ashes" (Job 42:3, 6).

We need to know our limits, and one of our limits is that we do not have the wisdom to out-talk God. No matter what we say, telling God that he ought to do this or shouldn't do that, our words will never change his wise plan for ruling the universe. In the words of Derek Kidner, "Whatever brave words we may multiply about man, or against his Maker, verses 10 and 11 remind us that we shall not alter the way in which we and our world were made."[11] In fact, the more we talk, the emptier our words will sound. To help keep us in our place, the Apostle Paul asked, "Who are you, O man, to answer back to God?" (Romans 9:20).

Rather than ending this part of his book with an argument, therefore, the Preacher closes with a couple of rhetorical questions: "For who knows what is good for man while he lives the few days of his vain life, which he passes like a shadow? For who can tell man what will be after him under the sun?" (Ecclesiastes 6:12).

These are basic questions about the meaning of life and death. The first question is about our present existence. The Preacher knows that life is short, like the shadow of a cloud scudding across the sky. He also knows that life is vanity, especially without God. He has been saying this repeatedly since the beginning of Ecclesiastes. But he still wants to know how to live a good life. He also wants to know what happens next. So his second question is about the life to come. Who knows what will happen afterward, whether on earth or in Heaven?

The Life to Come

With these words, we seem to have come all the way back to where Ecclesiastes began, with impossible questions about the meaning of life.

The Preacher still does not have all the answers, which is why some people find this chapter very pessimistic.

In knowing how to respond to this perspective, it will help us to remember where we are in Ecclesiastes, and where we are in the Bible as a whole. The Preacher began this chapter by talking about the evil that he had seen "under the sun." Although he has mentioned God from time to time, he has mainly been looking at life from a human perspective, which is true as far as it goes. We do suffer a good deal of disappointment in life. We also have questions that have never been answered to our satisfaction. But understand the Preacher's purpose: by talking openly about our disappointment with life, he is trying to awaken our longing for God. Some of our questions will get answered by the end of his book. Others will be left unanswered for the time being, but they do get answered in the gospel.

This is especially true of Qoheleth's final question: Is there a life to come? Some people deny it, although of course their case can never be proven. According to the British Humanist Association, "Life leads to nothing, and every pretense that it does not is a deceit."[12] But how can we possibly know that Heaven is a deception, that eternal life is a lie? Some skeptics are more careful. They may not believe in kingdom come, but they know they cannot deny the possibility. Thus they die in uncertainty, like Rabelais who said, "I am off in search of a great Perhaps," or Thomas Hobbes who famously described his death as the "last voyage, a great leap in the dark."[13]

People who believe the Bible know differently. If we leave God out of it, only looking at things "under the sun," we will never be certain what will happen when we die. But when we take God at his word and believe the promises he has made in the Bible, then we know there is a life to come. After he died for our sins and rose again, Jesus ascended into Heaven. He is there to prepare a place for us with him in the presence of God. The way to that blessed place is simply to trust in Jesus.

If there is no Heaven, then there is no way to escape the vanity of our existence. Nothing matters. Our longings will never be satisfied. Our appetites will keep wandering forever. As a result, sometimes we will be tempted to think that we would be better off dead, and no amount of complaining or arguing will change any of it. But if this life is a short preparation for a long eternity, then everything matters and there will be joy for us at the right hand of God.

I was reminded of this joy when our family visited the Narnia show at Philadelphia's Franklin Institute. The exhibition was dedicated to *Prince Caspian* and *The Lion, the Witch and the Wardrobe*—two films based on the famous children's stories by C. S. Lewis. The last gallery portrayed the throne room at Cair Paravel, Narnia's beautiful castle. I watched from behind as the three littlest Rykens passed through an honor guard of centaurs and approached the royal throne. There before us were four golden crowns—

movie props for the kings and the queens of Narnia, inscribed with the names of Peter, Susan, Edmund, and Lucy.

Then we heard a voice from the throne. It was the voice of Aslan, the great lion who rules the land of Narnia, saying, "Once a king or a queen in Narnia, always a king or a queen in Narnia." As we gazed at the crowns in childlike wonder, dreaming of an eternal kingdom, I whispered to the children, "Would you ever like to wear a crown?"

Of course they would! And so they shall by faith in Christ, for as we stood in the courts of Cair Paravel, behold, I could see us standing in the throne room of God, ready to receive the eternal crowns promised to us in Christ (see 2 Timothy 4:8; 1 Peter 5:4; Revelation 2:10). I could read the names inscribed for us: Kathryn the Pure, James the Just, Karoline the Brave, and Philip the Less (I think it said). There was a king on the throne—the Lion of the tribe of Judah—and with a loud voice he was saying, "Behold, I am making all things new!" (Revelation 21:5). So it shall be, by the grace of God, on the last of all days. We are here today, but we shall be crowned tomorrow!

14

Better and Better

ECCLESIASTES 7:1–12

A good name is better than precious ointment,
and the day of death than the day of birth.
It is better to go to the house of mourning
than to go to the house of feasting,
for this is the end of all mankind,
and the living will lay it to heart.

7:1–2

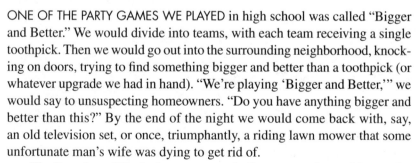

ONE OF THE PARTY GAMES WE PLAYED in high school was called "Bigger and Better." We would divide into teams, with each team receiving a single toothpick. Then we would go out into the surrounding neighborhood, knocking on doors, trying to find something bigger and better than a toothpick (or whatever upgrade we had in hand). "We're playing 'Bigger and Better,'" we would say to unsuspecting homeowners. "Do you have anything bigger and better than this?" By the end of the night we would come back with, say, an old television set, or once, triumphantly, a riding lawn mower that some unfortunate man's wife was dying to get rid of.

The Preacher of Ecclesiastes uses a similar strategy in teaching us the way of wisdom for life in this "all is vanity" world. At the end of chapter 6 the Preacher wondered how we can live well during our few and passing days on this earth. He answers that question in chapter 7 by making a series of "better than" comparisons. The Preacher is teaching us how to exercise discernment in choosing the way that we will live.

The Days of Birth and Death

As we consider Qoheleth's comparisons, it will help us to keep in mind that this section of his book is less tightly organized than the earlier chapters. Ecclesiastes is wisdom literature, and like many writings from the ancient Near East, it contains a wide variety of proverbs and other wise sayings. This is one reason why some scholars believe that Ecclesiastes was written by King Solomon. Some of the proverbs that we read here sound similar to what Solomon wrote in his book of Proverbs. Like the proverbs there, the ones we read in Ecclesiastes cover a wide range of topics. Yet many of them deal with related themes, as we find in the opening verses of chapter 7, where there are practical proverbs about the meaning of life and death (Ecclesiastes 7:1–4), about the difference between wise rebuke and foolish laughter (Ecclesiastes 7:5–6), and about waiting patiently as we look ahead to see what God will do (Ecclesiastes 7:7–10), followed by a statement summarizing the value of wisdom (Ecclesiastes 7:11–12).

The Preacher begins by offering us wisdom for understanding the great matters of life and death. He begins with a double comparison: "A good name is better than precious ointment, and the day of death than the day of birth" (Ecclesiastes 7:1). The first part of this proverb is similar to something that Solomon said elsewhere: "A good name is to be chosen rather than great riches" (Proverbs 22:1). Here in Ecclesiastes the Preacher compares a good reputation to the rich aroma of an exotic fragrance (see also Song 1:3). He does this by making a Hebrew wordplay that is hard to capture in English, but perhaps this paraphrase comes close: "Fair fame is better than fine perfume."[1] This proverb may have been a popular saying in those days. In the dusty communities of Biblical times, scented oils and other fragrances were valuable commodities. Yet having a name that people admire for integrity is even more valuable. With every comment we make and every action we take, we either build up or tear down our reputation.

Qoheleth calls us to wear the cologne of good character. Consider, therefore, what kind of name you are making for yourself. When people think of you, what character traits come to mind? Are they the characteristics of Christ? To give just a few examples: Are you known more for being cheerful or for having a critical spirit? Do you have a reputation for speaking the absolute truth or for coming up with stories that are hard to believe? Are you generous with what you have, or do you err on the side of stinginess? Character is as character does, and sooner or later you will be known for the character you keep. Make a good name—not for yourself but for Jesus.

The comparison in the first part of verse 1 sets up the comparison that follows, about birthdays and funerals. Here is how the verse fits together: "*As* a name is better than oil, *so* the day of death is better than the day of birth."[2] The second part of this comparison is so open-ended that it has been interpreted many different ways. Some scholars take it as a dark and cynical comment about the emptiness of our existence—"Qohelet's relief that life is finally over."[3] The Preacher had similar thoughts back in chapter 6, when he wondered if he would be better off dead (see Ecclesiastes 6:3–6). Somewhat more positively, his comparison between the days of birth and death might mean that some people have such a hard life that death will come as deliverance.

One good reason for taking this comparison more optimistically, however, is that the first half of the verse is so positive. Both precious perfume and a good reputation are wonderful to possess. Similarly, both the first and the last day of life have something to offer, especially to anyone who has a good name in the courts of Heaven through saving faith in Jesus Christ.[4] When Didymus the Blind studied this verse, he commented that a believer's dying day is best because it is "the end and termination of evil."[5] The Apostle Paul expressed a similar idea in his letter to the Philippians (1:21–23). In comparing life with death, Paul found it hard to decide which was better. "Which I shall choose I cannot tell," he said. "I am hard pressed between the two." On the one hand, the longer he lived, the more opportunities he had to do kingdom work. Yet as soon as he died, he would enter the presence of Christ, which would be far better. "For to me to live is Christ," Paul said, "and to die is gain."

This is why the day of a believer's death is the best day of all. "In the day of his birth he was born to die," wrote Thomas Boston, but "in the day of his death he dies to live."[6] Boston further described our dying day as the day we enter a better world, with higher perfection, greater purity, deeper rest, better company, higher perfection, and better employment than the world we entered on the day we were born.[7] Death is our entrance into glory—what Charles Spurgeon described as the day believers "reach their port, all danger over, and come to their desired haven."[8]

To understand how it is possible for our last day to be our best day, we need to go back to the day Christ was born, and the even better day when he died for our sins. The day Jesus was born was one of the best days ever—the coming of our God and King. The joy of that day is beautifully expressed in an old hymn by John Byrom:

> Christians, awake, salute the happy morn
> Whereon the Savior of the world was born.
> Rise to adore the mystery of love
> Which hosts of angels chanted from above,
> With them the joyful tidings first begun
> Of God incarnate and the Virgin's son.[9]

But even that blessed day is not the best day. We look beyond Bethlehem to Calvary, where the Savior in the manger died upon the cross. It is not the birth of Jesus that saves us, although of course he had to be born before he could die. Rather it is the *death* of Jesus that delivers—the shedding of his blood for the atonement of our sins. It is only because the day of his death was so good—Good Friday, we usually call it—that we can have any hope of life after our own death.

Some of the best Christmas carols speak to this great truth. In celebrating the birth of Christ, they also praise his life-saving death. "What child is this, who, laid to rest on Mary's lap is sleeping?" The carol answers: "Nails, spear shall pierce him through, the cross be borne for me, for you."[10] "Within a crib my Savior lay, a wooden manger filled with hay." Then these words: "Upon a cross my Savior died, to ransom sinners, crucified."[11] Or consider these beautiful words from a hymn by Paul Gerhardt: "He becomes the Lamb that taketh / Sin away and for aye full atonement maketh."[12] The truth we find in Ecclesiastes 7:1 is most perfectly expressed in the fragrant character, joyful birth, and atoning death of Jesus Christ.

The Way of All Flesh

There are several ways, then, to interpret what the Preacher says about the days of birth and death. But we understand him most clearly when we see his words in context. The main reason why the day of death is better than the day of birth is because, paradoxically, death has more to teach us about life: "It is better to go to the house of mourning than to go to the house of feasting, for this is the end of all mankind, and the living will lay it to heart. Sorrow is better than laughter, for by sadness of face the heart is made glad. The heart of the wise is in the house of mourning, but the heart of fools is in the house of mirth" (Ecclesiastes 7:2–4). Matthew Henry summarizes by saying, "It will do us more good to go to a funeral than to go to a festival."[13]

This is not to deny that laughter and feasting have their place in life. The Preacher's comparison assumes that it is good to celebrate, especially when we do it for the glory of God. Jesus himself was known to feast on occasion, and the banqueting table is one of the Bible's most positive images of divine blessing (e.g., Song 2:4; Luke 15:22–23). Yet even the happiest celebrations tend to be fairly superficial. As Derek Kidner wisely observes, "At a birth (and on all festive and gay occasions) the general mood is excited and expansive. It is no time for dwelling on life's brevity or on human limitations: we let our fancies and our hopes run high. At the house of mourning, on the other hand, the mood is thoughtful and the facts are plain. If we shrug them off, it is our fault: we shall have no better chance of facing them."[14] Going to a funeral is better in this sense: it teaches us to be wise in the way we live and prepare to die.

When the Preacher mentions "the house of mourning," he is talking about visiting a home where someone has died. In those days it was customary for people to pay their last respects in people's homes. Jesus did this when Lazarus died; he went to comfort Mary and Martha. Today we say our last farewells in church or at a funeral home, but whatever the custom, it is good to have a direct encounter with death.

This goes against the prevailing attitude of our culture, which does as much as it can to deny the reality of our mortality. In secular society, wrote Susan Sontag, "death is the obscene mystery, the ultimate affront, the thing that cannot be controlled. It can only be denied."[15] And deny it we do. It is increasingly rare for people to encounter dead bodies, or to watch coffins get lowered into the ground, or even to mention the word *death*. The so-called "departed" pass away, or are not with us anymore, or go to a better place— anything except what they actually did, which was to die.

It is better for us to deal with death directly, to know that this is the way of all flesh, and to lay it to heart. According to Martin Luther, it is good for us to "invite death into our presence when it is still at a distance and not on the move."[16] Charles Spurgeon gave similar counsel at greater length:

> It is much nearer to us than we think. To those of you who have passed fifty, sixty, or seventy years of age, it must, of necessity, be very near. To others of us who are in the prime of life, it is not far off, for I suppose we are all conscious that time flies more swiftly with us now than ever it did. The years of our youth seem to have been twice as long as the years are now that we are men. It was but yesterday that the buds began to swell and burst, and now the leaves are beginning to fall, and soon we shall be expecting to see old winter taking up his accustomed place. The years whirl along so fast that we cannot see the months which, as it were, make the spokes of the wheel. The whole thing travels so swiftly that the axle thereof grows hot with speed. We are flying, as on some mighty eagle's wing, swiftly on towards eternity. Let us, then, talk about preparing to die. It is the greatest thing we have to do, and we have soon to do it, so let us talk and think something about it.[17]

Going to a good funeral helps us think wisely about death. It causes us to mourn, which enables us to receive the comfort that Jesus promised to those who mourn (Matthew 5:4). Going to a funeral encourages sober contemplation of our own mortality, and this in turn teaches us how to live. The prayer of Moses is good for all of us: "So teach us to number our days that we may get a heart of wisdom" (Psalm 90:12). One place to get that wise heart is at a good funeral, where we recall that our own days are numbered and recommit ourselves to make every day count for eternity.

A good funeral also helps us prepare to die. Many people are not prepared to die at all, to their own folly. In his novel *The Second Coming*, Walker Percy writes:

The present-day unbeliever is crazy because he finds himself born into a world of endless wonders, having no notion how he got here, a world in which he eats, sleeps . . . works, grows old, gets sick, and dies . . . takes his comfort and ease, plays along with the game, watches TV, drinks his drink, laughs . . . for all the world as if his prostate were not growing cancerous, his arteries turning to chalk, his brain cells dying by the millions, as if the worms were not going to have him in no time at all.[18]

The believer in Christ, by contrast, is ready to die. One of the solemn duties of every believer is to die well, and this takes a lifetime of preparation:

Hanging on the edge of a precipice, engulfed by terror, is not the time or place to learn about emergency rock-climbing procedures; you have to learn about them before you start the expedition. Likewise, we have to start learning about death now, while we are still healthy . . . before we are blinded by denial and fighting valiantly for hope.[19]

One of the best ways to learn about death, while we still have time, is to help people bury their dead, especially when this is done with faith in the resurrection power of Jesus Christ.

The Preacher is right: it *is* better to go to a house of mourning than to a house of mirth. We gain more wisdom from going to one good funeral than we do from going to a whole year's worth of birthday parties. Dealing with death is good for the heart—a word the Preacher mentions repeatedly in verses 2–4. The heart is the center of who we are—the thinking, feeling, willing core of our being. Verse 3 says that "sorrow is better than laughter" because it makes the heart glad. More literally, by sadness the heart "is made better" (KJV). The point is not so much the gladness as it is the soundness of the heart. Dealing with death, in all its sorrow, makes us better people.

These Biblical truths cause me to reflect on what I have learned from some of the funerals I have attended. I remember when Sheri Nystrom died, from my church back home. Sheri is one of the most vibrant, fun-loving people I have ever met. To give just one example, when she was a little girl she and a friend mailed some goldfish to our pastor as a prank (do not try this at home; the fish did not survive). We were desperately sad when Sheri was killed in a car accident after college, newly married, with a child in her womb. Yet the visitation and burial were scenes of surprising joy, with the whole church family—people of all ages—crying, laughing, singing, and holding on to one another in Christian love. Most of us stayed until the very end, when Sheri's coffin was lowered into the ground and her father cast rose petals on the casket.

From this experience I learned the pain of a family's loss and the passion of a church's love, with the joy of grieving in the resurrection power of Jesus Christ. In the house of mourning I laid it to heart, and it made my heart better than it was before. To this day I sometimes sing my children a song that Sheri taught our youth group to sing, based on Jude 24: "Now to him who is able to keep you, who is able to keep you from stumbling, and to make you stand in his presence, without fault, blameless, with great joy." By the grace of God and through faith in Jesus Christ, even death can be used by the Holy Spirit to bring us life and joy.

Wisdom's Correction

As he talked about the houses of mirth and mourning (Ecclesiastes 7:4), the Preacher drew a contrast between wise and foolish hearts. The same contrast recurs when Qoheleth introduces a new topic with another comparison: "It is better for a man to hear the rebuke of the wise than to hear the song of fools. For as the crackling of thorns under a pot, so is the laughter of the fools; this also is vanity" (Ecclesiastes 7:5–6). The point of these verses, simply stated, is that wisdom's rebuke is better than folly's laughter. One of the best ways to learn how to live well in this vain world is to receive correction from people who are wiser than we are.

This is not what most people want to hear. They would prefer to listen to what the Preacher calls "the song of fools" (Ecclesiastes 7:5). Maybe he is thinking here of the silly things that some people sing when they are drunk. Or perhaps he has in mind the ungodly lyrics that people so often sing about violence, sex, and the worship of other gods.

In describing this kind of foolishness, the Preacher draws a vivid analogy, in which he compares "the laughter of fools" to "the crackling of thorns under a pot" (Ecclesiastes 7:6). This verse is partly a play on words because the Hebrew terms for "thorn" and "pot" sound very similar. We can come close to capturing this in English by saying that the laughter of fools is "like nettles crackling under kettles."[20]

Whenever we encounter a metaphor like this, we need to look for the point of comparison. In what way is foolish laughter like an open fire fueled by branches from a thorn bush? To begin with, they sound somewhat similar. The noise made by the crackling of a fire is like the cackling of fools. More importantly perhaps, a fire made of thorns is very short-lived. Although it will flame up very quickly (another point of comparison—the fool is ready to laugh at anything), it will not keep burning for long, the way a fire does when it is fueled by logs or burning coals. As a result, a thorny burning does not give off very much heat—"more flame than fire."[21]

So it is with foolish people. Their laughter does not have very much warmth. It has all the frivolity without the jollity. Although laughter may come easily to the fool, it dies out quickly. He who laughs the loudest will not necessarily laugh the longest. Indeed, Jesus said, "Woe to you who laugh now, for you shall mourn and weep" (Luke 6:25). Our Savior was thinking of the fires of the final judgment, when foolish laughter will perish forever.

This fits in well with the serious attitude that Ecclesiastes teaches us to have about life and death. Some people simply laugh their lives away. When the popular philosopher George Santayana considered the days of birth and death, he said, "There is no cure for birth and death but to enjoy the interval."[22] Thus some people try to laugh their way all the way to the grave. Consider the well-known epitaph of the English poet John Gay: "Life's a jest, and all things show it. / I thought so once, and now I know it." Thus says the fool. But there is nothing funny about death, or about the Hell that comes afterward for anyone who dies without Christ.

This is why the Preacher says it is much better for us to hear the rebuke of the wise. Someone who cares enough to confront will tell us to get serious about life and death. Listening to the constructive criticism of a godly friend can save our soul. Wise people will say all of the things that Ecclesiastes says. They will tell us that living for pleasure and working for selfish gain are striving after wind. They will tell us that God has a time for everything, including a time to be born and a time to die. They will tell us that two are better than one in facing all of the toils and trials of life. They will tell us that because God is in Heaven and we are on earth, we should be careful what we say. They will tell us that money will never satisfy our souls. In short, they will teach us not to live for today but to live for eternity.

Be wise, therefore, and go to the places where you can receive wise and life-giving correction. Read the Bible. Listen to Christ-centered, Spirit-filled preaching. Spend more time with people who are farther along in their spiritual pilgrimage than you are. When you hear something serious about spiritual things, do not laugh it off, but take it to heart.

Looking Ahead

The last comparison in these verses teaches us how to have a godly perspective about what is happening in the world. The Preacher has instructed us about birth and death, as well as wisdom and folly. Now, after a brief warning about the danger of power ("Surely oppression drives the wise into madness, and a bribe corrupts the heart," Ecclesiastes 7:7), he tells us to look ahead and take a long-term view: "Better is the end of a thing than its beginning, and the patient in spirit is better than the proud in spirit" (Ecclesiastes 7:8).

As usual, some scholars take the beginning of verse 8 as a dark and cynical comment about the vanity of life. The sooner we get done with all this, the better! Yet it is clear from what the Preacher goes on to say that he is making a positive point. When he talks about the "end" of something, he is talking about its result or outcome—the end product. Many things that do not seem all that promising at the beginning turn out well in the end. This is always true of anything that has the blessing of God. All's well that ends well in his gracious plan because "we know that for those who love God all things work together for good" (Romans 8:28).

A notable example comes from the history of Israel. When the people of God returned to Jerusalem after their long exile in Babylon, they built another temple. As construction began, some people frankly doubted whether it would be very impressive. Yet the prophet Zechariah promised that "whoever has despised the day of small things shall rejoice" (Zechariah 4:10). Although the new temple was starting small, by the grace of God its end would be better than its beginning.

We often see this principle worked out in our own lives. A few simple steps of obedience eventually lead to a stronger life of prayer or greater generosity in kingdom giving. We see it in our families, where sons and daughters who have so much to learn in life gradually grow more mature until finally they are able to offer useful service to the kingdom of God. We see it in church planting, where the vision and prayers of just a handful of people may eventually produce a congregation with hundreds of members. The end of a thing is better than its beginning.

We see this most clearly of all in God's plan of salvation. Go to Bethlehem, and what do you see? A young bride with her older husband, a humble stable, a few lowly shepherds, and a baby in a manger. Who would ever imagine that this was the start of an empire, that the baby would become a king, and that by offering himself as a sacrifice, he would gain the forgiveness of sins for people from all nations? Yet the end will be much better than the beginning. What began with the coming of the Christ-child will end with the consummation of his eternal kingdom.

Seeing the full scope of God's plan also helps us to avoid another error—one the Preacher warns about in verse 10: "Say not, 'Why were the former days better than these?' For it is not from wisdom that you ask this" (Ecclesiastes 7:10). If the temptation in verse 8 was pessimism about the future, the temptation here is nostalgia for the past. Some people like to talk about "the good old days." They want to go back to the way things were (possibly because they forget how bad some things were back then). Rather than looking forward, they always seem to be looking backward.

Some Israelites made this mistake when the temple was being rebuilt in the days of Ezra and Nehemiah. The old-timers said that the Second Temple was not nearly as beautiful as the one that Solomon built (see Ezra 3:12–13; Haggai 2:3). But the Solomon who wrote Ecclesiastes would have told them to let bygones be bygones. Instead of longing for better days, we should look to the future. God is still working his plan, and therefore the best is yet to come. This was true for the people of God in the days of the Second Temple as they waited for Christ to come—the living temple (see John 1:14; 2:19–22). It is true for us as we wait for Jesus to come again and make all things new. We should be looking forward, not backward, because our "salvation is nearer to us now than when we first believed" (Romans 13:11).

Take a godly perspective of what is happening in the world. Wait for God to work his plan, believing that the best is yet to come. Looking at life this way requires the attitude that the Preacher talks about in verse 8, where he says that patience is better than pride. Rather than arrogantly assuming that we know best, we should humbly submit to God as we wait for him to work things out. This applies to our own sanctification in all the areas where we still need to grow. It applies to marriage and family problems when we are tempted to give up instead of press on. It applies to ministry in the church whenever we wish that other people would catch the same vision that we have for what God can do. It applies to any area in life where we think we know best and wish that God would hurry up and do something, when in fact he wants us to hurry up and wait.

One of the easiest ways to tell whether we really trust God's timing or not is to see how angry we get when things do not go our way—the sin of exasperation. The Preacher gives us this command: "Be not quick in your spirit to become angry, for anger lodges in the bosom of fools" (Ecclesiastes 7:9). The connection between anger and folly is well known. Solomon gave similar advice in his book of Proverbs: "A man of quick temper acts foolishly" (14:17), and "he who has a hasty temper exalts folly" (14:29). Here the Preacher-King has a particular kind of anger in mind—the rash anger that explodes whenever we think that something is not happening as quickly as it should. Usually we tell ourselves that we have a right to be angry. But Ecclesiastes sees our anger for what it is—sinful folly, spiritual immaturity, and an underlying mistrust of the sovereignty of God. As soon as we start to get impatient, we need to ask the Holy Spirit to keep us from the folly of rash anger.

The Value of Wisdom

In all of these varied exhortations about life and death, about wisdom and folly, about waiting patiently to see what God will do, the Preacher is teaching us the right way to live and to look at life. He ends these exhortations by restating the value of wisdom, which he says "is good with an inheritance, an advantage to those who see the sun. For the protection of wisdom is like the protection of money, and the advantage of knowledge is that wisdom preserves the life of him who has it" (Ecclesiastes 7:11–12).

The connection that the Preacher makes here is very surprising. After everything else he has said about money and the way it fails to satisfy our soul, we hardly expect him to say that wisdom is like money. If we know the book of Proverbs, then we are even more surprised, because there Solomon says that wisdom is priceless (e.g., 8:11)! But here the Bible merely says that wisdom is "as good as an inheritance," which is another way to translate verse 11, and that the insurance it affords "is like the protection of money." The Preacher knows all too well that money does not last forever. But as long as we have it, money is useful in providing some protection against the practical difficulties of daily life. Similarly, wisdom is a protection for the soul. It helps us deal with the reality of death. It guards us against the folly of rash anger. It helps us take a long-term view of what God is doing in the world. Wisdom may even save our souls, for the Preacher claims that it "preserves the life of him who has it" (Ecclesiastes 7:12). True spiritual wisdom gives us spiritual vitality as long as we live, and when it comes time for us to die, it will lead us to everlasting life.

Charles Ward had this kind of wisdom. Ward served in the Union Army as a sergeant with the Thirty-second Massachusetts Volunteers. In one of his last letters home, he wrote, "I hope I may come home again but life here is uncertain." The soldier was right about the uncertainties of life and death because a few days later he was mortally wounded in the bloody wheat field at Gettysburg. Although he lingered for a little while, Ward died within the week. In his last letter home he wrote, "Dear Mother, I may not again see you but do not fear for your tired soldier boy. Death has no fears for me. My hope is still firm in Jesus. Meet me and Father in Heaven with all my *dear friends*. I have no special message to send you but bid you all a happy farewell. Your affectionate and soldier son, Charles Ward."[23]

If we are wise, we will follow Ward's example. By laying death to heart and looking ahead to what God has planned for us in Christ, we will live wisely . . . and die well.

15

The Crook in the Lot

ECCLESIASTES 7:13–18

*Consider the work of God: who can make
straight what he has made crooked?*

7:13

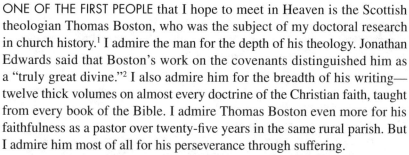

ONE OF THE FIRST PEOPLE that I hope to meet in Heaven is the Scottish
theologian Thomas Boston, who was the subject of my doctoral research
in church history.[1] I admire the man for the depth of his theology. Jonathan
Edwards said that Boston's work on the covenants distinguished him as
a "truly great divine."[2] I also admire him for the breadth of his writing—
twelve thick volumes on almost every doctrine of the Christian faith, taught
from every book of the Bible. I admire Thomas Boston even more for his
faithfulness as a pastor over twenty-five years in the same rural parish. But
I admire him most of all for his perseverance through suffering.

Thomas Boston was a melancholy man, prone to seasons of discouragement in the Christian life. He was often in poor health, even though he never
missed his turn in the pulpit. His wife suffered from chronic illness of the
body and perhaps also the mind. But perhaps the couple's greatest trial was
the death of their children: they lost six of their ten babies.

One loss was especially tragic. Boston had already lost a son named
Ebenezer, which in the Bible means "Hitherto hath the Lord helped us"
(1 Samuel 7:12, KJV). When his wife gave birth to another son, he considered
naming the new child Ebenezer as well. Yet the minister hesitated. Naming
the boy Ebenezer would be a testimony of hope in the faithfulness of God.
But what if this child died, too, and the family had to bury another Ebenezer?
That would be a loss too bitter to bear. By faith Boston decided to name his

son Ebenezer. Yet the child was sickly, and despite the urgent prayers of his parents, he never recovered. As the grieving father wrote in his *Memoirs*, "it pleased the Lord that he also was removed from me."[3]

After suffering such a heavy loss, many people would be tempted to accuse God of wrongdoing, or to abandon their faith, or at least to drop out of ministry for a while. But that is not what Thomas Boston did. He believed in the goodness as well as in the sovereignty of God. So rather than turning *away* from the Lord in his time of trial, he turned *toward* the Lord for help and comfort.

Boston's perseverance through suffering is worthy not only of our admiration but also of our imitation. One way to learn from his example is to read his classic sermon on the sovereignty of God, which is one of the last things he prepared for publication before he died. Boston called his sermon *The Crook in the Lot*.[4] It was based on the command and the question that we read in Ecclesiastes 7:13: "Consider the work of God: who can make straight what he has made crooked?"

Good Days, Bad Days

The command in this verse is a call to a careful observation of the way God works. The man who wrote Ecclesiastes—the Preacher who called himself Qoheleth and who may well have been King Solomon himself—took careful notice of the world around him. He studied the seasons of life, learning when it was time for this and time for that. He watched the way people worked and played. He saw how they lived and how they died. Here in Ecclesiastes 7 he invites us to consider God's work in the world. Then he asks a rhetorical question: Who has the power to straighten out what God has made crooked? The answer, of course, is no one. Things are the way God wants them to be; we do not have the ability to overrule the Almighty.

When the Preacher talks about something "crooked," he is not referring to something that is morally out of line, as if God could ever be the author of evil. Instead he is talking about some trouble or difficulty in life we wish we could change but cannot alter. This happens to all of us. We struggle with the physical limitations of our bodies. We suffer the breakdown of personal or family relationships. We have something that we wish we did not have or do not have something that we wish we did. Sooner or later there is something in life that we wish to God had a different shape to it. What is the one thing that you would change in your life, if you had the power to change it?

According to Ecclesiastes, God has given each of us a different situation in life. Thomas Boston explained it like this: "There is a certain train or course of events, by the providence of God, falling to every one of us during our life in this world: and that is our lot, as being allotted to us by the sovereign God." We all have our own lot in life. Furthermore, we all have things in life that we wish we could change. Boston continues:

> In that train or course of events, some fall out *cross* to us, and against the grain; and these make *the crook* in our lot. While we are here, there will be cross events, as well as agreeable ones, in our lot and condition. Sometimes things are softly and agreeably gliding on; but, by and by, there is some incident which alters that course, grates us, and pains us. . . . Every body's lot in this world has some crook in it. . . . There is no perfection here, no lot out of heaven without a crook.[5]

When some people hear Ecclesiastes say this, they assume that the Preacher is being fatalistic. Some things are straight in life, other things are crooked; but whether they are crooked or straight, there is absolutely nothing that we can do about it. It all comes down to fate, or maybe predestination. Therefore, this passage is about "the powerlessness of human beings over against God"[6]—a powerlessness that can only lead to fatalism.

There is another way to look at these verses, however—not as an expression of fatalism but of Calvinism! In other words, the Preacher is telling us that whether things seem crooked or straight, we need to see our situation in terms of the sovereignty of God. According to Thomas Boston, if God is the one who made the crook in our lot, then we need to see that crook as the work of God, which it is vain for us to try to change. "What God sees meet to mar" we "will not be able to mend." "This view of the matter," said Boston, "is a proper means, at once to silence and satisfy men, and so to bring them unto a dutiful submission to their Maker and Governor, under the crook in their lot."[7]

One way to see the difference between the despair of fatalism and the hope of Calvinism is to compare Ecclesiastes 7:13 to what the Preacher said back at the beginning, in Ecclesiastes 1:15. The wording of that verse is almost identical: "What is crooked cannot be made straight." But the first time the Preacher said this, he was leaving God out of the picture. He was looking at the world without God and telling us how meaningless it all is. But here in chapter 7 he brings God back into the picture. He is looking at the world according to God; he is putting both the straight things and the crooked things in life under his divine sovereignty.

It is still true, of course, that there is nothing we can do to straighten out what is crooked. We cannot change what God has done unless and until God wants to change it. We are under the power of the sovereign and omnipotent ruler of the entire universe. We do not have the power to edit his plan for our lives. But far from driving us to despair, the sovereignty of God gives us hope through all the trials of life. We do suffer the frustration of life in a fallen world. But the Bible says that we suffer these things by the will of a

God who is planning to set us free from all this futility and who is working all things together for our good (see Romans 8:20, 28).

Trusting in the sovereign goodness of God helps us know how to respond to all the joys and trials of life. Whether we are having a good day or a bad day, there is always a way for us to glorify God. The Preacher says, "In the day of prosperity be joyful, and in the day of adversity consider: God has made the one as well as the other, so that man may not find out anything that will be after him" (Ecclesiastes 7:14).

By saying this, Qoheleth puts today and every day under the sovereignty of God. Some days are full of prosperity. The sun is shining, the birds are singing, and all is right with the world. There is food on the table and money in the bank. If there is work to do, it is the kind of work that we enjoy doing. If we are taking the day off, we get to spend it the way we want to spend it, with the people we love. Every such day is a gift from God that calls us to be joyful. Here the Preacher celebrates the kind of meaningful hedonism that he has talked about several times already. Every fine day, every good meal, every financial windfall, every meaningful conversation, every pleasurable experience, every success in ministry—every blessing of any kind at all—is another reason to return praise and thanks to God. To be joyful is to find our fundamental satisfaction in God and then to receive every pleasure in life as a gift of his grace.

Not every day is like that, of course. Some days are full of adversity rather than prosperity. The sun is not shining, the birds are not singing, and nothing seems right with the world. There may be food on the table, but there is no money in the bank. Work is a chore, vacation is boring, and we may feel as if we do not have even one single friend in the world. Yet this day too is a day that comes from the hand of God, a day that is under his sovereign control. The Preacher does not have the heart to tell us to be joyful on such a difficult day, but he does call us to a wise consideration of the ways of God. When adversity comes, recognize that this too is a day that the Lord has made. "Shall we receive good from God," Job asked on the day of his adversity, "and shall we not receive evil?" (Job 2:10). We should acknowledge that both the good days and the bad days come from the hand of God.

The Preacher says further that it is impossible for us to know what will happen in the future. Given what he said at the beginning of verse 14, we might assume that the righteous people are the ones who prosper, while the wicked always suffer adversity. Yet sometimes exactly the opposite occurs: the righteous suffer adversity, while the ungodly prosper. Thus it is impossible for us to predict what will happen in coming days. As the Preacher says, "man may not find out anything that will be after him" (Ecclesiastes 7:14). We have no way of knowing whether the coming days will bring us greater prosperity or more adversity.

Living with this kind of uncertainty need not cause us anxiety or despair;

rather, it should teach us to leave our future in the hands of God. Most of us would prefer to control our own destiny. Instead we should entrust our lives to the loving care of our sovereign God. If we do this, we will be well prepared for both the good days and the bad days. In his comments on this verse, Martin Luther gave the following pastoral advice: "Enjoy the things that are present in such a way that you do not base your confidence on them, as though they were going to last forever . . . but reserve part of our heart for God, so that with it we can bear the day of adversity."[8]

This is all part of what it means to "consider the work of God." When the Preacher tells us to "consider," he is telling us to do something more than simply see what God has done. He is telling us to accept what God has done and surrender to his sovereign will. He is telling us to praise God for all our prosperity and trust God through every adversity. The Puritan Richard Baxter said it well: "Take what He gives, / And praise Him still, / Through good or ill, / Who ever lives."[9]

Two Dangers That Lead to Destruction

It is one thing to say that we believe in the sovereignty of God, but another thing to live that out in a world that often seems meaningless. No sooner has the Preacher told us to consider the works of God than he struggles with God's sovereignty.

Remember, Qoheleth is totally committed to telling us the truth about life, in all its vanity. Here he tells us that sometimes life seems desperately unfair. "In my vain life I have seen everything," he says. "There is a righteous man who perishes in his righteousness, and there is a wicked man who prolongs his life in his evildoing" (Ecclesiastes 7:15).

This is exactly the opposite of what most people would expect in a world that is governed by a good and righteous God. The righteous people are the ones who ought to rejoice in their prosperity, while the wicked suffer adversity until finally they are forced to admit that God is in control. All too often what we see instead is what the Preacher saw: righteous people dying before their time, while the ungodly keep on living.

This paradox almost seems to contradict what the Bible says in other places. God told his people that if they did what he said, he would bless them with long life in the land of promise (e.g., Deuteronomy 4:40). He also threatened to punish his enemies with death for their disobedience. But sometimes things are not the way they are supposed to be. Godly pastors are martyred for their faith, while their enemies live to terrorize the church another day. Innocent victims get cut down in the prime of life; their killers get convicted, but instead of dying, they get life in prison. It's just not fair!

These injustices are some of the crooked things in life that we wish we could straighten out. But knowing that we cannot do this, the Preacher gives us some practical advice: "Be not overly righteous, and do not make yourself too wise. Why should you destroy yourself? Be not overly wicked, neither be a fool. Why should you die before your time?" (Ecclesiastes 7:16–17).

Some scholars believe that these verses are cynical, and maybe they are. Maybe the Preacher is saying, "Look, if the righteous perish while the wicked live to prosper, then why be good? Take my advice: don't try to be a goody two-shoes. I'm not telling you to be evil, of course. It would be foolish to tempt fate by living a wicked life. I'm just saying that if only the good die young, then there is nothing to be gained by trying to be good."

On this interpretation, the Preacher is advising "a kind of middle-of-the-road approach to life, not overzealous about wisdom or foolishness, righteousness or wickedness."[10] This kind of reasoning would have been right at home with the ancient Greek and Roman philosophers, who often advocated a life of moderation. Do not be too good or too evil, they said. Too much piety or too much iniquity will lead to an early grave. This also happens to be the way many people think today. They know better than to live a life of total wickedness because deep down they believe that God will judge people for their sins. Yet secretly they suspect that trying to be holy will take the fun out of life. Generally speaking they try to be good, and they hope they are good enough to get by on the Day of Judgment. But their consciences are troubled too little by their sins. As long as they are not overly righteous or overly wicked, they are happy the way they are.

If this is what the Preacher means, then he must be looking at life "under the sun" again, leaving God out of the picture for the moment and thinking about good and evil the way only an unbeliever can.

There is an alternative, however. When he tells us not to be "overly righteous," he might be telling us not to be *self*-righteous. Grammatically speaking, the form of the verb that the Preacher uses in verse 16 may refer to someone who is only *pretending* to be righteous and is playing the wise man.[11] In that case, the person the Preacher has in mind is too righteous by half. He does not have the true holiness that comes by faith, but only the hypocritical holiness that comes by works.

After all, if God's standard is perfection—if we are called to love him with all our heart, soul, mind, and strength—then how could anyone ever be "overly righteous"? No, our real problem is thinking that we are more righteous than we really are. Somehow there never seems to be any shortage of people who think they are good enough for God. This leads H. C. Leupold to suspect that a "peculiar type of righteousness was beginning to manifest itself in Israel, an overstrained righteousness which lost sight of the ever-present sinful imperfections of men and felt strongly inclined to argue with God and to find fault with Him because He was apparently not rewarding those righteous men as they deemed they deserved to be rewarded."[12]

In response, the Preacher warns us not to be self-righteous. We should not think that trying to be more righteous will save us on the Day of Judgment. Nor should we think that we are so righteous that we do not deserve to suffer any adversity, that it is unfair for someone like us ever to have a crook in our lot. When we think too highly of ourselves, resting on our own righteousness, then it is easy for us to say, "I don't deserve to be treated like this. Doesn't God know who I am?" It is also a very short step from there to saying, "Who does God think he is?" So the Preacher cautions us not to be, as it were, "too righteous." In saying this, he is warning against a conceited righteousness that "stands ready to challenge God for His failure to reward" us as much as we think we deserve.[13]

This is not to say that we should be *unrighteous*, of course. The Preacher warns against this mistake in verse 17 when he tells us not to be too wicked. His point is *not* that it is okay for us to be a little bit wicked, as if there were some acceptable level of iniquity. When it comes to sin, even a little is too much. His point rather is that there is great danger in giving ourselves over to evil. It is one thing to sin from time to time, as everyone does. The Preacher will say as much in verse 20: "Surely there is not a righteous man on earth who does good and never sins." But there is a world of difference between committing the occasional sin and making a deliberate decision to pursue a lifestyle of theft, deception, lust, and greed. "Don't be a fool," the Preacher is saying. "If you live in sin, you will perish."

So there are two dangers. One is a temptation for the religious person—self-righteousness. The other is even more of a temptation for the non-religious person—unrighteousness. Both of these errors will lead to destruction; they may even lead to an untimely death. But there is a way to avoid both of these dangers, and that is to live in the fear of God. Qoholeth says, "It is good that you should take hold of this, and from that withhold not your hand, for the one who fears God shall come out from both of them" (Ecclesiastes 7:18).

This verse is difficult to understand, but when the Preacher tells us to "take hold of this" and not to withhold our hand "from that," he is looking back to the advice that he gave in verses 16–17. He is saying something like, "The right life walks the path between two extremes, shunning self-righteousness, but not allowing one's native wickedness to run its own course."[14] When we do this, we will avoid the death and destruction that will surely befall us if we live sinfully and self-righteously.

To say this more simply, the right way for us to live is in the fear of God. Notice in verse 18 that the person who "fears God" will escape the dangers of death and destruction. The fear of God is one of the great themes of the second half of Ecclesiastes, as the book moves from the vanity of life to the fear of its Creator. When we get to the very end of Ecclesiastes, the Preacher will tell us to "fear God and keep his commandments" (Ecclesiastes 12:13). Here he tells us to fear God and escape the coming judgment.

To fear God is to revere God. It is to know that he is God and we are not. It is to hold him in awe for his majestic beauty. It is to have respect for his mighty and awesome power. Having the true and proper fear of God will help us not to be so self-righteous. We will know that God sees us as we really are, and this will teach us not to pretend to be something we are not. The fear of God will also keep us from living a wicked life, because when we understand his holiness, the last thing we will want to do is fall under his judgment.

Why God Allows Suffering

This passage began with a call to consider the work of God. As we contemplate the way that God works in the world, he teaches us the right way to live. We learn to praise God for prosperity and to trust God through adversity. We learn to live a God-fearing life that is free from wickedness and self-righteousness. These are lessons it takes a lifetime to learn. But maybe the hardest lesson of all is the one with which we began in verse 13: learning to look beyond our present difficulties and see the work of God, accepting all of the crooked things in life until he chooses to make them straight.

At the beginning of this chapter we encountered Thomas Boston and his sermon on Ecclesiastes 7:13. Boston ended that sermon by listing some of the many reasons why God makes some things crooked.[15] These were Biblical lessons that he had confirmed through his own experience of grief and pain—lessons about the sovereign purposes of God that can help us in our suffering. Why does God make some things crooked, even when we pray for him to make them straight?

First, said Boston, *the crooked things in life are a test to help us determine whether we really are trusting in Christ for our salvation.* Think of Job, for example, who was afflicted with many painful trials in order to prove the genuineness of his faith. Our own sufferings have the same purpose: by the grace of God, they confirm that we are holding onto Christ. Or perhaps they reveal exactly the opposite, that we have never fully trusted in Christ at all but still need to trust him for our salvation.

Second, *whatever crooks there are in our earthly lot turn our hearts away from this vain world and teach us to look for happiness in the life to come.* Suffering is part of our preparation for eternity. Consider the Prodigal Son, who did not head back home to his father until he lost everything he had. When something in life seems crooked, remember that the day is coming when God will make it straight.

Third, *the crooked things in life convict us of our sins.* The reason that anything is crooked at all is because there is sin in the world, including our own sin. The Holy Spirit often uses the crooks in our lot to touch our conscience, reminding us of some particular sin that we need to confess.

Remember Joseph's brothers. When things went badly for them in Egypt, they thought at once of their guilt before God for selling their brother into slavery many years before (see Genesis 42:21). It would be a mistake to think, every time we suffer, that it must be because of our sins. But it would also be a mistake to miss the opportunity that every suffering brings to repent of any unconfessed sin.

Fourth, *the crooked things in life may correct us for our sins.* There are times when suffering serves as an instrument of God's justice, as a punishment (or, for the believer, a chastisement) for our sin. So it was for David, after he had murdered Uriah: the sword never departed from his house (see 2 Samuel 12:10). When we suffer, it may be that as a consequence for our sin we are under the judgment or the discipline of God.

These are not the only reasons why God makes some things crooked. Thomas Boston listed several others. Sometimes God allows us to suffer in order to keep us from committing a sin, or else to uncover a sinful attitude of the heart so deep that it could only be revealed by suffering a painful trial. Or maybe—and this is the happiest reason of all—God puts a crook into our lot in order to display his grace in our godliness. We are prone to what Boston called "fits of spiritual laziness," in which our graces lie dormant. But when we have a crook in our lot, it rouses us from our spiritual slumber and produces "many acts of faith, hope, love, self-denial, resignation, and other graces."[16]

The Shepherd's Crook

The point of listing these possible reasons for our suffering is not to suggest that we can always figure out why God has put some particular crook in our lot. The point rather is that *God* knows why he has put it there. When something in life seems crooked, we are usually very quick to tell him how to straighten it out. Instead we should let God straighten *us* out! In his sovereignty over our suffering, God is hard at work to accomplish our real spiritual good, not just in one way but in many ways. Therefore, we are called to trust in him, even for things that seem crooked.

Whenever we are having trouble believing that God knows what he is doing, the first thing we should do is consider the work of our Savior. Remember that our Good Shepherd once had a crook in his lot—a crook that came in the shape of a cross. In his prayer at the Garden of Gethsemane, Jesus asked his Father if there was any way to make Calvary straight instead of crooked. But there was no other way. As Jesus considered the work of God, he could see that the only way to make atonement for his people's sin was to die in their place. So Jesus suffered the crooked cross that it was his God-given lot to bear. And he trusted his Father, waiting for him to straighten things out when the time was right by raising him up on the third day.

If God could straighten out something as crooked as the cross, then surely he can be trusted to do something with the crook in our lot! This was the testimony that James Montgomery Boice gave the last time he spoke to his congregation at Philadelphia's Tenth Presbyterian Church. Dr. Boice had been diagnosed with a fatal and aggressive cancer; he only had weeks to live. This was the crook in his lot. So Dr. Boice raised a question that was based on the sovereignty and the goodness of God. "If God does something in your life," he asked, "would you change it?" To say this the way Qoheleth would have said it, "If God gave you something crooked, would you make it straight?"

Well, would you? Would you change your disability or disease? Would you change your job or your finances? Would you change your appearance, or your abilities, or your situation in life? Or would you trust God for all the crooked things in life and wait for him to make them straight, just like Jesus did when he died for you on the cross?

Dr. Boice answered his own rhetorical question by testifying to the goodness of God's sovereign will. He said that if we tried to change what God has done, then it wouldn't be as good; we would only make it worse.[17] The Preacher who wrote Ecclesiastes said something similar. "Consider the work of God," he said. "Do not try to straighten out what God has made crooked." Our Savior would tell us the same thing. "When you consider the work of God," he would say, "remember my love for you through the crooked cross, and trust our Father to straighten everything out in his own good time."

16

Wisdom for the Wise

ECCLESIASTES 7:19–29

All this I have tested by wisdom. I said,
"I will be wise," but it was far from me.
That which has been is far off, and deep,
very deep; who can find it out?

7:23–24

BELIEVE IT OR NOT, the English Department at the University of Wyoming offers a class to teach its students how to communicate with aliens. "Interstellar Message Composition," the course is called, and it is sponsored by a grant from the National Aeronautics and Space Administration (NASA). According to Wyoming's Web site, it is "the first class to enlist creative writers in a potential cosmic conversation." "We've thought a lot about how we might communicate with other worlds," the professor says, "but we haven't thought much about what we'd actually say."

One of the first assignments the instructor gives his students is to summarize the human condition in ten words or less—a short, simple statement they could send as an S.O.S. to the universe. One English major completed the assignment in just nine words: "We are an adolescent species searching for our identity."[1]

If this is what passes for higher education in America these days, then it is hard to know whether to laugh or cry. But we should also respond with pity for what it tells us about the condition of fallen humanity. People are searching for meaning, calling in the darkness and hoping there is someone out there who can tell us who we are.

Have you discovered the meaning of life, or are you still searching? Do you understand your place in the universe, or are you still trying to figure out who you are and what you are doing here?

The Strength of Wisdom

The Preacher-King who wrote Ecclesiastes was still on his spiritual quest. From the beginning of this book he has been trying and often failing to figure out what matters in life. "Vanity of vanities," he said. "It is all vanity!" Yet even when he did not have all the answers, the Preacher still wanted to know the right way to live. So throughout chapter 7 he has been praising the value of wisdom and showing its practical benefits. Ecclesiastes is wisdom literature, and like most wisdom literature from the ancient world, it celebrates wisdom as a precious gift.

Elsewhere the Bible says that wisdom is pricier than pearls (Job 28:18) and "better than jewels" (Proverbs 8:11). "How much better to get wisdom than gold!" King Solomon said in one of his wise proverbs (Proverbs 16:16). "The fountain of wisdom is a bubbling brook" (Proverbs 18:4). Earlier in this very chapter the Preacher told us that wisdom can be a lifesaver (see Ecclesiastes 7:12). Here he says that it will make us strong: "Wisdom gives strength to the wise man more than ten rulers who are in a city" (Ecclesiastes 7:19).

In this simple analogy, the Preacher imagines a city governed by a council of ten. Most cities would be fortunate to have even one wise leader to protect the city. But there is strength in numbers, and this particular city has ten good rulers to govern its civic affairs. A wise person has the strength of a well-governed city. Wisdom governs thought; so the wise person knows how to think about things in a God-centered way. Wisdom governs the will; so the wise person knows what choices to make in life. Wisdom governs speech; so the wise person knows what to say and what not to say. Wisdom governs action; so the wise person knows what to do in any and every situation. Take hold of wisdom, and it will make you strong.

We get a practical example of that strength in these verses when the Preacher says, "Do not take to heart all the things that people say, lest you hear your servant cursing you" (Ecclesiastes 7:21). This is the kind of wise, Biblical counsel that ought to be better known and more frequently followed. It is excellent advice, says Derek Kidner, "since to take too seriously what people say of us is asking to get hurt, and in any case we have all said some wounding things in our time."[2]

Even if we do not have servants to curse us, sooner or later we are bound to overhear somebody saying something about us that may be unkind or untrue. Usually our first reaction is to get angry. What we ought to do instead is let it go, realizing that it was never intended for us to hear anyway and may well have been spoken in a moment of weakness or misjudgment. It is foolish for us to eavesdrop. "If all men knew what each said of the other," Pascal darkly observed, "there would not be four friends in the world."[3] If we are wise, we will be careful not to take too much interest in what other people say about us: "Listeners, standing upon the tip-toe of suspicion, seldom hear good of themselves."[4]

This is a lesson that Lucy learned when she looked inside the magician's book, a story told in *The Voyage of the Dawn Treader* by C. S. Lewis. As she was leafing through a book of magical incantations, Lucy saw a spell that would enable her to hear what her friends were saying about her. Her curiosity got the best of her, and foolishly she cast the spell. Soon she could overhear Marjorie Preston telling Anne Featherstone that although Lucy was "not a bad little kid in her way," she "was getting pretty tired of her before the end of term."[5] It would have been wiser for Lucy to leave well enough alone rather than to ruin a reasonably good friendship.

The same thing will happen to us if we insist on knowing what people are saying about us. Know what to hear and what to ignore, especially when it comes to criticism. This is one of the ways that wisdom makes us strong: it helps us not to be overly concerned about what other people say. It teaches us not to take offense but to respond with gentleness and grace, even when the things that people say may seem unfair. One wise man responded to criticism by saying, "He didn't insult me at all; in fact, he was talking about another man: the man he thought I was."

To help put this counsel into perspective, Qoheleth gently reminds us that our own words are not always charitable either: "Your heart knows that many times you yourself have cursed others" (Ecclesiastes 7:22). It is true: to our own shame, we have often said things behind people's backs that we would never dream of saying to their faces. Sometimes we have spoken out of frustration; it was only after we had a chance to calm down that we could see the situation properly and speak with something closer to the truth. Sometimes we have spoken unkindly about people without fully understanding their situation. On other occasions, our criticisms have indicated more about what is wrong with us than what is wrong with someone else.

Whatever our reasons, there are times when we are guilty of unkind speech. We are the living proof of verse 22, and also verse 20, which says, "Surely there is not a righteous man on earth who does good and never sins" (cf. Psalm 143:2). We all fail to meet God's standard of perfect speech. So we should be slow to judge other people for not living up to that standard either. If we are wise, we will let our own sinful words remind us not to take what other people say too much to heart, but make allowances for them instead, offering them the same grace that we ourselves need so often. How do you respond to the criticism you get at home or the comments people make at school or the snide remarks you hear at work? Do you have the self-control to hold your tongue, or do you tend to make the situation worse by answering back with angry words of your own?

When he was still a young man, Jonathan Edwards made a personal resolution "never to say anything at all against anybody, but when it is perfectly agreeable to the highest degree of Christian honor, and of love to mankind, agreeable to the lowest humility, and sense of my own faults and failings, and agreeable to the Golden Rule."[6] This resolution is in keeping with the Bible's high standard for personal integrity. If we are wise, we will make sure that our own words pass a few simple tests before we dare to speak. Would I say this if that person could hear me say it, and is this the way that I would say it? Am I saying this for the glory of God and for the love of my brother or sister, or am I only saying it to vent my own frustration?

If we are wise, we will also follow the instructions that Paul told Pastor Titus to give the people in his church: "to speak evil of no one, to avoid quarreling, to be gentle, and to show perfect courtesy toward all people" (Titus 3:2). Paul went on to explain the reason why. It is because we ourselves have been guilty of many malicious sins, including hateful words. But God showed us mercy, saving us by the righteous works of his right-speaking Son and washing us by the cleansing power of the Holy Spirit. His saving and sanctifying grace comes with the strength of wisdom to know what to hear and what not to hear, how to speak and how not to speak.

The Search for Wisdom

It is hard to be wise in the use of our words. In fact, no sooner has the Preacher spoken about wisdom's strength than he tells us how hard wisdom is to find. Here was a man who had dedicated his whole life to the pursuit of wisdom, who had searched long and hard for the meaning of life. Notice the active verbs he uses to describe his quest. "All this I have *tested* by wisdom," he says (Ecclesiastes 7:23). Or again, "I turned my heart to *know* and to *search out* and to *seek* wisdom and the scheme of things, and to *know* the wickedness of folly and the foolishness that is madness" (Ecclesiastes 7:25).

As the Preacher describes his quest for knowledge, he is not just talking about the many things that he investigated in chapter 7—the value of a good name, the way adversity brings more wisdom than prosperity, how to accept what God has made crooked, and so forth. His words actually apply to everything that he has investigated since the beginning of Ecclesiastes, when he said, "I applied my heart to seek and to search out by wisdom all that is done under heaven" (Ecclesiastes 1:13).

Has any man ever made a more serious attempt to understand the meaning of life than the Solomon of Ecclesiastes? "I will be wise," he said (Ecclesiastes 7:23), and then over the course of many years he tried everything to learn the secrets of wisdom. Yet at the end of all his questing he had to admit—very reluctantly—that he had failed to find the wisdom he had been seeking all his life. "It was far from me," he lamented. "That which has been is far off, and deep, very deep; who can find it out?" (Ecclesiastes 7:23–24). At this point it almost seems as if the whole book of Ecclesiastes may end in failure. Qoheleth is looking for wisdom that he cannot find. His quest has failed. He is unable to explain the purpose of life, or explain why everything matters.

Derek Kidner describes these verses as "the epitaph of every philosopher."[7] Indeed, many philosophers have come to this point in their search for meaning and have struggled to go any farther. According to Horace, "Life's short span forbids us to enter on far reaching hopes."[8] Or consider the words of Pascal, from his famous *Pensées*:

> When I consider the short duration of my life, swallowed up in the eternity that lies before and after it, when I consider the little space I fill and I see, engulfed in the infinite immensity of spaces of which I am ignorant, and which know me not, I rest frightened, and astonished, for there is no reason why I should be here rather than there. Who put me here? Why now rather than then?[9]

Sooner or later almost everyone has the same questions, with the same doubts. What is the meaning of my existence, if there is any meaning at all? I have searched hard for wisdom, digging deep for the purpose of life. Yet I still have not found what I am looking for. So what do I do next?

At this point there are two main choices. One is to give up completely and give in to despair. But Qoheleth never did that, and neither should we. The best alternative is to admit that we do not have all the answers, but also to believe that God still does, and then to wait for whatever wisdom he provides. This is the way of humility and faith—what Calvin once called a "learned ignorance."[10] We should try as hard as we can to understand the meaning of life. But we should also be content to confess that there are some mysteries we do not understand. "Doubt wisely," wrote the preacher and poet John Donne.[11] Knowing the limits of wisdom is part of wisdom. The more we know, the more we should realize how little we know, and that whatever wisdom we gain comes as a gift from God.

A Deadly Trap

As frustrating as it was to fail to find the meaning of life, what the Preacher found next was even more discouraging. He was still on his quest for wisdom, and we are following the meanderings of his inquisitive mind. In verse 24 he announced that wisdom was too deep for anyone to get to the bottom of it. Verse 25 tells us that he kept looking anyway, trying to understand the difference between the wise way and the foolish way to live. Yet what he discovered was the darkest mystery and the deepest problem of all—the depravity of the human heart. In one way or another, the troubles of life always come back to the problem of sin. As disappointed as the Preacher was with life in general, his biggest disappointment was with other people.

By way of example, Qoheleth describes one kind of woman that it would be wise to avoid: "I find something more bitter than death: the woman whose heart is snares and nets, and whose hands are fetters. He who pleases God escapes her, but the sinner is taken by her" (Ecclesiastes 7:26).

The Preacher-King compares this woman's heart to a trap, like the kind of net or snare that a fowler would lay for a bird. But who was she? The Preacher seems to have someone in mind. If we wanted a Biblical example, the first woman who comes to mind is Delilah, who entangled Samson's long hair in her loom and eventually robbed that strong man of his godliness (Judges 16). Some commentators make a comparison with the book of Proverbs, where Solomon personifies wisdom and folly as two women in the street calling out to passersby. According to Proverbs, "The woman Folly . . . is seductive" (9:13). Perhaps Qoheleth was talking about the same woman in Ecclesiastes—not a literal person but a metaphor for foolish living. Some scholars claim that the Preacher was referring specifically to pagan philosophy.[12]

The trouble with these interpretations is that they are based more on what the Bible says in other places than on what the Bible says in Ecclesiastes 7. Here the Preacher does not make any wider comparisons to wisdom and folly but tells us something that he has learned from his own experience. Somewhere along the way he met a woman who tried to destroy him (cf. Proverbs 2:18–19; 5:4–5). He is not saying that all women are like this, but some of them are, and a wise person will heed his warning to flee from their temptations.

The warning is open-ended enough that it could apply to many situations in life, but one obvious way to apply it is by turning away from the seductions of sexual sin, including the temptations that come on television or over the computer. People call it virtual reality, but the danger is actual. When temptation comes, rather than getting lured in by sinful desire, remind your heart that the seductive woman is a trap! If you give in to her enticements, the result will be more bitter than death. She will lead you into soul-destroying sin, your capacity for true intimacy will be destroyed, and you will never become the man (or the woman) that God is calling you to become.

Know this: there is a way to escape. Ecclesiastes says that although the rebellious sinner will be trapped by the temptress, the person who pleases God will find a way to flee. Never say that you cannot stop sinning; always believe that by the power of God the Holy Spirit there is a way to run away from temptation, as Joseph did when he was caught in the clutches of Potiphar's wife (Genesis 39). Believe the gospel. Take your sin straight to the cross and confess it. Grow in the knowledge of God through the ministry of his Word. Pray for holiness, and ask a friend to help you pray. Get the shepherding help of a pastor or elder in the church. Seek the pleasure of God, and by his grace he will deliver you from the power of sin.

By telling us that there is a way of escape (see 1 Corinthians 10:13), the Preacher made it clear that he believed in the possibility of holiness. But he was still disappointed by all the ungodliness around him. If he had met one sinful woman, he had met a thousand. Listen to the futility of his quest to find someone living a wise and righteous life: "Behold, this is what I found, says the Preacher, while adding one thing to another to find the scheme of things—which my soul has sought repeatedly, but I have not found. One man among a thousand I found, but a woman among all these I have not found" (Ecclesiastes 7:27–28). Although the Preacher does not come right out and say it, the implication seems to be that he was looking for a wise or righteous person. Out of a thousand men, he could find only one who did not disappoint him, and out of a thousand women, none at all.

Before we accuse the Preacher of being sexist,[13] we need to see these verses in their total context. Taken as a whole, the Bible has as much (if not more) to say about sinful men than sinful women. Iniquity is an equal opportunity employer. We see that here in Ecclesiastes. Lest we think that the Preacher viewed men any more positively than women, we need to remember what he said in verse 20: "Surely there is not a righteous man on earth who does good and never sins." Even the one good man that he found in a thousand was still a sinner. If he speaks to us about the wickedness of men, we should not be offended when he also talks about the folly of women.

In addition to seeing verses 27–28 in their Biblical context, we also need to understand their personal context. The writer is not telling us about all people everywhere but is testifying to his own personal experience, which may say as much about him as it says about anyone else. Remember that these verses may well have been written by King Solomon, who knew some wise and godly men, like the prophet Nathan, but who also had a thousand wives and concubines in his royal harem—unbelieving women who worshiped foreign gods (see 1 Kings 11:3). Does it really surprise us to learn that not one of them was known for her godliness? The Bible says that these women turned Solomon away to the worship of other gods (see 1 Kings 11:1–8). Their hearts were the bitter trap that led to his tragic downfall.

The Bible praises many women for their godliness, like the beautiful bride in Psalm 45 or the virtuous woman in Proverbs 31 or the single women in Luke 8 who supported Jesus in his earthly ministry. All of these women were characterized by single-hearted devotion to God and, if they were married, by complete fidelity to their marriage covenant. Apparently the Preacher-King who wrote Ecclesiastes did not know any women like that, which is what a man gets for trying to love a thousand godless women! But we can praise God for the many godly women whom we meet in the church of Jesus Christ. Martin Luther was thinking of them when he said, "there is [nothing] on earth so lovely as a woman's heart, with God's grace to guide its love."[14] This teaches us how to pray for our mothers, wives, sisters, daughters—that they will become the one woman in a thousand who has a gracious heart guided by the love of God.

Our Fallen Estate

Even the best of women is nothing more than a sinner saved by grace. We are reminded of this by the last verse in Ecclesiastes 7, which brings the Preacher's quest for human wisdom to its unhappy conclusion. He laments, "See, this alone I found, that God made man upright, but they have sought out many schemes" (Ecclesiastes 7:29).

Here we have a broad indictment against humanity—what Charles Bridges called a "humbling testimony to the universal and total corruption of the whole race of man."[15] The Preacher takes the entire human race and places it under the category of iniquity. There is no use arguing about who is more or less righteous than whom or quibbling with Qoheleth for saying that the men he knew were one-tenth of one percent more likely to be righteous than the women he knew. Sin is the great equalizer. Every man, every woman, and every child is a sinner.

Theologians have long recognized Ecclesiastes 7:29 as an important verse for Christian doctrine, a verse that teaches us about both Creation and the Fall. It begins at the beginning, with the way that God made us in the first place. Many people try to blame God for everything that is wrong with the world, but he is not the one to blame! According to this verse (which agrees with what we read in the opening chapters of Scripture), "God made man upright." This is the Biblical doctrine of *original righteousness*.

When the Preacher says "man," he uses the word *adam*, or Adam, who was the father of us all. In his created condition, Adam was perfectly righteous. But Adam chose to eat the forbidden fruit, and in making that choice he doomed all of his children to depravity. This is the Biblical doctrine of *original sin*, which proves that God is not to blame for the sin of our race. By "his own free will," wrote Charles Bridges, Adam "became the author of his own ruin."[16] Not just his own ruin: Adam's sin is the ruin of us all. John Calvin thus compared Adam to a root that goes rotten and then ruins a whole tree.[17] This is the story of the family tree of humanity. To come from "the Lord Adam and the Lady Eve," said C. S. Lewis, "is both honor enough to erect the head of the poorest beggar, and shame enough to bow the shoulders of the greatest emperor on the earth."[18] By virtue of the sin that we have inherited from Adam, what Ecclesiastes says is true of all of us: we have pursued a wide variety of wicked and devious schemes—what the old King James Version called "many inventions."

This may not have been the answer that the Preacher was hoping to find when he started looking for the meaning of life, but it is essential to knowing true wisdom. One of the first things we need to understand is the human condition. What doctrine has greater explanatory power than the doctrine of total depravity, which teaches that the problem with the world is not God but us and our sin? Depravity is the one doctrine of the Christian faith that can be proven empirically. Mark Twain may not have been much of a theologian, but as an astute observer of human nature he made this wry remark about the effect of Adam's sin: "Whoever has lived long enough to find out what life is, knows how deep a debt of gratitude we owe to Adam, the first great benefactor of our race. He brought death into the world."[19] The Apostle Paul would agree: "sin came into the world through one man, and death through sin, and so death spread to all men because all sinned" (Romans 5:12).

This is as far as Ecclesiastes 7 can take us, but not as far as we should go. If we stop with the doctrine of sin, we stop short of salvation, and all will be lost. As Pascal once said, "Knowing our own wretchedness without knowing God makes for despair."[20] Thank God that the Bible does not stop with Creation and the Fall but goes on to teach redemption by grace. The first Adam is not the only Adam. There is also the Last Adam (1 Corinthians 15:45), which is one of the noble titles that the Bible gives to Jesus Christ. Seeing that the first Adam failed to remain upright, we should turn to the Last Adam for our salvation, asking him to help us stand firm at the final judgment.

Jesus Christ is the only man who ever remained totally upright and never fell into sin. By virtue of his perfect life and atoning death, he offers to forgive us for all our wicked schemes. Although it is true that "many died through one man's trespass," it is also true that those who "receive the abundance of grace and the free gift of righteousness" will live "through the one man Jesus Christ" (Romans 5:15, 17). Even if we do not have the wisdom to solve all the deep mysteries of life or to figure out everything there is to know about our place in the universe, we should at least be wise enough to see the deadly sin in our own hearts and to ask Jesus to be our Savior.

17

Command and Consent

ECCLESIASTES 8:1–9

Who is like the wise?
And who knows the interpretation of a thing?
A man's wisdom makes his face shine,
and the hardness of his face is changed.
I say: Keep the king's command,
because of God's oath to him.

8:1–2

HELMUTH VON MOLTKE was drafted to work in counterintelligence for Nazi Germany; yet his Christian faith made him a resolute opponent of Adolf Hitler. Although he believed it would be wrong for him to use violent force against the Nazis, von Moltke used his high position to rescue many prisoners from certain death. Not surprisingly, eventually he was accused of treason, put on trial, and sentenced to die.

In his final letter home to his beloved wife Freya, Helmuth described the dramatic moment at his trial when the judge launched into a tirade against his faith in Christ. "Only in one respect does the National Socialism resemble Christianity," he shouted: "we demand the whole man." Then the judge asked the accused to declare his ultimate loyalty: "From whom do you take your orders, from the other world or from Adolf Hitler? Where lie your loyalty and your faith?"[1]

Von Moltke knew exactly where his loyalty lay. He had put all his hope and trust in Jesus Christ. Therefore, he stood before his earthly judge as a Christian and nothing else. His faith had enabled him to act wisely in government service, and now it enabled him to act wisely when he faced his final hour. As a believer in Christ, von Moltke understood the difference between the proper exercise of authority and the abuse of power. He also knew the wise course of action when he was under someone else's control and in danger for his very life.

The Face of Wisdom

Ecclesiastes 8 teaches us how to exercise the same kind of wisdom in our own submission to authority. These verses give us practical guidance for dealing with earthly government, whether good or evil, even in matters of life and death.

The opening verse of this (loosely organized) passage is transitional. It summarizes what chapter 7 said about wisdom while at the same time preparing the way for what the rest of chapter 8 says about things that are outside of our control. The Preacher-King asks a rhetorical question, then praises the gift of wisdom: "Who is like the wise? And who knows the interpretation of a thing? A man's wisdom makes his face shine, and the hardness of his face is changed" (Ecclesiastes 8:1).

What is the answer to Qoheleth's questions? Who really is wise, and who has the skill to explain something that is hard to interpret? Some scholars think the answer is, "No one." These questions expect a negative answer, they say, especially after what the Preacher said in chapter 7 about how far away wisdom is and how hard it is to dig deep enough to find it (see vv. 23–24). There is no one wise; no, not one.

The trouble with this interpretation is that the second half of the verse is so positive. It says that true wisdom will transform a person's countenance. But why would the Preacher say this if no one is wise? There must be at least some people who possess wisdom. Thus the Preacher's rhetorical questions must have a slightly different force. He is not saying that no one is wise, but that wisdom is rare, and that no one can compare with a person who is truly wise. If wisdom is as hard to find as the Preacher said in chapter 7, then not many will find it—only one man out of a thousand (Ecclesiastes 7:28). Nor will we be able to find very many people who know how to interpret things. Think how hard it can be to understand the difficult teachings of the Bible (including some of the verses in this very passage). Or, to think more widely, consider how hard it is to explain the mysterious providence of God, the way he makes things crooked or straight in the world. Is my suffering a sign of God's judgment and thus a call for repentance, or is it an opportunity for God's grace and thus a test of my faith?

The man who has the wisdom to solve such vexing problems is rare indeed. Yet some individuals do have the gift of interpretation. To give just one notable example, consider the life and ministry of the prophet Daniel. When he was a young man, Daniel was carried off to captivity in Babylon, where he was trained at the court of Nebuchadnezzar. Only Daniel (with a few of his friends) was wise enough not to eat the meat that the Babylonians offered to their gods. The Bible says further that "in every matter of wisdom and understanding" Daniel knew ten times as much as any of the scholars or magicians in Babylon (Daniel 1:20). Later on he turned out to be the only man in the entire kingdom who was wise enough to reveal and interpret the king's dream (Daniel 2).

Not many people have as much wisdom as Daniel. He is such a glowing example that he matches the description given in the second half of Ecclesiastes 8:1. Wisdom made his face shine. In fact, even the Babylonians could see that his appearance was better than the appearance of their own young men (Daniel 1:15).

It is strange but true: godly wisdom makes a difference in the way people look. People who live without God in the world often show the proud demeanor or stern expression that comes from a heart hardened by sin— what the Preacher called "hardness of . . . face." But the wisdom of the gospel turns the frown of sin into the smile of grace. Thus the Preacher contrasts the face of a hardened sinner with "the wise man who is visibly gracious in his demeanor, and whose gentleness is obvious in his facial expression."[2] In saying this, he is not just telling us to "put on a happy face." Instead, he is saying what the psalmist said, that people who look to the Lord "are radiant, and their faces shall never be ashamed" (Psalm 34:5; cf. Exodus 34:29–35; Proverbs 15:13). This is more than a metaphor. True wisdom brings a joy to life that changes everything, including people's appearance.

A striking example comes from a 2008 essay by a prominent atheist about a strange phenomenon he had observed in Africa. The journalist Matthew Parris wrote a piece for *The Times* entitled "Why Africa Needs God." Although Parris made it clear that he does not believe in God at all, he admitted that Christianity made a tangible difference in the lives of people he knew in his boyhood home of Malawi and in other countries across Africa. Not only did he admire the good work that Christians were doing to care for the poor and sick, but he also liked the way they looked. "The Christians were different," he wrote. "Their faith appeared to have liberated and relaxed them. There was a liveliness, a curiosity, an engagement with the world. . . . Whenever we entered a territory worked by missionaries, we had to acknowledge that something changed in the faces of the people we passed and spoke to: something in their eyes."[3]

Biblical wisdom brings personal transformation. It makes a difference in our witness, showing people the joy of knowing Christ. It also makes a difference in our relationships. Instead of going around grumpy all the time (which is tempting for all of us), wise people have an inner joy that radiates out to other people. Have you ever seen this joy in the face of an older, wiser believer? Is God making your own face shine? As we pray for our spiritual progress, we should ask God for greater wisdom to bring growing joy to life in our witness for Jesus Christ. As his face shines upon us (see Numbers 6:25), our own faces will shine with the wisdom of his radiant grace (see 2 Corinthians 3:18).

The Divine Right of Kings

After telling us how wisdom looks, the Preacher shows us what wisdom does in dealing with people in absolute authority: "I say: Keep the king's command, because of God's oath to him. Be not hasty to go from his presence. Do not take your stand in an evil cause, for he does whatever he pleases. For the word of the king is supreme, and who may say to him, 'What are you doing?'" (Ecclesiastes 8:2–4).

In their original context, these verses applied most specifically to life at the royal court, like the palace where Daniel served in Babylon. The Preacher is talking about the divine right of kings, such as the monarchs who ruled over ancient Israel. These principles can also be applied to other forms of government, however, or even more generally to any situation in which we are called to submit to God-given authority.

There are hints throughout the passage that the king in question may or may not exercise his governance in a godly way. In fact, verse 9 indicates that earthly authority is often abused: "All this I observed while applying my heart to all that is done under the sun, when man had power over man to his hurt." This passage is not simply about the use of power but also about its abuse. From what the Preacher had seen, whenever one person has power over another person, there is always a strong possibility that it will be used in a destructive way. R. N. Whybray captures well the ambivalence in Qoheleth's attitude toward political authority: "on the one hand he counsels obedience and submission to it on the grounds of prudence, while on the other he does not hide the fact that he regards it as brutal and tyrannical."[4]

To Hear Is to Obey

What is the wise and godly way for us to live under authority? This question is not just for courtiers; it is relevant for every citizen, every employee, and every other person who is called to submit to any authority that God has put in place. How do we honor God by honoring the king?

Our first duty is obedience. So the Preacher begins by telling us to "keep the king's command" (Ecclesiastes 8:2). A wise servant will do what the king tells him to do. He will say, "Your wish is my command" or "To hear is to obey, my lord."

The general principle here is submission to the governing authorities— something the Bible also teaches in other places. Jesus told his disciples to "render to Caesar the things that are Caesar's" (Luke 20:25). Paul told every person to "be subject to the governing authorities"—what William Tyndale famously called "the powers that be" (Romans 13:1). Martin Luther called this the duty of "political obedience."[5] Every Christian is called to be a law-abiding citizen and to respond to any godly request the government makes for help. This includes everything from paying our full taxes to answering the president's call to volunteer service.

There are several good reasons to obey the king. The most important is theological: "Keep the king's command, because of God's oath to him" (Ecclesiastes 8:2). What the Scripture literally says is, "because of the oath of God." It is not entirely clear whether this refers to an oath that the citizen makes or an oath that God makes. Some scholars take it as a vow of loyalty made by the people of Israel. There are a few examples of such oaths in the Old Testament—the vows of public officials to be loyal to their king (e.g., 1 Chronicles 29:24). If that is what the Preacher means here, he is reminding members of the royal court that they have promised to obey the king.

There is another way to take this verse, however. The "oath of God" may be a divine rather than a human promise—the promise that God had made when he put his king on the throne. Remember that the rightful kings of Israel were the recipients of a royal promise. God had sworn to King David that one of his sons would sit on Israel's throne forever. This is the covenant that God made to David in 2 Samuel 7 and that David himself repeated in Psalm 110: "The Lord says to my Lord: 'Sit at my right hand, until I make your enemies your footstool'" (v. 1). The people of God were obliged to obey their earthly king because he was anointed by Almighty God. To obey the king, therefore, was to give honor to God.

We honor God the same way. Admittedly, our own rulers have not received the covenant that God promised to David. That solemn oath was fulfilled with the coming of Christ, who will reign forever as God's anointed King. But in the exercise of his royal and universal authority, Jesus has appointed the leaders of our own government: "There is no authority except from God, and those that exist have been instituted by God. Therefore whoever resists the authorities resists what God has appointed" (Romans 13:1–2). Our submission to authority on earth is one important part of our submission to Christ in Heaven.

People often wonder whether this obedience has any limits. Must I always submit to the governing authorities, or are there times when it is my duty as a Christian to disobey? The simple answer is the one that Peter gave when the rulers of Jerusalem told him to stop preaching the gospel: "We must obey God rather than men" (Acts 5:29). When it comes to a conflict between God and man, we must obey the higher authority.

What the Preacher gives us in Ecclesiastes 8 is practical wisdom for when we are under an earthly authority that is not entirely righteous and we might not be certain what to do. Verse 3 seems to assume a situation in which a public official disagrees with the command of his king. Here the Preacher gives a word of caution: "Be not hasty to go from his presence. Do not take your stand in an evil cause, for he does whatever he pleases" (Ecclesiastes 8:3).

When he tells us not to be hasty, the Preacher is not telling us how fast to walk when we leave the White House. In the ancient world, an audience with the king was a matter of life and death. For example, when Esther went in to the throne room of King Ahasuerus, she was putting her life into his hands ("If I perish, I perish;" Esther 4:16). In this cultural context, a hasty departure from the throne room was really a sign of disrespect, a way of turning one's back on authority. The Preacher is not saying that we never have a duty to disobey the government in order to fulfill our higher obligation to God. But he is telling us not to be hasty to walk away from any authority that God has put in place.

He also cautions us not to take our stand "in an evil cause" (Ecclesiastes 8:3). This would be good advice in any case, but given the context, the Preacher may have something specific in mind. When people are under the rule of ungodly authority, it is tempting to rebel in an unrighteous way. Instead the Preacher tells us to fight evil with godliness. A good example is the stand that Daniel's friends took against King Nebuchadnezzar when he commanded all of his subjects to worship him. Hananiah, Mishael, and Azariah (to use their proper Hebrew names) peacefully refused to worship anyone except God alone (see Daniel 3). Another notable example is Helmuth von Moltke—the man mentioned in the introduction to this chapter. Although he resisted Hitler at every turn, von Moltke refused to resort to violence, for fear that this would make him little better than a Nazi.

This is not to say that there is never a time to fight against tyranny, including by the rightful use of force, if this is a calling that we have been given by God. But Ecclesiastes cautions us not to respond to evil with evil. Nations apply this principle by following Biblical principles for the just practice of war, including the safe treatment of prisoners. But we can also apply this principle personally anytime we feel the urge to fight against the abuse of authority. When suffering oppression at home or at work or in society, do not let the desire for revenge turn your heart to ungodliness.

The most important reason to obey the king's command is theological. But the Preacher also gives us a good practical reason to do our royal duty, namely, that it will keep us from harm. Remember that the word of the king is law, that the earthly authority of government is absolute: "The word of the king is supreme, and who may say to him, 'What are you doing?'" (Ecclesiastes 8:4). Therefore, if we are unwise in the way that we challenge the king's authority—or worse, if our resistance is evil—then we may fall under his judgment (see Romans 13:4).

Some commentators get the impression that because he does "whatever he pleases" (Ecclesiastes 8:3), this particular king may be somewhat unpredictable, even dangerous.[6] Whether that is the case or not, it is good to be careful around an all-powerful ruler! If we disobey the king, we are likely to arouse his anger (see Proverbs 14:35; 16:14; 20:2). According to Derek Kidner, therefore, there are times when "wisdom has to fold its wings and take the form of discretion, content to keep its possessor out of trouble."[7] Yet the Preacher offers us this encouragement: "Whoever keeps a command will know no evil thing, and the wise heart will know the proper time and the just way" (Ecclesiastes 8:5). This is not an absolute promise, but it is a valid principle. Obedience has God's blessing. Submitting to the rule of law will keep us safe from harm. This is one of the blessings of wisdom: it helps us know the right way to live, which includes submitting to our government, the way a loyal citizen should.

Death, War, and the Future

Everything we have said thus far is aptly summarized in one of the Biblical proverbs: "My son, fear the LORD and the king, and do not join with those who do otherwise" (Proverbs 24:21). What is somewhat harder to understand is the advice that follows. After telling us that a wise person "will know the proper time and the just way," the Preacher assures us that "there is a time and a way for everything" (Ecclesiastes 8:5–6). In other words, the wise person knows the right thing to do and the right time to do it. Yet the Preacher goes on to say that "man's trouble lies heavy on him. For he does not know what is to be, for who can tell him how it will be?" (Ecclesiastes 8:6–7).

Once again we find ourselves up against the limits of earthly wisdom. The wise person has a sense of God's timing. This is in keeping with what the Preacher said earlier, that there is "a time for every matter under heaven" (Ecclesiastes 3:1). If the Preacher is still thinking about kings and governments, he is saying that there is a time to obey the king and a time to leave his presence, or even to start a righteous rebellion. We can apply the same principle to other situations that involve authority. There is a time to submit and a time to stand against oppression. To give just one example, there is a time to stay and make a marriage work, but there is also a time to leave an abusive or adulterous spouse.

The problem is that it is hard to know what time it is, which often makes it hard to know the wise thing to do. The troubles and frustrations of life are many, as the Preacher never fails to remind us. We do not know what the future will bring. Nor can anyone tell us exactly what will happen in days to come. Will I be able to achieve my ambitions? Will God bless me with the situation I desire in life? Which nations will rise and fall? Will the economy be good or bad? Will the church thrive or only survive? These are only some of the many uncertainties that we have about the future.

Then there is the biggest uncertainty of all, which is the time of death. This too is beyond our control. The Preacher says, "No man has power to retain the spirit, or power over the day of death" (Ecclesiastes 8:8). Although the word "spirit" sometimes means "wind" (e.g., Ecclesiastes 1:6), its connection here to "the day of death" makes it clear that the Preacher is thinking of "spirit" as the breath of life (cf. Ecclesiastes 3:19; 12:7). No mere human being has power over the life and death of the spirit. Someday soon we will take our very last breath, and when that day comes, there will be absolutely nothing we can do to extend it. The Scripture says, "It is appointed for man to die once" (Hebrews 9:27), but that appointment is on God's agenda, not our own. It also says that there is "a time to die" (Ecclesiastes 3:2), but that time is not on our timetable. The last breath we take is the last breath we get, and there will be no way for us to take even one more breath after that.

To give a specific example of the uncertainty of life and death—an example that relates to the power of earthly kings—the Preacher considers the case of a soldier in wartime: "There is no discharge from war, nor will wickedness deliver those who are given to it" (Ecclesiastes 8:8). The Bible generally regards military service as a noble calling. For example, John the Baptist told soldiers in the Roman army(!) not to quit their post but to honor God in the way they did their duty (Luke 3:14).

Here the Preacher tells soldiers the same thing, but he does so realizing that warfare is a dangerous occupation. A good soldier cannot stay out of harm's way. The Law of Moses made provision for cowardly men to get an exemption from military service (see Deuteronomy 20:8). But when it was time to fight, soldiers on active duty were forbidden to flee. This is the universal custom of every respectable army. A soldier cannot buck the system, dodge his service, or go absent without leave. Not even wickedness on the battlefield can relieve him of his responsibility to stand and fight.[8]

The situation of the soldier brings together two of the main themes of this passage (which, it should be noted again, has a loose structure, following the stream of the author's consciousness). Of all the things that a government commands people to do, this is the most demanding, namely, to defend their country. It is also the duty that brings the most danger, and with that danger, the most uncertainty about the future. A soldier in wartime deals with the real possibility of death at any moment. He of all people knows that he does not have knowledge of the future or power over the day of death. Nevertheless, a soldier must do what he is commanded to do. Incidentally, this is one of the many reasons why it is important for us to pray for military personnel, especially in time of war: they are dealing with the great matters of life and death every day.

This is our own situation, too, if only we will see it. All of us are under the authority of others. We all face an uncertain future. We do not control our own destiny or determine the days of our lives. We do not even know how to interpret everything that happens in our lives. What, then, is the wise way for us to live?

The wise way to live is by submitting to the sovereignty of God and entrusting our lives—body and soul—to the lordship of Jesus Christ. Jesus Christ is the wisdom of God (1 Corinthians 1:30); so if we want to know the wise way to live, we must go to him. Jesus Christ is the King of kings (Revelation 19:16); so when we submit to any earthly government, we are really honoring his eternal kingship. Jesus Christ is the Savior who died at his own appointed time, patiently surrendering his spirit to the Father (see Luke 23:46) as he offered his life on the cross for our sins. Jesus Christ is the Lord of eternal life (John 6:68); so he is able to deliver us from death and give us fullness of joy in the everlasting presence of God. Give your life to Christ, and he will save you forever. Your future will be secure, despite all the troubles and uncertainties of life.

In the last days of his life on earth, Helmuth von Moltke experienced the comfort of knowing Christ. Although he was innocent of all charges, once he was convicted by the Nazis, von Moltke knew that he was a dead man. Any day could be his last. Nevertheless, in his last letter home he was filled with joy and confidence in the goodness of God. Von Moltke was suffering the evil described in Ecclesiastes 8:9, in which one man has the power to hurt another. Yet at the same time he had the wisdom that comes from knowing Christ. Thus he was able to tell his beloved wife Freya that "the agony of parting, the terror of death, and the fear of hell" had no power over him. Instead, he was overwhelmed with faith, hope, and charity. "I know that I am living only in his grace," von Moltke said. He also quoted a line from a favorite hymn: "He for death is ready, who living clings to Thee."[9]

If we are wise, we too will cling to Jesus Christ, living only in his grace, and in this way we will be ready for death and everything else that happens in life.

18

Final Justice

ECCLESIASTES 8:10–15

*Though a sinner does evil a hundred times
and prolongs his life, yet I know that it will
be well with those who fear God, because they
fear before him. But it will not be well with the
wicked, neither will he prolong his days like a
shadow, because he does not fear before God.*

8:12–13

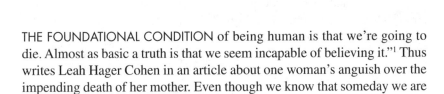

THE FOUNDATIONAL CONDITION of being human is that we're going to die. Almost as basic a truth is that we seem incapable of believing it."[1] Thus writes Leah Hager Cohen in an article about one woman's anguish over the impending death of her mother. Even though we know that someday we are going to die, we have trouble believing it.

Yet there are times when death confronts us so personally and so directly that we cannot deny it. We hear the news that some famous person is dead. We attend the funeral of a loved one. We visit a grave site. Or maybe we simply daydream about the end of our own existence. In a moment of crystal clarity we suddenly remember that life ends in death, and this changes everything.

Grave's End

The Preacher-King who wrote Ecclesiastes had a moment of clarity about the great matters of life and death. He had been thinking about the power of earthly kings and their God-given authority to rule (Ecclesiastes 8:2–4). He had also been meditating on God's sovereignty over life and death, reminding us that we do not determine the day we will die (Ecclesiastes 8:8). He was thinking about these things because he wanted to know the wise way to live. Suddenly he had an experience that shifted his whole perspective on life and death. "Then I saw the wicked buried," he said. "This also is vanity" (Ecclesiastes 8:10). Maybe the Preacher actually attended the burial service, or perhaps he saw the funeral procession going down the street. But in any case he witnessed the burial of a wicked man, which gave him greater wisdom.

Death has a way of bringing perspective to life. "The sight of a funeral," said Charles Spurgeon, "is a very healthful thing for the soul."[2] Similarly, Columba Stewart said, "Awareness of mortality exerts a unique power to focus the mind and heart on essentials."[3] It is easy to get so distracted by the pleasures and problems of everyday life that we give little thought to the future or to the end of our days. But when we stand beside a grave, we remember something that most people try hard to forget: death is coming sooner than we think.

This sad and sober reality helped the Preacher understand and accept something that was troubling his soul. As far as he could tell, bad people seemed to have a good life. If God is just, then he ought to judge the wicked. Yet as the Preacher looked around, he saw exactly the opposite. He was like Asaph, who admitted that he was "envious of the arrogant when I saw the prosperity of the wicked" (Psalm 73:3). Asaph makes this complaint in Psalm 73, where he also writes, "They have no pangs until death; their bodies are fat and sleek. They are not in trouble as others are; they are not stricken like the rest of mankind" (vv. 4–5). In other words, God's enemies seem to get all the blessing. They make more money, have more power, and experience more pleasure than people who try to do what God says.

This is what Asaph saw, and the Preacher saw it too. Here was his epitaph for the wicked: "They used to go in and out of the holy place and were praised in the city where they had done such things" (Ecclesiastes 8:10). It is not entirely certain which "holy place" the Preacher had in mind. Maybe he was referring to Jerusalem, the holy city of God. Or perhaps he was referring more specifically to the temple in Jerusalem. This led Martin Luther to believe that the people who "go in and out of the holy place" were the priests who led worship at the house of God, in which case the Preacher was talking about Israel's religious leaders.[4] But whoever they were and wherever they went, they used to come and go in freedom.

Most translations give the impression that these wicked people were popular, that they "were *praised* in the city" (Ecclesiastes 8:10). Some commentators also think this refers to their funerals: in spite of their wickedness, these people were eulogized when they were buried, which is something they never deserved.[5] Sometimes kind words are spoken at the funerals of evil people, but we can only interpret Ecclesiastes this way if we amend the text. It is much more likely that we should read the verse the way it reads in most manuscripts, which is also the way it is translated in the note for the English Standard Version: the wicked "were *forgotten* in the city." Solomon said something similar in the book of Proverbs: "The memory of the righteous is a blessing, but the name of the wicked will rot" (10:7). This is part of the perspective that death brings. Although wicked people are prominent in the city, and sometimes even in the church, when they are dead they will be forgotten.

But we are getting ahead of ourselves. As far as this present life is concerned, the wicked often seem to get what they do *not* deserve. Qoheleth writes about this injustice in Ecclesiastes 8:14: "There is a vanity that takes place on earth, that there are righteous people to whom it happens according to the deeds of the wicked, and there are wicked people to whom it happens according to the deeds of the righteous. I said that this also is vanity."

Oh, the injustice of it all! If God is righteous, then we would expect him to reward the righteous and punish the wicked. Yet often he seems to do exactly the opposite. Good people have troubles that only bad people deserve, while bad people get what only good people deserve. Cruel dictators drive out free governments. The man who robs investors of their inheritance gets a huge bonus, while hardworking people lose their jobs and their homes. Suffering pastors are put in prison, while the persecutors of the church grow strong in their cruel power. To bring things down to the personal level, the student who cheated on a difficult exam gets an A, but all you get is a C-. The worker who stabbed you in the back gets the promotion, while you remain stuck at the same pay grade. Or you make a commitment to chastity, and although you are still single, the girl who throws herself at men gets a ring on her finger and a long white dress.

The Preacher is telling us that in this life there is a reversal of retribution and reward. This is not just the way things seem, but the way they actually are. So what is the use of being righteous? If bad people get a good life, then what do we gain by godliness? The Preacher called this "vanity." The Reformation theologian Theodore Beza called it "repugnant to reason."[6] I would call it an absurd injustice.

The Delay That Leads to Depravity

To make matters worse, the apparent inequity between the rewards of the righteous and the unrighteous makes some people more likely to do evil. Notice what happens when the sins of the wicked go unpunished: "Because the sentence against an evil deed is not executed speedily, the heart of the children of man is fully set to do evil" (Ecclesiastes 8:11; cf. 7:29).

Here we get an ugly glimpse into the total depravity of the human heart. If evil deeds were punished right away, then people would be deterred from doing wickedness (like the kind of evil described back in verse 9, where one man had the power to hurt another man). But justice is so painfully slow that some people think they can get away with murder, both literally and figuratively. To give an example from the world of sports, one of the reasons why famous athletes like Barry Bonds and Alex Rodriguez kept using steroids, even though such drugs had been banned from professional baseball, is because steroid users were not being punished.[7] If there are never any consequences, then why not go ahead and sin?

When people operate unrighteously, they are taking advantage of God's mercy. The reason God does not throw thunderbolts from the sky is because he is so patient. He is "slow to anger, and abounding in steadfast love" (Exodus 34:6). Judgment is coming—maybe sooner than we think (see Psalm 55:23) but God is giving us more time to repent. The way to respond to this patient delay is to ask him to have mercy on our sins. The Scripture says, "God's kindness is meant to lead you to repentance" (Romans 2:4). Yet many people abuse the patience of God by making it an excuse for their immorality. If there is a final judgment, they assume that it is a long way off. More likely, though, they laugh at the very idea that God will ever judge them at all. They are like the scoffers about whom Peter warned, who follow their own sinful desires and say, "Where is the promise of his coming? For ever since the fathers fell asleep, all things are continuing as they were from the beginning of creation" (2 Peter 3:4).

Cornell University's William Provine makes this exact argument in his book on Darwinism. "When you die," he says, "you're not going to be surprised, because you're going to be completely dead. Now if I find myself aware after I'm dead, I'm going to be really surprised! But at least I'm going to go to Hell, where I won't have all of those grinning preachers from Sunday morning." Then Provine summarizes his own worldview, which has no room for God or for a final judgment:

> There are no gods, no purposes, and no goal-directed forces of any kind. There is no life after death. When I die, I am absolutely certain that I am going to be dead. That's the end of me. There is no ultimate foundation for ethics, no ultimate meaning in life. . . . Since we know that we are not going to live after we die, there is no reward for suffering in this world. You live and you die.[8]

Dr. Provine offers a long list of things that he "knows," yet they are actually things that he *believes*, since none of them are capable of rational or scientific proof. But notice how similar his worldview is to the one we are warned about in Ecclesiastes. When people do not believe in God, they misunderstand why life matters and lose their foundation for righteous living, and therefore they turn their hearts toward evil.

After That, the Judgment

One of the best ways to regain God's perspective on good and evil is to do what the Preacher did and go to someone's grave, especially the grave of someone evil. In his struggle over witnessing injustice, the Preacher also needed to see the end of the story. So do we, if we hope to keep our spiritual sanity in a fallen world.

In her memoirs, Svetlana Alliluyeva describes the death of a cruel tyrant who murdered millions of people. It was her father, Joseph Stalin. If ever a man set his heart to do evil, it was that wicked man. Here is how his youngest daughter describes his final breath:

> At what seemed like the very last moment he suddenly opened his eyes and cast a glance over everyone in the room. It was a terrible glance, insane or perhaps angry, and full of fear of death and the unfamiliar faces of the doctors bent over him. The glance swept over everyone in a second.
>
> Then something incomprehensible and awesome happened, that to this day I can't forget and don't understand. He suddenly lifted his left hand as though bringing down a curse on us all. The gesture was incomprehensible and full of menace, and no one could say to whom or what it might be directed. The next moment, after a final effort, the spirit wrenched itself free of the flesh.[9]

What happened after that? This is the ultimate question. What happens after we die? The Preacher believed there would be a final righting of all wrongs. True, he was troubled by the common injustices of life in a fallen world. But he was also convinced that God would make things right in the end: "Though a sinner does evil a hundred times and prolongs his life, yet I know that it will be well with those who fear God, because they fear before him. But it will not be well with the wicked, neither will he prolong his days like a shadow, because he does not fear before God" (Ecclesiastes 8:12–13).

Taken by themselves, these verses might possibly refer to our present existence. Whether or not things will go well for us depends on whether or not we honor God. But given the verses that come before (in which the Preacher talks about death; see Ecclesiastes 8:10–11) and the verse that comes after (in which he describes the vanity of earthly injustice; see Ecclesiastes 8:14), it seems more likely that he is looking ahead to the future. Even if he does not explain exactly what happens after death, Qoheleth knows that justice will be done. Although he knows that the world is full of injustice, he also believes in the final justice of God.

Things will not turn out well for the wicked, who will come to a bad end. Whether they sin a hundred times or a thousand, there is no blessing beyond the grave. One day they will be dead and buried, for as the Preacher reminds us in verse 10, the wicked will not live forever. T. M. Moore offers the following paraphrase: "And then they die. The funeral's nice enough: we give the guy his due; his loved ones weep; his friends all say they'll miss him; then we bury him away from sight, and everyone forgets him."[10]

Verses 12–13 tell us more. Verse 12 tells us that the wicked want to prolong their days. Because they do not have the assurance of Heaven, they cling to life for dear life, desperately trying to live as long as they can. But verse 13 tells us that they will not get even one more day than God gives them. The shadows lengthen at the end of the day, but the wicked cannot prevent the nightfall of death. David said something similar: "I am gone like a shadow at evening" (Psalm 109:23; cf. Psalm 102:11).

The Preacher says further, and rather ominously, that "it will not be well with the wicked" (Ecclesiastes 8:13; cf. Isaiah 3:11). If he is thinking about what happens after death, he is absolutely right. After they die, the wicked will face the judgment (see Hebrews 9:27). Their sins will be counted against them, their souls will be condemned to Hell, and they will be banished from God's presence forever. Do not envy the wicked, even when they seem to prosper. It will not go well for them on the Day of Judgment! No indeed, for the Bible says that they will be "thrown into the outer darkness," where there will be "weeping and gnashing of teeth" (Matthew 8:12).

All's Well That Ends Well

The Preacher is far more hopeful about people who lead a godly life. "I know that it will be well with those who fear God," he says, "because they fear before him" (Ecclesiastes 8:12). Usually the Preacher tells us what he "saw," but this time he chooses a different verb and tells us something that he "knows." This is not something that he has seen from a distance, but something he has grasped with the rational conviction of his own mind. His reply "is not an observation, but the answer of faith."[11] He believes what he cannot see—that one day all will be well for everyone who lives in the fear of God.

When the Bible talks about "the fear of God," it does not mean simply that people are afraid of God, although that may be part of it. Rather, the fear of God is what Michael Eaton calls "the awe and holy caution that arises from realization of the greatness of God."[12]

In this case, the realization of God's greatness also comes with a realization of his nearness. Those who fear God are said to "fear before him" (Ecclesiastes 8:12), meaning that they know they are in his presence. Most people, including many Christians, go through life hardly realizing that they are constantly in the presence of God. But the person who fears God knows that God is always near. He is with us when we are on our beds at night, worrying about tomorrow. He is with us when we have an opportunity for witness and are not sure what to say. He is with us when we have a sudden emergency and need supernatural help. To live a God-fearing life is to live in constant awareness of the presence of God, who is even closer than a prayer away. He is with us in the bedroom and the kitchen, in the car and on the bus, at the grocery store and at the football game. He is with us wherever we go.

The proper fear of God is an important theme throughout Ecclesiastes, but especially at the end. The Preacher has told us to fear God because he is sovereign over the times of life (Ecclesiastes 3:14) and also to fear God when we go into his house for worship (Ecclesiastes 5:1, 7). Later he will tell us to fear God by keeping his commandments (Ecclesiastes 12:13). Here he says that if we fear God, it will go well for us in days to come.

This promise will be fulfilled completely at the final judgment. Remember the words of the thief on the cross next to Christ. Two thieves were crucified that day, one on either side of Jesus. One of them mocked our Lord, but the other thief rebuked him by saying, "Do you not fear God?" (Luke 23:40). Then he demonstrated his own fear of God by asking the crucified Christ to be his Savior. "Jesus," he said, "remember me when you come into your kingdom" (Luke 23:42). This is the way for anyone to begin living in the fear of God: Ask Jesus to save you!

Anyone who asks for forgiveness will receive the same promise of eternal life that the thief received when he was dying on the cross next to Jesus. Jesus will say to us what he said to that thief: "You will be with me in Paradise" (Luke 23:43). It is for this reason, and for this reason alone, that all "will be well" for the man, the woman, or the child who fears God. It is only because Jesus died for our sins on the cross.

Do not use the delay of judgment as an excuse for not repenting of your sins or trusting in Jesus. According to Ecclesiastes 8—as well as what we read everywhere else in the Bible—there are only two kinds of people: those who fear God and those who don't! The Bible is equally clear that things will only go well for those who do. It may not always seem that way in this life. In fact, in all honesty sometimes it seems exactly the opposite, as Qoheleth tells us. But there will be final justice. The wicked will be buried, and after that they will be punished for their sins. As for the righteous, they will be vindicated by the grace of God. Justice is coming; it is only a matter of time.

It Is Well

One day all will be well for the God-fearing people of God. In the meantime, the Preacher has practical advice about the way we ought to live. The same fear of God that will lead us to eternal life also helps us find enjoyment in the here and now: "And I commend joy, for man has no good thing under the sun but to eat and drink and be joyful, for this will go with him in his toil through the days of his life that God has given him under the sun" (Ecclesiastes 8:15).

What the Preacher says here is similar to what he has said before in the so-called enjoyment passages of Ecclesiastes (see 2:24–26; 3:12–13, 22; 5:18–20). In spite of all the vanity "under the sun," it is possible for us to find genuine joy in the ordinary things of daily life. Indeed, that is one of the main points of this book. Here is how Augustine summarized its message: "Solomon gives over the entire book of Ecclesiastes to suggesting, with such fullness as he judged adequate, the emptiness of this life, with the ultimate objective, to be sure, of making us yearn for another kind of life which is no unsubstantial shadow under the sun but substantial reality under the sun's Creator."[13]

Some scholars offer a very different interpretation of verses like Ecclesiastes 8:15. They say that the Preacher is simply making the best of a bad situation, that Solomon is a cynic. If we are all going to die anyway, then why not seize the day? This verse, they say, "can only be understood as the expression of resignation."[14] Eat, drink, and be joyful, for tomorrow we die!

The problem with this view is that it does not do full justice to what the Preacher says. Nor does it recognize the genuine joy that we can experience while we are still waiting for final justice. Notice that the Preacher is giving us a God-centered perspective and that in verse 15 he is talking about the days of our lives as a gift from God. Notice as well that he mentions joy twice in this verse and describes it as something we can experience all through life. If God is always by our side, then we always have the deep contentment of knowing that he is near, even in our darkest trials.

Furthermore, the Preacher is growing more and more confident about this joy. Earlier he told us that he had found "nothing better" than joy (Ecclesiastes 2:24) and that he had "seen" joy (Ecclesiastes 5:18), but here he urges us to experience God's joy for ourselves. "I commend joy," he says (Ecclesiastes 8:15), and the word he uses for "commend" is a Hebrew word for praise (*shabach*). Yes, there is vanity under the sun. Yes, we see injustice that is hard to accept or understand. Yes, we have a lot of hard work to do. Nevertheless, there is joy for us in the ordinary things of life—eating, drinking, and sharing fellowship with the people of God. Dietrich Bonhoeffer wrote, "Our life is not only a great deal of trouble and hard work; it is also refreshment and joy in God's goodness. We labor, but God nourishes and sustains us. There is a reason to celebrate. . . . God is calling us to rejoice, to celebrate in the midst of our working day."[15]

Without the saving, personal knowledge of Jesus Christ and the certainty of eternal life, it is hard to have much joy at all. Even the best moments in life are tinged with sadness because we know that life will not last forever. One day we will have to die, and unless we know Christ, we live in the fearful expectation of judgment. The humanist Marghanita Laski was brutally honest about this when she summarized the human condition for a radio audience in Britain: "We are lonely, we are guilty and we are going to die."[16]

Contrast Laski's despair with the faith and joy of Lewis de Marolles, an old French Protestant who in 1685 was imprisoned for his faith in Jesus Christ (this was following the infamous revocation of the Edict of Nantes). De Marolles suffered many inhumane hardships for many years as he was put in chains, moved from dungeon to dungeon, and forced to serve as a galley slave. His captors constantly tried to persuade him to renounce his confession of faith. Indeed, they tried to crush his confidence in God and his hope of eternal life.

But de Marolles did not despair. He continued to call God his "dear and true friend." He fully resigned himself to the will of God. He wrote, "I am persuaded, that all states and conditions in which it shall please him to put me, are those states, in which he judges I shall glorify him *better* than in an infinite number of others which he might allot me." This is not to say that Lewis de Marolles never struggled with the injustice of it all. Indeed, in the last year of his life he went through a period of deep spiritual despondency, in which constant solitude and perpetual darkness presented his soul with "frightful and terrifying ideas" that made "fatal impressions" on his mind and plunged him "into a profound abyss of affliction."[17] Yet de Marolles had prayed for the grace to continue faithful unto death. Whenever doubts arose about the goodness of God, as they sometimes did, he comforted himself with the same truth that we read in Ecclesiastes 8:12. He said to himself, "It is—and it shall be—well."[18]

This is the testimony of everyone who believes in Jesus Christ and the grace that comes from his cross and the empty tomb. In spite of our present sufferings, it is well, for God is near. And it shall be well, because the God of justice and mercy will save us on the final day.

19

The Living and the Dead

ECCLESIASTES 8:16—9:6

*But he who is joined with all the living has
hope, for a living dog is better than a dead lion.
For the living know that they will die, but the
dead know nothing, and they have no more
reward, for the memory of them is forgotten.*

9:4–5

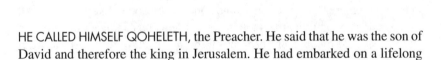

HE CALLED HIMSELF QOHELETH, the Preacher. He said that he was the son of
David and therefore the king in Jerusalem. He had embarked on a lifelong
quest to discover the meaning of life, as told in the book of Ecclesiastes.

Qoheleth's quest did not end the way that one might expect, however.
Usually when people try to figure out what life is all about, they hope to come
up with a simple, unambiguous answer—something memorable enough to
print on a poster and hang on a bedroom wall. But the Preacher-King never
seemed to get a final answer. The more he looked into things, the more he
struggled to make sense of his world.

Undoubtedly Qoheleth would have sympathized with the frustration that
Samuel Johnson felt when he finally published his famous dictionary. By the
time he was finished with his lexical masterpiece, Dr. Johnson had a definition for nearly every word in the English language. Yet not for a moment did
he think that he knew all the answers. Here is what he wrote in his preface:
"I saw that one enquiry only gave occasion to another, that book referred to
book, that to search was not always to find, and to find was not always to be
informed; and that thus to pursue perfection was . . . to chase the sun."[1]

So it was for the Preacher. Looking for the meaning of life was like chasing the sun. This helps us understand Ecclesiastes. It is not the kind of book that we keep reading until we reach the end and get the answer, like a mystery. Instead it is a book in which we keep struggling with the problems of life, and as we struggle, we learn to trust God with the questions even when we do *not* have all the answers. This is how the Christian life works: it is not just about what we get at the end, but also about what we become along the way. Discipleship is a journey, and not merely a destination.

A Frustrated Philosopher

At the end of Ecclesiastes 8, we find the Preacher still struggling with many of the same questions. The advice that he gave in verse 15 was good as far as it went, but it did not give him all of the answers that he was hoping to find. Thus he gives us the testimony of a frustrated philosopher:

> When I applied my heart to know wisdom, and to see the business that is done on earth, how neither day nor night do one's eyes see sleep, then I saw all the work of God, that man cannot find out the work that is done under the sun. However much man may toil in seeking, he will not find it out. Even though a wise man claims to know, he cannot find it out. (Ecclesiastes 8:16–17)

From everything that we have read so far (e.g., Ecclesiastes 1:13), we know that the Preacher is telling us the honest truth about his spiritual quest. He has been trying to learn as much about life as he can. Both by personal experience and by careful observation, he has tried to discover the truth about things as they actually are.

What has he learned so far? Only this: life is a weary business, and it is impossible to know for certain what God is doing in the world. If anyone tries to tell us any different—if anyone claims to have figured out the meaning of life or to have unlocked the secret plans of God—he is only telling a lie.

When the Preacher talks about sleepless days and nights, he may be telling us about his own insomnia.[2] The more he tried to figure out the meaning of life, the more anxious he became; he was up all night, trying to understand the ways of God and man. More likely, though, he is telling us the truth about our own restless days and sleepless nights. We are so busy that we never seem to get the rest we need. I sometimes dream about getting a Grunsday—an extra twenty-four hours tucked in between Wednesday and Thursday. Grunsday is a day for catching up—no one is allowed to make any phone calls or set up any appointments. Yet the sad reality is that not even Grunsday would help us. Give us eight days a week, and we would fill them with nine days of work. We never seem to get enough rest.

Then there is the weary business of trying to understand the work of

God. We see God's work, but we fail to understand it. No matter how wise we are, and no matter how much we "toil in seeking" (Ecclesiastes 8:17), we fail to comprehend his holy ways. Here Ecclesiastes confronts us with the limits of human knowledge. As of 2006, researchers estimated that the world generated almost 200 billion gigabytes of digital information every year.[3] Yet none of that data could even begin to explain the mysteries of the sovereignty of God. Many things in the divine government of the universe are simply beyond our capacity to know.

What is the best way for us to respond to this limitation? Some people look at all the confusion in the world and conclude that there is no God. Life is only "a tale told by an idiot, full of sound and fury, signifying nothing."[4] Others think that although there may be a God, he has no idea what he is doing. He is like the deity that Thomas Hardy wrote about—"the dreaming, dark, dumb Thing that turns the handle of this idle Show."[5]

Qoheleth does not give in to this kind of thinking. As skeptical as he is about his ability to know the mind of God, he nevertheless believes that what happens in the world is "the work of God" (Ecclesiastes 8:17). If we are wise, we too will admit there are many mysteries about life that we cannot comprehend, but we will admit this without doubting the existence of God or deciding that he is limited in his understanding.

Some people expect to have all the answers, and when they fail to find them, they get angry with God about what is happening (or not happening) in their lives. It is wiser for us humbly to admit that we are finite beings with fallen minds and that therefore we are incapable of understanding everything that happens. Francis Bacon was right when he warned us not to "draw down or submit the mysteries of God to our reason."[6] Instead we should lift our hearts to the praise of God, as Paul did when he confessed his faith in the great mysteries of the mind of God: "Oh, the depth of the riches and wisdom and knowledge of God! How unsearchable are his judgments and how inscrutable his ways! 'For who has known the mind of the Lord, or who has been his counselor?'" (Romans 11:33–34).

Rather than getting frustrated with all the things that we do not know about the world or do not understand about the ways of God, we are invited to rest content with our own limitations and to worship God for his superior wisdom. "Where reason fails, with all her powers," wrote Isaac Watts at the end of one of his many hymns, "there faith prevails, and love adores."[7]

In God's Hands

As Qoheleth wrestled with the ways of God, he had not yet reached the place of adoring love, but his faith did prevail. In the opening verses of chapter 9, we see him affirm his belief in the sovereignty of God and then wrestle with some of that doctrine's practical implications.

There may have been many things that the Preacher failed to understand, but he never gave up his faith that God was in charge: "But all this
I laid to heart, examining it all, how the righteous and the wise and their
deeds are in the hand of God" (Ecclesiastes 9:1). With these words, the
Preacher leaves God's people in God's hands. The Bible uses the image of
"the hand of God" to express God's power, love, supervision, and control.
Here the metaphor expresses his sovereign supervision of his people and
their actions. God really does have "the whole world in his hands," as the old
gospel song says. "Each one of us," writes T. M. Moore, "without regard for
what we've done in life, or whom we know, or what place we might occupy
in our society—each one is in the hand of God, and he decides for each of
us just what will be for us throughout our lives."[8]

For the faithful believer in Jesus Christ, the hand of God is an image
of comfort and assurance. We know that the hand of God is a hand of love.
We know this because we know that the hands of Jesus were pierced for our
transgressions when he was nailed to the tree. This gives us the hope and the
faith to leave everything in God's hands—all our burdens, all our trials, and
all our cares. The Savior who loves us and died for us will also care for us.

This is not the Preacher's perspective, however. He is writing before
the cross, of course, but he is also writing out of his struggle to understand
what God is doing in the world. His uncertainty comes out very clearly in
the second half of Ecclesiastes 9:1: "Whether it is love or hate, man does not
know; both are before him."

The meaning of this verse is debatable. The Preacher may be talking
about love and hate as human emotions. That is certainly what he means
in verse 6, where he talks about "*their* love and *their* hate." So perhaps in
verse 1 he is saying that human beings have trouble discerning the difference
between love and hate. Yet it is hard to see how this idea fits very well into
the flow of his argument. It seems better, therefore, to see love and hate as
attributes of God. When the Bible applies these terms to God, "love" refers
to his acceptance, and "hate" refers to his rejection. For example, when the
Lord says, "Jacob I loved, but Esau I hated" (Romans 9:13), he means that
Jacob is accepted by faith, but Esau is rejected in his unbelief.

The problem is that it is difficult (if not impossible) for us to know
whether God loves us or hates us, whether he will accept us or reject us.
Qoheleth is dealing here with the very real issue of where we stand before
God: "Whether it is love or hate, man does not know." Qoheleth has never
lost his grip on the sovereignty of God; so he knows that our fate is in God's
hands. What he does not know, however, is whether God's hand is for us
or against us. The Scripture says that God's "right hand is filled with righteousness" (Psalm 48:10), that we are "the sheep of his hand" (Psalm 95:7),
and that no one can ever snatch us out of his hand (John 10:28), even when
it comes time for us to die (Psalm 31:5). Yet the Scripture also says, "It is

a fearful thing to fall into the hands of the living God" (Hebrews 10:31). Therefore, it is not enough to know that we are in God's hands. Everyone is in God's hands. The question is whether God's hand is for us or against us. Is he our friend or our foe?

The Same Fate Happens to All

As the Preacher struggled with this question—is God for us or against us?—he discovered that it was virtually impossible to answer this question simply by looking at people's circumstances. Many people assume that if there is a God, he will reward his followers with earthly prosperity. If we want to know whether God is for someone or against someone, therefore, all we have to do is count their earthly blessings. This is not how God operates, however. As far as the Preacher could tell, he seems to treat everyone more or less the same, which makes it hard to figure out whether he "loves" us or "hates" us:

> It is the same for all, since the same event happens to the righteous and the wicked, to the good and the evil, to the clean and the unclean, to him who sacrifices and him who does not sacrifice. As the good one is, so is the sinner, and he who swears is as he who shuns an oath. This is an evil in all that is done under the sun, that the same event happens to all. (Ecclesiastes 9:2–3)

Earlier the Preacher assured us that things would go well for the righteous, but not for the wicked (Ecclesiastes 8:12–13). This will be true enough on the Day of Judgment. But in the meantime, the Preacher struggled to understand why the righteous were not blessed and the wicked were not cursed. Back in Ecclesiastes 8:14 he talked about a reversal of fortune, in which good people get what bad people deserve and vice versa. In Ecclesiastes 9:2–3 he makes a different point—not that there is a reversal of fortune, but that everyone suffers the same misfortune. One reason it is so hard to tell whether God is for us or against us is because the same things happen to everyone.

In saying that "it is the same for all," the Preacher carefully distinguishes between two kinds of people. One group is described as "righteous," "good," and "clean"; they offer sacrifices to God. The other group is described as "wicked," "evil," and "unclean." Not surprisingly, these people do not make any holy sacrifices to God. There is also a contrast between the vows that these people take. It is hard to be completely certain whether the Preacher thinks it is better to swear or to shun an oath. Earlier he warned against taking any hasty vows (Ecclesiastes 5:3–4). But here in chapter 9, where the positive side of each pair comes first, he seems to be saying that righteous people make a holy commitment to God (see, e.g., Deuteronomy 6:13), whereas wicked people refuse to enter into covenant with him. Either way, though, the overall comparison is clear: some people honor God, but other people do not.

Yet, strangely, both groups suffer the same fate. "It is the same for all," the Preacher says, and "the same event happens to all" (Ecclesiastes 9:2–3). If there are heavy storms, the righteous get flooded out with the wicked. If there is an earthquake, both of their houses fall down, and if there is a depression, they both go broke. Thinking more optimistically, when times are good, the rising tide will lift all boats. Therefore, we will never be able to separate the righteous from the wicked on the basis of what happens in the world. Since God "sends rain on the just and on the unjust" (Matthew 5:45), it is impossible to tell who has and who does not have God's eternal favor.

This frustrated the Preacher no end. In fact, he begins verse 3 by saying that the equivalence of earthly outcomes is an evil thing. Then he ends the verse by saying, once again, that human beings are desperately wicked: "Also, the hearts of the children of man are full of evil, and madness is in their hearts while they live, and after that they go to the dead" (Ecclesiastes 9:3; cf. 7:29; 8:11).

This is as frustrating as anything we have seen in Ecclesiastes. It all seems so futile. Does anything really matter? The Preacher ended chapter 8 by denying that anyone can understand the work that God does in the world. For a moment he gave us some hope that our lives were in the hands of a sovereign God, but then he said that it was impossible for us to know whether God is for us or against us—the same fate awaits us all. Here he tells us how desperately and discouragingly sinful we are.

The human heart is full of so much evil that it almost drives us out of our minds. The "madness" that the Preacher mentions may be defined as "a moral wildness that is impetuous and irrational."[9] People commit acts of lawless violence, like killing police officers. They pursue self-destructive addictions, like sex and drugs. They hurt the people they love the most and need the most, including the members of their own families. We are living in a mad, mad, mad, mad world.

Worst of all, we all die in the end. "After that," the Preacher says, "they go to the dead" (Ecclesiastes 9:3). Death is the great leveler. No matter who we are or how well we live, our time on earth will end in death—"the universal obliterator."[10] In the words of one bumper sticker, "Eat well, stay fit, and die anyway."

Better Alive Than Dead

Once again the Preacher is confronting us with our own mortality. Most people try to avoid even thinking about death, but Qoheleth talked about it as often as he could. Here he gives us another *memento mori*, or reminder of death, from the Latin phrase which means "remember that you must die."

What the Preacher says about death here is that it is better to be alive than dead. Sooner or later death will take us all. But:

> He who is joined with all the living has hope, for a living dog is better than a dead lion. For the living know that they will die, but the dead know nothing, and they have no more reward, for the memory of them is forgotten. Their love and their hate and their envy have already perished, and forever they have no more share in all that is done under the sun. (Ecclesiastes 9:4–6)

In order to compare life and death, the Preacher repeats a memorable proverb, which contrasts a living dog with a dead lion. The lion is a noble beast, as everyone knows (see Proverbs 30:30). This was especially true in Biblical times, when the lion served as the royal insignia of the house of David—the emblem of our Messiah (see Genesis 49:9). By contrast, few animals were more despised than dogs. Some people are fond of dogs, but in those days they were considered wild and filthy animals. The kind of dog that Qoheleth has in mind is not a household pet but a "contemptible cur who ranged the streets as a scavenger."[11] To get a sense of the way people regarded dogs in those days, think of Goliath's taunt to the boy David: "Am I a dog, that you come to me with sticks?" (1 Samuel 17:43).

Even the most ardent dog-lover would admit that dogs are no comparison to lions. When people go to the zoo, for example, they do not go to see the hyenas (if the zoo even has any). They want to see the lion exhibit, of course. Yet the situation changes if the lion happens to be dead. Then the dog comes out on top because at least he is alive!

The simple point is that living is better than dying. Here the Preacher mentions some of the problems with death. Death brings ignorance, for the dead know nothing—at least nothing about what is happening on earth. The end of verse 6 makes it clear that the Preacher is not denying the afterlife but is describing the totally permanent end that death brings to our earthly existence. As soon as we die, we forever forfeit our "share in all that is done under the sun" (Ecclesiastes 9:6). Death also brings irreparable loss, for the dead do not gain any earthly reward (or heavenly reward, for that matter, if they die outside of Christ). Death also brings oblivion; no one remembers the dead when they are gone. Even the earthly emotions that make us feel the most alive—feelings like the love and hatred and envy that the Preacher mentions in verse 6—will all disappear when we die.

When we consider all of the things that we lose through death—the people whom we love and all the little joys of life on this beautiful planet—it ought to make us appreciate the fact that we are still alive and breathing. However difficult life may be, at least it is better than the alternative! Where there's life, there's hope.

Life after Death

Yet what hope does life really give us? In verse 4 the Preacher refers to this hope in general terms, but in verse 5 he gets more specific: "the living know that they will die." This may seem like small comfort. Relatively speaking, life is better than death, but the main advantage of living turns out to be the knowledge of dying. How hopeful is that? According to some Bible scholars, this is only "a sarcastic or bitter preference."[12] Life may be better than nothing, but not by much.

It is possible to see what the Preacher says in a somewhat more positive light, however. It is better to be conscious than unconscious, so what the Preacher says is true: better alive than dead. Furthermore, it is good for us to know that we will die because this gives us time to prepare for death, and also for eternity.

Nevertheless, we need to acknowledge that this is one of the most pessimistic passages in Ecclesiastes. According to Derek Kidner, this section of the book "confronts us with the little that we know, then with the vast extent of what we cannot handle: in particular, with death."[13] It does this without giving any clear indication of a life to come. But if life only ends in death, what hope is there at all?

The British preacher and evangelist David Watson tells about a medical student who came to see him after dissecting his first cadaver. The student was deeply shaken by the experience, because as he cut through muscle and other tissue to expose the body's internal organs, he said to himself, "If this is all that we become at death, what is the point of anything?"[14]

To answer this question, we need to look beyond this chapter to the end of the book, where the Scripture says that this life is not the only life there is. Ecclesiastes 9 tells us about life "under the sun," which raises the possibility of some other kind of life, in some other place. When we get to chapter 12, we discover that there is also a life above, where "the spirit returns to God who gave it" (v. 7), and a life to come, when "God will bring every deed into judgment" (v. 14).

We also need to look beyond Ecclesiastes to the gospel of Jesus Christ and the promise of the resurrection. Ecclesiastes does not have all the answers, nor does it claim to. Remember, this is not the kind of book that we keep reading until we get the answer, but the kind of book that helps us know how to serve God when we do *not* have all the answers. It is also part of a larger book that gives fuller answers to many of the same questions that Ecclesiastes only begins to address. This book, says Derek Kidner, "pushes us towards a synthesis which lies mostly beyond its own pages; in this case, the prospect of reward and punishment in the world to come."[15] Therefore, we always need to read Ecclesiastes in the context of the whole Bible.

What does the rest of the Bible teach us about the life to come? It teaches us that Jesus Christ, the Son of God, has gone ahead of us into glory. First Jesus gave his life for our sins by dying on the cross. Then he was buried in the ground; he was as dead as dead could be. But on the third day he rose to immortality, bringing eternal life out of the deadly grave.

Now the promise of God for every believer in Christ is that we too shall live. "Our belief in Christ raises us up to heaven and promises eternity to our souls."[16] This means that our lives will not end in mindless oblivion. We will never suffer endless loss. On the contrary, death will be our passage to glory. "Blessed are the dead," the Bible says, "who die in the Lord" (Revelation 14:13). We will rest from all our labors. We will enter the presence of God and know the fullness of his joy. Our bodies will rise, never to die again. By the mercy of God, we will be "born again to a living hope through the resurrection of Jesus Christ from the dead, to an inheritance that is imperishable, undefiled, and unfading" (1 Peter 1:3–4). All of this is only the beginning, because "no eye has seen, nor ear heard, nor the heart of man imagined, what God has prepared for those who love him" (1 Corinthians 2:9).

What hope these promises bring to life, and what confidence they give us for the day of death! Consider the dying words of the infamous Giacomo Casanova. Like the Solomon of Ecclesiastes, Casanova had tasted almost everything that life has to offer, including many sinful pleasures. We know from his writings that none of these experiences ever satisfied his soul. Yet we also know, by the testimony of multiple witnesses, that his last words expressed his hope in resurrection life. "I have lived as a philosopher," Casanova said, "and die as a Christian."[17]

As we read Ecclesiastes, we learn something about what it means to live as a philosopher. With the Preacher as our guide, we experience almost everything that life has to offer and struggle to find the answers to life's questions. Many of us have learned some of the same lessons from our own experiments with life and our own experiences of suffering. Like Casanova, we have "lived as philosophers."

But will we die as Christians? This is the most important question of all. If we are wise, we will get ready to die now by asking Jesus to forgive our sins and by trusting him to raise our dead bodies to eternal life. Then, when we come to the last of our days, we will be ready to die with full confidence in Christ.

20

The Good Life

ECCLESIASTES 9:7–10

Go, eat your bread with joy,
and drink your wine with a merry heart,
for God has already approved what you do.
Let your garments be always white.
Let not oil be lacking on your head.

9:7–8

PEOPLE MAY NOT SING IT MUCH ANYMORE, but the following song was popular in its day:

> You're gonna take that ocean trip, no matter come what may;
>   You've got your reservations made, but you just can't get away.
> Next year for sure, you'll see the world, you'll really get around;
>   But how far can you travel when you're six feet under ground?

Then the refrain:

> Enjoy yourself, it's later than you think!
>   Enjoy yourself, while you're still in the pink.
> The years go by, as quickly as a wink,
>   Enjoy yourself, enjoy yourself, it's later than you think.[1]

"Enjoy Yourself" was written in the 1930s and popularized in the 1950s, but its perspective on life is as old as Ecclesiastes. Our time on earth is short, so we had better make the most of it, finding joy in its many pleasures.

Making the Most of It

This may seem like a surprising perspective for Qoheleth to take. From the opening words of Ecclesiastes, he has been telling us mostly about the troubles of life. Our existence under the sun is vanity and striving after the wind. Yet this is not the Preacher's only theme. He speaks to pleasure as well as to pain, especially in the so-called "enjoyment passages" of Ecclesiastes. At the end of chapter 2 he talked about eating and drinking (vv. 24–26). In the middle of chapter 3 he spoke about joyfully doing good as long as we live (vv. 12–13). In chapter 5 he explained how "good and fitting" it is for us to find enjoyment in our work, because this is our lot in life (v. 18). Then in chapter 8 he went farther and commended joy as a lifestyle (v. 15).

These passages pose a major challenge in interpreting the book of Ecclesiastes because they seem to contradict what the Preacher says about the frustration of life under the sun. For this reason some commentators see them as ironic: when the Preacher tells us to enjoy life, he is speaking cynically or sarcastically. According to this interpretation, the Preacher's attitude is encapsulated in the old Latin expression *carpe diem*: "Seize the day!"[2] Since life has nothing better to offer than pleasure, we might as well get as much of it as we can. "Let us eat and drink, for tomorrow we die" (1 Corinthians 15:32). This is the best that a man (or woman) can get.

Some commentators also draw comparisons with similar passages in other ancient writings. By way of example, consider these words from *The Epic of Gilgamesh*, an Akkadian poem from the time of Abraham, or even earlier:

> Gilgamesh, fill your belly—
> Day and night make merry,
> Let days be full of joy,
> Dance and make music day and night.
> And wear fresh clothes,
> And wash your head and bathe.
> Look at the child that is holding your hand,
> And let your wife delight in your embrace.
> These things alone are the concern of men.[3]

The point these scholars make is not that Ecclesiastes is based on *Gilgamesh*, as if this were a case of literary dependency, but that Qoheleth has the same attitude toward life. We find something similar in writings from ancient Egypt: "Flow thy desire, so long as thou livest. Put myrrh on thine head, clothe thee in fine linen, and anoint thee . . . and vex not thine heart—until that day of lamentation cometh to thee."[4]

There are at least two good reasons why we should be careful not to minimize what the Preacher says about joy, but rather take it seriously as part of the truth about life. First, the enjoyment passages give us a balanced perspective. It is true that Qoheleth has a lot to say about vanity and striving after wind. Yet it should not surprise us that he also has something to teach us about joy, because this is the way life really is. For all our difficulty and despair, there are also many things that we are able to enjoy. Life is bitter and sweet, and if we fail to perceive both of these tastes, we fail to experience life as it actually should be lived.

The Preacher saw life in its full complexity, and he wants us to see it too. We have tried to give full weight to all of the struggles he had with life under the sun. But if we want to gain the man's wisdom, we need to see his optimism as well as his pessimism. The same Preacher who said "all is vanity" also came to believe that there is joy to life, which is part of having a balanced view. According to Martin Luther, the Solomon of Ecclesiastes "is not urging a life of pleasure and luxury characteristic of those who do not sense this vanity, for that would be putting oil on fire; but he is speaking of godly men, who sense the vexation and troubles of the world. It is their downcast hearts that he wants to encourage."[5]

Another reason why we need to hear the Preacher's call to joy is because all of the passages where he gives this call have God at their center. This immediately distinguishes Ecclesiastes from ancient writings like *The Epic of Gilgamesh*. Why should we enjoy eating and drinking and working? In chapter 2 it is because these activities come "from the hand of God" (v. 24). In chapter 3 it is because these activities are "God's gift to man" (v. 13). The same is true in chapter 5, which also says that God keeps us "occupied with joy" in our hearts (v. 20). The Preacher may be frustrated with life in this fallen world, but he still acknowledges the gifts that come from the hand of God.

We see this perhaps most clearly in Ecclesiastes 9, where the Preacher tells us to enjoy bread and wine because "God has already approved what you do" (v. 7). This is not a blanket endorsement of everything that people do, as if God would ever approve of wickedness. Nor is it a full statement of the doctrine of justification—that we are accepted by the righteousness of God. Primarily the Preacher is saying that our eating and drinking enjoy the blessing of God. Life's enjoyments are not guilty pleasures but godly pleasures—or at least they ought to be. A merry heart has God's approval. It is part of his gracious will for our lives.

The Pleasures of Life

What kinds of pleasure has God given his people to enjoy? The Preacher mentions at least three pleasures in particular: contentment, comfort, and companionship.[6]

He begins with the basic pleasures of eating and drinking: "Go, eat your bread with joy, and drink your wine with a merry heart" (Ecclesiastes 9:7). The word "go" conveys a sense of urgency. This statement is not descriptive but imperative. We are hereby commanded to eat our bread and drink our wine (yes, wine) with joyful hearts. It is not so much the eating and drinking that the Preacher is after, but the heartfelt joy. As we share table fellowship with one another—as we break fresh bread, sip fine wine, and taste all the other good food and drink that God provides—we are charged to receive each pleasure with God-centered joy in the heart.

The celebration continues in verse 8: "Let your garments be always white. Let not oil be lacking on your head." White garments were the "dress-up clothes" of the ancient Near East. Many festive occasions were adorned with robes of white. They were worn by war heroes in a victory parade, by slaves on the day they gained their freedom, and by priests on the high holy days of Israel (e.g., 2 Chronicles 5:12). To put this into a contemporary context, the Preacher is telling us to put on tuxedos and evening gowns so we can dance the night away.

Qoheleth also tells us to wear sweet perfume. To anoint someone's head with oil (see Psalm 23:5) was to pour out something richly scented, like cologne—what the Bible terms "the oil of gladness" (Psalm 45:7). This is an important part of getting ready for a celebration—not just looking good but also smelling good, especially in a hot climate. The Preacher is telling us to prepare for a party.

There is more. The Preacher also invites us to "enjoy life with the wife whom you love" (Ecclesiastes 9:9). Literally he says, "with the woman you love," but he is not just saying, "Love the one you're with." As Tremper Longman has argued persuasively in his commentary, the woman in view is understood to be the man's beloved wife.[7] The Preacher is commending the daily pleasures of marriage and family life.

Here it seems appropriate to give a word of practical exhortation to married couples. We could apply the principle of this verse to other relationships, of course. The love between a man and his wife is not the only pleasure we can experience in human friendship. But here the Bible gives a specific command to husbands, who need to pay attention to exactly what the Preacher says.

Every husband is called to enjoy his wife. This means spending time together as friends. In all the busy demands of life, set aside time to do things together that you both enjoy. It means prizing one another as lovers. Speak terms of affection and get away—just the two of you—to fuel the fires of romantic love. Enjoying one's wife also means valuing her as a person. Listen carefully to what she says, without immediately pointing out where she's wrong or trying to solve problems that she's not even asking you to solve until she has been understood. These are only a few of the many ways that husbands are called to enjoy their wives.

At this point some husbands (and not a few wives) will be tempted to complain that their wives (or husbands) are not always easy to enjoy. The romance of marriage is long gone, and sometimes even the friendship seems to be over. If that is the case, then we need to notice exactly how the Preacher words this command: the wife whom we are told to "enjoy" is also the wife whom we are said to "love." Maybe your wife or your husband is hard to enjoy very much right now, but can you at least obey God's command to love? For husbands, this means loving their wives with the same costly, sacrificial love that Jesus demonstrated when he died for our sins on the cross (see Ephesians 5:25–30). It is hard to see how any man will enjoy his wife (or how she can possibly enjoy him) unless he is committed to loving her in a Christlike way.

Love and enjoyment go together (as we see from Solomon's love poems in the Song of Songs). If you love one another, be intentional about enjoying one another. But if you are having trouble staying in love, ask God for the grace to love again, the way you used to, or maybe the way you never have but know you should. Here the Preacher says what the Bible says to husbands again and again and, frankly, what most husbands need to hear all the time: love your wives (cf. Ephesians 5:25, 28, 33).

Surprisingly, the call to marital love is only a short-term calling; it is only for this life, not for eternity. Thus the Preacher tells husbands to enjoy their wives "all the days of your vain life that he has given you under the sun, because that is your portion in life" (Ecclesiastes 9:9). This is hardly the kind of statement that a woman is hoping to find written on her anniversary card! The Preacher is no more sentimental about marriage than he is about anything else in life. But this does not make him a cynic. On the contrary, he is giving a serious view of life that makes room for joy but also faces up to the sober realities of life in a fallen world and the inevitable reality of death.

When Qoheleth says that life is "vain," he uses the same word for vanity (*hebel*) that he has used throughout the book of Ecclesiastes. In this particular context he is not saying that life is meaningless but rather that life is short. Our earthly existence passes quickly, like smoke blown away by the wind. Thus we should engage in love while we still have the time.

The last pleasure that the Preacher mentions is work, which is part of our portion in life: "Enjoy . . . your toil at which you toil under the sun" (Ecclesiastes 9:9). The phrase "under the sun" does not refer to backbreaking labor in the heat of the day but to the regular calling of our earthly existence—whatever God has called us to do. Whether we labor in law or science or education or construction or medicine or ministry or the arts (or in all of these areas through the high calling of homemaking), God has given us good work to do. As the Preacher has said before, this work is a gift from God that we should enjoy as long as we can.

He goes on in verse 10 to reinforce what he says about work by giving a strong command: "Whatever your hand finds to do, do it with your might" (Ecclesiastes 9:10). Here the Bible tells us what to do, namely, whatever lies near at hand. The point is not that we should work randomly or do whatever we please. Rather, in the course of God's providence some things lie in the path of our duty—things that are pleasing to God. But we can only do what God has given us to do, not the things that he has placed out of our reach. In his sermon on this verse Charles Spurgeon described a young man who dreamed of standing under a banyan tree and preaching eloquent sermons to people in India. "My dear fellow," said Spurgeon, "why don't you try the streets of London first, and see whether you are eloquent there!"[8] Each one of us should do whatever work God has given us to do, not what he has given someone else to do.

The Preacher also tells us the way to do this work—not just what to do but *how* to do it: with all our might (cf. Romans 12:11; Colossians 3:23). As we have the opportunity, we should work with all our strength. How easy it is to while away the hours, not focusing on the things we know God wants us to do but idling away our time with lots of little distractions. Are you giving God 100 percent of your working time, or are you giving him something less than your very best? The Puritan William Perkins said, "We must take heed of two damnable sins. . . . The first is idleness, whereby the duties of our callings . . . are neglected or omitted. The second is slothfulness, whereby they are performed slackly and carelessly."[9] Ecclesiastes 9:10 is the perfect remedy for both of these sins because it tells us both what to do and how to do it: whatever we are called to do, with all our strength.

Pleasure's Danger

The spirit of what the Preacher says about the pleasures of wine, women, and work is captured well by Eugene Peterson's loose paraphrase in *The Message*:

> Seize life! Eat bread with gusto,
> Drink wine with a robust heart.
> Oh yes – God takes pleasure in your pleasure!
> Dress festively every morning.
> Don't skimp on colors and scarves.
> Relish life with the spouse you love
> Each and every day of your precarious life.
> Each day is God's gift. It's all you get in exchange
> For the hard work of staying alive.

Make the most of each one!

Whatever turns up, grab it and do it! And heartily! (Ecclesiastes 9:7–10)

There are millions of ways to apply this passage, with its call to Christian hedonism. This is a beautiful, bountiful world, and we were designed to enjoy its pleasures. So make the most of every day. This week I have tasted some of the little joys of life (most of them free): a warm piece of cornbread, fresh from the oven; the sight of two hawks soaring high over the city on their daily hunt; an evening with friends; shooting baskets and playing catch with my sons; a good strong hug from each of my three daughters. To have these joys is to know my Father's grace.

But there is also a deadly spiritual danger in the pursuit of pleasure. We may get so distracted by earthly pleasures that we lose our passion for God. How tempting it is to worship the gift and forget the Giver!

Some people live for food. They make a god out of their belly (Philippians 3:19), and thus they are guilty of gluttony (which has little or nothing to do with how much people weigh, but everything to do with our attitude toward food). Some people are addicted to wine or strong drink. They are guilty of drunkenness and dissipation (Luke 21:34). Others live for a relationship. Maybe it is the romance they have, which has turned inward rather than outward, in service to others. Or maybe it is the relationship they do not have, which has become one of their main frustrations in life. Then there are all the people who live for their work, when in fact they are living for the money that their work produces, or for prestige and approval, or to avoid problems at home.

The pleasures that people pursue are usually good in themselves. The danger comes when they take the place of God. "Sin is not just the doing of bad things," writes Tim Keller, "but the making of good things into *ultimate* things. It is seeking to establish a sense of self by making something else more central to your significance, purpose, and happiness than your relationship to God."[10] The list of good things that can get in the way of God is endless. For some people it may be new clothes or video games. For others it may be antiques and opera music, or sports, or academics, or the hobby that takes up all their weekends. The world is full of good things that bring pleasure to life but were never intended to satisfy the soul. When we pursue these things apart from a relationship with God, we end up losing the joy that they can bring to life.

The Grace of Gratitude

Some Christians deal with this danger by self-denial. Rather than letting certain pleasures lead them astray, they deny them altogether. They follow the rules that the Colossians used to make: "Do not handle, Do not taste, Do not touch" (Colossians 2:21).

Admittedly, there may be some pleasures that some people should deny—not as an absolute rule for all Christians everywhere, but as a matter of personal wisdom. "'All things are lawful,'" the Scripture says, "but not all things are helpful" (1 Corinthians 10:23). For example, it may be wise for someone who has abused alcohol to vow never to take another sip of wine. Or it may be wise for someone who watches too much television to lock the TV set in the closet for a year. Things that are not wrong in themselves may nevertheless be wrong for a particular person or at a particular time.

In general, though, this is not the approach that the Bible teaches us to take with the good things of life. What it tells us to do instead is to receive pleasure with gratitude, returning our thanks to God. One of the best ways for us to keep the good things of life in their proper perspective is to praise the Giver for all of his gifts. "Everything created by God is good," the Scripture says, "and nothing is to be rejected *if* it is received with thanksgiving" (1 Timothy 4:4).

This gives us a good test to use for all our earthly pleasures. We can ask ourselves: When I pray, is this something I would feel good about including in my thanksgiving, or would I be embarrassed to mention it? Am I thanking God for this pleasure, or have I been enjoying it without ever giving him a second thought? When we are enjoying legitimate pleasures in a God-honoring way, it seems natural to include them in our prayers. But when we pursue them for their own sake, usually we do not pray about them much at all (or about anything else, for that matter).

God alone "is the source of all the gifts of earthly life: its bread and wine, festivity and work, marriage and love."[11] Every pleasure comes from the God of all pleasure, and therefore it should be received with thanksgiving and praise. Elizabeth Barrett Browning wrote, "Earth's crammed with heaven, / And every common bush afire with God; / But only he who sees, takes off his shoes / The rest sit round it and pluck blackberries."[12] See the gifts that God has given to you, and then respond with holy praise.

This is why we pray before we eat (and maybe afterward, too, the way my grandparents always did). We are giving thanks to the God who put bread on our table and drink in our glass. We should view marriage the same way—as something good that is intended to point us to God. The Puritan Caroline Perthes gave this advice to her married daughter: "Your mutual love can be a means of happiness and blessing, only as it increases your love to God."[13] Our work can give us the same kind of blessing, provided that we receive it as a gift from God and then offer it back to him in joyful service. For people who enjoy as many blessings as we do, the words "Thank you, Father" should never be far from our grateful lips.

This is especially true for everyone who knows the grace of God through the saving work of Jesus Christ—his death on the cross for our sins and his return from the grave with the free gift of eternal life. We have even more to celebrate than the Preacher of Ecclesiastes because we know "the good news of great joy" that God announced through the coming of Christ (see Luke 2:10). It is for this reason, most of all, that we are able to eat our bread with joy, drink wine with a merry heart, enjoy life with the people we love, and find enjoyment in the hard work of our daily calling. It is all because we know the Savior.

The pleasures in Ecclesiastes 9 are all pleasures that Jesus enjoyed during his earthly ministry or enjoys now in his eternal kingdom. When Jesus broke bread for his disciples (see John 6:11) and when he lifted up the cup of their salvation (see Luke 22:19–20), he gave thanks to his Father in Heaven. Whatever work Jesus ever did for our salvation, he did with all his might. "My food," he said, "is to do the will of him who sent me and to accomplish his work" (John 4:34). Now Jesus is waiting for his eternal bride, which is one of the common metaphors the Bible uses for the people of God (e.g., Ephesians 5:31–32). Jesus desires to enjoy life with us, the people he loves.

One of the best ways for us to enjoy life with Jesus is by sharing in his pleasures. All of the good things mentioned in Ecclesiastes 9 symbolize the gifts of his grace. Jesus gives us our daily bread (see Luke 11:3). He makes our hearts glad with the bread and the wine of the Lord's Supper. He has anointed our heads with oil—the oil of the Holy Spirit. He has invited us to the wedding supper of Heaven, where he will be our worthy groom and we will be his beautiful bride (see Revelation 19:7, 9). He has promised to give us spotless white to wear in his eternal kingdom, where we will join the celebration that never ends (see Revelation 7:9, 14). From here to eternity, every pleasure we enjoy is a gift from our everlasting Savior.

Numbering Our Days

In the meantime, Jesus has given us good work to do—the work of his kingdom. We should do this work as well as we can, for as long as we have the opportunity, because—as usual—the Preacher ends by reminding us that our days are numbered. Here is his sober motivation for working with all our might: "for there is no work or thought or knowledge or wisdom in Sheol, to which you are going" (Ecclesiastes 9:10).

The word "Sheol" is not a synonym for Hell but simply refers to the place of the dead, whether good or evil. Martin Luther said it well: Sheol is "the hidden resting-place . . . outside of the present life, where the soul departs to its place."[14] When the Preacher says that there is no work or wisdom there, he may sound as if he denies the afterlife.[15] But the Preacher is not trying to answer our questions about what does or does not happen to us after we die; to answer those questions we need to turn to other places in Scripture. He simply is saying that we are all going to die and that when we do, it will be the end of our work on earth, the end of everything we know about what is happening in the world, and the end of all our earthly pleasures.

If it is true that our work time is limited, then we need to be sure that we do the most important work of the soul, which is to repent of our sin and believe in Jesus Christ for our salvation. Once we have done that, we may enjoy the good life that God has given to us as long as we can and work hard at living for Jesus, sharing the gospel, loving our neighbors, and doing all of the other kingdom things that God has called us to do. Jesus said something similar: "We must work the works of him who sent me while it is day; night is coming, when no one can work" (John 9:4).

The time is short. This makes some Christians think that we do not have time for the joyous activities described in Ecclesiastes 9, like celebrating, and maybe even marrying. But these things still have their place in life. In fact, the right kind of enjoyment will prove to be one of our best preparations for eternity. Our earthly pleasures are telling us that we were made for another world. Every honest day's work brings us one day closer to our eternal rest. Every good meal is a reminder that we have been invited to the last and the best of all banquets. Every God-centered party anticipates the heavenly celebration that will never end.

Marriage too is part of our preparation for glory. In his book on marriage, Bishop Jeremy Taylor acknowledged that one day everything that pleases us about marriage will pass away. "At the resurrection," he said, "there shall be no relation of husband and wife, and no marriage shall be celebrated but the marriage of the Lamb." Nevertheless, Taylor said, we will all remember that there was such a thing on earth as marriage, and we will see for ourselves that it was part of our preparation for eternity. Whenever we saw an eager groom and his bride dressed in white, we were catching a glimpse of the eternal love that Jesus has for all his people.

One day we will enter the full joy of that love. Taylor described what that day will be like for Christian couples: even though they will no longer be married, they will nevertheless "pass to the spiritual and eternal, where love shall be their portion, and joys shall crown their heads, and they shall lie in the bosom of Jesus, and in the heart of God, to eternal ages."[16]

These joys are not just for husbands and wives but for all the children of God. What Bishop Taylor said about marriage is true of every good thing in life. One day love will be our portion, joy will crown our heads, and we will rest with Jesus in the heart of our God forever. When we receive these pleasures in Heaven, we will realize that we first experienced them here on earth. Every earthly joy is the foretaste of a better life to come, in the Paradise where God has promised us pleasures forevermore (Psalm 16:11).

21

Man Knows Not His Time

ECCLESIASTES 9:11–18

Again I saw that under the sun the race is
not to the swift, nor the battle to the strong,
nor bread to the wise, nor riches to the intelligent,
nor favor to those with knowledge,
but time and chance happen to them all.
For man does not know his time.

9:11–12

YOU NEVER KNOW what will happen next. Disaster can strike at any time, including the moment when you least expect it.

Consider the curious case of Molière, the French actor and playwright. While performing the title role in the final scene of his own drama *The Hypochondriac, or The Imaginary Invalid*, Molière was seized by a violent coughing fit. As it turned out, his malady was no imagination. Molière died just a few hours later.[1]

Or consider the sad fate of America's leading psychic, Jeanne Dixon. On January 2, 1997 Dixon predicted that a "famous entertainer will leave a nation in mourning within weeks." Whether the nation mourned or not, just three weeks later Dixon herself died of a heart attack.[2] It is doubtful that she ever saw it coming.

Here is another example. Bob Cartwright was disappointed when he was unable to accept an invitation to fly to New York with his friend Tyler Stanger and the professional baseball player Cory Lidle for a playoff game between the Yankees and the Tigers. He felt differently when he saw the news that Stanger and Lidle had crashed into an apartment building and perished. "I was supposed to be on that plane," Cartwright said. Yet just one month later Cartwright died in another plane crash, near his mountain home in California.[3]

Then there is Donald Peters, who bought two Connecticut lottery tickets on November 1, 2008—just as he had for the previous twenty years. As it turned out, one of his tickets was worth $10 million. But Peters was not as lucky as one might think, because he died of a heart attack later on the very day that he bought the winning ticket.[4]

None of these unfortunate, unexpected events would have surprised the Preacher who wrote Ecclesiastes. "Time and chance happen to them all," he would have said. "Man knows not his time."

Time and Chance

Once again Ecclesiastes confronts us with one of the frustrations of life in a fallen world. Earlier we learned, somewhat to our surprise, that good things do not necessarily happen to good people: "The same event happens to the righteous and the wicked" (Ecclesiastes 9:2). When he said this, the Preacher was thinking in moral categories. The same things happen to everyone, whether good or evil.

Verse 11 takes the same basic principle and applies it to people's various talents. Ordinarily we would expect things to go well for people with strong abilities. Often they do, but having speed or strength or smarts does not guarantee success. So the Preacher said, "Again I saw that under the sun the race is not to the swift, nor the battle to the strong, nor bread to the wise, nor riches to the intelligent, nor favor to those with knowledge, but time and chance happen to them all" (Ecclesiastes 9:11).

The Preacher mentions five kinds of people that one would expect to be winners, yet sometimes turn out to be losers. Usually the fastest person wins the race, but not always. Think of the tortoise and the hare. Or, to give a little-known but striking example from Scripture, think of Asahel and Abner. Asahel was as fast as a gazelle; so when he pursued Abner in battle, Abner had no chance to outrun him. But Abner did have a weapon, and he knew how to use it. So when Asahel overtook him, Abner impaled the faster man with a spear (2 Samuel 2:17–23). Speaking of battles, usually the strongest man wins the fight, but sometimes the weaker man wins. The most famous example, of course, is David and Goliath—the story that gives hope to every underdog. The Olympic slogan says *citius, altius, fortius*—swifter, higher, stronger! But the race is not always won by the swift, nor the battle always by the strong.

Then the Preacher augments his list of physical attributes by mentioning several intellectual abilities. Ordinarily we would expect someone with a superior mind to be worth a fortune, or at least to make a good living. But when the markets crash, even the sharpest financial adviser suddenly realizes that he is not as smart as he thought he was. At the same time, some of the people living at a homeless shelter are smarter than average. What the Preacher says is true: the wise do not always have bread, intelligence does not guarantee a good income, and having a lot of knowledge will not necessarily do us any favors.

In short, human ability is no guarantee of success in life. Disaster can overtake any one of us. As the Preacher says, "time and chance" happen to us all. This phrase does not deny the sovereignty of God. We know that God "works all things according to the counsel of his will" (Ephesians 1:11). Everything is under his wise providence and sovereign control. What happens in life is not arbitrary, therefore, but is subject to God's authority.

From our perspective, however, there is still a problem: we do not necessarily know what God is doing. No matter how strong we are, or how smart, many bad things happen to us in life, and there is no way for us to predict when they will happen. Earlier Qoheleth told us that there is a time for everything (Ecclesiastes 3:1–8). Here he tells us that we do not know when that time will be: "Man does not know his time" (Ecclesiastes 9:12).

The Preacher illustrates this truth with a pair of vivid images, drawn from nature: "Like fish that are taken in an evil net, and like birds that are caught in a snare, so the children of man are snared at an evil time, when it suddenly falls upon them" (Ecclesiastes 9:12). The fish and the birds get caught before they know it. If they had realized they were swimming into a net or flying into a snare, they would have gone the opposite direction. But by the time they were trapped, it was too late to escape.

The same thing happens to human beings. "Time" and "chance" happen to us all. The word "time" may refer generally to the seasons of life. In the words of Martin Luther, "You should understand 'time' here not to refer only to the end of life but to every appointed time and outcome."[5] The word can also be used more specifically to refer to an appointed time of divine judgment (e.g., Ezekiel 7:7). Either way, the time will come when events overtake us. Before we know it, we will get trapped in a bad situation at work, or afflicted with a fatal disease, or caught in a financial tsunami. At the very end, of course, the time will come for us to die and go to judgment—a time that God knows, but we do not.

If "time" does not overtake us, then "chance" will. This word does not mean something like "fate" but refers to an occurrence—something that happens to us in life. From the rest of verse 12, which talks about "an evil net" and "an evil time," it is clear that when the Preacher talks about "chance," he is not talking about something good that happens but something bad. In a fallen world, many unhappy things happen every day, from natural disasters and environmental catastrophes to military conflicts and economic downturns.

Life is unpredictable; its misfortunes are inevitable and often inescapable.

In his mercy God tells us to expect the unexpected. When hardship comes, even when it comes very suddenly, we should not be surprised. Nor, when life is good, should we think that our own natural abilities will spare us from having hard times. No matter how gifted we are or how well prepared or how many advantages we have in life, we too may suffer an evil day.

Wisdom Exemplified

How should we respond when the evil day comes? And how should we live with the uncertainty of knowing that something bad could happen at any time?

At this point, some people are tempted to give up and to think there is nothing we can do except resign ourselves to our fate. If the race does not go to the swift, then why run at all? If the battle is not won by the strong, then why prepare for war? If getting smart will not get you more money, then why bother to develop your mind? Since it all comes down to chance anyway, fatalism might appear to be the only honest option.

The Preacher gives a different response. He commends the relative value of earthly wisdom, telling us to live wisely. The Preacher does this first by giving us the example of someone wise (Ecclesiastes 9:13–15) and then by comparing wisdom to several (less advantageous) alternatives (Ecclesiastes 9:16–18). We can add to this by making our own application of wisdom to daily life—wisdom exemplified, wisdom prioritized, and wisdom applied.

Here is the Preacher's example: "I have also seen this example of wisdom under the sun, and it seemed great to me. There was a little city with few men in it, and a great king came against it and besieged it, building great siegeworks against it. But there was found in it a poor, wise man, and he by his wisdom delivered the city" (Ecclesiastes 9:13–15).

Although some commentators have treated this story as a parable, most regard it as the true account of an historical event. It was something the Preacher had seen for himself, not something he invented: a poor man who was wise enough to save his entire city. Some scholars have even tried to determine the precise historical context. Certainly we know similar stories from the Bible. In 2 Samuel we read about a wise woman who saved the city of Abel by sacrificing the life of one evil man (20:14–22). Wise King Hezekiah saved Jerusalem a different way—by praying to God for deliverance (2 Kings 19). There are examples from ancient history as well, like Archimedes who reportedly saved Syracuse from the Romans by sinking their ships.

Sometimes one man is wise enough to save a metropolis. In this particular case the Preacher does not tell us how he did it. Nor are we likely to figure it out because according to verse 15, "no one remembered that poor man." He never became famous like Archimedes. Yet the fact remains that his wisdom saved a city.

The Preacher saw the city's deliverance as something "great," in the sense that it was significant or that it taught an important lesson. The city had almost no chance to survive. Its defenders were totally outnumbered. Their enemies were led by a powerful king who had the latest military technology. Humanly speaking, the city didn't have a prayer. But the battle is not always to the strong. Praise God! In this particular case, one man knew exactly what to do. For the Preacher, this was an example of what wisdom can do. Happy is the city that has even one person who is wise enough to rescue its citizens.

Wisdom Prioritized

Admittedly, the man who saved this particular city was soon forgotten.[6] Here again we see the realism—not to say, pessimism—of Ecclesiastes. Despite the good deed that he had done, "no one remembered that poor man" (Ecclesiastes 9:15). People are fickle, and fame is fleeting.

There are examples of this in the Bible as well. Think of Joseph, who helped Pharaoh's butler when both men were in prison. Joseph had good reason to hope that the butler would help him get out of jail, too, but as soon as he was set free, the butler forgot all about him (Genesis 40). Or consider Mordecai, who uncovered a plot against King Ahasuerus but at the time did not receive any reward (Esther 2:21–23; 6:1–13). People are like that. Life is like that too: even life-saving wisdom is soon forgotten.

Yet wisdom still has its advantages. Yes, human wisdom has its limitations. It may not make us famous, any more than it will guarantee us a fortune. But it is relatively valuable nonetheless. People may forget who gave them wise counsel. They may even refuse to listen to the wise counsel we give. But wisdom is still better than the alternative!

The Preacher proves this by making several comparisons. In verses 13–15 wisdom was *exemplified*; in verses 16–18 wisdom is *prioritized*. Qoheleth loved to show the relative value of something by claiming that one thing was better than another. Here he says that wisdom is "better," or more valuable, than physical or military strength: "But I say that wisdom is better than might, though the poor man's wisdom is despised and his words are not heard" (Ecclesiastes 9:16).

Fortunately, the poor man who saved the city was able to get people to listen to what he had to say. It does not always work out that way, however. Sometimes people refuse to listen to words of wisdom. Nevertheless, brains are better than brawn.

This is all the more true when the words of the wise are actually heeded. This is one of the Preacher's main points throughout this section: if we are wise, we will listen to wise counsel. This is the advantageous situation described in verses 17–18: "The words of the wise heard in quiet are better than the shouting of a ruler among fools. Wisdom is better than weapons of war, but one sinner destroys much good."

The last phrase is a sober reminder of the damage that one sinful person can do, especially someone in power. Although wisdom has its advantages—we will say more about them in a moment—"it does not take much to spoil the good that it might produce."[7]

Verse 17 describes a loud-mouthed leader. Yet we know that the loudest voice is not always the wisest voice (in fact, usually it is *not* the wisest voice). This particular man got his own way by shouting everyone else down. Not that his advisers would have given him good advice anyway, for he was surrounded by "fools"! It happens all the time: a man tries to rule his family or run his business or take control of his church by throwing his weight around, usually doing a lot of yelling in the process. How easy it is for one proud or angry man to wreck a marriage or divide a church!

There is a better way to lead, however, and the Preacher commends it to us. A wise man does not feel the need to do a lot of shouting. He knows it is not the loud word that moves people's hearts and changes the world for good, but the wise word. Thus he lets the wisdom of what he says speak for itself, and as a result his quiet advice is always worth hearing (even if it is not always followed). The Preacher says, "The words of the wise heard in quiet are better than the shouting of a ruler among fools" (Ecclesiastes 9:17).

This is especially true in times of conflict. With apologies to Teddy Roosevelt, we might paraphrase verse 18 by saying, "Speak softly, and do not carry a big stick." The Preacher is not denying that there is a time for war. Nor is he denying the usefulness of weapons when it is time to fight. But he is saying that wisdom is superior to weaponry.

We can apply this principle to the home, where a few quiet words are usually more honoring to God and almost always more effective—especially in the long run—than a lot of shouting. We can also apply this principle to the church, where honest conversation and genuine communication usually help avoid a major conflict. Then we can apply this principle to the government of cities and nations. There is a time for war, as the Preacher told us back in 3:8, but even the weapons of war are used best by someone who listens to wise counsel. Wisdom is always better.

Wisdom Applied

How then should we live, especially in a world where "time and chance" happen to us all? Life is so uncertain. We may suffer loss or hardship at any moment. Even if we are swift, we may lose the race. Even if we are strong, we may get defeated in battle. Even if we are smart, we may suffer poverty. Nor do we know how much time we have left. So what is the wisest way for us to use the time we have left? Having seen wisdom exemplified and prioritized, how should it be *applied*?

The first thing we need to do is to give our lives to Jesus Christ. This means asking him to be our Savior, praying that he will forgive our sins by the blood that he shed on the cross. It also means submitting to him as our Lord, offering our whole lives for his service. This is the wisest thing that anyone can do.

Ecclesiastes mainly looks at things from the perspective of human wisdom, which is valuable as far as it goes. But there is also a divine wisdom, which alone can save us. The Bible says that the foolishness of God, so to speak, is wiser than the wisdom of men (1 Corinthians 1:25). The point is not that God is foolish, of course, but that if he were, even his foolishness would be wiser than all our wisdom. If we want to be wise, therefore, we need the wisdom of God. The way to get that wisdom is simply to ask God for it. "If any of you lacks wisdom," the Scripture says, "let him ask God, who gives generously to all without reproach, and it will be given him" (James 1:5). The primary way that God answers our prayer for wisdom is by giving us his Son, Jesus Christ, whom the Bible identifies as the very wisdom of God (1 Corinthians 1:30).

One way to see the wisdom of Jesus is to see how perfectly he illustrates the story that the Preacher told about a city saved by wisdom. The story is not a direct prophecy of Jesus Christ, but it is a fair analogy for his saving work. Jesus was as poor as anyone. He was homeless and destitute, and therefore he was totally dependent on God the Father for his daily bread. Jesus was also wiser than anyone, as we know from all the wise things he said. By his wisdom Jesus delivered the lost city of fallen humanity. The devil was coming against that city with all the powers of Hell. But Jesus delivered us, all by himself. How did he do it? He did it through something that seemed foolish at the time but actually turned out to be wise for salvation. Jesus saved our city by dying on the cross and then rising again.

Giving our lives to Jesus Christ, in all his wisdom, is the wisest decision that we can ever make. Now our future is totally secure. We know for certain that when we die, we will go to Heaven. We also know that whatever happens in life, we have a loving Lord and Savior who will be with us to help us and to care for us. Time and chance may happen to all, but they also happen to be under God's control. When we trust in him, therefore, we know that our lives are kept safe in the hands of our Savior, which is by far the wisest place for us to be.

Once we do give our lives to Christ, there are many other things it is wise for us to do, especially in uncertain times. Even though our days are numbered, and even though time and chance will happen to us all, there is still a long list of things that are wise to do—not just in human and practical terms, but also in supernatural and spiritual terms. As a tool for self-examination, consider which items from the following list are the most important for you to hear and obey:

It is wise for us to be *thankful*. When trouble overtakes us—when we lose the race we thought we were fast enough to win or the battle we thought we were strong enough to fight—it is easy to get discouraged. Things may not be going very well at home, at school, or at work. But if we are wise, we will remember to celebrate God's blessings every day. We will thank God with joy for the basic provision of our daily bread, for the blessing of our brothers and sisters in Christ, for the beautiful world that he has made, and for all the benefits that we have in Jesus.

At the same time, we will be *content*. When life has turned out to be a huge disappointment, and our future seems uncertain, it is easy to complain that God is not giving us what we want or telling us what we need to know. But wisdom is content with whatever God gives and whatever God does not give (including, usually, very limited information about the future). Either we can go through life grumbling (which never changes anything anyway and can only add to our unhappiness) or we can accept whatever God decides to do (or not to do).

It is also wise for us to be *prayerful*. This is wise because God loves to answer godly prayer. Therefore, if there are things we truly need, we should go to God and ask for them. Prayer is wise because it helps to remind us who is in charge. *God* is in charge, so we come to him asking rather than dictating. Prayer also gives us something to do with our worry. God does not want us to be anxious about anything but to trust him for everything (see Philippians 4:6).

Prayer also teaches us to be *humble*, which is another important part of wisdom. Rather than putting confidence in our own abilities, whether physical or intellectual, the vagaries of time and chance should teach us not to think too highly of ourselves but to let God use our talents however he wants them to be used.

If we are wise, we will strive to be *generous*. In difficult times, it is tempting to want to hold on to everything we have. But God has promised to bless the cheerful giver (2 Corinthians 9:7). If we feel uncertain about the future, we should give more of our stuff and more of ourselves away for kingdom work, because only what is done for Jesus will last.

Wisdom is also *faithful*. If the swift and the strong do not always win, it is tempting to think that nothing we do matters. But wisdom teaches us exactly the opposite. If the future is unpredictable, then we need to leave the results of what we do up to God. Still, we need to do the things that God has called us to do and then trust him to use what we do however he pleases to use it.

As we do this, we of all people ought to be *hopeful*. Far from making us fatalistic, knowing that "time and chance happen to . . . all" should teach us to put our hope in God. Despite our best efforts, we cannot control what happens. But if we are wise, we will put our confidence in the God who knows the future. We will remind ourselves, again and again, that Jesus is coming soon. We may not know our time, but we do know Jesus, which also means that we know what will happen to us at the end of the world: our wise Savior will deliver us from all our troubles.

All of this helps us to know how to handle life's setbacks and live with life's uncertainties. A practical, down-to-earth example comes from a missionary partner serving in the Muslim Middle East.[8] Her family had been going through hard times, but she knew how to handle them wisely. In a letter to her supporters back home, she listed some of those hardships. But she also listed, right next to them, a better and wiser way of looking at each circumstance:

- Deep spiritual oppression and harassment //
  - Privileged to shine as stars in this inky black night
- Mail, packages, and a wallet stolen, phone tapped //
  - Great reminders that our lives are not our own
- No longer do we have the convenience of a car //
  - No longer do we have the expense of a car
- Very dangerous driving conditions and traffic //
  - A good public transportation system to use
- Tight and challenging times facing us now //
  - Many opportunities to prayerfully trust Him
- Mud-colored tap water flows from our faucets //
  - Sparkling, life-giving water flows from our lives
- Many aggressive viruses and lingering illnesses //
  - Truly thankful spirits for His healing touch
- A cold apartment when you have the flu //
  - Hot drinks, blankets, massages and prayers that warm us up

If we are wise, we will ask God for the grace to live the same way—thankful for our many blessings, content with what we have, prayerful about every difficulty, faithful in doing God's work, and hopeful about the future. Even though we do not know how much time we have, we will use our time wisely, taking every chance we have as an opportunity to trust in Jesus and live for him.

22

No Foolin'

ECCLESIASTES 10:1–11

Dead flies make the perfumer's
ointment give off a stench;
so a little folly outweighs wisdom and honor.

10:1

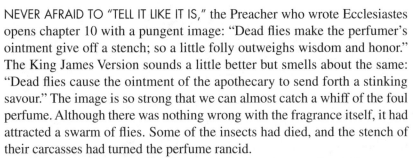

NEVER AFRAID TO "TELL IT LIKE IT IS," the Preacher who wrote Ecclesiastes opens chapter 10 with a pungent image: "Dead flies make the perfumer's ointment give off a stench; so a little folly outweighs wisdom and honor." The King James Version sounds a little better but smells about the same: "Dead flies cause the ointment of the apothecary to send forth a stinking savour." The image is so strong that we can almost catch a whiff of the foul perfume. Although there was nothing wrong with the fragrance itself, it had attracted a swarm of flies. Some of the insects had died, and the stench of their carcasses had turned the perfume rancid.

The Solomon of Ecclesiastes never forgot that smell, and he uses it here as an analogy for folly. Wisdom is sweet, like fragrant perfume. But it does not take much foolishness to turn things sour because folly stinks. All it takes is one rash word, one rude remark, one hasty decision, one foolish pleasure, or one angry outburst to spoil everything. As Derek Kidner observes, "It is easier to make a stink than to create sweetness."[1]

When it comes to sweetness, Ecclesiastes can help because it was written to grace our lives with the fragrance of godly wisdom. Such wisdom is not learned from a single example or a short list of commands but from a lifetime of thoughtful reflection on the experiences of life and careful study of the Word of God. This explains why Qoheleth spends so much time musing about wisdom and sharing his wide-ranging thoughts. Chapter 9 ended with wisdom exemplified, prioritized, and applied. Chapter 10 warns us to stay away from folly, which is the antithesis of wisdom.

Defining Folly

This part of Ecclesiastes is not a carefully constructed argument but includes a variety of short stories, case studies, maxims, proverbs, comparisons, and exhortations. Although the apparent lack of organization may be frustrating to some readers, it is a lot like life itself, in which one thing often runs into another without any obvious point of connection. But through it all the Preacher makes a clear contrast between two entirely different ways to live— the wise way and the foolish way (cf. Ecclesiastes 2:19). As we work through the passage, the question to ask is, "Am I living wisely or foolishly?"

It is vital to know the difference between wisdom and folly. Most Christians can distinguish good from evil. We know that some things are morally right, while others are morally wrong. So we try to do the right things instead of the wrong things. This kind of thinking is fine, as far as it goes. The trouble, however, is that some of the most important choices in life are not between good and evil but between wisdom and folly.

To understand the difference, we need to know the Biblical definition of folly. A "fool" in the Biblical sense is not necessarily someone with below-average intelligence. Folly does not always show up on the low end of the IQ scale. Rather, the term refers to someone who lacks the proper fear of God and therefore is prone to go the wrong direction in life. It is the fool who "says in his heart, 'There is no God'" (Psalm 14:1).

To be sure, folly is often closely associated with wickedness. The Preacher put them together just a few chapters earlier: "Be not overly wicked, neither be a fool" (Ecclesiastes 7:17; cf. Jeremiah 4:22). However, folly is not exactly the same thing as wickedness; it is an important Biblical category in its own right. Many wicked people are deliberately malicious. But the fool is characterized instead by impulsive disobedience, self-centered arrogance, and rash disregard for the holiness of God. In the words of Dan Allender, he or she is guilty of "hot anger (directed at self or others), self-centeredness, and hatred of discipline and wisdom."[2]

The Preacher has told us many things about the fool already. He is lazy (Ecclesiastes 4:5), ill-tempered (7:9), and morally blind (2:14). He refuses to take advice (9:17). His life is not pleasing to God (5:4). Here the Preacher adds that the fool is directionally-challenged: "A wise man's heart inclines him to the right, but a fool's heart to the left" (10:2). This verse defines folly with a short, memorable contrast—what a literary scholar would call an *antithetical proverb*. Perhaps this contrast is captured best in the Jerusalem Bible: "The wise man's heart leads him aright, the fool's heart leads him astray."

With apologies to left-handers, the Bible generally treats the right side as the good side: "The right hand was associated with a strength which saves, supports and protects."[3] In addition, the right hand was used to convey blessing, such as the time that Jacob crossed his arms to place his right hand on Ephraim's head and thus give him the greater blessing (Genesis 48:13–20; cf. Proverbs 3:16). The right hand was also associated with authority, which is why Jesus sits on the right hand of the Father (e.g., Colossians 3:1). Given this background, it is not surprising that at the final judgment, the sheep will be on the right, but the goats will be on the left (Matthew 25:31–33).

When the Preacher says that the fool is on the left, therefore, he is telling us that the man is going the wrong direction in life. There are plenty of examples in the Bible. Think of the contrast between Abraham and his cousin Lot. When the two men divided the land of promise (see Genesis 13), Abraham was content with what God provided. Lot, on the other hand, chose the better territory for himself (or so he thought). Foolishly, he moved to Sodom, an evil city that was later destroyed by God. There is a similar contrast between Ruth, who remained faithful to Naomi and the people of the one true God, and her sister-in-law Orpah, who abandoned Naomi and went back to the worship of pagan idols (Ruth 1:6–18).

Which direction are you going in life? Are you moving toward temptation or away from evil? Are you moving the right way in discipleship or falling away spiritually? Are you drawing closer to the people of God or going off by yourself? Only a fool would go the wrong direction in life.

Notice the reason why the fool goes this way: it is because his "heart" is leaning in the wrong direction. The heart is the core of a person's being—the inside part of every person that either loves or does not love God. Charles Bridges defined the heart as "the center of affection—the seat of knowledge—the source of purpose and emotion—the very soul of the spiritual life."[4] Everything in life follows the heart. The wise man goes the right way because his heart leans the right way, but the wicked man's heart leans in the opposite direction, which is where he ends up going. Wisdom and folly are inclinations of the heart.

Which way is your heart leaning—toward God or away from him? Do you have a growing appetite for the Word of God, or does the Bible taste stale? Are you moving toward or away from God in prayer? Are you getting more serious about sin, or have you stopped pursuing personal sanctification? Understand that the leaning of the heart determines the direction of the life.

Many people want to know which way to go in life. They are looking for direction. Well, the place to start is by making sure that our heart is in the right place—or at least that it is leaning in the right direction—because if it is, we will end up in the right place on the right road.

The fool is on the wrong road completely, but sadly, he does not even realize it. According to verse 3, "Even when the fool walks on the road, he lacks sense, and he says to everyone that he is a fool." This is part of the definition of a fool: he seems to be the only person who does not know that he is a fool! According to an ancient Malayan proverb, "A fool is like the big drum that beats fast but does not realize its hollowness." Dan Allender says it well: the fool "will follow a path that seems to be right, even when the blacktop gives way to gravel and gravel to dirt and dirt to rocks and debris. Almost nothing will stop the fool from plunging ahead into peril."[5]

There are at least two ways to take the second half of verse 3 ("he says to everyone that he is a fool"). One is to take it literally, in which case the fool is always busy telling other people that they are fools. He is not saying that he himself is a fool, but rather that everyone else is foolish. This certainly is what fools usually believe—that they alone are wise and that everyone else is a fool (which, of course, is a very foolish thing to think!).

It is also possible that verse 3 should be taken metaphorically. The fool does not literally "say" that he is a fool, yet this is exactly what his words and his actions communicate. He (or she) has such an obvious lack of spiritual good sense that his (or her) folly is evident to everyone. Fools have a way of refusing to listen to good advice (see Proverbs 12:15; 18:2; 23:9) or of saying the wrong thing at the wrong time (see Proverbs 18:6) or of doing something else that shouts, "Look at me, I'm a fool!" As it says in the book of Proverbs, "a fool flaunts his folly" (Proverbs 13:16; cf. 12:23).

The application of these verses is simple: Don't be a fool! One of the reasons why the Bible defines the difference between wisdom and folly is so we can choose well how to live. Do not be the kind of person who refuses to listen to constructive criticism or ignores what godly people are trying to say or erupts with disproportionate anger every time something goes wrong. Instead turn your heart toward God and ask him for the grace to go the right way rather than the wrong way—his way rather than your own way.

Dealing with Folly

In addition to telling us how to avoid folly ourselves, the Preacher also tells us how to respond to folly in the lives of others. Whereas verses 1–3 defined the difference between wisdom and folly, verses 4–7 give us practical advice for dealing with the many foolish people we meet in the world.

There are so many foolish people around—so many people who do not fear God but live for themselves instead—that sooner or later we will be frustrated by their folly. Some of us live with fools, and their foolish behavior disrupts the life of our home. Some of us work with fools, and their laziness or their selfish demands or their erratic decision-making make the workplace miserable.

Then there are all the fools in government. Most Americans, at least, can relate to one of Mark Twain's frequently-quoted witticisms: "Suppose you were an idiot. And suppose you were a member of Congress. But I repeat myself." Twain's remark may seem overly sarcastic, but it is in keeping with what Ecclesiastes says about political leadership: "There is an evil that I have seen under the sun, as it were an error proceeding from the ruler: folly is set in many high places, and the rich sit in a low place. I have seen slaves on horses, and princes walking on the ground like slaves" (Ecclesiastes 10:5–7).

Once again the Preacher is reporting what he has seen. This time he offers a notable example of what he was talking about in verse 1, when he said that "a little folly outweighs wisdom and honor." In the words of Martin Luther, "just as dead flies ruin the best of ointments, so it happens to the best of counsel in the state, in the senate, or in war; along comes some wicked rascal and ruins everything."[6]

Unfortunately, there are many foolish people in government. As foolish as they are, they nonetheless manage to work their way into positions of political leadership. Some are completely incompetent. Others use their position for personal advantage. They are more interested in status than service. By the time their folly is exposed, it is too late—the damage has been done. Afterward people wonder how they ever managed to get put in charge.

When the wrong people get into power, everything gets turned upside down. The Preacher says in verse 5 that errors in leadership produce evil in society. Then he describes some of the bad things that happen. For example, "the rich sit in a low place" (Ecclesiastes 10:6). In a different context, this reversal might indicate the triumph of justice, as the filthy rich finally get put in their place. But here it means that people with financial resources do not have the power to use them for the public good. Verse 7 sounds like something out of Mark Twain's famous novel *The Prince and the Pauper*, in which two men with similar looks but different social positions switch places. In Biblical times, horses were strongly associated with power, wealth, and royal authority (e.g., Esther 6:7–9). Slaves generally did not ride on horseback but walked in front of or behind their masters. But when folly sits on the throne, everything is topsy-turvy. Slaves ride, while princes walk.

As a Bible teacher, it is not my place to say which political leaders are wise and which are foolish. Sometimes this is unnecessary anyway, because as the Preacher has said, the fool lets everyone know that he is a fool. But whenever we see things turned upside down—whenever a society celebrates immorality, perpetrates wrongful violence, punishes righteousness, denies the authority of God, or persecutes his people—we may be sure that folly is in control.

How should we respond? The Preacher's answer may surprise us. "If the anger of the ruler rises against you," he says, "do not leave your place, for calmness will lay great offenses to rest" (Ecclesiastes 10:4). Rather than running away from tyranny or taking the law into our own hands or claiming that we have a right to be angry or saying that we do not have to obey a foolish government, the Preacher recommends a calm and quiet response that turns away wrath. This is the Biblical way to deal with fools—not by sharing in their folly but by living out the character of Christ.

Qoheleth's command applies most specifically to members of the royal court. Ecclesiastes 9:17 described a loud-mouthed ruler. Ecclesiastes 10:4 describes someone similar—a bad-tempered leader who gets mad at one of his officials. Rather than getting angry about this or walking away as a matter of principle, the official should stick to his post and speak words of gentle wisdom. In the words of one commentator, "The anger of a ruler must be soothed with a calm forbearance that neither panics in fear nor deserts in bitterness."[7]

The same counsel applies to many other situations in life. The Preacher is not condoning verbal abuse. Nor is he saying there is never a time for people in authority to put down a tyrant or for someone to walk away from a fight. In fact, back in Ecclesiastes 8:3 he seemed to indicate that on certain occasions we *should* walk away. But here the Preacher is saying that ordinarily the best response to anger is to stay, not to run away, and to remain calm, not to get angry. Getting angry would only make things worse, for as Derek Kidner explains, "it is better to have only one angry person than to have two!"[8]

This is good counsel for workers with an angry boss, for students with an angry teacher, for parents with an angry child, and for wives with an angry husband (or vice versa). It is good counsel for all the situations in life when someone else is suddenly provoked to anger and it makes us mad that he or she is angry. Just because someone else gets upset does not mean that we have the right to walk away from a relationship, especially if that relationship is ordained by God and is sealed with a promise (the way marriage is, for example). The way to deal with foolish anger is not to be intimidated by it or to respond in kind but to keep calm, which we can only do by the power of the Holy Spirit.

When someone gets angry, it is tempting to say, "I'm not going to take this anymore!" Admittedly, there are times when Christians are called to leave a bad work situation, or when we have Biblical grounds for separation and divorce, or when we need to hold an angry person accountable so that the poor fool can get the help he or she needs. But even then we should act calmly and carefully rather than angrily and hastily. Usually the wisest thing for us to do is to remain in the situation. Staying calm is part of God's winning strategy for dealing with foolish anger.

The Apostle Peter gave similar advice. He knew what it was like to deal with angry people, like the fools who told him to stop preaching the gospel. Yet Peter commended a life of quiet gentleness. He told Christians to submit to the governing authorities, *even when* they were persecuting the church, because by doing good deeds, the suffering church would "put to silence the ignorance of foolish people" (1 Peter 2:13–15). He told servants to respect their masters, *even if* they were unjust, for it is a gracious thing to endure injustice (1 Peter 2:18–19). He told wives to submit to their husbands, *even if* they were unbelievers, so that by pure and respectful conduct they might win their husband's heart for Christ (1 Peter 3:1–2).

If we doubt the wisdom of Peter's counsel—or if we think that it is impossible for us to follow—then we should remember the example that Peter gives. Why should we keep serving people who make us suffer? Peter said, "Because Christ also suffered for you, leaving you an example, so that you might follow in his steps" (1 Peter 2:21).

Then Peter pointed out that Jesus did exactly what Ecclesiastes tells us to do. Angry rulers rose against him—foolish men who treated him with angry contempt until finally they crucified him. Yet Jesus refused to leave his place of service or to fight anger with anger. Instead he calmly did the work that he was called to do: "When he was reviled, he did not revile in return; when he suffered, he did not threaten" (1 Peter 2:23). By his calm response, Jesus laid great offenses to rest, carrying our sins upon the cross and forgiving everyone who trusts in him, including some of the very men who crucified him.

Now Jesus calls us to follow in his footsteps. Who is the angry or foolish person in your life, and how will you respond? The way to glorify God and to lay great offenses to rest is by keeping the calm of Christ.

Folly Destroyed

The Preacher gives us further encouragement for wise living when he tells us that folly is self-destructive: "He who digs a pit will fall into it, and a serpent will bite him who breaks through a wall. He who quarries stones is hurt by them, and he who splits logs is endangered by them" (Ecclesiastes 10:8–9).

Qoheleth may simply be telling us to be careful. This world is not a safe place, and if we are wise, we will watch out for danger.

> Here an innocent person is simply engaged in his occupation, and he is accidentally injured. This is the first of four illustrations of people who are simply doing their jobs and who fall prey to the dangers that are inherent in their occupations. Their injuries are simply accidental. They are not punishments for bad behavior, and they are not mentioned so that the wise person can avoid them; they are unavoidable accidents.[9]

Certainly this interpretation is true to life. Ditchdiggers do not always fall into the holes they dig. Nor do stonecutters always get injured by falling rocks. But sometimes they do, and this fits in well with what Ecclesiastes says elsewhere about life's many misfortunes.

It does not fit in quite as well with the immediate context, however. The end of chapter 9 and most of chapter 10 are about wisdom and folly, and this may be true here as well. Pit-digging can be an act of treacherous violence, and there are examples of this in the Bible. On occasion the psalmist complained that someone had "dug a pit" to capture him and kill him (e.g., Psalm 35:7).

In this case, however, the foolish (and probably evil) man fell into his own pit! This was not an accident of misfortune but an act of poetic and presumably divine justice.[10] David talked about a similar incident in Psalm 7: "He makes a pit, digging it out, and falls into the hole that he has made. His mischief returns upon his own head, and on his own skull his violence descends" (vv. 15–16). Something similar happens to the man who knocks down a wall, heedless of danger, breaking a boundary that was never meant to be broken. Folly can be deadly. In the words of Charles Bridges, "Evil shall fall upon the heads of its own authors."[11]

For every folly, there is an equal and opposite self-destruction. The addict seeks the calm of the drink or the thrill of the hit but ends up wasting away. The lusty sinner wants sexual pleasure but by gratifying desire outside the holy bonds of matrimony ends up spiritually unsatisfied. The selfish husband or wife wants to have things his or her own way but in trying to get it ruins the relationship and loses everything. The angry father or mother wants more control, but angry emotions set everyone on edge, which only leads to more chaos, more anger, and ultimately less control. These are some of the pitfalls of folly. Dig the pit, and you will fall in. Break down the wall, and the snake of sin will come back to bite you.

There is a wiser and safer way to live, but it will take some patience. The Preacher shows this by drawing a couple of analogies, one from a blacksmith and one from a snake charmer: "If the iron is blunt, and one does not sharpen the edge, he must use more strength, but wisdom helps one to succeed. If the serpent bites before it is charmed, there is no advantage to the charmer" (Ecclesiastes 10:10–11).

When the Bible uses images like this, we need to slow down to understand them, puzzling over them like riddles instead of skimming over them like stories. Verse 10 compares wisdom to a sharpened blade. It takes more strength to wield an axe or a sword when the blade is dull, and to cut something in two, a man has to keep hacking away at it. Yet this is exactly the way foolish people live. They keep flailing away at their work or their relationships without ever making much progress, especially spiritually. It would be wiser to sharpen the edge of the blade, so it can slice through something with a single blow.

If we are wise, therefore, we will take the time to prepare our blade. This principle applies to education. Be sure to get the best training, sharpening skills for effective service in the kingdom of God. It applies to relationships: a prudent courtship is far more likely to lead to a more successful marriage than a whirlwind romance. It applies to ministry. Before starting something new—planting a church, for example—make sure that you have everything you need to succeed.

How sharp is your blade? Are you hacking away at life like a fool or staying on the sharp edge of wisdom? Living wisely may take more time at the beginning, but it saves time in the long run. Make sure you have the right tools for the job God has given you to do, and then take the time to prepare them well.

Verse 11 is more difficult to interpret, but it seems to make nearly the opposite point. Here the danger lies in acting too slowly: "one who is able to handle a difficult matter (*a charmer*) fails for lack of promptitude (*the serpent bites . . . before charmed*)."[12] Once a snake is charmed, it can be kept under control. But until then it is very dangerous (there are examples in the Bible; see Psalm 58:3–5; Jeremiah 8:17). Thus it is vitally important for a snake charmer to get busy and charm his snake before it bites, which would be too bad for the snake charmer! Foolish delay will come back to bite you.

Taken together, verses 10–11 show us why we need wisdom from God. Sometimes it is important to take more time to prepare. Other times we need to act before it is too late. Wisdom comes in knowing the difference. Ovid, the famous Roman poet, is reported to have said, "At times it is folly to hasten, at other times, to delay. The wise do everything in its proper time." Thus the wise person is never early and never late but always right on time.

Some of this timely wisdom comes from life experience. Some of it comes from talking with people who are wiser (and usually older) than we are. But the best way to gain true spiritual wisdom is by listening to the words of Jesus.

Like the Solomon of Ecclesiastes, Jesus knew the difference between wisdom and folly. Once he told a story to show the difference—the story of a wise man and a foolish man. The wise man "built his house on the rock. And the rain fell, and the floods came, and the winds blew and beat on that house, but it did not fall, because it had been founded on the rock" (Matthew 7:24–25). The foolish man was much less fortunate. He "built his house on the sand. And the rain fell, and the floods came, and the winds blew and beat against that house, and it fell, and great was the fall of it" (Matthew 7:26–27).

Jesus not only believed there was a difference between wisdom and folly; he also believed that it was the difference between life and death. But what exactly made the difference? The wise man built his house upon the rock, but what did the rock represent? According to Jesus, the wise person is the one "who hears these words of mine and does them" (Matthew 7:24). More than anything else, what makes a fool a fool is not listening to Jesus and not doing what he says. If we are wise, therefore, we will build our lives on the solid rock of Jesus and his Word—the Word that is able to make us "wise for salvation through faith in Christ Jesus" (2 Timothy 3:15).

23

A Word to the Wise

ECCLESIASTES 10:12–20

The words of a wise man's mouth win him favor,
but the lips of a fool consume him.

10:12

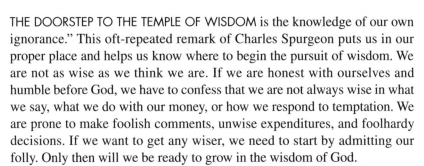

THE DOORSTEP TO THE TEMPLE OF WISDOM is the knowledge of our own ignorance." This oft-repeated remark of Charles Spurgeon puts us in our proper place and helps us know where to begin the pursuit of wisdom. We are not as wise as we think we are. If we are honest with ourselves and humble before God, we have to confess that we are not always wise in what we say, what we do with our money, or how we respond to temptation. We are prone to make foolish comments, unwise expenditures, and foolhardy decisions. If we want to get any wiser, we need to start by admitting our folly. Only then will we be ready to grow in the wisdom of God.

Ecclesiastes invites us to enter the temple of divine wisdom. The Preacher has been showing us the difference between wisdom and folly in daily life, helping us in the many practical situations where wisdom is required. At the end of chapter 10 he continues in the same vein, teaching us about the wise employment of words (vv. 12–14, 20), the wise exercise of leadership (vv. 16–17), and the wise expenditure of effort (vv. 18–19).

Wise Words

Eventually every wise teacher has something to say about what we say, because the way we use our words is "the acid test of wisdom."[1] If the mouth only speaks what is in the heart, then every time we say something, we reveal the wisdom or the folly inside.

The wise person speaks wisdom. The Preacher says, "The words of a wise man's mouth win him favor" (Ecclesiastes 10:12). This may simply mean that someone who speaks wisdom will gain a good reputation. No one knew this better than Solomon, who became world-famous for his royal wisdom. Yet perhaps we should take the verse more literally. The word "favor" is really the Hebrew word for "grace" (*hen*), favor that is undeserved. A wise person's words show this kind of grace to other people—they are messages of blessing. The point of the verse, then, is not that wise speech will get us something *from* other people (namely, their favor) but that they will enable us to give something *to* other people (namely, the gracious love of God): "Words from the mouth of a wise man are gracious" (Ecclesiastes 10:12, NASB).

This is exactly the opposite of the way most people use words most of the time. Words have the power to help us get what we want. We use them to get a laugh, or to get attention, or to get someone to do something for us. We use our words to get a job or to get a girl (or a guy, as the case may be). We use our words to build ourselves up and tear other people down. But do we use our words as instruments of grace? Do we speak for the good of others or as a way of achieving our own agenda?

A wise person is slow to speak (Ecclesiastes 6:11; cf. James 1:19) because sometimes it is better not to say anything at all. Wisdom chooses each word carefully. But when we do speak, there are many wise things to say. By way of application, therefore, consider some of the many wise ways to speak, not as a list of rules to obey but as a lifestyle to pursue:

- A wise person offers verbal praise and audible thanksgiving to God—not cursing him but blessing him. This is wise because it reminds us who we are. We are creatures made in the image of God and designed to give him the glory. If "the fear of the LORD is the beginning of knowledge" (Proverbs 1:7), then one of the first ways to show wisdom is by speaking or singing words of worship.
- When a wise person speaks to other people, he or she uses more words of encouragement than criticism. Usually the way to bring out the best in other people is not by finding fault but by building them up. Instead of boasting, the wise person uses words to make other people look good.
- A wise person speaks "the truth with his neighbor" (Ephesians 4:25), not stretching it for personal advantage, but saying what needs to be said in a loving way. This includes speaking out against injustice and confronting someone who is doing the wrong thing, if it is our God-given place to do so. The wise person uses wise words to speak hard truths

when they need to be spoken—what the Bible calls "a word in season" (Proverbs 15:23; cf. 25:11).

- A wise person speaks with gentleness, never in unrighteous anger. Wisdom waits until emotions are under better control. Then whatever words we speak can offer genuine grace. According to Proverbs, "The heart of the righteous ponders how to answer, but the mouth of the wicked pours out evil things" (15:28).
- A wise person also knows how to use reconciling words like "I'm sorry" and "Please forgive me." Although there are times when we are called to speak in our own defense, a wise person is never defensive but instead is content to give a quiet answer and then let God bring vindication in his good time. Nor does a wise person lash out with cruel or cutting remarks, even when provoked, knowing that it is the "soft answer" that "turns away wrath" (Proverbs 15:1).
- A wise person speaks words of love and affection. For example, a wise husband is not content to let his actions speak for themselves but makes his wife secure by affirming his love. Sometimes wisdom is as simple as saying, "I love you."

These are some of the many ways that wisdom speaks. Are you choosing your words wisely? Unfortunately, most of us are not as wise with our speech as we ought to be. What, then, would it take for us to be wiser in what we say?

Since it is "out of the abundance of the heart" that "the mouth speaks" (Matthew 12:34), wise speech requires a heart overflowing with the love of God. Remember what the Preacher said at the beginning of this chapter: a wise heart inclines us to do the right thing (Ecclesiastes 10:2). Therefore, wise speech can only come from a wise heart, and this is a gift from God, whose Son lives in our hearts through faith (Ephesians 3:17).

A wise heart is a humble heart: it fears God and puts other people first. When we have such a heart, it is only natural for us to use our words to give praise to God and to speak his grace to other people. *A wise heart is a true heart*: it moves our lips to speak the truth. *A wise heart is a gentle heart*: it makes our speech tender and mild. *A wise heart is a loving heart*—a heart that speaks words of affection.

In other words, a wise person has the heart of Jesus and therefore speaks words that demonstrate his grace. If ever a man uttered words of wisdom, it was Jesus Christ. The Bible says that when he spoke, people "marveled at the gracious words that were coming from his mouth" (Luke 4:22). This was in keeping with the Messianic prophecy of Psalm 45:2—that God would pour grace on the Savior's lips. It was also in keeping with the wisdom of Ecclesiastes: "The words of a wise man's mouth win him favor" (10:12). Jesus spoke this way because his heart was perfectly humble, loving, and true. When we ask the Holy Spirit to give us the heart of Jesus, he will empower us and enable us to speak words of his wisdom and grace.

Foolish Words

The words of a fool are not so wise. To help us see the difference between wisdom and folly, Qoheleth mentions some of the many problems we have with foolish speech. In fact, he spends more time talking about the lips of a fool than about the mouth of a wise man, presumably because speech is such a difficult area of sanctification for most of us. The Apostle James said, "if anyone does not stumble in what he says, he is a perfect man" (James 3:2). But who is ever that perfect?

The Preacher mentions several danger areas for foolish speech, and they are struggles for all of us. To begin with, the words of a fool are *self-destructive*. Rather than winning him favor, like the wise man, "the lips of a fool consume him" (Ecclesiastes 10:12). Literally, his words eat him up. When the fool opens his mouth to say something, the words that come out turn right around to swallow him whole.

There are many ways that words can destroy. Sometimes a fool says something that gets him into trouble. His rash words make someone else angry, and that person destroys him. Sometimes a fool says something that ruins a relationship. She carelessly reveals something that would be better left unsaid, but once it is said, the damage is done. There are thousands of ways for foolish words to destroy the person who utters them.

The Preacher gives us one specific example at the end of the chapter: "Even in your thoughts, do not curse the king, nor in your bedroom curse the rich, for a bird of the air will carry your voice, or some winged creature tell the matter" (Ecclesiastes 10:20).

One of the riskiest things for foolish people to do with their words is to criticize people in authority—in this case, people with power and political influence. In some countries, criticizing the government is tantamount to treason. That is especially true in an absolute monarchy, which in Biblical times would have included most nations. Gossip about the government—even in secret—and your words may well get you into trouble. Cursing political leaders is wrong in itself, which is something Christians who live in a democracy need to remember before, during, and after every election cycle. According to the Law of Moses, "You shall not . . . curse a ruler of your people" (Exodus 22:28). But in addition to being wrong in themselves, our foolish criticisms may come back to haunt us.

Here the Preacher uses the ancient and familiar image of a bird overhearing what is said and then repeating it to someone else. He is not claiming that flying animals have the power of speech, of course, but is using a familiar metaphor for the rapid dissemination of foolishness: "A little bird told me." Say something stupid, and before you know it, the whole world knows about it.

So be careful what you say! Sooner or later what we say to one person will get repeated to another person, with varying degrees of accuracy. Once the words leave our mouths, we lose control over where they go. If the wrong word reaches the ear of the wrong person, there may be serious repercussions. How easy it is to send a quick electronic message, but how difficult it is to undo the damage done by words that are personally insulting or sexually inappropriate. It would be wiser not even to think such things, let alone say them, especially because God knows all our thoughts (e.g., Psalm 139:4).

Not only are foolish words self-destructive, but they are also *evil*. Verse 13 describes a downward spiral: "The beginning of the words of his mouth is foolishness, and the end of his talk is evil madness." At first the fool's words were merely foolish, which was bad enough, but then things went from bad to worse. By the time he was through, the fool had degenerated into "evil madness"—a phrase that indicates both moral depravity and mental disability.

It is important not to make a habit of using unwise words. At first a fool's speech may simply be silly, but it will not stay that way for long. A person who is foolish enough to tell a "little white lie" or say something behind someone's back will not stop there. Soon the fool will be using words in ever more destructive ways. If we are wise, we will guard our speech carefully, knowing that folly is the gateway to depravity.

Nor will we let foolish words go uncorrected when they come from the lips of our children. Paul Tripp offers wise counsel in his book *War of Words*, a practical guide to knowing the difference between wise and foolish speech. Here is Dr. Tripp's list of questions for self-examination:

> Listen to the talk that goes on in your home. How much of it is impatient and unkind? How often are words spoken out of selfishness and personal desire? How easily do outbursts of anger occur? How often do we bring up past wrongs? How do we fail to communicate hope? How do we fail to protect? How often do our words carry threats that we have "had it" and are about to quit? Stop and listen, and you will see how much we need to hold our talk to this standard of love, and how often the truth we profess to speak has been distorted by our sin.[2]

There is yet another problem with the words of a fool: they are *presumptuous*. In other words, fools make arrogant and boastful claims about what they know and about what they will do, but they are unable to back up their words with knowledge or action. So the Preacher says, "A fool multiplies words, though no man knows what is to be, and who can tell him what will be after him?" (Ecclesiastes 10:14).

Fools are usually quite opinionated; they tend to be big talkers. For some reason, a fool is seldom content to keep his folly to himself but insists on sharing it with others. Words multiply. Fools go on and on, even when they do not know what they are talking about. As someone once said, "Wise men speak because they have something to say; fools because they have to say something."

One of the many things that foolish people like to talk about is the future. No one knows what will happen in days to come, but for some reason this does not stop the fool from predicting the future. Some fools have fanciful theories about global disasters. Others have big plans for the future. To hear them talk about it, they are always one lucky break from striking it rich or landing their dream job. They boast about a "done deal" before the deal is actually done. This is all very foolish, because if there is one thing we can never presume, it is to know the future.

If we are wise, we will follow the counsel of James, who sounds as if he must have been familiar with Ecclesiastes:

> Come now, you who say, "Today or tomorrow we will go into such and such a town and spend a year there and trade and make a profit"—yet you do not know what tomorrow will bring. What is your life? For you are a mist that appears for a little time and then vanishes. Instead you ought to say, "If the Lord wills, we will live and do this or that." (James 4:13–15)

To avoid the evil, presumption, and self-destruction of foolish speech, we need to choose our words carefully:

> Winning the war of words involves choosing our words carefully. It is not just about the words we say, but also about the words we choose not to say. Winning the war is about being prepared to say the right thing at the right moment, exercising self-control. It is refusing to let our talk be driven by passion and personal desire but communicating instead with God's purposes in view. It is exercising the faith necessary to be part of what God is doing at that moment.[3]

Wise and Foolish Government

To this point, the Preacher has been talking about the way we employ our words. In verse 16 he turns to consider another area where spiritual wisdom is badly needed but is usually in short supply—the exercise of political leadership. Government is a recurring theme in Ecclesiastes, which is one of the reasons why many people think the book may have been written by

King Solomon himself. Here he says that wise leadership is a blessing, but foolish government is a curse: "Woe to you, O land, when your king is a child, and your princes feast in the morning! Happy are you, O land, when your king is the son of the nobility, and your princes feast at the proper time, for strength, and not for drunkenness!" (Ecclesiastes 10:16–17).

These verses tell the story of a national disaster, with someone completely incompetent in charge. The word "child" may indicate that the ruler is a youngster, like a boy king. On rare occasions this can turn out to be a blessing. A notable example is King Josiah, who ascended to the throne of Judah at the tender age of eight. The Bible says that when he was only sixteen, Josiah "began to seek the God of David his father" (2 Chronicles 34:3). Josiah must be the exception that proves the rule, however, because more often than not, inexperienced leaders cause all kinds of trouble.

The word "child" (na'ar) is not limited to people under a certain age, however. It may refer, especially in a political context, to someone older who is still immature. King Solomon used the word this way when he first took the throne of Israel. "I am but a little child," he said, acknowledging his lack of experience before asking God for the wisdom to rule (1 Kings 3:7). Solomon's son Rehoboam was not nearly as wise. Although he was forty-one when he began to reign (2 Chronicles 12:13), Rehoboam had no idea what he was doing. His court was corrupt, his judgment was unsound, and soon his kingdom was divided.

To show how much trouble a country can get into when it lacks mature leadership, Qoheleth describes a kingly court where gluttonous princes feast every morning. The Preacher is not talking about having a hearty breakfast but about a royal banquet that includes enough alcohol to get wasted. Instead of getting up in the morning to improve and defend their country, these princes lie about in a drunken stupor. They take "a dissolute, slothful approach to life, with emphasis on luxury and personal indulgence."[4]

A notable example from European history is Charles XII, who became the king of Sweden when he was only a teenager. The wild behavior of Charles and his friends included riding on horseback through his grandmother's apartment, knocking people to the ground in the city streets, and practicing firearms by shooting out the windows of the palace. In response, the leading preachers of Stockholm all agreed to preach from Ecclesiastes 10:16 on the same Sunday, pronouncing woe on a land with a child for a king and princes that feasted in the morning.[5]

The Preacher is not saying there is anything wrong with a proper feast at the proper time and for the proper purpose. Verse 17 praises the courtiers who sit down to a good dinner and gain strength for their kingdom work. After all, the king's table is supposed to be set with a royal feast, which Solomon knew as well as anyone. But the Bible everywhere condemns the kind of bad behavior that is described in verse 16: excessive feasting, especially in the morning (e.g., Isaiah 5:11), and drunkenness on any occasion (e.g., Proverbs 23:20). It also condemns people who use their position of privilege for selfish pleasure.

The words of the Preacher call us to wise government. We can apply his words to nations and kingdoms. Politicians who rule for personal advantage bring disaster to the people they lead. Woe to any nation characterized by sinful entertainment, lazy self-indulgence, and the widespread abuse of alcohol and other drugs, especially among its national leaders.

We can also apply the same principles at the personal level. There is a time and a place for feasting in the Christian life. But there is also a danger of wasting our lives by living for our pleasures. How do you spend your mornings? Here is a word to the wise: get up early to do whatever kingdom work God has given you to do. What is your relationship to food and alcohol? Here is another word to the wise: do not eat and drink to sinful excess, but exercise self-control by the power of the Holy Spirit. "Put on the Lord Jesus Christ," the Scripture says, "and make no provision for the flesh, to gratify its desires" (Romans 13:14).

If we want to govern ourselves wisely, we do well to follow the example of our King. Although verse 17 is not a direct prophecy of Jesus Christ, it aptly describes his wisdom and the character of his kingdom. As the Son of David and the Son of God, Jesus is "the son of the nobility" twice over. He knew when to feast, as he did with his disciples. But his first priority was the work of God's kingdom. Therefore, on many occasions he fasted, feeding only on the Word of God (e.g., Luke 4:1-4).

As the born-again children of God, we are princes and princesses of his kingdom. We should know the time to feast, which includes keeping the regular feast of the Lord's Supper as well as the occasional celebrations of the Christian life, all of which remind us that our King has a feast waiting for us in Heaven.

We should also learn when *not* to feast, which is an important part of living for Christ. This includes refraining from all drunkenness, which empties us of the Holy Spirit (Ephesians 5:18). But it also includes other forms of fasting, in which we say no to the pleasures of this world so we can find more satisfaction in God himself. Jesus Christ is the soul's greatest pleasure, but to discover this for ourselves, sometimes we need to fast for a while from lesser pleasures that may distract us from the kingdom of God (like eating good food, for example, or watching sports or doing something else that may be in danger of ruling our hearts). According to the New Testament (e.g., Matthew 6:16–18), such fasting should be a regular part of the Christian life. It is a form of self-government—a wise way to live in greater dependence on the Lord our God. It is also a wise way to follow the example of Jesus Christ, who did not serve his own pleasures but gave himself up for our salvation by dying on the cross.

Working Wisely

The last subject that the Preacher addresses in Ecclesiastes 10 is one that he has addressed before (e.g., Ecclesiastes 2:18–26)—the wise expenditure of effort. The subject of work came up when he talked about princes having champagne for breakfast instead of getting an early start on their kingdom work (Ecclesiastes 10:16). It also came up in verse 15, when he said, "The toil of a fool wearies him, for he does not know the way to the city."

Ironically, a lazy fool gets worn out by his work—not because he is working hard, but because he is fooling around when he ought to be working. This is an important insight for someone who quickly gets tired of working but never has very much to show for his (or her) work. Merely playing at work wearies the soul, because deep down we know that we ought to be more productive. The feelings of guilt that we have as a result are exhausting (especially when we realize that we still have a lot of work to do that we should have done already). The wise man gets energized by working hard; his service for the Lord satisfies his soul. But the fool is exhausted. He may try to convince himself (or others) that he is working hard, when in fact he is wearing himself out by hardly working at all.

Maybe it is not surprising that the fool has never learned how to work. After all, the poor man is so lost that he cannot even find his way to the big city! This seems to be the meaning of verse 15. Although people may have trouble locating a small town, it is hard to miss a major metropolis. Yet somehow the fool manages to lose his way. "So the picture begins to emerge," writes Derek Kidner, "of a man who makes things needlessly difficult for himself by his stupidity."[6] The fool never seems to get anywhere in life. He will not get very far in the life to come either but will get lost somewhere on his way to God's everlasting city.

The end result of all his laziness comes out clearly in verse 18, with its memorable image of a house that is falling apart: "Through sloth the roof sinks in, and through indolence the house leaks." Some maintenance is always required. Neglect regular upkeep of the roof, and soon every rainstorm will be another opportunity to unfold an umbrella! The Preacher imagines a fool who is so lazy that his whole house will collapse before he climbs up the ladder to patch his crumbling roof.

This image of fatal decay helps us see that sloth is a deadly sin. It will destroy the soul that is too lazy to seek its own spiritual progress. But that is not the only thing that sloth will destroy. It will destroy a relationship when people turn to their own interests rather than working hard at intimacy. It will destroy a church that rests on what it has already accomplished rather than doing everything it still has an opportunity to do for Christ. Sloth can even destroy a kingdom, especially when people have more of a sense of entitlement than a sense of responsibility. Only a fool would neglect something as important as personal sanctification or family unity or effective service to church and country.

In contrast to a lazy fool, a hard-working individual has everything that he or she needs. Verse 19 is sometimes criticized for taking a cynical approach to life's necessities and pleasures. In this context, however, it shows the wisdom of hard work, as compared with the folly of lazy ease. The Preacher says, "Bread is made for laughter, and wine gladdens life, and money answers everything."

Money does have its limitations, of course, which is why the Bible often warns us not to trust it (e.g., Hebrews 13:5) or worship it (e.g., Matthew 6:24). But from the practical standpoint, what the Preacher says remains true: if we have enough money, we can buy anything else we need. Bread is a daily necessity. Fine wine is a delicious pleasure. But if we have the money, we can buy both bread and wine, plus anything else that we need or want. According to Charles Bridges, someone who has money lacks "nothing that this world can give. It supplies a thousand advantages—not only the necessaries, but the conveniences, indulgences, and embellishments of life."[7]

There is something else that money can do, which is to advance the kingdom of God by supporting the ministry of a local church and its missionary work around the world. A wise person works hard to get enough money not only to pay for daily necessities but also to honor God by celebrating the good things of this world and, more importantly, by making a major investment in the work of God's kingdom.

A Wise Example

When I think of everything that is involved in living wisely, I often think of Frank Ryken, my paternal grandfather. Grandpa Ryken received only an eighth-grade education, and as a result his children and grandchildren have academic achievements and intellectual accomplishments that he could only begin to understand. But it is doubtful whether any of us will ever surpass his wisdom.

Grandpa Ryken was wise enough to fear God, which is the beginning of wisdom, and also to believe in Jesus Christ, who is the very wisdom of God. Grandpa was slow to speak, but when he did talk, it was usually about something important—his daily work, the weather (which is always serious business to a farmer), friends and family, or the ministry of the church where he served as an elder. When my grandmother multiplied words, as she sometimes did, he would wisely and cheerfully say, "Now, Mother . . . " and she would know where the limit was for godly speech.

My grandfather did not presume upon the future but was content to leave his life and everything he loved in the hands of his sovereign God. Even in his retirement, he was exceptionally hard-working. He was not worn out by foolish striving but slept well and rose up early in the morning to work another day. Like most farmers, he had the skills to do just about anything, including keeping his property well maintained. No leaky roof for him! He had everything he needed in life, with more than enough money to support the work of his church. His farmer's table was a place for wholesome feasts of fresh meat, corn on the cob, homemade applesauce, and cherry pie. All of this good food was received with thanksgiving, consecrated through prayer, and often shared with the many guests who loved to visit his home.

In his own simple way, therefore, my grandfather lived the kind of life taught in Ecclesiastes. He was wise in his speech, his leadership, and his labor. Everything the Preacher said about such a man is true. His words have won him the favor of his children's praise. At the proper time, he took his rightful place at the last and greatest feast. Now, by the grace of God, he is a prince in the house of the High King—that noble Son, the Lord Jesus Christ. Life and laughter are his forever, and also *yours* forever if you will listen to the whisper of the Holy Spirit and believe the words that God speaks to the wise.

24

You Never Know

ECCLESIASTES 11:1–6

In the morning sow your seed, and at
evening withhold not your hand, for you do
not know which will prosper, this or that,
or whether both alike will be good.

11:6

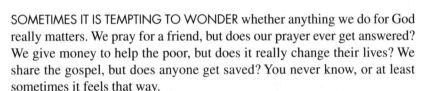

SOMETIMES IT IS TEMPTING TO WONDER whether anything we do for God really matters. We pray for a friend, but does our prayer ever get answered? We give money to help the poor, but does it really change their lives? We share the gospel, but does anyone get saved? You never know, or at least sometimes it feels that way.

Yet there are also times when we catch a glimpse of what God is doing, when we see something we did for Jesus make a difference in someone's life. A Presbyterian elder from Mississippi had this experience in Eastern Europe. Every year he traveled to Ukraine for street preaching and door-to-door evangelism. Some people responded to the gospel, and some didn't, but even the ones who prayed to receive Christ sometimes failed to follow through in Christian discipleship.

One day the elder was out with friends and asked a stranger to take their picture. Afterward the man who took the photo had something he wanted to say:

> You probably don't remember me, but four years ago you came to my apartment and shared the good news of Jesus Christ, how He died for sinners like me. I prayed that prayer, but I was just going through the motions to please my mother. I was in a very bad condition for about two years after

253

that. I completely lost hope. I was drugging and drinking intending just to kill myself, but in God's mercy I remembered what you told me, that Christ died for sinners and His blood was for my sins. I prayed again and this time I meant it. He really did come into my heart. I have been delivered. You probably wonder, sometimes, if what you are doing really does any good. For me God used it to save my life and my soul.[1]

Even when we do not know how God will use our work to advance his kingdom, we should continue to pray, continue to serve, and continue to hope, "knowing that in the Lord your labor is not in vain" (1 Corinthians 15:58). The Preacher takes this perspective in Ecclesiastes 11, where he tells us to live boldly, not letting the uncertainties of life hold us back from taking risks by faith for the glory of God. The better part of spiritual wisdom is not caution but courage through Christ.

Cast Your Bread upon the Waters

The chapter begins with a pair of commands that are hard to interpret. The commands themselves are simple enough ("cast" and "give"), but the poetic images in these verses are difficult to define: "Cast your bread upon the waters, for you will find it after many days. Give a portion to seven, or even to eight, for you know not what disaster may happen on earth" (Ecclesiastes 11:1–2).

What exactly does Qoheleth mean when he says, "cast your bread upon the waters"? The image always puzzled me when I was a child because I assumed that the Bible was speaking literally. I imagined fresh loaves of white bread bobbing along a river, getting soggy, or perhaps wrapped in brightly colored plastic. But if the bread floated down the river, who would ever find it again? And if someone found it "after many days," who would want to eat it? By then it would be moldy. So why not just keep the bread rather than sending it down the river?

Some commentators think these verses are about philanthropy: the Preacher is encouraging us to be generous in giving to the poor. Bread "cast . . . upon the waters" is shared with someone who needs help. The point is that if we are generous with others when they are in need, eventually we ourselves will get help in time of trouble. Some commentators draw a comparison to an ancient Arabian proverb: "Do a good deed and throw it into the river; when this dries up you shall find it."[2] Others remember the words of Jesus: "Give, and it will be given to you. Good measure, pressed down, shaken together, running over, will be put into your lap" (Luke 6:38).

Similarly, the portions of seven or eight mentioned in verse 2 may be offered to the poor. In Biblical times it was customary for a family to share a feast with neighbors in need. For example, when Ezra read the Law of God in Jerusalem, and the people celebrated, Nehemiah told them, "Eat the fat and drink sweet wine and send portions to anyone who has nothing ready, for this day is holy to our Lord" (Nehemiah 8:10). To give a portion, then, is to share the good things of this life. To share seven portions would be the height of generosity. To share eight is to do even more: it is to do everything we can to help others, not using the fear of some coming disaster as an excuse to be stingy, but giving and giving and giving some more. Martin Luther said, "Be generous to everyone while you can, use your riches wherever you can possibly do any good."[3]

There is another way to take these verses, however—not as a call to generous philanthropy, but as a call to prudent industry. On this interpretation, the images in verses 1–2 come from the business of agriculture.

Some older commentators believed that the image of casting bread referred to the sowing of seed in a floodplain. Charles Bridges used the annual inundation of the Nile as an example: "The time for sowing the seed, is just when the waters are going down, leaving a loamy bed, in which the seed apparently lost is deposited, and produces a most luxuriant harvest."[4] On this interpretation, what a person finds "after many days" is a harvest of grain. Thus the farmer gets a good return for sowing his seed, although it is a little difficult to understand why the Preacher would describe this as "casting bread" rather than casting seed.

Another interpretation, however, may be the most likely of all. To "cast [one's] bread upon the waters" is to engage in international trade, sending one's grain or other produce out to sea and then waiting for the ships to return with fine goods from foreign lands. To "find it after many days," therefore, is to receive the reward that eventually comes after taking the risk of a wise investment. Nothing ventured, nothing gained.

The Preacher invites us to handle our spiritual business the same way. What we invest in the kingdom of God—our time, our talent, our treasure— is never wasted. But if we want the blessings that God loves to give, we need to exercise our faith:

> Ships on commercial voyages might be long delayed before any profit resulted. Yet one's goods had to be committed to them. Solomon's fleet which brought back "gold, silver, ivory, apes, and peacocks" (1 Kings 10:22) sailed once in three years. Similarly the preacher has called his readers to take life as from the hand of God, and to enjoy it despite its trials and perplexities. Such a life contains within it the elements of trust and adventure (*Cast*), demands total commitment (for *your bread* is used in the sense of "goods, livelihood," as in Deut. 8:3, Prov. 31:14), and has a forward look to it (*you will find*), a reward which requires patience (*after many days*).[5]

Verse 2 makes a similar but slightly different point. To "give a portion to seven, or even to eight" is a way of saying, "do not put all your eggs in one basket." In business this would be called "diversifying investments." Rather than focusing narrowly on a single product or service, many companies try to widen their interests.

One of the main reasons for adopting this strategy is that "you know not what disaster may happen on earth." Once again Qoheleth reminds us of the mysteries of the future and the many misfortunes of life—war, pestilence, famine, and financial collapse. Rather than simply taking our chances, we will plan for an uncertain and possibly unfortunate future. If we are wise, we will invest widely. Hopefully, if one investment does poorly it will be counterbalanced by another source of revenue that is doing somewhat better.

There are ways to apply this sound financial advice to the spiritual business of God's kingdom. Qoheleth's concern, writes Michael Eaton, is "that the wise man will invest everything he has in the life of faith."[6] Rather than holding on to what we have, hoarding it all for ourselves—which is the error that the man with one talent made in a parable that Jesus told (Matthew 25:24–28)—God invites us to be venture capitalists for the kingdom of God. This is not exclusively or even primarily about money. It is about having the holy boldness to do seven (or even eight) things to spread the gospel and then waiting for God's ship to come in. Some of the things that we attempt may fail (or at least seem to fail at the time)—some of the ministries we start, for example, or the churches we plant, or the efforts we make to share the good news of the cross and the empty tomb. But we should never stop investing with the gospel in as many places as we can. Whenever we engage in kingdom enterprises, we offer the Holy Spirit something he can and often will use to save people's souls.

The Wind and the Clouds

Some people—including many Christians—have a completely different attitude toward spiritual business. They are so risk averse that they keep waiting until conditions are perfect before they do the work that God is calling them to do. Sometimes they end up waiting forever. "If the clouds are full of rain, they empty themselves on the earth, and if a tree falls to the south or to the north, in the place where the tree falls, there it will lie. He who observes the wind will not sow, and he who regards the clouds will not reap" (Ecclesiastes 11:3–4).

These two verses warn us what will happen if we do not obey the commands in verses 1–2. If we fail to invest wisely and give generously, we will never do any productive spiritual work that will yield a kingdom harvest. To show this, the Preacher pictures a farmer standing out in his field. The clouds are heavy with rain—part of a familiar cycle in nature. Nearby a tree has fallen to the ground, possibly as the result of a storm. There is nothing the farmer can do about either the rain or the tree; these natural and seemingly random events are far outside his personal control.

The one thing that the farmer can control is when he will sow his seed and harvest his crops. But this particular farmer is just standing there—watching the wind and the clouds, but not farming his field. The implication is that he is trying to guess when he can safely cast his seed or harvest his grain. Although there is "a time to plant, and a time to pluck up what is planted" (Ecclesiastes 3:2), apparently this man is not sure what time it is! Back in chapter 10, the Preacher introduced us to a foolish homeowner who was too lazy to fix his roof (v. 18). The farmer in chapter 11 also refuses to work, but he is a different kind of fool. He keeps watching and waiting, but never sowing or reaping. Why not? Because rather than getting on with his work, he keeps hoping for better conditions.

By showing us this farmer, the Preacher is giving us a practical warning that we can apply to many situations in life. How do you respond when things seem out of your control or when you have reason to fear that something bad might happen? Some people get paralyzed with fear. Or they procrastinate. Instead of doing what they know they ought to be doing, they keep putting things off. There is always some plausible excuse for delay. Maybe the weather will be better tomorrow!

As long as we keep thinking this way, we will never accomplish anything in life. At planting time there is always a chance that the weather will stay dry, in which case the seed we sow will shrivel and die. At harvesttime, there is always a chance that a storm will strike before we get all the grain safely into the barn. There are no guarantees in life. "Time and chance happen to [us] all" (Ecclesiastes 9:11). You never know. Nevertheless, the Preacher says, you will never reap if you never sow!

Rather than watching the wind and the clouds, imagining all the difficulties and waiting for better circumstances, we should try and do what we can with whatever God has given us in life. Pursue the dream you believe that God has given for your calling in life. Get involved in ministry. Show mercy to someone in need. Start a friendship with a neighbor, and pray that God will use that relationship to lead your neighbor to Christ.

Do not hold back because of fear, but step out by faith—not faith that your own efforts will succeed, necessarily, but faith that God will take what you offer and use it in some way for his glory. But whatever you do, do not use the sovereignty of God or the uncertain difficulties of life as an excuse for not doing anything at all. "If there are risks in everything," Derek Kidner writes, "it is better to fail in launching out than in hugging one's resources to oneself."[7] When it comes to kingdom work, we should always be venture capitalists, willing to take risks for the glory of God (cf. Luke 19:11–27).

The Mysteries of Providence

Chapter 11 began by commanding us to "cast" and to "give," even if we do not know what blessings or disasters may lie in the future (Ecclesiastes 11:1–2). Then the Preacher warned us what will happen if we refuse to act, like the farmer who watches the weather but never does any farming (Ecclesiastes 11:3–4).

Now in verse 5 he uses an analogy to remind us how little knowledge we have compared to God, and this will set up his concluding command, which basically repeats what he said in verses 1–2. Here, then, is the Preacher's analogy: "As you do not know the way the spirit comes to the bones in the womb of a woman with child, so you do not know the work of God who makes everything."

The word "spirit" (*ruach*) might just as well be translated "wind," as in verse 4. In that case the Preacher really draws two analogies. The first analogy points to the wind as an analogy for the mysterious purposes of God: we do not know which way the wind will blow. Jesus used the same analogy when he was teaching Nicodemus about the born-again mystery of regeneration: "The wind blows where it wishes, and you hear its sound, but you do not know where it comes from or where it goes. So it is with everyone who is born of the Spirit" (John 3:8).

Yet it is just as likely, if not more so, that the Preacher is talking about the human spirit and the way it animates the human body. What divine mysteries unfold when a child grows in his mother's womb! We know more, perhaps, than Solomon did about the growth of a child from conception to birth, but this knowledge does not diminish our sense of wonder. In fact, the more we know about life in the womb, the more amazing it seems. One whole new person (sometimes more than one) grows inside the body of another person. I say "person" because the Preacher clearly states that the child in the womb is not merely a body but also a living spirit. Who can possibly explain the mystery of how the life of a soul animates flesh and blood and bone? We are indeed "fearfully and wonderfully made" (Psalm 139:14).

This is not the only work of God that goes beyond our understanding, however. The Preacher uses the mysteries of the womb as an analogy for all the other wonders that are beyond human thought—the mysteries of creation and the providence of God.

Consider God's work in creation. In 2004 the Hubble Space Telescope photographed a tiny sliver of space through prolonged exposures that lasted for more than eleven days. Then astronomers counted the number of galaxies in the photograph. In that one little subsection of the universe, there were ten thousand galaxies, each containing one hundred billion stars. Who can explain how all those stars came into being? Or go to the other end of the scale, where scientists are trying to discover tangible evidence for the "last" atomic particle, the Higgs boson. Yet as soon as they observe it—if they ever do—they will wonder if there is something even smaller. Truly, God "does great things and unsearchable, marvelous things without number" (Job 5:9). The whole universe is full of mysteries, from inside the atom to the farthest star in space and everything in between.

What God does in our own lives is no less mysterious. Why did he take something away that we were hoping to keep or give us something that we never wanted to have? Why did our prayers go unanswered and our dreams go unfulfilled? But there are also happier mysteries, including the mystery of our own salvation. What made the Son of God willing to suffer and to die for our sins, bearing our guilt and shame on the cross where he died naked and totally alone? Why did God choose us, of all people, to believe in Jesus and to receive life in his name? How did the Holy Spirit enable us to believe that the Bible really is the Word of God?

Then there are the mysteries that surround the work of the church. Why does the gospel spread faster in one place than another? What is God's plan for vast nations of people that are lost in sin? Why does the suffering church seem to produce more spiritual fruit? What on earth is God doing? As we consider such questions, we find ourselves agreeing with the Preacher's testimony that we "do not know the work of God who makes everything" (Ecclesiastes 11:5).

Reaping What You Sow

These great mysteries are a call to humility. Every time we encounter something that only God knows, we are reminded that he is God and we are not. These mysteries are also a call to faith. When we do not know what God is doing, we may still trust that *he does* know what he is doing. But the Preacher uses the mysteries of God as a call to faithful obedience. Here is his concluding command: "In the morning sow your seed, and at evening withhold not your hand, for you do not know which will prosper, this or that, or whether both alike will be good" (Ecclesiastes 11:6).

Some people use the mysterious ways of God as an excuse for giving up on their work or holding back in their witness. If God is sovereign over everything in the universe, including what will happen in the future, then why bother to do anything?

Ecclesiastes teaches us to take the opposite approach. It may be true that, to paraphrase this passage, "you never know," but it is equally true that "you will never reap if you never sow." So work hard for the kingdom of God. Live boldly and creatively. Try something new! Be a spiritual entrepreneur. Even if you are not completely sure what will work, try everything you can to serve Christ in a world that desperately needs the gospel. Work hard from morning till night, making the most of your time by offering God a full day's work. Then leave the results to him, knowing that he will use your work in whatever way he sees fit.

The Preacher's practical exhortation to sow good seed is not just for farmers, of course. It applies to many areas of life. But the Bible most frequently uses the imagery of sowing and reaping to talk about what we do with the Word of God. Jesus told a famous parable about a farmer who sowed his seed on four different types of soil. When he explained this parable to his disciples, he told them that "the sower sows the word" (Mark 4:14). Of all the things that we ought to be sowing, therefore, the most important is the living Word of God.

We sow the Word when we read it, study it, and memorize it for ourselves, listening to the voice of God. We sow the Word when we teach it to our children at bedtime or around the family dinner table. We sow the Word when we give someone a Bible or use a simple verse from Scripture with a friend who needs to know Jesus. We sow the Word when we take it to the prison, the nursing home, and the college or university campus. We sow the Word when we support sound Biblical preaching in our own local congregation, as well as through missions and ministries that broadcast the gospel around the world. There is no one single way to share the gospel; the best way to do it is every way we can.

From time to time we may wonder whether any gospel ministry ever accomplishes anything. But the Bible encourages us with many wonderful promises about the work that the Holy Spirit will do with the Word of God:

> For as the rain and the snow come down from heaven
>> and do not return there but water the earth,
> making it bring forth and sprout,
>> giving seed to the sower and bread to the eater,
> so shall my word be that goes out from my mouth;
>> it shall not return to me empty,
> but it shall accomplish that which I purpose,
>> and shall succeed in the thing for which I sent it. (Isaiah 55:10–11)

> Whoever sows sparingly will also reap sparingly, and whoever sows bountifully will also reap bountifully. (2 Corinthians 9:6)

> And let us not grow weary of doing good, for in due season we will reap, if we do not give up. (Galatians 6:9)

Jesus Christ is the Lord of the harvest, which will come at the proper time. This was true in his own life and ministry. Jesus said, "Unless a grain of wheat falls into the earth and dies, it remains alone; but if it dies, it bears much fruit" (John 12:24). Jesus was talking about his own death on the cross and burial in the ground, as well as the resurrection that followed. It was not just words that Jesus sowed but his very life itself, when he offered his blood on the cross for our sins. The gospel harvest of his saving work is forgiveness and eternal life for everyone who believes in him. Jesus does not offer this grace in portions to seven, or even to eight, but to millions and millions of sinners who turn to him in faith and repentance.

Now Jesus sends us out to do a little sowing of our own. He is the Lord of the surprising harvest (surprising to us, not to him). We do not always know what God will do with what we sow. But if we keep sowing, the day will come when God will reap a harvest of salvation.

One of my favorite examples of God's surprising harvest is the conversion of Luke Short at the tender age of 103. Short was sitting under a hedge in Virginia when he happened to remember a sermon he had once heard preached by the famous Puritan John Flavel. As he recalled the sermon, Short asked God to forgive his sins right then and there, through the death and resurrection of Jesus Christ. He lived for three more years, and when he died, the following words were inscribed on his tombstone: "Here lies a babe in grace, aged three years, who died according to nature, aged 106." But here is the remarkable part of the story: the sermon that old Mr. Short remembered had been preached *eighty-five* years earlier, back in England! Nearly a century had passed between Flavel's sermon and Short's conversion, between the sowing and the reaping.[8]

So cast your bread upon the waters. Give a portion to seven, or even to eight. In the morning sow your seed, and at evening withhold not your hand. What God will do, you never know; but you will never reap if you never sow!

25

Young and Old

ECCLESIASTES 11:7—12:7

*Remember also your Creator in the days
of your youth, before the evil days come
and the years draw near of which you
will say, "I have no pleasure in them."*

12:1

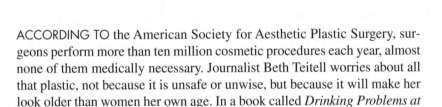

ACCORDING TO the American Society for Aesthetic Plastic Surgery, sur-
geons perform more than ten million cosmetic procedures each year, almost
none of them medically necessary. Journalist Beth Teitell worries about all
that plastic, not because it is unsafe or unwise, but because it will make her
look older than women her own age. In a book called *Drinking Problems at
the Fountain of Youth*, Teitell comments that no one is safe from this fear,
not even the rich:

> I know women who worked hard to get into good colleges, worked their
> connections to land enviable jobs, married well, produced children who
> could pose for Ralph Lauren ads, vacation on the right islands with the
> right beach towels and the right heiresses—they have fractional owner-
> ships in Cessnas, for heaven's sake—and yet if they have furrows and
> hints of upper-lip lines and puppet mouth when those around them are
> smoother than freshly ironed Pratesi linens, what's it all worth? In a word,
> nothing.[1]

Whether she knows it or not, Teitell is confronting one of the reigning
idolatries of modern times—the cult of youth. For people who know they are
getting older, worshiping this god or goddess demands endless efforts to stay

young. But many young people worship the same deity. Rather than respecting their elders, they look down on people or ideas that seem old-fashioned. They want everything new and trendy. It is hard for them to imagine that they will ever grow old. Given the choice, some would rather die first.

Whether we are young or old or somewhere in between, Ecclesiastes can help us. The Preacher who wrote this book teaches us to celebrate the joys of life at any age. But he is also honest about the troubles that come with growing old. By the wisdom of the Spirit, he gives a series of calls that can help us live well, however young or old we happen to be—two calls to rejoice, one call to remove, and one call to remember.

Sweetness and Light

The first call is to rejoice in the goodness of life, even though we know that life is vanity. The Preacher says, "Light is sweet, and it is pleasant for the eyes to see the sun. So if a person lives many years, let him rejoice in them all; but let him remember that the days of darkness will be many. All that comes is vanity" (Ecclesiastes 11:7–8).

This call is especially for old people—people who have lived "many years." It is good to find joy in the pleasures of life. Many things in life are "sweet," like the taste of golden honey or the soft fold of skin on a baby's neck or the sound of the sweet spot on a baseball bat when it connects for a home run. Many things in life are also bright—the first shaft of morning sunshine over a shimmering sea, a full rainbow against dark clouds, a blazing campfire on a warm summer's night, the twinkling lights of home after a long journey. How sweet life is, and how bright are its many blessings!

What a joy it is, therefore, to live for many years—not only because we have more time to serve the Lord in sowing and reaping (see Ecclesiastes 11:1–6), but also because we have more opportunity to enjoy the goodness of life. I often remember the words of one old saint who was feeling the effects of his age. When I worried that he might be discouraged, he said, "Not at all, because with the Lord, life gets better and better!" For the faithful believer, long life is a blessing from God (Psalm 91:16).

The right way to respond is by rejoicing. Praise God for the goodness of life! Praise him for everything sweet you taste and everything bright you see. The living God is the Lord of light. When he said, "Let there be light!" (Genesis 1:3), there was light, and that light has been shining ever since. According to the prophets, "the sun of righteousness shall rise with healing in its wings" (Malachi 4:2). Now the God of light deserves our praise. We should praise God the way Francis of Assisi did when he said, "Be praised, my Lord, through all your creatures, especially through Brother Sun, who brings the day; you give light through him. And he is beautiful and radiant in all his splendor! Of you, Most High, he bears the likeness."[2]

Yet even as we rejoice, we need to remember that there is more to life than sweetness and light, which is something that Qoheleth never lets us forget. If we live for "many years," he says, "the days of darkness will be many" (Ecclesiastes 11:8), and we will taste what is bitter in life as well as what is sweet. Sooner or later we will suffer loss, disappointment, injustice, and grief. "All that comes"—including the years when we are old and gray— "is vanity" (Ecclesiastes 11:8). At the beginning of Ecclesiastes we were told that "all is vanity" (Ecclesiastes 1:2). If life has no unmitigated joys or undiminished pleasures, then why should our later years be any different?

Some commentators think the Preacher is confused here, that he is "giving the contradictory advice that his reader should both enjoy life but also remember that he is going to die."[3] This is not confusion but clarity. Ecclesiastes gives us a realistic view of life that is joyful about its happy pleasures while at the same time sober about its many sorrows. The book steadfastly refuses to show us anything less than the whole of life as it actually is.

When the Preacher tells us that we will have many dark days, he is not being cynical or trying to rob us of all our joy. Instead he is telling us to enjoy life as much as we can for as long as we can. "The days of darkness" qualify what he says about rejoicing in the light, but they do not negate it. To the end of our days there is sweetness in the world, and therefore we are called to rejoice. Do not take life for granted. Do not complain about all your problems, the way older people sometimes do. But greet each new day the way the Psalmist did, saying, "This is the day that the LORD has made; let us rejoice and be glad in it" (Psalm 118:24).

Young at Heart

The call to rejoice is not just for the elderly but also for youngsters. While old people are to praise God for the length of their days, young people are to praise God for the strength of their youth. Hence the Preacher's second call: "Rejoice, O young man, in your youth, and let your heart cheer you in the days of your youth. Walk in the ways of your heart and the sight of your eyes" (Ecclesiastes 11:9).

Young people enjoy many blessings in life. They have fewer of the cares that come with having adult responsibilities. Their bodies are strong and getting stronger. Their hearts are full of good cheer and easy laughter. The future is full of possibilities. There is freedom to take risks and time to go a new direction in life. Young people still dare to dream that they can make a difference in the world. These are all reasons for the young to rejoice.

And yet once again the Preacher sounds a cautionary note. What he says about following one's heart might lead some people to think they can do whatever they please, which frankly is the way many young people operate.

They think mainly of themselves. They expect everyone else to operate on their schedule. Living for the moment, they do not stop to think about the consequences of their actions. They buy on impulse. Rather than cleaning up after themselves, they leave a mess behind. They take the immediate pleasure of sex without making the long-term love commitment of marriage. To make it clear, then, that young people are called to holiness, the Preacher says, "Walk in the ways of your heart and the sight of your eyes. But know that for all these things God will bring you into judgment" (Ecclesiastes 11:9).

The Preacher knows that young people face many temptations. He also believes that God is a righteous judge who will hold every one of us accountable for what we do. Therefore, he reminds us that every time we follow our hearts and do what looks good to us, we have to answer to God for what we have done. Young people, especially, should beware of "the lust of the flesh, and the lust of the eyes, and the pride of life" (1 John 2:16, KJV). The Preacher does not say this to suck all the joy out of life or to give us the impression that God is out to get us, but to remind us that we live before God and are called to rejoice in him.

The word "judgment" at the end of verse 9 is literally "*the* judgment," and thus it may refer to the last of all judgments—the great day when "God judges the secrets of men by Christ Jesus" (Romans 2:16). That day may seem like it is a long way off—too far to make any difference in our daily decision-making. But the Judge is always near. He sees everything that we do. God "looks to the ends of the earth and sees everything under the heavens" (Job 28:24). This means that everything we do and everything we decide matters for eternity. How we spend our money, what we do with our bodies, the way we use our time, what we decide about our future, how we handle our relationships—what we touch, taste, hear, and see—all of this matters to our Judge and therefore ought to matter to us as well.

Rejoice responsibly. Enjoy life's pleasures, but not in sinful ways. Celebrate the gift of youth, but at the same time follow God's command to "flee youthful passions and pursue righteousness, faith, love, and peace, along with those who call on the Lord from a pure heart" (2 Timothy 2:22).

Pain Remedy

After his call for old people and young people to rejoice, the Preacher gives a call to remove: "Remove vexation from your heart, and put away pain from your body, for youth and the dawn of life are vanity" (Ecclesiastes 11:10).

With these words, the Preacher advises us to eliminate the bad things in life that trouble our bodies and our souls. A "vexation" is any problem that causes us worry and concern, that "angers, grieves or irritates."[4] It is "the bitterness provoked by a hard and disappointing world."[5] There is little point in listing examples. With so much trouble in the world, it would be hard to know where to start or how to end. Furthermore, the vexations are different for each one of us. What angers or irritates one person may or may not anger or irritate someone else. Yet we can all agree that life is full of vexation. It is also full of physical pain.[6] Whether from illness, accident, or disability, we all suffer bodily pains.

Once again the Preacher is honest about the troubles of life, both physical and psychological. He also has some advice for us: we should do what we can to remove discouragement from our souls and to minimize damage to our bodies. This is not a call to deny the very real suffering that everyone experiences. Nor is it a call to escape pain by living for pleasure. Rather, it is a call to take care of our mental and physical health.

If we are getting discouraged by various vexations, and if we are tempted therefore to become depressed or disillusioned, we should do what the Preacher says and remove those vexations from our hearts. This starts with refusing to feel sorry for ourselves. Rather than dwelling on all the things that are going wrong, we should count our blessings. We should also seek the care of a pastor or the counsel of Christian friends—brothers and sisters in Christ who are sympathetic to our situation but also able to see our situation for what it is and tell us what we need to hear, especially from the Scriptures.

But the very best remedy for vexation is to go to God in prayer, telling him all our troubles. "Do not be anxious about anything"—or *vexed* about anything, we might say—"but in everything by prayer and supplication with thanksgiving let your requests be made known to God." This command is then followed by a promise: "And the peace of God, which surpasses all understanding, will guard your hearts and your minds in Christ Jesus" (Philippians 4:6–7). The Biblical way of removing vexation is to cast our cares on God.

If our sufferings are physical, it is right and good for us to seek a way to ease the pain. When the Bible tells us to put away pain, it is not giving us license to drown our sorrows in alcohol or to use life-destroying drugs. But physical pain is an evil that we are right to avoid, when we are able to do it in a way that honors God. Ecclesiastes 11:10 thus provides part of the Biblical rationale for good medical care.

One of the reasons why the Preacher tells us to remove pain and vexation is because he knows that we cannot stay young forever: "youth and the dawn of life are vanity" (Ecclesiastes 11:10). This does not mean that youth is meaningless. The Preacher has already told us to rejoice in our youth and to enjoy its many pleasures. But youth is vain or empty (*hebel*) in the sense that it is elusive and ephemeral. It is like smoke that disappears into thin air or mist that vanishes with the morning sun. One day we are young and strong, but almost before we know it, those days are gone. Thus the Preacher advises us to live free from care as long as we can.

This is not cynicism or pessimism but realism about the limitations of human life. In fact, we might even call it a kind of optimism because the Preacher is helping us make the most out of life. God "has made everything beautiful in its time" (Ecclesiastes 3:11). There is a time to be young and strong, and as long as we are in that season of life, we should celebrate its blessings.

I remember tasting this kind of joy on the basketball court when I was about twenty-five years old. I had just raced down the court and nailed a three-pointer—*swish!*—one of the greatest feelings in life. As I ran back to play defense, I thought to myself, "Enjoy this feeling now, and praise God for it, because the day will come when you are no longer able to play basketball." Knowing the vanity of life helped me to enjoy that game more and at the same time helped prepare me in some small way for old age. God gave me the grace both to enjoy my youth and to learn wisdom for growing old.

Everything the Preacher has said to young people about rejoicing in life, about removing pain and vexation, and about loving God rather than living for youthful lusts is well expressed in a majestic hymn by Margaret Clarkson:

> We worship you, Lord Christ,
> Our Savior and our King,
> To you our youth and strength
> Adoringly we bring:
> So fill our hearts, that all may view
> Your life in us, and turn to you.[7]

This Old House

The Preacher's last instruction is mainly for young people, although maybe the people who understand it the best are older. It is a call is to remembrance: "Remember also your Creator in the days of your youth, before the evil days come and the years draw near of which you will say, 'I have no pleasure in them'" (Ecclesiastes 12:1).

Here Qoheleth is calling us to live a God-centered life, making the God who made the universe our first and highest priority. In fact, this is the key to all the other things that he has called us to do in this passage. The reason we are able to rejoice in our long years of life or else in our youth and strength is because every day is a gift from our Creator God. The reason we need to walk in holy ways is because our Maker is also our Judge. The best remedy for any pain or vexation is to cast our care upon the God who made us and knows all about us. Everything that the Preacher says in this passage assumes and requires the close presence of God.

To remember God is to live our whole lives for him. It is to be mindful of God in every circumstance—including him in all our plans, praising him for all his blessings, and praying to him through all our troubles. Such remembrance, writes Derek Kidner, is "no perfunctory or purely mental act; it is to drop our pretense of self-sufficiency and commit ourselves to Him."[8]

The best time in life to do this is when we are still young enough to give a whole lifetime to God's service. Do not wait until you are so old that you do not have much desire to do anything because life has lost its pleasure. Rather, give your life to God now, while you still have enough passion to make a difference in the world. Remember God when at home and at school. Remember him when outside in his creation or indoors in the kitchen or the bedroom. Remember him at work and at play—playing baseball or playing the violin. Do not forget about God, but remember him in everything you do.

To help prove his point, the Preacher gives us one of the most memorable poems in the Bible. The poem is about the reality of mortality. A literature professor would call it a "character sketch"—"a generalized and figurative description of old age in its physical manifestations."[9] It also happens to be the most beautiful poem ever written about growing old. The time to remember our Creator is

> before the sun and the light and the moon and the stars are darkened and the clouds return after the rain, in the day when the keepers of the house tremble, and the strong men are bent, and the grinders cease because they are few, and those who look through the windows are dimmed, and the doors on the street are shut—when the sound of the grinding is low, and one rises up at the sound of a bird, and all the daughters of song are brought low—they are afraid also of what is high, and terrors are in the way; the almond tree blossoms, the grasshopper drags itself along, and desire fails. (Ecclesiastes 12:2–5)

Verse 2 compares the troubles of old age to a gathering storm. Both night and day are darkened by clouds, and after the rain falls, the storm clouds gather again. This is what happens as people grow old. When we are young, there is still time for the sky to clear, but when we are old, we suffer one trouble after another, with little or no time to recover. The light of life grows dim. Derek Kidner says that this scene is:

> somber enough to bring home to us not only the fading of physical and mental powers but the more general desolations of old age. There are many lights that are liable then to be withdrawn, besides those of the senses and faculties as, one by one, old friends are taken, familiar customs change, and long-held hopes now have to be abandoned.[10]

Verses 3–5 compare an elderly person to a house that is slowly crumbling with decay.[11] "The keepers of the house" are a person's arms, which start to tremble. "The strong men" are legs, which are bent with age. "The grinders" are teeth, of course, if any are left. "The windows" are eyes dimmed by cataracts or a general loss of vision. "The doors" are ears that are deaf or hard of hearing and thus closed to the hustle and bustle of a noisy street. Michael Eaton thinks that "the grinding of grain must have been a common cheerful indication that younger folk were going about their business, while the elderly found themselves increasingly shut off from the hum of daily life."[12] "The daughters of song" are vocal cords that no longer have the elastic strength to make sweet music. Since almond trees are pale in the springtime, the phrase "the almond tree blossoms" indicates that someone's hair has turned white with age.

Nor are these the only problems that come with growing old. According to verse 4, old people have trouble sleeping; they are up with the first songbirds, before dawn. According to verse 5, they are afraid—afraid of falling or of being attacked along the road. They suffer from diminished desire, which may include sexual desire but is not limited to that. One thinks of old Barzillai's lament when King David invited him to the royal palace in Jerusalem: "I am this day eighty years old. Can I discern what is pleasant and what is not? Can your servant taste what he eats or what he drinks? Can I still listen to the voice of singing men and singing women?" (2 Samuel 19:35).

Then one day the crumbling old house will collapse. The Preacher prepares us for this with the image of the grasshopper in verse 5. Typically grasshoppers spring up in the air. So a grasshopper stiffly scraping itself along the ground is a goner. Yet the same fate awaits us all—not just the diminishment of old age but the dust of death. This too is a reason to remember our Creator while we are still young: "because man is going to his eternal home, and the mourners go about the streets—before the silver cord is snapped, or the golden bowl is broken, or the pitcher is shattered at the fountain, or the wheel broken at the cistern, and the dust returns to the earth as it was, and the spirit returns to God who gave it" (Ecclesiastes 12:5–7).

These are all memorable descriptions of death. To die is to go to our eternal home. We will not live here forever. Today we are young and strong, but already we are getting older, and tomorrow the mourners will carry our bodies out for burial.

Death is like the snapping of a silver cord and the shattering of a golden bowl. This may refer to a golden lamp suspended by a silver chain (in which case the light of life has been snuffed out). But in any case something precious and beautiful is broken. To change the metaphor, death is like a wheel broken and a jar shattered at a well for drawing water. The apparatus is destroyed beyond repair, and thus it is useless for drawing any life-giving water.

What else can we say about death? To die is to return to the dust—the curse that God pronounced on Adam and all our sin (see Genesis 3:19). This is the same curse that Jesus suffered on the cross, for in the psalm of the God-forsaken servant we hear him say to his Father, "you lay me in the dust of death" (Psalm 22:15). We too are made of dust (Genesis 2:7; Psalm 103:14), and to the dust we shall return. One day our bodies will go into the ground, and our souls will return to their Maker as death separates body from soul until the resurrection.

These are the sober realities of life and death that everyone has to face in a fallen world. The call of the Preacher is to remember our Creator *now*, before all of these things happen to us.

Young Again

Bono has written: "Ecclesiastes is one of my favorite books. It's a book about a character who wants to find out why he's alive, why he was created. He tries knowledge. He tries wealth. He tries experience. He tries everything. You hurry to the end of the book to find out why, and it says, 'Remember your Creator.' In a way, it's such a letdown. Yet it isn't."[13] No, it isn't. Getting to know our Creator *before* we grow old and die is the most important thing we can ever do.

This call is especially for young people. Remember God now, while you still have your wits about you. Remember God now, while you are still charting your course in life and making important decisions about what to do with your talents. Remember your Creator now, before you forget the God who made you and make a lot of bad decisions that you will regret later. Remember God now, while you still have a whole lifetime to live for his glory. As Charles Bridges once said, "Many have remembered too late—none too soon."[14]

This passage is not just for young people, however. It is also for people who are growing old. Admittedly, taken by itself, the Preacher's poem does not seem very encouraging. However honest it may be, it hardly seems very hopeful! Yet there is genuine encouragement here for older saints.

Be encouraged by the beauty of this poem. Growing old and facing death are some of the hardest experiences in life. The Bible is honest about this, but not bitter. In fact, this passage contains some of the most beautiful words ever breathed. The Holy Spirit took special pains to treat aging and dying with dignity. This shows God's loving care for his people all through life, even down to old age, and then on to the grave. The Scripture says, "Precious in the sight of the LORD is the death of his saints" (Psalm 116:15). But it is not only the death of his saints that is precious to God—they are precious to him throughout the whole process of aging.

Be encouraged by this as well: your Creator remembers you, even if you do not always remember him. The security of our salvation does not depend on our remembrance of God but on his promise to remember us. So the psalmist prayed, "O God, from my youth you have taught me, and I still proclaim your wondrous deeds. So even to old age and gray hairs, O God, do not forsake me" (Psalm 71:17–18).

By the time he was in his early nineties, my grandfather found it hard to remember much of anything, including, on occasion, who he was. This was extremely distressing for him because he knew that he was confused but didn't know why. "I can't remember who I am!" he said to my mother. "That's okay, Dad," she said, "I know who you are, and I can take care of everything you need."

There is even more security for every believer in the remembrance of God. The great thing is not that we remember our Creator, although of course we are called to remember him. The great thing is that God remembers us now and will remember us all our days. Jesus said, "And this is the will of him who sent me, that I should lose nothing of all that he has given me, but raise it up on the last day. For this is the will of my Father, that everyone who looks on the Son and believes in him should have eternal life, and I will raise him up on the last day" (John 6:39–40). Jesus has promised to remember us from now until the last of all days, when he will raise us up to everlasting life.

Be encouraged by the promise of the resurrection, that those who die believing in Christ will live again and will be young forever. Like the Preacher of Ecclesiastes, the Apostle Paul understood that one day the old house of our earthly body will be destroyed. But as the servant of a Savior who rose from the grave, he also believed that our bodies will be rebuilt: "For we know that if the tent that is our earthly home is destroyed"—an image similar to the collapsed house in Ecclesiastes 12—"we have a building from God, a house not made with hands, eternal in the heavens" (2 Corinthians 5:1). This new house is the resurrection body of everyone who believes in Jesus, his cross, and his empty tomb.

Maybe this is why some old saints are so young at heart that they hardly seem to grow old at all. I love the promise of Psalm 92, which compares the righteous to a palm tree growing in the house of God. "They still bear fruit in old age," the psalmist says; "they are ever full of sap and green" (v. 14). Even as they grow old, the righteous are alive by the power of the Holy Spirit living in them. Though outwardly they are "wasting away," inwardly they are "being renewed day by day" (2 Corinthians 4:16). They live in the hope of an eternal home, where they know they will be young again.

26

The End of the Matter

ECCLESIASTES 12:8–14

The end of the matter; all has been heard.
Fear God and keep his commandments, for
this is the whole duty of man. For God will
bring every deed into judgment, with every
secret thing, whether good or evil.

12:13–14

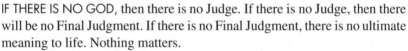

IF THERE IS NO GOD, then there is no Judge. If there is no Judge, then there will be no Final Judgment. If there is no Final Judgment, there is no ultimate meaning to life. Nothing matters.

This is the logic of Quentin's argument in *After the Fall* by Arthur Miller. Quentin says:

> For many years I looked at life like a case at law. It was a series of proofs. When you're young you prove how brave you are, or smart; then, what a good lover; then, a good father; finally, how wise, or powerful. . . . But underlying it all, I see now, there was a presumption. That one moved . . . on an upward path toward some elevation, where . . . God knows what . . . I would be justified, or even condemned. A verdict anyway. I think now that my disaster really began when I looked up one day . . . and the bench was empty. No judge in sight. And all that remained was the endless argument with oneself, this pointless litigation of existence before an empty bench. . . . Which, of course, is another way of saying—despair.[1]

If there is no God to judge the world, then human existence is a pointless litigation that ends in meaningless despair. The Preacher who wrote

273

Ecclesiastes would have agreed. From the beginning of his book he has been saying that if there is no God, there is no meaning. Nothing matters.

What He Said

"Vanity of vanities . . . all is vanity" (Ecclesiastes 12:8). These are the Preacher's first and also his last words (see Ecclesiastes 1:2)—a literary technique known as *inclusio*. The writer begins and ends his composition by saying exactly the same thing.

The Hebrew word for vanity (*hevel*) is the Preacher's multipurpose metaphor to express the futility of life in a fallen world. Taken literally, the word refers to a breath or vapor, like the steam rising from a boiling kettle. Such is life. It is impossible to grasp, and before you know it, life is gone; it vanishes into thin air.

The vapor of our existence is dramatically expressed in *Breath*, a play by Samuel Beckett that lasts a mere thirty-five seconds. As the curtain opens, there is a pile of rubbish on the stage, illuminated by a single light. The light dims and then brightens a little before going completely out. There are no words or actors in the drama, only a sound track with a human cry, followed by an inhaled breath, an exhaled breath, and another cry. The play thus depicts what King David wrote in the psalms: "mankind is a mere breath" (Psalm 39:5, 11).

By beginning and ending with the same statement, the structure of Ecclesiastes reinforces one of its main points—namely, that "there is nothing new under the sun" (Ecclesiastes 1:9). As it was before, so it is now, and so it will ever be. Vanity of vanities! All is vanity, all the time. Thus we end up right back where we began.

We should not think, however, that the Preacher merely repeats himself. Ecclesiastes 12:8 does bring us back to the same place where we began, but we are not the same people. Reading Ecclesiastes has given us a bigger perspective on life. The Preacher has shown us how vain life is; so when we hear him make the same statement at the end of his book, it strikes us with much greater force.

Now we know that work is vanity, that there is nothing for us to gain from all our restless toil under the sun (e.g., Ecclesiastes 1:3). It is all "vanity and striving after wind" (Ecclesiastes 1:13–14; 2:18–23). We know that human wisdom is vanity, that it only increases our "sorrow" and "vexation" (Ecclesiastes 1:18). Whether we are wise or foolish does not even matter because we will all die in the end (Ecclesiastes 2:15–16). We know that pleasure is vanity. Wine, women, and song; parks, houses, and vineyards; gold, silver, and treasure—there is "nothing to be gained under the sun" (Ecclesiastes 2:11).

It is all vanity. Power is vanity: there is no one to comfort the tears of the oppressed (Ecclesiastes 4:1). Money is vanity, too, because it causes no end of trouble as we look after our possessions, which may all be lost at a moment's notice (Ecclesiastes 5:11–14). But even if we manage to hold on to our money, it cannot satisfy our souls (Ecclesiastes 5:10).

Then there is the last of all vanities, which is the vanity of death. Nearly all of us will have to endure the indignities of growing old (Ecclesiastes 12:1ff.), and after that, the final vanity of returning to the ground from which we were made. Dust we are, and to the dust we shall return (Ecclesiastes 3:20).

Not that we never have any joy, of course. In spite of all the vanity, we can still rejoice in life's many blessings. The Preacher has encouraged us to eat and drink and find satisfaction in our work (e.g., Ecclesiastes 2:24). He has told us that there is a time for healing and harvesting, a time for laughing and dancing, a time for loving and making peace (Ecclesiastes 3:1–8). He has told us to rejoice in the prosperity that God so richly provides (Ecclesiastes 5:19; 7:14) and to enjoy life with the one whom we love (Ecclesiastes 9:9). There is joy in the world under the blessing of a faithful God.

Yet what the Preacher mainly wants us to see is how meaningless life is without God, how little joy there is under the sun if we try to leave our Creator out of his universe. By the time we get to the end of Ecclesiastes, we have to admit that he has proved his case. "Nothing in our search has led us home," says Derek Kidner; "nothing that we are offered under the sun is ours to keep."[2] Vanity of vanities! It is all vanity.

How He Said It

Yet "vanity" does not get the last word, either in the Bible or in the Christian life. Ecclesiastes might well have ended with chapter 12, verse 8 as a suitable summary of everything Qoheleth said. Instead it closes with further remarks that help us put the entire book into perspective.

The epilogue to Ecclesiastes may have been written by another author. The Preacher is still speaking in verse 8, but when we get to verse 9 there is a shift. Someone refers to the Preacher in the third person, as if to say, "Now let me give you my own perspective on all this."[3] Some scholars even think there may be two epilogues, one in verses 9–11 from someone who agrees with the Preacher and one in verses 12–14 from someone who tries to correct him.[4]

It may well be that these verses were written by someone other than the Preacher-King. But when we look carefully, we find the epilogue affirming both what Qoheleth said and the way that he said it, before applying his teaching in a practical way to the life that we live before God.

Up until now Ecclesiastes has told us what the Preacher said. Now the book tells us *how* he said it: "Besides being wise, the Preacher also taught the people knowledge, weighing and studying and arranging many proverbs with great care. The Preacher sought to find words of delight, and uprightly he wrote words of truth" (Ecclesiastes 12:9–10). Although these verses refer most specifically to what we read in Ecclesiastes, at the same time they tell us some important things about how the whole Bible was written.

The Preacher wrote with *logical clarity*. He took the time and trouble to evaluate all the wise sayings that he had heard and then included only the ones that were weighty enough to demand our full attention— proverbs like "anger lodges in the bosom of fools" (Ecclesiastes 7:9), for example, or "who can make straight what he [God] has made crooked?" (Ecclesiastes 7:13).

If the Preacher was King Solomon, as many people think, then what Ecclesiastes says about studying proverbs would help us make sense of the book of Proverbs, which mainly came from Solomon's pen. King Solomon heard many wise sayings over the course of his lifetime but only included in the Bible the ones that were wise and true—some three thousand proverbs in all (see 1 Kings 4:32).

Not only did the Preacher assess these proverbs studiously, but he also arranged them carefully. There is a logic to the way this book is put together. It is not the logic of a history or an epistle but of a collection of proverbs. Ecclesiastes was not thrown together but constructed as a complete work of literature. After an opening statement of theme (Ecclesiastes 1:1–11), the Preacher told us the story of his quest to find meaning in life (Ecclesiastes 1:12–6:12). Then, to help us know how to live for God in this vain world, he showed the difference between wisdom and folly (Ecclesiastes 7—11). He ended, appropriately enough, by talking again about death and dying (Ecclesiastes 12:1–7), before restating his primary theme—the vanity of all vanity (Ecclesiastes 12:8).

In addition to writing with logical clarity, the Preacher also wrote with *literary artistry*. He sought to find "words of delight" (Ecclesiastes 12:10)—a marvelous phrase that expresses the beauty of the Bible. Whether people agree with the Preacher or not, no one criticizes his writing style. The famous American writer Tom Wolfe described Ecclesiastes as "the highest flower of poetry, eloquence, and truth"—"the greatest single piece of writing I have known."[5] This is the book that gave us phrases like "the sun also rises" (Ecclesiastes 1:5, NKJV), "to everything there is a season" (Ecclesiastes 3:1), "eternity in the hearts of men" (Ecclesiastes 3:11, NIV), "cast your bread upon the waters" (Ecclesiastes 11:1), "the almond tree blossoms" (Ecclesiastes 12:5), and "man does not know his time" (Ecclesiastes 9:12).

Praise God for the beauty of Ecclesiastes—not just what the book says, but also the way the book says it. This is one of the many ways that God reveals his character and shows us his grace. He is a God of exquisite beauty. It is only appropriate, then, for the book that tells the story of his salvation to please the ear, inspire the imagination, fascinate the mind, and delight the soul.

The Preacher also wrote with *intellectual integrity*. Once he had found words of delight, "uprightly he wrote words of truth" (Ecclesiastes 12:10). To be of real spiritual help, it is not enough for someone to write clearly and stylishly; he must also write truthfully. If there is one thing we can always count on the Preacher to do, it is to tell us the truth—not just the truth about God but also the truth about life in a fallen world. This is why *Moby Dick* describes Ecclesiastes as "a fine-hammered steel of woe."[6] Whether he is talking about the agonies of old age or the anguish of losing a fortune, the Preacher never holds back from telling us what life is like under the sun.

The author of Ecclesiastes wrote with clarity, artistry, and integrity. Thus his book instructs our minds, touches our hearts, and guides us in the wisdom of God.

Why He Said It

Knowing what the Preacher said and how he said it, we still need to ask the question why. Are these "words of delight" also words of purpose? If so, what was the Preacher's reason for telling us about the vanity of life? Ecclesiastes closes with a clear purpose statement: "The words of the wise are like goads, and like nails firmly fixed are the collected sayings; they are given by one Shepherd" (Ecclesiastes 12:11).

The words of the Preacher—like the words of many other wise men— are like the goads that farmers use to drive their oxen down the road. A "goad" is one of the tools of a shepherd's trade, a sharp stick that spurs a stubborn beast to keep moving. It is not designed to injure the animal, of course, but to inflict just enough pain to get his full cooperation!

Ecclesiastes does the same thing for people of faith. Although its words may be pleasing, they also inflict a certain amount of pain. They are goads to the conscience, making us uncomfortable enough to turn away from sin. They are a stimulus to the soul, steering us back onto the right spiritual path. In the days of the early church, Gregory Thaumaturgos said, "the mind is roused and spurred by the instructions of wise people just as much as the body is by an ox-goad being applied."[7]

Think of Ecclesiastes, then, as God's cattle prod. The Preacher's words push us not to expect lasting satisfaction in money or pleasure but only in the goodness of God. They steer us away from foolish rage and mocking laughter. They spur us on to patience, contentment, humility, and joy. When we forget about God, the Preacher prods us to remember our Creator, and the moment we begin to think that we will live forever, he pokes us in the ribs and reminds us that soon we will die.

Ecclesiastes also compares the Preacher's words to "nails firmly fixed."

This is not a prophecy of the crucifixion but an image of permanence and fixity. Some commentators believe that the nails in question are part of the farmer's cattle prod. But the Bible may simply mean that once a wise saying is driven into the mind, it stays there, like a nail pounded deep into a block of wood. Life may be a vapor, but wisdom can help us pin it down, giving us a place to hang our experience.

The Biblical proverbs have a way of nailing us right in the conscience. They also have a way of sticking into our brains. They are so memorable that once we hear them, we never forget them. There are many such proverbs in Ecclesiastes: "Two are better than one . . . a threefold cord is not quickly broken" (Ecclesiastes 4:9, 12), "the race is not to the swift, nor the battle to the strong . . . but time and chance happen to them all" (Ecclesiastes 9:11), and so forth.

All of these words—the wise sayings that get nailed into our hearts and that goad us into action—are "given by one Shepherd" (Ecclesiastes 12:11). Possibly this refers to the Preacher himself, since a pastor is a kind of shepherd. Furthermore, the Preacher has identified himself as "king over Israel in Jerusalem" (see Ecclesiastes 1:12), and in the ancient world kings were often identified as the shepherds of their people.

What seems more likely, however, is that the "shepherd" is none other than God himself (which is why the term is capitalized in the English Standard Version and some other translations). This is the first time that the title "shepherd" has appeared in Ecclesiastes, which seems to distinguish the Shepherd from the Preacher rather than to identify the two.[8] Furthermore, "Shepherd" is one of the noble titles for God in the Old Testament, not only in Psalm 23 but also in places like Psalm 80, where he is called "Shepherd of Israel" (v. 1). Thus the "one Shepherd" in Ecclesiastes 12 is the one and only Shepherd—God Almighty.

This makes Ecclesiastes 12:11 an important verse for the Biblical doctrine of the inspiration of Scripture (see also 2 Peter 1:21). Ecclesiastes is the very Word of God. The Preacher's words are not merely the musings of some skeptical philosopher; they are part of the inspired, infallible, and inerrant revelation of Almighty God. Therefore, it is not enough merely to admire their artistry and respect their integrity—we must also submit to their authority. As the Shepherd of our souls, God uses this book—as he uses everything written in the Bible—to prod us into spiritual action.

What Ecclesiastes says about the Shepherd's words takes on even greater force when we remember that our Shepherd is also our Savior. Jesus Christ is the Good Shepherd who lays down his life for his sheep (see John 10:11). Thus the words that we read in Ecclesiastes are really his words. Jesus is the one who calls us away from the vanity of life without God to find joy and meaning in his grace. We are not just living "under the sun." We are living under the Son—the Son of God who "loved us and gave himself up for us" (Ephesians 5:2).

Books without End

To read Ecclesiastes is to hear our Shepherd's voice. We should be very careful to listen to him, therefore, building our life on the Word of God and not on anything more or less. Thus the Bible gives us this warning: "My son, beware of anything beyond these. Of making many books there is no end, and much study is a weariness of the flesh" (Ecclesiastes 12:12).

What Ecclesiastes says about writing and reading can be confirmed by every scholar who has ever lived. Already in the ancient world, royal libraries were full of books. Today more than a million new books are published every year.[9] So what the Bible says is true: of the making of many books there is no end, and studying even some of them is enough to wear anyone out.

Not that we should never read any books (or write any books, for that matter). There is a place in Christian discipleship for the life of the mind. But we should always remember that human wisdom and man-made philosophy are extremely limited. How many books have been written! Yet how little most of them are able to teach us about the knowledge of God or the way of everlasting life. By far the most important book for us to study is the Bible, including everything written in Ecclesiastes. Therefore, be careful of trying to go farther than the Word of God.

In his novel *The Great Divorce*, C. S. Lewis describes a man from the suburbs of Hell who has spent his whole life seeking the truth, or so he says. The man wanders somewhere near the borders of Heaven, where, by the gracious invitation of God, he is invited to enter. But the Spirit warns him, "I can promise you . . . no scope for your talents; only forgiveness for having perverted them. No atmosphere of inquiry, for I will bring you to the land not of questions but of answers, and you shall see the face of God."

The man is not ready to let go of his quest, however. He wants to study some more before he accepts anyone else's conclusions. So he says, "We must all interpret those beautiful words in our own way! For me there is no such thing as a final answer. The free wind of inquiry must *always* continue to blow through the mind, must it not?"

"Listen!" God's Spirit says to the man. "Once you were a child. Once you knew what inquiry was for. There was a time when you asked questions because you wanted answers, and were glad when you had found them. Become that child again: even now." Yet, sadly, the man refuses. "When I became a man," he says, "I put away childish things." The conversation suddenly ends when the man remembers that he has an appointment, makes his apologies, and hurries off to a discussion group in Hell.[10]

Are you still seeking spiritual truth? End that quest and surrender to the God who knows the answers. Do not be like the person Paul warned about in the New Testament—"always learning and never able to arrive at a knowledge of the truth" (2 Timothy 3:7). Be content with what the Bible says. Do not accept anything less, and do not demand anything more (cf. Revelation 22:18–19).

All There Is

Ecclesiastes ends with the practical application of Biblical truth. We have heard what the Preacher said, as well as how and why he said it. How then should we respond? What is the book's conclusion? What should we take with us as we leave Ecclesiastes?

The book's final words provide an ethical and eschatological conclusion: "The end of the matter; all has been heard. Fear God and keep his commandments, for this is the whole duty of man. For God will bring every deed into judgment, with every secret thing, whether good or evil" (Ecclesiastes 12:13–14).

This is not the first time that Ecclesiastes has told us to fear the living God. To fear God is to honor and revere him, to worship him as God. At various points the Preacher has told us to fear God because his work is eternal (3:14) and because he demands holy worship (5:7). He has told us to fear God in times of adversity as well as prosperity (7:14–18). He has told us that if we do fear God, it will go well with us (8:12). Now we are told to fear God and to obey him because one day we will stand before him for judgment.

When the Bible says that "this is the whole duty of man," it literally says that "this is the whole of man." The word "duty" may well be implied, but Ecclesiastes is making a wider point. To say, "this is the whole of man" is to say, "this is all there is to man."[11] In other words, "this is what life is all about." The most important thing for any person to do is to worship God and obey his holy commandments. This is more than simply a man's duty. According to Charles Bridges, it is "his whole happiness and business—the total sum of all that concerns him—all that God requires of him—all that the Savior enjoins—all that the Holy Spirit teaches and works in him."[12] The greatest thing in life is to come before the one true God in worship and obedience.

Whether we are ready to come before God now or hope to avoid it, the truth is that one day every one of us will stand before God for judgment. "Life down here," wrote D. R. Davis, "is only a prelude to a greater life in the hereafter."[13] One day God will expose every secret sin and uncover every anonymous kindness. He will bring every last deed to judgment, whether it is good or evil, including every casual thought and every careless word (see

Matthew 12:36). He "will bring to light the things now hidden in darkness and will disclose the purposes of the heart" (1 Corinthians 4:5).

Ecclesiastes has mentioned all of this before as well. When the Preacher told us to rejoice in the strength of our youth, he also reminded us that one day God will bring us to judgment (see 11:9). And so he will. After all our days of questing, at the end of our spiritual road we will arrive at the throne of eternal justice and meet the Great Judge.

Why does Ecclesiastes tell us about the final judgment here? Because it means that everything matters. The Preacher began and ended his spiritual quest by saying that everything is vanity and that without God there is no meaning or purpose to life. "Is that all there is?" he kept asking. "Isn't there more to life than what I see under the sun?" If there is no God, and therefore no final judgment, then it is hard to see how anything we do really matters. But if there is a God who will judge the world, then *everything* matters.

This is *not* all there is. There is a God in Heaven who rules the world. There is a life to come after this life. One day the dead will be raised and every person who has ever lived will stand before God for judgment. When that day comes, it will be revealed that everything anyone ever did or said or thought has eternal significance.

At the final judgment, it will matter how we used our time, whether we wasted it on foolish pleasures or worked hard for the Lord. It will matter what we did with our money, whether we spent it on ourselves or invested it in the eternal kingdom. It will matter what we did with our bodies—what our eyes saw, our hands touched, and our mouths spoke. Whether we obeyed our father and mother will matter; so will the look we gave them and the little comment we made as we were walking away. What we did for a two-year-old will matter—the way we made time for her and got down on her level. What we said about someone else's performance will matter—the sarcastic remark or the word of genuine praise. The proud boast and the selfless sacrifice will matter. The household task and the homework assignment will matter. The cup of water, the tear of compassion, the word of testimony—all of it matters.

The final message of Ecclesiastes is not that nothing matters but that *everything* does. What we did, how we did it, and why we did it will all have eternal significance. The reason everything matters is because everything in the universe is subject to the final verdict of a righteous God who knows every secret.

What matters most of all, therefore, is the personal decision that each person makes about Jesus Christ. Ecclesiastes does not end with a promise of grace but with the warning of judgment. Nevertheless, this book has the gracious purpose of pointing us to the gospel. If it is true that God will bring everything to judgment, then it is desperately important for us to make sure that we will be found righteous on that awesome and momentous day. The only way to be sure is to entrust our lives to Jesus Christ, who alone has the power to save us from the wrath of God.

Into this vain world the Savior came. Like us, he suffered all of its futility and frustration. But Jesus did more. When the time was right, he took the judgment that we deserve by dying for our sins on the cross. His body returned to the dust, like the Preacher said. But on the third day he rose again, bringing life out of the grave.

Soon Jesus will come again, "on that day when, according to my gospel, God judges the secrets of men by Christ Jesus" (Romans 2:16). The Bible says that God "has fixed a day on which he will judge the world in righteousness by a man whom he has appointed; and of this he has given assurance to all by raising him from the dead" (Acts 17:31). When that day comes, everyone who believes in Jesus will stand before the righteous Judge and look into the eyes of a loving Savior. Trust Jesus, whose victory saves us from life's vanity—praise God!

Soli Deo gloria!

Notes

Preface and Acknowledgments

1. For a full account, see J. N. D. Kelly, *Golden Mouth: John Chrysostom—Ascetic, Preacher, Bishop* (Grand Rapids, MI: Baker, 1995), pp. 147–149.

Chapter One: Vanity of Vanities

1. Jonathan Kozol, *Amazing Grace: The Lives of Children and the Conscience of a Nation* (New York: HarperCollins, 1995), pp. 23, 44.
2. Rabbi Tanhum, *Mishnah Shabbat*, quoted in Tremper Longman III, *The Book of Ecclesiastes*, New International Commentary on the Old Testament (Grand Rapids, MI: Eerdmans, 1998), p. 27.
3. "Assessment of Ecclesiastes," in J. R. Dummelow, ed., *A Commentary on the Holy Bible* (New York: Macmillan, 1952), p. 391.
4. Curt Kuhl, *The Old Testament, Its Origin and Composition* (Richmond, VA: John Knox, 1961), pp. 264–265.
5. Herman Melville, *Moby Dick* (Boston: C. H. Simonds Co., 1892), p. 400.
6. Derek Kidner, *The Message of Ecclesiastes*, The Bible Speaks Today (Downers Grove, IL: InterVarsity, 1976), p. 15.
7. Norbert Lohfink, *Qoheleth*, trans. Sean McEvenue, A Continental Commentary (Minneapolis: Fortress, 2003), p. 1.
8. This remark come from Manfred O. Garibotti, who served as a ruling elder of Philadelphia's Tenth Presbyterian Church for more than fifty years.
9. Kidner, *The Message of Ecclesiastes*, 13.
10. R. N. Whybray, *Ecclesiastes*, The New Century Bible Commentary (Grand Rapids, MI: Eerdmans, 1989), p. 2.
11. Michael V. Fox, *A Time to Tear Down and a Time to Build Up: A Rereading of Ecclesiastes* (Grand Rapids, MI: Eerdmans, 1999), p. 159.
12. For a good example of what scholars have learned from this body of literature, see Tremper Longman III, *Fictional Akkadian Autobiography* (Winona Lake, IN: Eisenbrauns, 1991).
13. H. C. Leupold, *Exposition of Ecclesiastes* (Grand Rapids, MI: Baker, 1952), p. 15.
14. Kidner, *The Message of Ecclesiastes*, p. 17.
15. Fox, *A Time to Tear Down and a Time to Build Up*, p. 30.
16. Gerhard von Rad, quoted in Whybray, *Ecclesiastes*, p. 12.
17. Whybray, *Ecclesiastes*, p. 17.
18. Fox, *A Time to Tear Down and a Time to Build Up*, p. 147.
19. See especially Longman, *Ecclesiastes*, pp. 37–39.
20. Michael Eaton writes: "It is very odd to imagine an 'editor' issuing a work with which he disagrees but adding extensive notes and an epilogue to compensate. Why should an orthodox writer reproduce a skeptical book at all, let alone add orthodox glosses to produce a noticeably mixed bag? It is quite conceivable that an editor sent out Ecclesiastes with a commendatory note, but it is scarcely likely that anyone would do this if he were unhappy with the content of the work. No wisdom document exists in two recensions with opposite theologies; it is doubtful if one ever did" (*Ecclesiastes: An Introduction and Commentary*, Tyndale Old Testament Commentaries [Downers Grove, IL: InterVarsity, 1983], pp. 40–41).

21. From the entry to John Wesley's journal for January 2, 1777, as quoted in Whybray, *Ecclesiastes*, pp. xii–xiii.

Chapter Two: Same Old, Same Old

1. Stephen Crane, *The Black Riders and Other Lines* (Boston: Copeland and Day, 1896), p. 25.
2. Socrates, quoted in Suzy Platt, ed., *Respectfully Quoted: A Dictionary of Quotations* (New York: Barnes and Noble, 1992), p. 42.
3. Jerome, quoted in J. L. Crenshaw, *Ecclesiastes*, Old Testament Library (Philadelphia: Westminster, 1987), p. 63.
4. Roger Waters, "Time," *The Dark Side of the Moon* (Harvest, 1973).
5. Oscar Hammerstein II, "Ol' Man River," *Show Boat* (1927).
6. See Mark Kurlansky, *Cod: A Biography of the Fish That Changed the World* (New York: Penguin, 1998).
7. Matt Millen, quoted by David Jones and Bob Flounders, in "Lions were never all angels," *The Patriot News* (July 27, 2008).
8. For an overview of ancient civilizations in the Western hemisphere, consult Charles Mann, *1491: New Revelations of the Americas before Columbus* (New York: Vintage Books, 2006).
9. Derek Kidner, *The Message of Ecclesiastes*, The Bible Speaks Today (Downers Grove, IL: InterVarsity, 1976), p. 20.
10. H. C. Leupold, *Exposition of Ecclesiastes* (Grand Rapids, MI: Baker, 1952), p. 28.
11. Charles Bridges, *Ecclesiastes* (Carlisle, PA: Banner of Truth, 1998), pp. xiv–xv.
12. Didymus the Blind, *Commentary on Ecclesiastes*, 46.7, in *Ancient Christian Commentary on Scripture IX*, ed. J. Robert Wright (Downers Grove, IL: InterVarsity Press, 2005), p. 213.
13. T. M. Moore, *Ecclesiastes: Ancient Wisdom When All Else Fails: A New Translation and Interpretive Paraphrase* (Downers Grove, IL: InterVarsity, 2001), p. 11.

Chapter Three: Humanity's Search for Meaning

1. Douglas Adams, *The Hitchhiker's Guide to the Galaxy* (London: Pan Books, 1979), p. 162.
2. Derek Kidner, *The Message of Ecclesiastes*, The Bible Speaks Today (Downers Grove, IL: InterVarsity, 1976), p. 28.
3. R. N. Whybray, *Ecclesiastes*, The New Century Bible Commentary (Grand Rapids, MI: Eerdmans, 1989), p. 48.
4. Tremper Longman III, *The Book of Ecclesiastes*, New International Commentary on the Old Testament (Grand Rapids, MI: Eerdmans, 1998), p. 80.
5. See, e.g., Michael V. Fox, *A Time to Tear Down and a Time to Build Up: A Rereading of Ecclesiastes* (Grand Rapids, MI: Eerdmans, 1999), p. 171.
6. Leonard Woolf, quoted in *Wireless Age* (September/November 1998).
7. Whybray, *Ecclesiastes*, p. 49.
8. Francis Schaeffer, *Death in the City* (Downers Grove, IL: InterVarsity, 1970), p. 98.
9. Stephen Hawking, quoted in George Johnson, "The Theory That Ate the World," *The New York Times Book Review* (August 24, 2008), p. 16.
10. Longman, *The Book of Ecclesiastes*, p. 77.
11. See http://www.quoteland.com/topic.asp?CATEGORY_ID=89.
12. Richard Dawkins, *River out of Eden* (New York: Basic Books, 1995), p. 96.
13. Orhan Pamuk, *Other Colors: Essays and a Story*, as quoted by Colin Thubron, "Locked in the Writer's Room," *The New York Review of Books*, Vol. LIV (November 8, 2007): p. 4.
14. H. C. Leupold, *Exposition of Ecclesiastes* (Grand Rapids, MI: Baker, 1952), p. 55.

15. Kidner, *The Message of Ecclesiastes*, p. 31.
16. Leupold, *Exposition of Ecclesiastes*, p. 55.

Chapter Four: Meaningless Hedonism

1. "Is That All There Is?" by Jerry Leiber and Mike Stoller, as recorded in *Peggy Lee's All-Time Greatest Hits, Volume 1* (Curb Records).
2. U2, "The Wanderer," as sung with Johnny Cash on *Zooropa* (Island Records, 1993).
3. Derek Kidner, *The Message of Ecclesiastes*, The Bible Speaks Today (Downers Grove, IL: InterVarsity, 1976), p. 31.
4. T. M. Moore, *Ecclesiastes: Ancient Wisdom When All Else Fails: A New Translation and Interpretive Paraphrase* (Downers Grove, IL: InterVarsity, 2001), p. 23.
5. H. C. Leupold, *Exposition of Ecclesiastes* (Grand Rapids, MI: Baker, 1952), p. 60.
6. Moore, *Ecclesiastes: Ancient Wisdom When All Else Fails*, p. 23.
7. Kidner, *The Message of Ecclesiastes*, p. 32.
8. Michael A. Eaton, *Ecclesiastes: An Introduction and Commentary*, Tyndale Old Testament Commentaries (Downers Grove, IL: InterVarsity, 1983), p. 67.
9. Kidner, *The Message of Ecclesiastes*, p. 31.
10. Gregg Easterbrook, *The Progress Paradox: How Life Gets Better While People Feel Worse* (New York: Random House, 2003), p. 124.
11. Harold Kushner, *When All You've Ever Wanted Isn't Enough: The Search for a Life That Matters* (New York: Summit, 1986), pp. 17–18.
12. Interview available at http://www.cbsnews.com/stories/2005/11/03/60minutes/main 1008148_page3.shtml.
13. C. S. Lewis, *Mere Christianity* (New York: Macmillan, 1943), p. 119.
14. Andrew Delbanco, *The Real American Dream: A Meditation on Hope*, quoted in Easterbrook, *The Progress Paradox*, p. 248.
15. Mark Driscoll, "Setting the Record Crooked," *Preaching Today* (issue 266).
16. Christina Rossetti, "Jesus Alone," *Christina Rossetti: The Complete Poems* (New York: Penguin Classics, 2001), p. 588.
17. *Time* (January 24, 1964), quoted in Michael Cassidy, *Chasing the Wind: Answers for Life's Questions* (London: Hodder and Stoughton, 2002), pp. 24–25.
18. Martin Luther, "Notes on Ecclesiastes," in *Luther's Works*, trans. and ed. Jaroslav Pelikan, 56 vols. (St. Louis: Concordia, 1972), 15:30.
19. R. Kent Hughes quoted this testimony in a sermon entitled "Set Apart to Save: Hedonism," preached at College Church in Wheaton on November 11, 2001, and also in his book *Set Apart: Calling a Worldly Church to a Godly Life* (Wheaton, IL: Crossway, 2003), p. 40.

Chapter Five: Wisdom and Mad Folly

1. This short story is available in several Welsh and English editions, including the one that Penguin Books published in London in 1996.
2. William Shakespeare, *Macbeth*, Act V, scene v.
3. Michael V. Fox, *A Time to Tear Down and a Time to Build Up: A Rereading of Ecclesiastes* (Grand Rapids, MI: Eerdmans, 1999), p. 182.
4. Michael A. Eaton, *Ecclesiastes: An Introduction and Commentary*, Tyndale Old Testament Commentaries (Downers Grove, IL: InterVarsity, 1983), p. 68.
5. T. M. Moore, *Ecclesiastes: Ancient Wisdom When All Else Fails: A New Translation and Interpretive Paraphrase* (Downers Grove, IL: InterVarsity, 2001), p. 25.
6. Gregg Easterbrook, *The Progress Paradox: How Life Gets Better While People Feel Worse* (New York: Random House, 2003), p. 209.
7. Woody Allen, quoted in Steven Pinker, "The Brain: The Mystery of Consciousness," *Time* (January 19, 2007), p. 70.
8. John Blanchard recounts this story in *Where Do We Go from Here?* (Darlington, UK: Evangelical Press, 2008), p. 4.

9. Derek Kidner, *The Message of Ecclesiastes*, The Bible Speaks Today (Downers Grove, IL: InterVarsity, 1976), p. 34.

10. Fox, *A Time to Tear Down and a Time to Build Up: A Rereading of Ecclesiastes*, p. 184.

11. Voltaire, quoted in Charles Bridges, *A Commentary on Ecclesiastes* (1860; repr. Edinburgh: Banner of Truth, 1961), p. 41.

12. C. S. Lewis, "De Profundis," in *Spirits in Bondage*, quoted in Alan Jacobs, *The Narnian* (New York: Harper, 2005), p. 78.

13. Francois Mauriac, *The Knot of Vipers*, in *A Mauriac Reader* (New York: Farrar, Straus, and Giroux, 1968), p. 315.

Chapter Six: Working Things Out

1. Leland Ryken, "In Search of a Christian Work Ethic for the Christian Worker," *Business and Professional Ethics Journal*, Vol. 23, No. 4 (2004), pp. 153–170.

2. Leo Tolstoy, *A Confession*, quoted in Timothy Keller, *The Reason for God: Belief in an Age of Skepticism* (New York: Dutton, 2008), p. 201.

3. James Limburg, *Encountering Ecclesiastes: A Book for Our Time* (Grand Rapids, MI: Eerdmans), p. 33.

4. Warren Schmidt, played by Jack Nicholson, in *About Schmidt* (New Line Cinema, 2002).

5. Michael A. Eaton, *Ecclesiastes: An Introduction and Commentary*, Tyndale Old Testament Commentaries (Downers Grove, IL: InterVarsity, 1983), p. 73.

6. Martin Luther, "Notes on Ecclesiastes," in *Luther's Works*, trans. and ed. Jaroslav Pelikan, 56 vols. (St. Louis: Concordia, 1972), 15:46.

7. For example, on page 214 of *How to Read the Bible for All It's Worth* (Grand Rapids, MI: Zondervan, 1993), Gordon Fee and Douglas Stuart say, "The bulk of the book, everything but two final verses, represents a brilliant, artful argument for the way one would look at life—*if* God did *not* play a direct, intervening role in life and *if* there were no life after death." The book thus offers us "the secular, fatalistic wisdom that a *practical* atheism produces."

8. Tremper Longman III, *The Book of Ecclesiastes*, New International Commentary on the Old Testament (Grand Rapids, MI: Eerdmans, 1998), p. 107.

9. Elizabeth Huwiler, "Ecclesiastes," in Roland Murphy and Elizabeth Huwiler, *Proverbs, Ecclesiastes, Song of Songs*, New International Biblical Commentary, Old Testament (Peabody, MA: Hendrickson, 1999), 12:165.

10. The cartoon is quoted in Robert K. Johnston, *Useless Beauty: Ecclesiastes through the Lens of Contemporary Film* (Grand Rapids, MI: Baker, 2004), p. 169.

11. Ray Stedman, *Is This All There Is to Life?* (Grand Rapids, MI: Discovery House, 1999), pp. 651–654.

12. John Milton, *Paradise Lost*, Book IV, lines 618–620.

13. Dorothy L. Sayers, *Creed or Chaos?* (New York: Harcourt, Brace, 1949), p. 53.

14. Derek Kidner, *The Message of Ecclesiastes*, The Bible Speaks Today (Downers Grove, IL: InterVarsity, 1976), p. 36.

15. Martin Luther, from his sermon on Matthew 6:24–34, as quoted in Ewald M. Plass, *What Luther Says: An Anthology* (St. Louis: Concordia, 1959), p. 560.

16. Thomas Hughes, *Tom Brown's Schooldays*, quoted in F. W. Boreham, *In Pastures Green: A Ramble through the Twenty-third Psalm* (London: Epworth, 1954), pp. 46, 48

Chapter Seven: To Everything a Season

1. Bruce Kuklick, *To Every Thing a Season: Shibe Park and Urban Philadelphia* (Princeton, NJ: Princeton University Press, 1991).

2. Plautus, quoted by A. Cornelius Gellius in his *Attic Nights (Noctes Atticae)*, Book III, section 3.

3. Horace Mann, quoted in Elizabeth M. Knowles, ed. *The Oxford Dictionary of Quotations*, 5th edition (Oxford: Oxford University Press, 1999), p. 493.

4. H. L. Ginsberg, "The Structure and Contents of the Book of Koheleth," in *Wisdom in Israel and in the Ancient Near East*, ed. M. Noth and D. W. Thomas (1955), quoted in Michael A. Eaton, *Ecclesiastes: An Introduction and Commentary*, Tyndale Old Testament Commentaries (Downers Grove, IL: InterVarsity, 1983), p. 77.

5. E. Jones, *Proverbs, Ecclesiastes*, Torch Bible Commentaries (1976), quoted in ibid.

6. H. C. Leupold, *Exposition of Ecclesiastes* (Grand Rapids, MI: Baker, 1952), p. 83.

7. Charles Bridges, *A Commentary on Ecclesiastes* (1860; repr. Edinburgh: Banner of Truth, 1961), p. 48.

8. Ralph Wardlaw, *Lectures on the Book of Ecclesiastes* (1821), quoted in ibid., p. 49.

9. Martin Luther, "Notes on Ecclesiastes," in *Luther's Works*, trans. and ed. Jaroslav Pelikan, 56 vols. (St. Louis: Concordia, 1972), 15:51.

10. William F. Lloyd, "My Times Are in Thy Hand," 1824.

11. Vicomte de Turenne, quoted in Harold G. Moore and Joseph L. Galloway, *We Were Soldiers Once . . . and Young* (New York: HarperCollins, 1992), p. 321.

12. This story was reported by Reuters on November 1, 2006.

13. Stephen F. Olford, *A Time for Truth: A Study of Ecclesiastes 3:1–8* (Chattanooga: AMG, 1999), p. 9.

14. For a helpful summary of possible meanings for what Qoheleth says about casting away and gathering stones in verse 5, see Eaton, *Ecclesiastes: An Introduction and Commentary*, pp. 79–80.

Chapter Eight: All in Good Time

1. Don Richardson, *Peace Child* (Ventura, CA: Regal, 1974).

2. Don Richardson, *Eternity in Their Hearts* (Ventura, CA: Regal, 1981).

3. Derek Kidner, *The Message of Ecclesiastes*, The Bible Speaks Today (Downers Grove, IL: InterVarsity, 1976), p. 39.

4. Here the text reads "eternity," not "darkness," as some commentators have emended it to say.

5. Walter Kaiser, *Ecclesiastes: Total Life*, Everyman's Bible Commentary (Chicago: Moody Press, 1979), p. 66.

6. John Jarick, quoted in Tremper Longman III, *The Book of Ecclesiastes*, New International Commentary on the Old Testament (Grand Rapids, MI: Eerdmans, 1998), p. 121.

7. Woody Allen, quoted in Robert K. Johnston, *Useless Beauty: Ecclesiastes through the Lens of Contemporary Film* (Grand Rapids, MI: Baker, 2004), p. 55.

8. C. S. Lewis, *Mere Christianity* (New York: Macmillan, 1952), p. 120.

9. C. S. Lewis, *Till We Have Faces* (New York: Harcourt, 1956), p. 75.

10. C. S. Lewis, *The Weight of Glory and Other Addresses* (San Francisco: HarperSanFrancisco, 2001), pp. 30–31.

11. Charles Bridges, *A Commentary on Ecclesiastes* (1860; repr. Edinburgh: Banner of Truth, 1961), p. 66.

12. Longman, *The Book of Ecclesiastes*, p. 121.

13. Jean-Paul Sartre, quoted in Timothy Keller, *The Reason for God: Belief in an Age of Skepticism* (New York: Dutton, 2008), p. 127.

14. Thomas Boston, *The Complete Works of the Late Rev. Thomas Boston of Ettrick*, ed. Samuel M'Millan, 12 vols. (London, 1853; repr. Wheaton, IL: Richard Owen Roberts, 1980), 5:254.

15. Michael V. Fox, *A Time to Tear Down and a Time to Build Up: A Rereading of Ecclesiastes* (Grand Rapids, MI: Eerdmans, 1999), p. 213.

16. Longman, *The Book of Ecclesiastes*, p. 124.

17. Martin Luther, "Notes on Ecclesiastes," in *Luther's Works*, trans. and ed. Jaroslav Pelikan, 56 vols. (St. Louis: Concordia, 1972), 15:55.

18. Didymus the Blind, "Commentary on Ecclesiastes," 88.29, *Proverbs, Ecclesiastes, Song of Solomon*, ed. J. Robert Wright, Ancient Christian Commentary on Scripture, OT 9 (Downers Grove, IL: InterVarsity, 2005), p. 230.

19. Michael A. Eaton, *Ecclesiastes: An Introduction and Commentary*, Tyndale Old Testament Commentaries (Downers Grove, IL: InterVarsity, 1983), p. 48.

20. Kidner, *The Message of Ecclesiastes*, p. 40.

Chapter Nine: From Dust to Glory

1. *Nothing to be Frightened Of* was published by Knopf in 2008. The quotations here come from Garrison Keillor, "Dying of the Light," *The New York Times Book Review* (October 5, 2008), pp. 1, 10.

2. T. M. Moore, *Ecclesiastes: Ancient Wisdom When All Else Fails: A New Translation and Interpretive Paraphrase* (Downers Grove, IL: InterVarsity, 2001), p. 11.

3. Martin Luther, "Notes on Ecclesiastes," in *Luther's Works*, trans. and ed. Jaroslav Pelikan, 56 vols. (St. Louis: Concordia, 1972), 15:56.

4. Lana's story is recounted by Gary Lane, a reporter for CBN, in *The Voice of the Martyrs* (April 2008), pp. 4–5.

5. See Derek Kidner, *The Message of Ecclesiastes*, The Bible Speaks Today (Downers Grove, IL: InterVarsity, 1976), p. 42.

6. The practice of these monks is described by Haddon Robinson in "The Grim Shepherd," *Christianity Today* (October 23, 2000), p. 115.

7. Somerset Maugham, *The Summing Up*, quoted in Timothy Keller, *The Reason for God: Belief in an Age of Skepticism* (New York: Dutton, 2008), p. 127.

8. For this argument, see Michael A. Eaton, *Ecclesiastes: An Introduction and Commentary*, Tyndale Old Testament Commentaries (Downers Grove, IL: InterVarsity, 1983), pp. 87–89.

9. Olympiodorus, "Commentary on Ecclesiastes [3:21]," in *Proverbs, Ecclesiastes, Song of Solomon*, ed. J. Robert Wright, Ancient Christian Commentary on Scripture, OT 9 (Downers Grove, IL: InterVarsity, 2005), p. 233.

10. Samuel Wilkerson, quoted in Harry S. Stout, *Upon the Altar of the Nation: A Moral History of the Civil War* (New York: Viking-Penguin, 2006), pp. 240–241.

11. *The Voice of the Martyrs*, pp. 4–5.

Chapter Ten: Two Are Better Than One

1. David Wyss, quoted in Timothy Lamer, "Striving After Wind," *World* (August 13, 2005), p. 41.

2. Derek Kidner, *The Message of Ecclesiastes*, The Bible Speaks Today (Downers Grove, IL: InterVarsity, 1976), p. 46.

3. William P. Brown, *Ecclesiastes* (Louisville: John Knox, 2000), p. 50.

4. Anonymous, quoted in *The New Encyclopedia of Christian Quotations*, comp. Mark Water (Grand Rapids, MI: Baker, 2000), p. 224.

5. Kidner, *The Message of Ecclesiastes*, p. 52.

6. John Calvin, *Commentary on the Book of Psalms*, Vol. 1, trans. Rev. James Anderson (Grand Rapids, MI: Baker, 1999), p. xl.

7. John Calvin, *Institutes of the Christian Religion*, ed. John T. McNeill, trans. Ford Lewis Battles, 2 vols., Library of Christian Classics, 20–21 (Philadelphia: Westminster, 1960), I.xviii.4.

8. Kidner, *The Message of Ecclesiastes*, p. 46.

9. Robert K. Johnston cites this scene in his book *Useless Beauty: Ecclesiastes through the Lens of Contemporary Film* (Grand Rapids, MI: Baker, 2004), p. 60.

10. James Limburg reprints Goodman's column in *Encountering Ecclesiastes: A Book for Our Time* (Grand Rapids, MI: Eerdmans, 2006), pp. 61–63.

11. Irving Berlin, "I've Got My Love to Keep Me Warm" (1937).

Chapter Eleven: In Spirit and in Truth

1. Derek Kidner, *The Message of Ecclesiastes*, The Bible Speaks Today (Downers Grove, IL: InterVarsity, 1976), p. 52.
2. John Calvin, *Institutes of the Christian Religion*, ed. John T. McNeill, trans. Ford Lewis Battles, 2 vols., Library of Christian Classics, 20–21 (Philadelphia: Westminster, 1960), I.i.1.
3. See especially the works of Cornelius Van Til, such as the second edition of his *Christian Apologetics*, ed. William Edgar (Phillipsburg, NJ: P&R, 2003).
4. Gregory of Nyssa, "Answer to Eunomius's Second Book," in *Proverbs, Ecclesiastes, Song of Solomon*, ed. J. Robert Wright, Ancient Christian Commentary on Scripture, OT 9 (Downers Grove, IL: InterVarsity, 2005), p. 240.
5. Tremper Longman III, *The Book of Ecclesiastes*, New International Commentary on the Old Testament (Grand Rapids, MI: Eerdmans, 1998), p. 152.
6. Charles Bridges, *A Commentary on Ecclesiastes* (1860; repr. Edinburgh: Banner of Truth, 1961), p. 102.
7. Ibid., p. 105.
8. Longman, *The Book of Ecclesiastes*, p. 154.
9. Bridges, *A Commentary on Ecclesiastes*, p. 109.
10. T. M. Moore, *Ecclesiastes: Ancient Wisdom When All Else Fails: A New Translation and Interpretive Paraphrase* (Downers Grove, IL: InterVarsity, 2001), pp. 43–44.

Chapter Twelve: Satisfaction Sold Separately

1. Tremper Longman III, *The Book of Ecclesiastes*, New International Commentary on the Old Testament (Grand Rapids, MI: Eerdmans, 1998), p. 157.
2. Michael A. Eaton, *Ecclesiastes: An Introduction and Commentary*, Tyndale Old Testament Commentaries (Downers Grove, IL: InterVarsity, 1983), p. 101.
3. Martin Luther, "Notes on Ecclesiastes," in *Luther's Works*, trans. and ed. Jaroslav Pelikan, 56 vols. (St. Louis: Concordia, 1972), 15:5.
4. Longman, *The Book of Ecclesiastes*, p. 157.
5. O'Neill explains the term in her book *The Golden Ghetto: The Psychology of Affluence* (Center City, MN: Hazelden, 1996).
6. Charles Bridges, *A Commentary on Ecclesiastes* (1860; repr. Edinburgh: Banner of Truth, 1961), p. 115.
7. From the songs "Can't Buy Me Love" and "Money (That's What I Want)" on the *Hard Day's Night* (1964) and *With the Beatles* (1963) albums respectively.
8. Derek Kidner, *The Message of Ecclesiastes*, The Bible Speaks Today (Downers Grove, IL: InterVarsity, 1976), p. 56.
9. Oliver Goldsmith, *The Deserted Village*, in *The Poetical Works of Oliver Goldsmith: with a Life* (New York: Blakeman & Mason, 1862), p. 35.
10. Luther, "Notes on Ecclesiastes," 15:90.
11. Simon Dyson, quoted in John Blanchard, *Where Do We Go from Here?* (Darlington, UK: Evangelical Press, 2008), p. 6.
12. Luther, "Notes on Ecclesiastes," 15:91.
13. Randy Alcorn, *The Treasure Principle: Unlocking the Secret of Joyful Living* (New York: Doubleday, 2005), pp. 55–56.
14. Kidner, *The Message of Ecclesiastes*, p. 56.
15. Longman, *The Book of Ecclesiastes*, p. 168.
16. George Herbert, *George Herbert and the Seventeenth-Century Religious Poets*, ed. Marion A. D. Cesare (New York: Norton, 1978), p. 57.
17. Eaton, *Ecclesiastes: An Introduction and Commentary*, p. 104.

Chapter Thirteen: Here Today, Gone Tomorrow

1. Ronald Rolheiser, *The Holy Longing: The Search for a Christian Spirituality*, quoted by Richard A. Kauffman, in "The Human Condition," *Christianity Today* (July 2008), p. 46.
2. Jonathan Clements, "No Satisfaction: Why What You Have Is Never Enough," *Wall Street Journal* (May 2, 2007), D1.
3. Alexander Pushkin, *Eugene Onegin and Other Poems*, Everyman's Library Pocket Poets, trans. Charles Johnston (New York: Alfred A. Knopf), p. 11.
4. Martin Luther, "Notes on Ecclesiastes," in *Luther's Works*, trans. and ed. Jaroslav Pelikan, 56 vols. (St. Louis: Concordia, 1972), 15:94.
5. Derek Kidner, *The Message of Ecclesiastes*, The Bible Speaks Today (Downers Grove, IL: InterVarsity, 1976), p. 59.
6. Michael A. Eaton, *Ecclesiastes: An Introduction and Commentary*, Tyndale Old Testament Commentaries (Downers Grove, IL: InterVarsity, 1983), p. 106.
7. Kidner, *The Message of Ecclesiastes*, p. 60.
8. Karl Barth, *Dogmatics in Outline*, quoted in James Limburg, *Encountering Ecclesiastes: A Book for Our Time* (Grand Rapids, MI: Eerdmans, 2006), p. 84.
9. The excavation is described by Clovis G. Chappell in *Feminine Faces* (Grand Rapids, MI: Baker, 1978), n.p.
10. Luther, "Notes on Ecclesiastes," 15:101.
11. Kidner, *The Message of Ecclesiastes*, p. 62.
12. The British Humanist Association, quoted by John Blanchard in *Where Do We Go from Here?* (Darlington, UK: Evangelical Press, 2008), p. 10.
13. Both Rabelais and Hobbes are quoted in ibid., p. 9.

Chapter Fourteen: Better and Better

1. G. C. Martin, *Proverbs, Ecclesiastes, and Song of Songs*, in *The Century Bible: A Modern Commentary*, 33 vols., ed. Walter F. Adeney (London: Caxton, 1908), 13:253.
2. Michael A. Eaton, *Ecclesiastes: An Introduction and Commentary*, Tyndale Old Testament Commentaries (Downers Grove, IL: InterVarsity, 1983), p. 109.
3. Tremper Longman III, *The Book of Ecclesiastes*, New International Commentary on the Old Testament (Grand Rapids, MI: Eerdmans, 1998), p. 182.
4. In his sermon on this text, Thomas Boston draws a close connection between the two parts of the verse, arguing that it is specifically the man who has a good name whose dying day is better than his day of birth. See *The Complete Works of the Late Rev. Thomas Boston of Ettrick*, ed. Samuel M'Millan, 12 vols. (London, 1853; repr. Wheaton, IL: Richard Owen Roberts, 1980), 5:463, 480ff.
5. Didymus the Blind, "Commentary on Ecclesiastes," in *Proverbs, Ecclesiastes, Song of Solomon*, ed. J. Robert Wright, Ancient Christian Commentary on Scripture, OT 9 (Downers Grove, IL: InterVarsity, 2005), p. 249.
6. Boston, *The Complete Works*, 5:484.
7. Ibid., 5:486ff.
8. Charles H. Spurgeon, "The Believer's Deathday Better than His Birthday," *The Metropolitan Tabernacle Pulpit*, Vol. 27 (1882; repr. London: Banner of Truth, 1971), p. 149.
9. John Byrom, "Christians, Awake, Salute the Happy Morn," 1745.
10. "What Child Is This?" is a traditional English carol; the well-known words were adapted by William Dix around 1865.
11. "Within a Crib My Savior Lay," Timothy Dudley-Smith, 1968.
12. Paul Gerhardt, "All My Heart This Night Rejoices," 1653.
13. Matthew Henry, quoted in Charles Bridges, *A Commentary on Ecclesiastes* (1860; repr. Edinburgh: Banner of Truth, 1961), p. 135.
14. Derek Kidner, *The Message of Ecclesiastes*, The Bible Speaks Today (Downers Grove, IL: InterVarsity, 1976), p. 65.

15. Susan Sontag, quoted in Marvin Olasky, "Whistling past the graveyard," *World* (July/ August 2002), p. 58.

16. Martin Luther, quoted in Dennis Ngien, "Picture Christ," *Christianity Today* (April 2007), p. 68.

17. Charles Spurgeon, *The Metropolitan Tabernacle Pulpit* (Pasadena, TX: Pilgrim Publications, 1977), 54:3116.

18. Walker Percy, quoted in Marvin Olasky, "Wanting both: Looking for love in the right places," *World* (December 22, 2004), p. 96.

19. Virginia Morris, *Talking About Death Won't Kill You*, quoted in Olasky, "Whistling past the graveyard," pp. 55–56.

20. Moffatt, quoted in Eaton, *Ecclesiastes: An Introduction and Commentary*, p. 110.

21. Martin Luther, "Notes on Ecclesiastes," in *Luther's Works*, trans. and ed. Jaroslav Pelikan, 56 vols. (St. Louis: Concordia, 1972), 15:114.

22. George Santayana, quoted in Olasky, "Whistling past the graveyard," p. 56.

23. Charles Ward, quoted in Harry S. Stout, *Upon the Altar of the Nation: A Moral History of the Civil War* (New York: Viking–Penguin, 2006), p. 237.

Chapter Fifteen: The Crook in the Lot

1. See Philip Graham Ryken, *Thomas Boston as Preacher of the Fourfold State*, Rutherford Studies in Historical Theology (Carlisle, UK: Paternoster, 1999).

2. Jonathan Edwards, *The Works of Jonathan Edwards*, ed. John E. Smith (New Haven, CT: Yale University Press, 1957), 2:489.

3. Thomas Boston, *The Complete Works of the Late Rev. Thomas Boston of Ettrick*, ed. Samuel M'Millan, 12 vols. (London, 1853; repr. Wheaton, IL: Richard Owen Roberts, 1980), 12:205.

4. Thomas Boston, *The Crook in the Lot*, in *Complete Works*, 3:495–590.

5. Ibid., 3:499.

6. John Jarick, quoted in Tremper Longman III, *The Book of Ecclesiastes*, New International Commentary on the Old Testament (Grand Rapids, MI: Eerdmans, 1998), p. 191.

7. Boston, *The Crook in the Lot*, 3:498.

8. Martin Luther, "Notes on Ecclesiastes," in *Luther's Works*, trans. and ed. Jaroslav Pelikan, 56 vols. (St. Louis: Concordia, 1972), 15:120.

9. Richard Baxter, quoted in Derek Kidner, *The Message of Ecclesiastes*, The Bible Speaks Today (Downers Grove, IL: InterVarsity, 1976), p. 68.

10. Longman, *The Book of Ecclesiastes*, p. 196.

11. R. N. Whybray, *Ecclesiastes*, The New Century Bible Commentary (Grand Rapids, MI: Eerdmans, 1989), pp. 120–121.

12. H. C. Leupold, *Exposition of Ecclesiastes* (Grand Rapids, MI: Baker, 1952), p. 163.

13. Ibid., p. 164.

14. Michael A. Eaton, *Ecclesiastes: An Introduction and Commentary*, Tyndale Old Testament Commentaries (Downers Grove, IL: InterVarsity, 1983), p. 114.

15. Boston, *The Crook in the Lot*, 3:511–516.

16. Ibid., 3:515–516.

17. James Montgomery Boice, "Final Address at Tenth Presbyterian Church," in *The Life of Dr. James Montgomery Boice, 1938–2000*, ed. Philip G. Ryken (Philadelphia: Tenth Presbyterian Church, 2001), pp. 44–45.

Chapter Sixteen: Wisdom for the Wise

1. Information about this course comes from Ken Ham, "Talking to Aliens?" *answersupdate*, Vol. 15, No. 9, pp. 1–2.

2. Derek Kidner, *The Message of Ecclesiastes*, The Bible Speaks Today (Downers Grove, IL: InterVarsity, 1976), p. 69.

3. Blaise Pascal, *Thoughts*, The Harvard Classics, Vol. 48, trans. W. F. Trotter (New York: P.F. Collier & Son, 1910), p. 45.

4. Charles Bridges, *A Commentary on Ecclesiastes* (1860; repr. Edinburgh: Banner of Truth, 1961), p. 171.

5. C. S. Lewis, *The Voyage of the Dawn Treader* (London: Geoffrey Bles, 1952), p. 143.

6. Jonathan Edwards, "Resolutions," *Letters and Personal Writings (WJE Online)*, ed. George S. Claghorn, 16:751 (Resolution 31).

7. Kidner, *The Message of Ecclesiastes*, p. 71.

8. Horace, *Horace for English Readers: Being a Translation of the Poems of Quintus Horatius Flaccus into English Prose*, trans. E. C. Wickham (Oxford: Clarendon Press, 1903), p. 30.

9. Pascal, *Thoughts*, p. 78.

10. John Calvin, *Institutes of the Christian Religion*, ed. John T. McNeill, trans. Ford Lewis Battles, 2 vols., Library of Christian Classics, 20–21 (Philadelphia: Westminster, 1960), III.xxi.2.

11. John Donne, *Poems of John Donne*, ed. E. K. Chambers (New York: Charles Scribner's Sons, 1896), p. 188.

12. H. C. Leupold, *Exposition of Ecclesiastes* (Grand Rapids, MI: Baker, 1952), pp. 173–176.

13. For the view that Qoheleth is a misogynist, see Tremper Longman III, *The Book of Ecclesiastes*, New International Commentary on the Old Testament (Grand Rapids, MI: Eerdmans, 1998), pp. 203–207.

14. Martin Luther, quoted in Bridges, *A Commentary on Ecclesiastes*, p. 177.

15. Bridges, *A Commentary on Ecclesiastes*, p. 168.

16. Ibid., p. 179.

17. Calvin, *Institutes*, II.i.6, 7.

18. C. S. Lewis, *Prince Caspian* (New York: HarperCollins, 1979), p. 233.

19. Mark Twain, *The Tragedy of Pudd'nhead Wilson and the Comedy of the Extraordinary Twins* (New York: Harper & Brothers, 1922), p. 18.

20. Blaise Pascal, quoted in William Edgar, "Why Is Light Given to the Miserable?" *It Was Good—Making Art to the Glory of God*, ed. Ned Bustard (Baltimore: Square Halo, 2000), p. 45.

Chapter Seventeen: Command and Consent

1. Helmuth von Moltke, in a letter to his wife Freya, dated January 11, 1945, in *The Christian Lover: The Sweetness of Love and Marriage in the Letters of Believers*, ed. Michael A. G. Haykin and Victoria J. Haykin (Lake Mary, FL: Reformation Trust, 2009), p. 95.

2. Michael A. Eaton, *Ecclesiastes: An Introduction and Commentary*, Tyndale Old Testament Commentaries (Downers Grove, IL: InterVarsity, 1983), p. 117.

3. Matthew Parris, "As an atheist, I truly believe Africa needs God," *TimesOnline*, December 27, 2008; http://www.timesonline.co.uk/tol/comment/columnists/matthew_parris/article 5400568.ece.

4 R. N, Whybray, *Ecclesiastes*, The New Century Bible Commentary (Grand Rapids, MI: Eerdmans, 1989), pp. 134–135.

5. Martin Luther, "Notes on Ecclesiastes," in *Luther's Works*, trans. and ed. Jaroslav Pelikan, 56 vols. (St. Louis: Concordia, 1972), 15:135.

6. For example, see Tremper Longman III, *The Book of Ecclesiastes*, New International Commentary on the Old Testament (Grand Rapids, MI: Eerdmans, 1998), p. 212.

7. Derek Kidner, *The Message of Ecclesiastes*, The Bible Speaks Today (Downers Grove, IL: InterVarsity, 1976), p. 74.

8. Alternatively, the "wickedness" in verse 8 is unrelated to warfare but serves as a separate example of something in life that is out of our control: "the person who recognizes no law

but does exactly as he pleases might be expected to be an exception to the general rule that man is always the victim of circumstances; but even he will eventually be overtaken by them" (Whybray, *Ecclesiastes*, p. 134).

9. Von Moltke, quoted in Haykin, *The Christian Lover*, pp. 93, 95.

Chapter Eighteen: Final Justice

1. Leah Hager Cohen, "Rough Crossing," *New York Times Book Review* (January 4, 2009), p. 1.
2. Charles Spurgeon, "The Wicked Man's Life, Funeral, and Epitaph," *The New Park Street Pulpit* (Pasadena, TX: Pilgrim, 1975), p. 281.
3. Columba Stewart, *Prayer and Community: The Benedictine Tradition*, quoted in Richard A. Kauffman, "Benedictine Wisdom," *Christianity Today* (December 2008), p. 55.
4. Martin Luther, "Notes on Ecclesiastes," in *Luther's Works*, trans. and ed. Jaroslav Pelikan, 56 vols. (St. Louis: Concordia, 1972), 15:139.
5. Michael A. Eaton, *Ecclesiastes: An Introduction and Commentary*, Tyndale Old Testament Commentaries (Downers Grove, IL: InterVarsity, 1983), p. 121.
6. Theodore Beza, quoted in Charles Bridges, *A Commentary on Ecclesiastes* (1860; repr. Edinburgh: Banner of Truth, 1961), p. 204.
7. See David Epstein, "The Rules, the Law, the Reality," *Sports Illustrated* (February 16, 2009), pp. 30–31.
8. William Provine, from a 1994 debate with Phillip Johnson at Stanford University, "Darwinism: Science of Naturalistic Philosophy?"
9. Svetlana Alliluyeva, *Letters to a Friend*, quoted in John Blanchard, *Where Do We Go from Here?* (Darlington, UK: Evangelical Press, 2008), p. 3.
10. T. M. Moore, *Ecclesiastes: Ancient Wisdom When All Else Fails: A New Translation and Interpretive Paraphrase* (Downers Grove, IL: InterVarsity, 2001), 60.
11. Eaton, *Ecclesiastes: An Introduction and Commentary*, p. 123.
12. Ibid., pp. 122–123.
13. Augustine, "City of God," 20.3, in *Proverbs, Ecclesiastes, Song of Solomon*, ed. J. Robert Wright, Ancient Christian Commentary on Scripture, OT 9 (Downers Grove, IL: InterVarsity, 2005), p. 261.
14. Tremper Longman III, *The Book of Ecclesiastes*, New International Commentary on the Old Testament (Grand Rapids, MI: Eerdmans, 1998), p. 216.
15. Dietrich Bonhoeffer, *Life Together*, quoted in James Limburg, *Encountering Ecclesiastes: A Book for Our Time* (Grand Rapids, MI: Eerdmans, 2006), pp. 47–48.
16. Marghanita Laski, quoted in Blanchard, *Where Do We Go from Here?*, p. 7.
17. This quotation, as well as other details of de Marolle's imprisonment, come from Lewis de Marolles, *An Essay on Providence. To which is prefixed an abridgment of Mr. Jaquelot's History of the Sufferings and Martyrdom of Mr. De Marolles* (London, 1790).
18. Lewis de Marolles, quoted in Bridges, *A Commentary on Ecclesiastes*, p. 203.

Chapter Nineteen: The Living and the Dead

1. Samuel Johnson, from the preface to *A Dictionary of the English Language* (London, 1555).
2. This is the interpretation we find, for example, in H. C. Leupold, *Exposition of Ecclesiastes* (Grand Rapids, MI: Baker, 1952), p. 202.
3. Brian Bergstein, "Overload," *The Philadelphia Inquirer* (March 8, 2007), C1.
4. William Shakespeare, *Macbeth*, Act 5, scene 5.
5. Thomas Hardy, "The Dynasts" (1904–1908).
6. Francis Bacon, quoted in Charles Bridges, *A Commentary on Ecclesiastes* (1860; repr. Edinburgh: Banner of Truth, 1961), p. 207.
7. Isaac Watts, "We Give Immortal Praise," 1709.

8. T. M. Moore, *Ecclesiastes: Ancient Wisdom When All Else Fails: A New Translation and Interpretive Paraphrase* (Downers Grove, IL: InterVarsity, 2001), p. 65.
9. Michael A. Eaton, *Ecclesiastes: An Introduction and Commentary*, Tyndale Old Testament Commentaries (Downers Grove, IL: InterVarsity, 1983), p. 126.
10. Derek Kidner, *The Message of Ecclesiastes*, The Bible Speaks Today (Downers Grove, IL: InterVarsity, 1976), p. 82.
11. Leupold, *Exposition of Ecclesiastes*, p. 21.
12. Tremper Longman III, *The Book of Ecclesiastes*, New International Commentary on the Old Testament (Grand Rapids, MI: Eerdmans, 1998), p. 228.
13. Kidner, *The Message of Ecclesiastes*, p. 80.
14. David Watson, *Is Anyone There?* (London: Hodder and Stoughton, 1979), p. 66.
15. Kidner, *The Message of Ecclesiastes*, p. 82.
16. Jerome, Letter 108.27, in *Proverbs, Ecclesiastes, Song of Solomon*, ed. J. Robert Wright, Ancient Christian Commentary on Scripture, OT 9 (Downers Grove, IL: InterVarsity, 2005), p. 263.
17. Giacomo Casanova, quoted in Michael Dirda, "The Pleasures of Casanova," *The New York Review of Books* (May 31, 2007), p. 20.

Chapter Twenty: The Good Life

1. Herb Magidson, "Enjoy Yourself (It's Later than You Think)," 1934.
2. Tremper Longman III, *The Book of Ecclesiastes*, New International Commentary on the Old Testament (Grand Rapids, MI: Eerdmans, 1998), p. 229.
3. *The Epic of Gilgamesh*, in *Before Philosophy*, trans. H. Frankfort et al. (New York: Pelican, 1949), p. 226.
4. This Egyptian funeral song is found in *The Literature of the Ancient Egyptians*, trans. A. Erman (London: Methuen, 1927), p. 133.
5. Martin Luther, "Notes on Ecclesiastes," in *Luther's Works*, trans. and ed. Jaroslav Pelikan, 56 vols. (St. Louis: Concordia, 1972), 15:149.
6. Michael A. Eaton, *Ecclesiastes: An Introduction and Commentary*, Tyndale Old Testament Commentaries (Downers Grove, IL: InterVarsity, 1983), p. 129.
7. Longman, *The Book of Ecclesiastes*, pp. 230–231.
8. Charles Spurgeon, "A Home Mission Sermon," *The New Park Street Pulpit* (Pasadena, TX: Pilgrim, 1975), 5:274.
9. William Perkins, *Works*, 2 vols. (London, 1626), 1:752.
10. Tim Keller, *The Reason for God: Belief in an Age of Skepticism* (New York: Dutton, 2008), p. 162.
11. Derek Kidner, *The Message of Ecclesiastes*, The Bible Speaks Today (Downers Grove, IL: InterVarsity, 1976), p. 83.
12. Elizabeth Barrett Browning, *Aurora Leigh* (New York: Penguin, 1996), book 7.
13. Caroline Perthes, *Life of Perthes*, quoted in Charles Bridges, *A Commentary on Ecclesiastes* (1860; repr. Edinburgh: Banner of Truth, 1961), p. 221.
14. Luther, "Notes on Ecclesiastes," 15:150.
15. See Longman, *The Book of Ecclesiastes*, p. 231, for example.
16. Jeremy Taylor, *Marriage Ring*, quoted in Bridges, *A Commentary on Ecclesiastes*, pp. 222–223.

Chapter Twenty-One: Man Knows Not His Time

1. "Molière, The Imaginary Invalid," in the Literature, Arts, and Medicine Database of New York University.
2. As told by *Uncle John's Giant 10ᵗʰ Anniversary Bathroom Reader* (Ashland, OR: Bathroom Readers' Press, 1997), p. 156.
3. See http://www.msnbc.msn.com/id/15759622/?GT1=8717.

4. As reported in *China Daily* (January 5, 2009), p. 6.

5. Martin Luther, "Notes on Ecclesiastes," in *Luther's Works*, trans. and ed. Jaroslav Pelikan, 56 vols. (St. Louis: Concordia, 1972), 15:152.

6. According to an alternate interpretation, the poor man's advice was never heeded at all: although he *could have* saved the city, nobody listened to his wise counsel. This interpretation requires a fair amount of reading between the lines, however, so it is better to take the text as it stands. The man did in fact deliver the city, but afterward he was forgotten.

7. Tremper Longman III, *The Book of Ecclesiastes*, New International Commentary on the Old Testament (Grand Rapids, MI: Eerdmans, 1998), p. 237.

8. The name of this missionary partner is omitted for the protection of her family; she wrote her letter in February 2009.

Chapter Twenty-Two: No Foolin'

1. Derek Kidner, *The Message of Ecclesiastes*, The Bible Speaks Today (Downers Grove, IL: InterVarsity, 1976), p. 88.

2. Dan B. Allender and Tremper Longman III, *Bold Love* (Colorado Springs: NavPress, 1992), p. 256.

3. Michael A. Eaton, *Ecclesiastes: An Introduction and Commentary*, Tyndale Old Testament Commentaries (Downers Grove, IL: InterVarsity, 1983), p. 133.

4. Charles Bridges, *A Commentary on Ecclesiastes* (1860; repr. Edinburgh: Banner of Truth, 1961), p. 236.

5. Allender and Longman, *Bold Love*, p. 263.

6. Martin Luther, "Notes on Ecclesiastes," in *Luther's Works*, trans. and ed. Jaroslav Pelikan, 56 vols. (St. Louis: Concordia, 1972), 15:157.

7. Eaton, *Ecclesiastes: An Introduction and Commentary*, p. 134.

8. Kidner, *The Message of Ecclesiastes*, p. 90.

9. Tremper Longman III, *The Book of Ecclesiastes*, New International Commentary on the Old Testament (Grand Rapids, MI: Eerdmans, 1998), p. 244.

10. For an opposing view, see R. N. Whybray, *Ecclesiastes*, The New Century Bible Commentary (Grand Rapids, MI: Eerdmans, 1989), p. 153: "This saying has nothing to do with those passages in the Old Testament which speak of the wicked or malicious who themselves fall into pits which they have dug to encompass the destruction of others."

11. Bridges, *A Commentary on Ecclesiastes*, p. 243.

12. Eaton, *Ecclesiastes: An Introduction and Commentary*, p. 136.

Chapter Twenty-Three: A Word to the Wise

1. Michael A. Eaton, *Ecclesiastes: An Introduction and Commentary*, Tyndale Old Testament Commentaries (Downers Grove, IL: InterVarsity, 1983), p. 136.

2. Paul David Tripp, *War of Words: Getting to the Heart of Your Communication Struggles* (Phillipsburg, NJ: P&R, 2000), p. 229.

3. Ibid., p. 200.

4. Eaton, *Ecclesiastes: An Introduction and Commentary*, p. 137.

5. The story of young Charles XII is recounted by Dale Ralph Davis in *The Wisdom and the Folly: An Exposition of the Book of First Kings* (Fearn, Ross–Shire: Christian Focus, 2002), p. 188.

6. Derek Kidner, *The Message of Ecclesiastes*, The Bible Speaks Today (Downers Grove, IL: InterVarsity, 1976), p. 93.

7. Charles Bridges, *A Commentary on Ecclesiastes* (1860; repr. Edinburgh: Banner of Truth, 1961), p. 259.

Chapter Twenty-Four: You Never Know

1. This story comes from the ministry of elder Bo Bowen, as shared by his pastor, Dr. Ligon Duncan, of the First Presbyterian Church in Jackson, Mississippi.

2. This proverb is quoted in Michael A. Eaton, *Ecclesiastes: An Introduction and Commentary*, Tyndale Old Testament Commentaries (Downers Grove, IL: InterVarsity, 1983), p. 140.

3. Martin Luther, "Notes on Ecclesiastes," in *Luther's Works*, trans. and ed. Jaroslav Pelikan, 56 vols. (St. Louis: Concordia, 1972), 15:171.

4. Charles Bridges, *A Commentary on Ecclesiastes* (1860; repr. Edinburgh: Banner of Truth, 1961), p. 263.

5. Eaton, *Ecclesiastes: An Introduction and Commentary*, p. 140.

6. Ibid.

7. Derek Kidner, *The Message of Ecclesiastes*, The Bible Speaks Today (Downers Grove, IL: InterVarsity, 1976), p. 97.

8. See John Flavel, *The Mystery of Providence* (Edinburgh: Banner of Truth, 1963), p. 11.

Chapter Twenty-Five: Young and Old

1. Beth Teitell, *Drinking Problems at the Fountain of Youth* (New York: William Morrow, 2008), pp. 12–13.

2. Francis of Assisi, "The Canticle of the Sun."

3. Tremper Longman III, *The Book of Ecclesiastes*, New International Commentary on the Old Testament (Grand Rapids, MI: Eerdmans, 1998), p. 260.

4. Michael A. Eaton, *Ecclesiastes: An Introduction and Commentary*, Tyndale Old Testament Commentaries (Downers Grove, IL: InterVarsity, 1983), p. 146.

5. Derek Kidner, *The Message of Ecclesiastes*, The Bible Speaks Today (Downers Grove, IL: InterVarsity, 1976), p. 99.

6. The phrase "pain from your body" could also be translated "evil from your flesh," in which case the Preacher is still addressing the subject of sanctification, as he was in verse 9. But since "flesh" ordinarily refers to the human body (not to moral weakness, as it often does in the New Testament), the "evil" the Preacher has in mind is physical pain.

7. Margaret Clarkson, "We Come, O Christ, to You" (1957, 1985).

8. Kidner, *The Message of Ecclesiastes*, p. 100.

9. Leland Ryken, *The Literature of the Bible* (Grand Rapids, MI: Zondervan, 1974), p. 257.

10. Kidner, *The Message of Ecclesiastes*, p. 101.

11. According to an alternative interpretation, all of the images in this passage refer to a funeral procession and to the way that activity ceases in a village when someone dies. See Michael V. Fox, *A Time to Tear Down and a Time to Build Up: A Rereading of Ecclesiastes* (Grand Rapids, MI: Eerdmans, 1999), p. 37.

12. Eaton, *Ecclesiastes: An Introduction and Commentary*, p. 149.

13. Bono, quoted by Denis Haack, "Johnny Cash: Clouded by Sin, Colored by Grace," *byFaith* (July/August 2005), p. 39.

14. Charles Bridges, *A Commentary on Ecclesiastes* (1860; repr. Edinburgh: Banner of Truth, 1961), p. 294.

Chapter Twenty-Six: The End of the Matter

1. Arthur Miller, *After the Fall* (1964), quoted in Tim Keller, *The Reason for God: Belief in an Age of Skepticism* (New York: Dutton, 2008), pp. 156–157.

2. Derek Kidner, *The Message of Ecclesiastes*, The Bible Speaks Today (Downers Grove, IL: InterVarsity, 1976), p. 104.

3. Iain Provan, *Ecclesiastes/Song of Songs*, NIV Application Commentary (Grand Rapids, MI: Zondervan, 2001), p. 226.

4. R. N. Whybray, *Ecclesiastes*, The New Century Bible Commentary (Grand Rapids, MI: Eerdmans, 1989), p. 169.

5. Tom Wolfe, quoted in Robert Short, *A Time to Be Born—A Time to Die* (New York: Harper and Row, 1973), p. ix.

6. Herman Melville, *Moby Dick*, quoted in Robert K. Johnston, *Useless Beauty: Ecclesiastes through the Lens of Contemporary Film* (Grand Rapids, MI: Baker, 2004), p. 20.

7. Gregory Thaumaturgos, quoted in Tremper Longman III, *The Book of Ecclesiastes*, New International Commentary on the Old Testament (Grand Rapids, MI: Eerdmans, 1998), p. 280.

8. Michael A. Eaton, *Ecclesiastes: An Introduction and Commentary*, Tyndale Old Testament Commentaries (Downers Grove, IL: InterVarsity, 1983), p. 154.

9. The United Nations Educational, Scientific and Cultural Organization (UNESCO) publishes these statistics annually.

10. C. S. Lewis, *The Great Divorce* (London: Geoffrey Bles, 1945), pp. 40ff.

11. Kidner, *The Message of Ecclesiastes*, p. 107.

12. Charles Bridges, *A Commentary on Ecclesiastes* (1860; repr. Edinburgh: Banner of Truth, 1961), p. 310.

13. D. R. Davis, *The World We Have Forgotten*, quoted in Stephen F. Olford, *A Time for Truth: A Study of Ecclesiastes 3:1–8* (Chattanooga: AMG, 1999), p. 163.

Scripture Index

116:15	271	31:14	255
118:24	265	31:25	47
119:37	50		
139:4	245	*Ecclesiastes*	
139:13	81	1:1	36
139:14	258	1:1–11	276
141:3	86	1:1, 12	58
143:2	173	1:2	265, 274
147:18	31	1:3	21, 274
		1:3–11	36
Proverbs		1:5	276
1:7	21, 43, 96, 127, 242	1:6	188
2:18–19	176	1:9	60, 97, 274
3:16	233	1:11	63
5:4–5	176	1:12–15	58
6:17–19	82	1:12–6:12	276
8:11	158, 172	1:13	58, 174, 202
9:13	176	1:13–14	274
10:1	61	1:15	163
10:7	63, 193	1:16	16
10:23	47	1:16–18	58
12:15	234	1:17	58
12:23	234	1:18	19, 274
13:16	234	2:1–11	58
13:22	134	2:1ff.	95
14:17	158	2:4–9	69
14:29	158	2:9	16
14:31	101	2:11	19, 274
14:35	187	2:14	232
15:1	243	2:15–16	274
15:13	183	2:16	68
15:17	109	2:17	68
15:23	86, 243	2:18	140
15:28	243	2:18–23	274
16:14	187	2:18–26	249
16:16	172	2:19	232
18:2	234	2:24	110, 198, 213, 275
18:4	172	2:24–26	137, 198, 212
18:6	234	3:1	96, 102, 187, 276
20:1	47	3:1–8	223, 275
20:2	187	3:2	95, 102, 188, 257
22:1	150	3:11	79, 268, 276
23:9	234	3:12–13, 22	198, 212
23:20	248	3:13	213
24:21	187	3:14	197, 280
25:11	86, 243	3:19	188
26:19	47	3:20	275
27:14	86	4:1	275
29:9	47	4:5	232
30:30	207	4:9, 12	278
31	177	5:1, 7	197

General Index

Index of
Sermon Illustrations

The Preaching the Word series is written
by pastors for pastors and their churches.

crossway.org/preachingtheword